Human Development Report **2011**

Sustainability and Equity:
A Better Future for All

Published for the
United Nations
Development
Programme
(UNDP)

ISBN: 9780230363311

Palgrave Macmillan
Houndmills, Basingstoke, Hampshire RG21 6XS and
175 Fifth Avenue, New York, NY 10010

Companies and representatives throughout the world

Palgrave Macmillan in the UK is an imprint of Macmillan Publishers Limited,
registered in England, company number 785998, of Houndmills, Basingstoke,
Hampshire RG21 6XS.

Palgrave Macmillan in the US is a division of St Martin's Press LLC,
175 Fifth Avenue, New York, NY 10010.

Palgrave Macmillan is the global academic imprint of the above companies
and has companies and representatives throughout the world.

Palgrave® and Macmillan® are registered trademarks in the United States,
the United Kingdom, Europe and other countries.

A catalogue record for this book is available from the British Library and the Library of Congress.

Printed in the United States by Consolidated Graphics. Cover is printed on Tembec's 12 pt Kallima coated-one-side
paper. Text pages are printed on Cascades Mills' 60# Rolland Opaque Smooth text that is 50% de-inked post-
consumer recycled fibre. Both sheets are Forest Stewardship Council Certified, elemental chlorine-free papers and
printed with vegetable-based inks and produced by means of environmentally compatible technology.

Editing and production: Communications Development Incorporated, Washington DC
Design: Gerry Quinn

For a list of any errors or omissions found subsequent to printing please visit our
website at http://hdr.undp.org

Human Development Report 2011 team

The UNDP Human Development Report Office

The *Human Development Report* is the product of a collective effort under the guidance of the Director, with research, statistics, communications and publishing staff, and a team supporting National Human Development Reports. Operations and administration colleagues facilitate the work of the office.

Director and lead author

Jeni Klugman

Research

Francisco Rodríguez (Head), Shital Beejadhur, Subhra Bhattacharjee, Monalisa Chatterjee, Hyung-Jin Choi, Alan Fuchs, Mamaye Gebretsadik, Zachary Gidwitz, Martin Philipp Heger, Vera Kehayova, José Pineda, Emma Samman and Sarah Twigg

Statistics

Milorad Kovacevic (Head), Astra Bonini, Amie Gaye, Clara Garcia Aguña and Shreyasi Jha

Communications and publishing

William Orme (Head), Botagoz Abdreyeva, Carlotta Aiello, Wynne Boelt and Jean-Yves Hamel

National Human Development Reports

Eva Jespersen (Deputy Director), Mary Ann Mwangi, Paola Pagliani and Tim Scott

Operations and administration

Sarantuya Mend (Operations Manager), Diane Bouopda and Fe Juarez-Shanahan

Foreword

In June 2012 world leaders will gather in Rio de Janeiro to seek a new consensus on global actions to safeguard the future of the planet and the right of future generations everywhere to live healthy and fulfilling lives. This is the great development challenge of the 21st century.

The 2011 *Human Development Report* offers important new contributions to the global dialogue on this challenge, showing how sustainability is inextricably linked to basic questions of equity—that is, of fairness and social justice and of greater access to a better quality of life. Sustainability is not exclusively or even primarily an environmental issue, as this Report so persuasively argues. It is fundamentally about how we choose to live our lives, with an awareness that everything we do has consequences for the 7 billion of us here today, as well as for the billions more who will follow, for centuries to come.

Understanding the links between environmental sustainability and equity is critical if we are to expand human freedoms for current and future generations. The remarkable progress in human development over recent decades, which the global *Human Development Reports* have documented, cannot continue without bold global steps to reduce both environmental risks and inequality. This Report identifies pathways for people, local communities, countries and the international community to promote environmental sustainability and equity in mutually reinforcing ways.

In the 176 countries and territories where the United Nations Development Programme is working every day, many disadvantaged people carry a double burden of deprivation. They are more vulnerable to the wider effects of environmental degradation, because of more severe stresses and fewer coping tools. They must also deal with threats to their immediate environment from indoor air pollution, dirty water and unimproved sanitation. Forecasts suggest that continuing failure to reduce the grave environmental risks and deepening social inequalities threatens to slow decades of sustained progress by the world's poor majority—and even to reverse the global convergence in human development.

Major disparities in power shape these patterns. New analysis shows how power imbalances and gender inequalities at the national level are linked to reduced access to clean water and improved sanitation, land degradation and deaths due to indoor and outdoor air pollution, amplifying the effects associated with income disparities. Gender inequalities also interact with environmental outcomes and make them worse. At the global level governance arrangements often weaken the voices of developing countries and exclude marginalized groups.

Yet there are alternatives to inequality and unsustainability. Growth driven by fossil fuel consumption is not a prerequisite for a better life in broader human development terms. Investments that improve equity—in access, for example, to renewable energy, water and sanitation, and reproductive healthcare—could advance both sustainability and human development. Stronger accountability and democratic processes, in part through support for an active civil society and media, can also improve outcomes. Successful approaches rely on community management, inclusive institutions that pay particular attention to disadvantaged groups, and cross-cutting approaches that coordinate budgets and mechanisms across government agencies and development partners.

Beyond the Millennium Development Goals, the world needs a post-2015 development framework that reflects equity and sustainability; Rio+20 stands out as a key opportunity to reach a shared understanding of how to move forward. This Report shows that approaches that integrate equity into policies and programmes and that empower people to bring about change in the legal and political arenas hold enormous promise. Growing country experiences around the world have demonstrated the potential of these approaches to generate and capture positive synergies.

The financing needed for development—including for environmental and social protection—will have to be many times greater than current official development assistance. Today's spending on low-carbon energy sources, for example, is only 1.6 percent of even the lowest estimate of need, while spending on climate change adaptation and mitigation is around 11 percent of estimated need. Hope rests on new climate finance. While market mechanisms and private funding will be vital, they must be supported and leveraged by proactive public investment. Closing the financing gap requires innovative thinking, which this Report provides.

Beyond raising new sources of funds to address pressing environmental threats equitably, the Report advocates reforms that promote equity and voice. Financing flows need to be channelled towards the critical challenges of unsustainability and inequity—and not exacerbate existing disparities.

Providing opportunities and choices for all is the central goal of human development. We have a collective responsibility towards the least privileged among us today and in the future around the world—and a moral imperative to ensure that the present is not the enemy of the future. This Report can help us see the way forward.

Helen Clark
Administrator
United Nations Development Programme

The analysis and policy recommendations of this Report do not necessarily reflect the views of the United Nations Development Programme or its Executive Board. The Report is an independent publication commissioned by UNDP. The research and writing of the Report was a collaborative effort by the Human Development Report team and a group of eminent advisors led by Jeni Klugman, Director of the Human Development Report Office.

Acknowledgements

This is my third and final year of directing the global *Human Development Report*, which, as ever, has been an enormous collaborative effort. The hard work and dedication of the Human Development Report Office team anchor the work, supported by a much broader family of researchers, advocates and officials whose commitment and vision are equally critical to our success.

An academic advisory panel provided valuable guidance, for which we thank Bina Agarwal, Sabina Alkire, Anthony Atkinson, Tariq Banuri, François Bourguignon, William Easterly, Daniel Esty, Sakiko Fukuda-Parr, Enrico Giovannini, Stephany Griffith-Jones, Brian Hammond, Geoffrey Heal, Cesar Hidalgo, Richard Jolly, Gareth Jones, Martin Khor, Mwangi S. Kimenyi, Adil Najam, Eric Neumayer, Michael Noble, José Antonio Ocampo, Marcio Pochmann, Henry Richardson, Ingrid Robeyns, José Salazar-Xirinachs, Frances Stewart, Pavan Sukhdev, Miguel Székely, Dennis Trewin, Leonardo Villar and Tarik Yousef.

A reconstituted statistical advisory panel, comprising official statisticians and academic experts, provided excellent advice on the methodology and data sources related to the family of human development indices: Anthony Atkinson, Grace Bediako, Haishan Fu, Enrico Giovannini, Peter Harper, Gareth Jones, Irena Krizman, Charles Leyeka Lufumpa, Michael Noble, Eduardo Nunes, Marcio Pochmann, Eric Swanson, Miguel Székely and Dato' Hajan Wan Ramlah Wan Abd. Raof. More generally, the United Nations Statistical Commission provided useful feedback from member states.

An extensive series of consultations involved some 500 researchers, civil society advocates, development practitioners and policy-makers from around the globe. Twenty-six events were held between February 2010 and September 2011—in Amman, Bamako, Bangkok, Beijing, Berkeley, Bonn, Copenhagen, Dubai, Geneva, Kigali, Ljubljana, London, Nairobi, New Delhi, New York, Paris, Quito, San José—with the support of the United Nations Development Programme (UNDP) country and regional offices. Support from partnering institutions, listed at http://hdr.undp.org/en/reports/global/hdr2011/consultations, is also gratefully acknowledged.

Background research, commissioned on a range of thematic issues, is available online in our Human Development Research Papers series and listed in *References*. Special thanks to Sabina Alkire and the Oxford Human Development and Poverty Initiative for their continued collaboration and efforts to improve our measure of multidimensional poverty.

The statistics used in this Report rely on various databases. We are particularly grateful to the Carbon Dioxide Information Analysis Center of the US Department of Energy, Yale Center for Environmental Law and Policy, Robert Barro and Jong-Wha Lee, Food and Agricultural Organization, Gallup World Poll, Global Footprint Network, ICF Macro, International Monetary Fund, International Energy Agency, International Labour Organization, International Union for Conservation of Nature, Inter-Parliamentary Union, Luxembourg Income Study, United Nations Department of Economic and Social Affairs, United Nations Educational, Scientific and Cultural Organization Institute for Statistics, United Nations Children's Fund, World Bank and World Health Organization.

Claudio Montenegro conducted the analysis on the World Bank's International Income Distribution Database, Suman Seth on the European Union Statistics on Income and Living Conditions and Kenneth Harttgen on the ICF Macro Demographic and Health Surveys.

A UNDP Readers Group, representing all the regional and policy bureaus, and other colleagues, too numerous to list, provided valuable advice throughout the preparation of the Report. Particular thanks are due to Jennifer Laughlin, Charles MacPherson and colleagues at the Bureau of Development Policy. The HD Network, which comprises some 1,500 UNDP staff, academics and nongovernmental organizations, generated a range of useful ideas and feedback through online discussions. Martha Mai of the UN Office for Project Services provided administrative support.

Several hard working interns made important contributions over the course of the year: Raphaelle Aubert, Uttara Balakrishnan, Luis Fernando Cervantes, Nicole Glanemann, Faith Kim, Meng Lu, Francesca Rappocciolo, Andrés Méndez Ruiz, Fredrik M. Sjoberg and Seol Yoo.

A team at Communications Development Incorporated, led by Bruce Ross-Larson, with Meta de Coquereaumont, Rob Elson, Jack Harlow, Christopher Trott and Elaine Wilson, edited, proofread and laid out the Report. Gerry Quinn designed the Report and created the figures.

We thank all of those involved directly or indirectly in contributing to our efforts, while acknowledging sole responsibility for errors of commission and omission.

Directing the global *Human Development Report* has been a great experience for me, both personally and professionally over the past three years. The human development approach continues to demonstrate its value as a lens for critical and constructive thinking about some of the most fundamental challenges facing us today, and I am confident that the independent global reports, commissioned by UNDP, will remain as central as ever in key global debates. I wish my successor, Khalid Malik, the best of luck in taking this endeavour forward into the next decade.

Jeni Klugman
Director and lead author
Human Development Report 2011

Contents

STATISTICAL ANNEX

BOXES

FIGURES

MAP

TABLES

Overview

This year's Report focuses on the challenge of sustainable and equitable progress. A joint lens shows how environmental degradation intensifies inequality through adverse impacts on already disadvantaged people and how inequalities in human development amplify environmental degradation.

Human development, which is about expanding people's choices, builds on shared natural resources. Promoting human development requires addressing sustainability—locally, nationally and globally—and this can and should be done in ways that are equitable and empowering.

We seek to ensure that poor people's aspirations for better lives are fully taken into account in moving towards greater environmental sustainability. And we point to pathways that enable people, communities, countries and the international community to promote sustainability and equity so that they are mutually reinforcing.

Why sustainability and equity?

The human development approach has enduring relevance in making sense of our world and addressing challenges now and in the future. Last year's 20th anniversary *Human Development Report* (*HDR*) celebrated the concept of human development, emphasizing how equity, empowerment and sustainability expand people's choices. At the same time it highlighted inherent challenges, showing that these key aspects of human development do not always come together.

The case for considering sustainability and equity together

This year we explore the intersections between environmental sustainability and equity, which are fundamentally similar in their concern for distributive justice. We value sustainability because future generations should have at least the same possibilities as people today. Similarly, all inequitable processes are unjust: people's chances at better lives should not be constrained by factors outside their control. Inequalities are especially unjust when particular groups, whether because of gender, race or birthplace, are systematically disadvantaged.

More than a decade ago Sudhir Anand and Amartya Sen made the case for jointly considering sustainability and equity. "It would be a gross violation of the universalist principle," they argued, "if we were to be obsessed about *inter*generational equity without at the same time seizing the problem of *intra*generational equity" (emphasis in original). Similar themes emerged from the Brundtland Commission's 1987 report and a series of international declarations from Stockholm in 1972 through Johannesburg in 2002. Yet today many debates about sustainability neglect equality, treating it as a separate and unrelated concern. This perspective is incomplete and counterproductive.

Some key definitions

Human development is the expansion of people's freedoms and capabilities to lead lives that they value and have reason to value. It is about expanding choices. Freedoms and capabilities are a more expansive notion than basic needs. Many ends are necessary for a "good life," ends that can be intrinsically as well as instrumentally valuable—we may value biodiversity, for example, or natural beauty, independently of its contribution to our living standards.

Disadvantaged people are a central focus of human development. This includes people in the future who will suffer the most severe consequences of the risks arising from our activities today. We are concerned not only with what happens on average or in the most probable scenario but also with what happens in the less likely but still possible scenarios, particularly when the events are catastrophic for poor and vulnerable people.

Debates over what environmental sustainability means often focus on whether human-made capital can substitute for natural resources—whether human ingenuity will relax natural resource constraints, as in the past. Whether this will be possible in the future is unknown and, coupled with the risk of catastrophe, favours the position of preserving basic natural assets and the associated flow of ecological services. This perspective also aligns with human rights–based approaches to development. *Sustainable human development is the expansion of the substantive freedoms of people today while making reasonable efforts to avoid seriously compromising those of future generations.* Reasoned public deliberation, vital to defining the risks a society is willing to accept, is crucial to this idea.

The joint pursuit of environmental sustainability and equity does not require that the two always be mutually reinforcing. In many instances there will be trade-offs. Measures to improve the environment can have adverse effects on equity—for example, if they constrain economic growth in developing countries. This Report illustrates the types of joint impacts that policies could have, while acknowledging that they do not hold universally and underlining that context is critical.

The framework encourages special attention to identifying positive synergies and to considering trade-offs. We investigate how societies can implement win-win-win solutions that favour sustainability, equity and human development.

Patterns and trends, progress and prospects

Increasing evidence points to widespread environmental degradation around the world and potential future deterioration. Because the extent of future changes is uncertain, we explore a range of predictions and consider the insights for human development.

Our starting point, and a key theme of the 2010 *HDR*, is the enormous progress in human development over the past several decades—with three caveats:

- Income growth has been associated with deterioration in such key environmental indicators as carbon dioxide emissions, soil and water quality and forest cover.
- The distribution of income has worsened at the country level in much of the world, even with the narrowing of gaps in health and education achievement.
- While empowerment on average tends to accompany a rising Human Development Index (HDI), there is considerable variation around the relationship.

Simulations for this Report suggest that by 2050 the global HDI would be 8 percent lower than in the baseline in an "environmental challenge" scenario that captures the adverse effects of global warming on agricultural production, on access to clean water and improved sanitation and on pollution (and 12 percent lower in South Asia and Sub-Saharan Africa). Under an even more adverse "environmental disaster" scenario, which envisions vast deforestation and land degradation, dramatic declines in biodiversity and accelerated extreme weather events, the global HDI would be some 15 percent below the projected baseline.

If we do nothing to halt or reverse current trends, the environmental disaster scenario leads to a turning point before 2050 in developing countries—their convergence with rich countries in HDI achievements begins to reverse.

These projections suggest that in many cases the most disadvantaged people bear and will continue to bear the repercussions of environmental deterioration, even if they contribute little to the problem. For example, low HDI countries have contributed the least to global climate change, but they have experienced the greatest loss in rainfall and the greatest increase in its variability, with implications for agricultural production and livelihoods.

Emissions per capita are much greater in very high HDI countries than in low, medium and high HDI countries combined because of more energy-intensive activities—driving cars,

Sustainable human development is the expansion of the substantive freedoms of people today while making reasonable efforts to avoid seriously compromising those of future generations cooling and heating homes and businesses, consuming processed and packaged food. The average person in a very high HDI country accounts for more than four times the carbon dioxide emissions and about twice the methane and nitrous oxide emissions of a person in a low, medium or high HDI country—and about 30 times the carbon dioxide emissions of a person in a low HDI country. The average UK citizen accounts for as much greenhouse gas emissions in two months as a person in a low HDI country generates in a year. And the average Qatari—living in the country with the highest per capita emissions—does so in only 10 days, although that value reflects consumption as well as production that is consumed elsewhere.

While three-quarters of the growth in emissions since 1970 comes from low, medium and high HDI countries, overall levels of greenhouse gases remain much greater in very high HDI countries. And this stands without accounting for the relocation of carbon-intensive production to poorer countries, whose output is largely exported to rich countries.

Around the world rising HDI has been associated with environmental degradation —though the damage can be traced largely to economic growth. Countries with higher incomes generally have higher carbon dioxide emissions per capita. But our analysis finds no association between emissions and the health and education components of the HDI. This result is intuitive: activities that emit carbon dioxide into the atmosphere are those linked to the production of goods, not to the provision of health and education. These results also show the nonlinear nature of the relationship between carbon dioxide emissions per capita and HDI components: little or no relationship at low HDI, but as the HDI rises a "tipping point" is reached, beyond which appears a strong positive correlation between carbon dioxide emissions and income.

Countries with faster improvements in the HDI have also experienced faster increases in carbon dioxide emissions per capita. These changes over time—rather than the snapshot relationship—highlight what to expect tomorrow as a result of development today. Again, income changes drive the trend.

But these relationships do not hold for all environmental indicators. Our analysis finds only a weak positive correlation between the HDI and deforestation, for example. Why do carbon dioxide emissions differ from other environmental threats? We suggest that where the link between the environment and quality of life is direct, as with pollution, environmental achievements are often greater in developed countries; where the links are more diffuse, performance is much weaker. Looking at the relationship between environmental risks and the HDI, we observe three general findings:

- Household environmental deprivations— indoor air pollution, inadequate access to clean water and improved sanitation—are more severe at low HDI levels and decline as the HDI rises.
- Environmental risks with community effects—such as urban air pollution— seem to rise and then fall with development; some suggest that an inverted U-shaped curve describes the relationship.
- Environmental risks with global effects —namely greenhouse gas emissions— typically rise with the HDI.

The HDI itself is not the true driver of these transitions. Incomes and economic growth have an important explanatory role for emissions—but the relationship is not deterministic either. And complex interactions of broader forces change the risk patterns. For example, international trade allows countries to outsource the production of goods that degrade the environment; large-scale commercial use of natural resources has different impacts than subsistence exploitation; and urban and rural environmental profiles differ. And as we will see, policies and the political context matter greatly.

It follows that the patterns are not inevitable. Several countries have achieved significant progress both in the HDI and in equity and environmental sustainability. In line with our focus on positive synergies, we propose a multidimensional strategy to identify countries that have done better than regional peers in promoting equity, raising the HDI,

> **Where the link between the environment and quality of life is direct, as with pollution, environmental achievements are often greater in developed countries; where the links are more diffuse, performance is much weaker**

reducing household indoor air pollution and increasing access to clean water and that are top regional and global performers in environmental sustainability. Environmental sustainability is judged on greenhouse gas emissions, water use and deforestation. The results are illustrative rather than indicative because of patchy data and other comparability issues. Just one country, Costa Rica, outperforms its regional median on all the criteria, while the three other top performers display unevenness across dimensions. Sweden is notable for its high reforestation rate compared with regional and global averages.

Our list shows that across regions, development stages and structural characteristics countries can enact policies conducive to environmental sustainability, equity and the key facets of human development captured in the HDI. We review the types of policies and programmes associated with success while underlining the importance of local conditions and context.

More generally, however, environmental trends over recent decades show deterioration on several fronts, with adverse repercussions for human development, especially for the millions of people who depend directly on natural resources for their livelihoods.

- Globally, nearly 40 percent of land is degraded due to soil erosion, reduced fertility and overgrazing. Land productivity is declining, with estimated yield loss as high as 50 percent in the most adverse scenarios.
- Agriculture accounts for 70–85 percent of water use, and an estimated 20 percent of global grain production uses water unsustainably, imperilling future agricultural growth.
- Deforestation is a major challenge. Between 1990 and 2010 Latin America and the Caribbean and Sub-Saharan Africa experienced the greatest forest losses, followed by the Arab States. The other regions have seen minor gains in forest cover.
- Desertification threatens the drylands that are home to about a third of the world's people. Some areas are particularly vulnerable—notably Sub-Saharan Africa,

where the drylands are highly sensitive and adaptive capacity is low.

Adverse environmental factors are expected to boost world food prices 30–50 percent in real terms in the coming decades and to increase price volatility, with harsh repercussions for poor households. The largest risks are faced by the 1.3 billion people involved in agriculture, fishing, forestry, hunting and gathering. The burden of environmental degradation and climate change is likely to be disequalizing across groups—for several reasons:

- Many rural poor people depend overwhelmingly on natural resources for their income. Even people who do not normally engage in such activities may do so as a coping strategy during hardship.
- How environmental degradation will affect people depends on whether they are net producers or net consumers of natural resources, whether they produce for subsistence or for the market and how readily they can shift between these activities and diversify their livelihoods with other occupations.
- Today, around 350 million people, many of them poor, live in or near forests on which they rely for subsistence and incomes. Both deforestation and restrictions on access to natural resources can hurt the poor. Evidence from a range of countries suggests that women typically rely on forests more than men do because women tend to have fewer occupational options, be less mobile and bear most of the responsibility for collecting fuelwood.
- Around 45 million people—at least 6 million of them women—fish for a living and are threatened by overfishing and climate change. The vulnerability is twofold: the countries most at risk also rely the most on fish for dietary protein, livelihoods and exports. Climate change is expected to lead to major declines in fish stocks in the Pacific Islands, while benefits are predicted at some northern latitudes, including around Alaska, Greenland, Norway and the Russian Federation.

To the extent that women in poor countries are disproportionately involved in subsistence farming and water collection, they face greater adverse consequences of environmental degradation. Many indigenous peoples also rely heavily on natural resources and live in ecosystems especially vulnerable to the effects of climate change, such as small island developing states, arctic regions and high altitudes. Evidence suggests that traditional practices can protect natural resources, yet such knowledge is often overlooked or downplayed.

The effects of climate change on farmers' livelihoods depend on the crop, region and season, underlining the importance of in-depth, local analysis. Impacts will also differ depending on household production and consumption patterns, access to resources, poverty levels and ability to cope. Taken together, however, the net biophysical impacts of climate change on irrigated and rainfed crops by 2050 will likely be negative—and worst in low HDI countries.

Understanding the links

Drawing on the important intersections between the environment and equity at the global level, we explore the links at the community and household levels. We also highlight countries and groups that have broken the pattern, emphasizing transformations in gender roles and in empowerment.

A key theme: the most disadvantaged people carry a double burden of deprivation. More vulnerable to the wider effects of environmental degradation, they must also cope with threats to their immediate environment posed by indoor air pollution, dirty water and unimproved sanitation. Our Multidimensional Poverty Index (MPI), introduced in the 2010 *HDR* and estimated this year for 109 countries, provides a closer look at these deprivations to see where they are most acute.

The MPI measures serious deficits in health, education and living standards, looking at both the number of deprived people and the intensity of their deprivations. This year we explore the pervasiveness of environmental deprivations among the multidimensionally poor and their overlaps at the household level, an innovation in the MPI.

The poverty-focused lens allows us to examine environmental deprivations in access to modern cooking fuel, clean water and basic sanitation. These absolute deprivations, important in themselves, are major violations of human rights. Ending these deprivations could increase higher order capabilities, expanding people's choices and advancing human development.

In developing countries at least 6 people in 10 experience one of these environmental deprivations, and 4 in 10 experience two or more. These deprivations are especially acute among multidimensionally poor people, more than 9 in 10 of whom experience at least one. Most suffer overlapping deprivations: 8 in 10 multidimensionally poor people have two or more, and nearly 1 in 3 (29 percent) is deprived in all three. These environmental deprivations disproportionately contribute to multidimensional poverty, accounting for 20 percent of the MPI—above their 17 percent weight in the index. Across most developing countries deprivations are highest in access to cooking fuel, though lack of water is paramount in several Arab States.

To better understand environmental deprivations, we analysed the patterns for given poverty levels. Countries were ordered by the share of multidimensionally poor people facing one environmental deprivation and the share facing all three. The analysis shows that the shares of the population with environmental deprivations rise with the MPI, but with much variation around the trend. Countries with the lowest share of poor people facing at least one deprivation are mainly in the Arab States and Latin American and the Caribbean (7 of the top 10).

Of the countries with the fewest multidimensionally poor people with all three environmental deprivations, better performers are concentrated in South Asia—5 of the top 10. Several South Asian countries have reduced some environmental deprivations, notably access to potable water, even as other deprivations have remained severe. And five countries are in both top 10 lists—not only is their environmental poverty relatively low, it is also less intense.

The most disadvantaged people carry a double burden of deprivation: more vulnerable to the wider effects of environmental degradation, they must also cope with threats to their immediate environment posed by indoor air pollution, dirty water and unimproved sanitation

Performance on these indicators does not necessarily identify environmental risks and degradation more broadly, for example, in terms of exposure to floods. At the same time the poor, more subject to direct environmental threats, are also more exposed to environmental degradation writ large.

We investigate this pattern further by looking at the relationship between the MPI and stresses posed by climate change. For 130 nationally defined administrative regions in 15 countries, we compare area-specific MPIs with changes in precipitation and temperature. Overall, the poorest regions and locales in these countries seem to have gotten hotter but not much wetter or drier—change that is consistent with evidence exploring the effects of climate change on income poverty.

Environmental threats to selected aspects of human development

Environmental degradation stunts people's capabilities in many ways, going beyond incomes and livelihoods to include impacts on health, education and other dimensions of well-being.

Bad environments and health— overlapping deprivations

The disease burden arising from indoor and outdoor air pollution, dirty water and unimproved sanitation is greatest for people in poor countries, especially for deprived groups. Indoor air pollution kills 11 times more people living in low HDI countries than people elsewhere. Disadvantaged groups in low, medium and high HDI countries face greater risk from outdoor air pollution because of both higher exposure and greater vulnerability. In low HDI countries more than 6 people in 10 lack ready access to improved water, while nearly 4 in 10 lack sanitary toilets, contributing to both disease and malnourishment. Climate change threatens to worsen these disparities through the spread of tropical diseases such as malaria and dengue fever and through declining crop yields.

The World Health Organization's Global Burden of Disease database provides some striking findings on the repercussions of environmental factors, including that unclean water and inadequate sanitation and hygiene are among the 10 leading causes of disease worldwide. Each year environment-related diseases, including acute respiratory infections and diarrhoea, kill at least 3 million children under age 5—more than the entire under-five populations of Austria, Belgium, the Netherlands, Portugal and Switzerland combined.

Environmental degradation and climate change affect physical and social environments, knowledge, assets and behaviours. Dimensions of disadvantage can interact, compounding adverse impacts—for example, the intensity of health risks is highest where water and sanitation are inadequate, deprivations that often coincide. Of the 10 countries with the highest rates of death from environmental disasters, 6 are also in the top 10 in the MPI, including Niger, Mali and Angola.

Impeding education advances for disadvantaged children, especially girls

Despite near universal primary school enrolment in many parts of the world, gaps remain. Nearly 3 in 10 children of primary school age in low HDI countries are not even enrolled in primary school, and multiple constraints, some environmental, persist even for enrolled children. Lack of electricity, for example, has both direct and indirect effects. Electricity access can enable better lighting, allowing increased study time, as well as the use of modern stoves, reducing time spent collecting fuelwood and water, activities shown to slow education progress and lower school enrolment. Girls are more often adversely affected because they are more likely to combine resource collection and schooling. Access to clean water and improved sanitation is also especially important for girls' education, affording them health gains, time savings and privacy.

Other repercussions

Household environmental deprivations can coincide with wider environmental stresses, constricting people's choices in a wide range of contexts and making it harder to earn a living from natural resources: people have to work more to achieve the same returns or may

Environmental degradation stunts people's capabilities in many ways, going beyond incomes and livelihoods to include impacts on health, education and other dimensions of well-being even have to migrate to escape environmental degradation.

Resource-dependent livelihoods are time consuming, especially where households face a lack of modern cooking fuel and clean water. And time-use surveys offer a window into the associated gender-based inequalities. Women typically spend many more hours than men do fetching wood and water, and girls often spend more time than boys do. Women's heavy involvement in these activities has also been shown to prevent them from engaging in higher return activities.

As argued in the 2009 *HDR*, mobility—allowing people to choose where they live—is important for expanding people's freedoms and achieving better outcomes. But legal constraints make migration risky. Estimating how many people move to escape environmental stresses is difficult because other factors are in play, notably poverty. Nevertheless, some estimates are very high.

Environmental stress has also been linked to an increased likelihood of conflict. The link is not direct, however, and is influenced by the broader political economy and contextual factors that make individuals, communities and society vulnerable to the effects of environmental degradation.

Disequalizing effects of extreme weather events

Alongside pernicious chronic threats, environmental degradation can amplify the likelihood of acute threats, with disequalizing impacts. Our analysis suggests that a 10 percent increase in the number of people affected by an extreme weather event reduces a country's HDI almost 2 percent, with larger effects on incomes and in medium HDI countries.

And the burden is not borne equally: the risk of injury and death from floods, high winds and landslides is higher among children, women and the elderly, especially for the poor. The striking gender inequality of natural disasters suggests that inequalities in exposure —as well as in access to resources, capabilities and opportunities—systematically disadvantage some women by making them more vulnerable.

Children disproportionately suffer from weather shocks because the lasting effects of malnourishment and missing school limit their prospects. Evidence from many developing countries shows how transitory income shocks can cause households to pull children out of school. More generally, several factors condition households' exposure to adverse shocks and their capacity to cope, including the type of shock, socioeconomic status, social capital and informal support, and the equity and effectiveness of relief and reconstruction efforts.

Empowerment—reproductive choice and political imbalances

Transformations in gender roles and empowerment have enabled some countries and groups to improve environmental sustainability and equity, advancing human development.

Gender inequality

Our Gender Inequality Index (GII), updated this year for 145 countries, shows how reproductive health constraints contribute to gender inequality. This is important because in countries where effective control of reproduction is universal, women have fewer children, with attendant gains for maternal and child health and reduced greenhouse gas emissions. For instance, in Cuba, Mauritius, Thailand and Tunisia, where reproductive healthcare and contraceptives are readily available, fertility rates are below two births per woman. But substantial unmet need persists worldwide, and evidence suggests that if all women could exercise reproductive choice, population growth would slow enough to bring greenhouse gas emissions below current levels. Meeting unmet need for family planning by 2050 would lower the world's carbon emissions an estimated 17 percent below what they are today.

The GII also focuses on women's participation in political decision-making, highlighting that women lag behind men across the world, especially in Sub-Saharan Africa, South Asia and the Arab States. This has important implications for sustainability and equity. Because women often shoulder the heaviest burden of resource collection and are

A 10 percent increase in the number of people affected by an extreme weather event reduces a country's HDI almost 2 percent, with larger effects on incomes and in medium HDI countries the most exposed to indoor air pollution, they are often more affected than men by decisions related to natural resources. Recent studies reveal that not only is women's participation important but also how they participate—and how much. And because women often show more concern for the environment, support proenvironmental policies and vote for pro-environmental leaders, their greater involvement in politics and in nongovernmental organizations could result in environmental gains, with multiplier effects across all the Millennium Development Goals.

These arguments are not new, but they reaffirm the value of expanding women's effective freedoms. Thus, women's participation in decision-making has both intrinsic value and instrumental importance in addressing equity and environmental degradation.

Power disparities

As argued in the 2010 *HDR*, empowerment has many aspects, including formal, procedural democracy at the national level and participatory processes at the local level. Political empowerment at the national and subnational levels has been shown to improve environmental sustainability. And while context is important, studies show that democracies are typically more accountable to voters and more likely to support civil liberties. A key challenge everywhere, however, is that even in democratic systems, the people most adversely affected by environmental degradation are often the worst off and least empowered, so policy priorities do not reflect their interests and needs.

Evidence is accumulating that power inequalities, mediated through political institutions, affect environmental outcomes in a range of countries and contexts. This means that poor people and other disadvantaged groups disproportionately suffer the effects of environmental degradation. New analysis for this Report covering some 100 countries confirms that greater equity in power distribution, broadly defined, is positively associated with better environmental outcomes, including better access to water, less land degradation and fewer deaths due to indoor and outdoor

air pollution and dirty water—suggesting an important scope for positive synergies.

Positive synergies—winning strategies for the environment, equity and human development

In facing the challenges elaborated here, a range of governments, civil society, private sector actors and development partners have created approaches that integrate environmental sustainability and equity and promote human development—win-win-win strategies. Effective solutions must be context-specific. But it is important, nonetheless, to consider local and national experiences that show potential and to recognize principles that apply across contexts. At the local level we stress the need for inclusive institutions; and at the national level, the scope for the scaling up of successful innovations and policy reform.

The policy agenda is vast. This Report cannot do it full justice—but the value added is in identifying win-win-win strategies that demonstrate success in addressing our social, economic and environmental challenges by managing, or even bypassing, trade-offs through approaches that are good not only for the environment but also for equity and human development more broadly. To inspire debate and action, we offer concrete examples showing how the strategy of overcoming potential trade-offs and identifying positive synergies has worked in practice. Here, we present the example of modern energy.

Access to modern energy

Energy is central to human development, yet some 1.5 billion people worldwide—more than one in five—lack electricity. Among the multidimensionally poor the deprivations are much greater—one in three lacks access.

Is there a trade-off between expanding energy provision and carbon emissions? Not necessarily. We argue that this relationship is wrongly characterized. There are many promising prospects for expanding access without a heavy environmental toll:
- Off-grid decentralized options are technically feasible for delivering energy services

> **Meeting unmet need for family planning by 2050 would lower the world's carbon emissions an estimated 17 percent below what they are today**

to poor households and can be financed and delivered with minimal impact on the climate.

- Providing basic modern energy services for all would increase carbon dioxide emissions by only an estimated 0.8 percent—taking into account broad policy commitments already announced.

Global energy supply reached a tipping point in 2010, with renewables accounting for 25 percent of global power capacity and delivering more than 18 percent of global electricity. The challenge is to expand access at a scale and speed that will improve the lives of poor women and men now and in the future.

Averting environmental degradation

A broader menu of measures to avert environmental degradation ranges from expanding reproductive choice to promoting community forest management and adaptive disaster responses.

Reproductive rights, including access to reproductive health services, are a precondition for women's empowerment and could avert environmental degradation. Major improvements are feasible. Many examples attest to the opportunities for using the existing health infrastructure to deliver reproductive health services at little additional cost and to the importance of community involvement. Consider Bangladesh, where the fertility rate plunged from 6.6 births per woman in 1975 to 2.4 in 2009. The government used outreach and subsidies to make contraceptives more easily available and influenced social norms through discussions with opinion leaders of both sexes, including religious leaders, teachers and nongovernmental organizations.

Community forest management could redress local environmental degradation and mitigate carbon emissions, but experience shows that it also risks excluding and disadvantaging already marginalized groups. To avoid these risks, we underline the importance of broad participation in designing and implementing forest management, especially for women, and of ensuring that poor groups and those who rely on forest resources are not made worse-off.

Promising avenues are also emerging to reduce the adverse impacts of disasters through equitable and adaptive disaster responses and innovative social protection schemes. Disaster responses include community-based risk-mapping and more progressive distribution of reconstructed assets. Experience has spurred a shift to decentralized models of risk reduction. Such efforts can empower local communities, particularly women, by emphasizing participation in design and decision-making. Communities can rebuild in ways that redress existing inequalities.

Rethinking our development model—levers for change

The large disparities across people, groups and countries that add to the large and growing environmental threats pose massive policy challenges. But there is cause for optimism. In many respects the conditions today are more conducive to progress than ever—given innovative policies and initiatives in some parts of the world. Taking the debate further entails bold thinking, especially on the eve of the UN Conference on Sustainable Development (Rio+20) and the dawn of the post-2015 era. This Report advances a new vision for promoting human development through the joint lens of sustainability and equity. At the local and national levels we stress the need to bring equity to the forefront of policy and programme design and to exploit the potential multiplier effects of greater empowerment in legal and political arenas. At the global level we highlight the need to devote more resources to pressing environmental threats and to boost the equity and representation of disadvantaged countries and groups in accessing finance.

Integrating equity concerns into green economy policies

A key theme of this Report is the need to fully integrate equity concerns into policies that affect the environment. Traditional methods of assessing environmental policies fall short. They might expose the impacts on the path of future emissions, for example, but they are

> There are many promising prospects for expanding energy provision without a heavy environmental toll

often silent on distributive issues. Even when the effects on different groups are considered, attention is typically restricted to people's incomes. The importance of equity and inclusion is already explicit in the objectives of green economy policies. We propose taking the agenda further.

Several key principles could bring broader equity concerns into policy-making through stakeholder involvement in analysis that considers:

- Nonincome dimensions of well-being, through such tools as the MPI.
- Indirect and direct effects of policy.
- Compensation mechanisms for adversely affected people.
- Risk of extreme weather events that, however unlikely, could prove catastrophic.

Early analysis of the distributional and environmental consequences of policies is critical.

A clean and safe environment— a right, not a privilege

Embedding environmental rights in national constitutions and legislation can be effective, not least by empowering citizens to protect such rights. At least 120 countries have constitutions that address environmental norms. And many countries without explicit environmental rights interpret general constitutional provisions for individual rights to include a fundamental right to a healthy environment.

Constitutionally recognizing equal rights to a healthy environment promotes equity by no longer limiting access to those who can afford it. And embodying this right in the legal framework can affect government priorities and resource allocations.

Alongside legal recognition of equal rights to a healthy, well functioning environment is the need for enabling institutions, including a fair and independent judiciary, and the right to information from governments and corporations. The international community, too, increasingly recognizes a right to environmental information.

Participation and accountability

Process freedoms are central to human development and, as discussed in last year's *HDR*, have both intrinsic and instrumental value. Major disparities in power translate into large disparities in environmental outcomes. But the converse is that greater empowerment can bring about positive environmental outcomes equitably. Democracy is important, but beyond that, national institutions need to be accountable and inclusive—especially with respect to affected groups, including women —to enable civil society and foster popular access to information.

A prerequisite for participation is open, transparent and inclusive deliberative processes —but in practice, barriers to effective participation persist. Despite positive change, further efforts are needed to strengthen the possibilities for some traditionally excluded groups, such as indigenous peoples, to play a more active role. And increasing evidence points to the importance of enabling women's involvement, both in itself and because it has been linked to more sustainable outcomes.

Where governments are responsive to popular concerns, change is more likely. An environment in which civil society thrives also engenders accountability at the local, national and global levels, while freedom of press is vital in raising awareness and facilitating public participation.

Financing investments: where do we stand?

Sustainability debates raise major questions of costs and financing, including who should finance what—and how. Equity principles argue for large transfers of resources to poor countries, both to achieve more equitable access to water and energy and to pay for adapting to climate change and mitigating its effects.

Four important messages emerge from our financing analysis:

- Investment needs are large, but they do not exceed current spending on other sectors such as the military. The estimated annual investment to achieve universal access to modern sources of energy is less than an eighth of annual subsidies for fossils fuels.
- Public sector commitments are important (the generosity of some donors stands out), and the private sector is a major—and

> Traditional methods of assessing environmental policies are often silent on distribution issues. While the importance of equity and inclusion is already explicit in the objectives of green economy policies, we propose taking the agenda further

critical—source of finance. Public efforts can catalyse private investment, emphasizing the importance of increasing public funds and supporting a positive investment climate and local capacity.

- Data constraints make it hard to monitor private and domestic public sector spending on environmental sustainability. Available information allows only official development assistance flows to be examined.
- Funding architecture is complex and fragmented, reducing its effectiveness and making spending hard to monitor. There is much to learn from earlier commitments to aid effectiveness made in Paris and Accra.

Although the evidence on needs, commitments and disbursements is patchy and the magnitudes uncertain, the picture is clear. The gaps between official development assistance spending and the investments needed to address climate change, low-carbon energy, and water and sanitation are huge—even larger than the gap between commitments and investment needs. Spending on low-carbon energy sources is only 1.6 percent of the lower bound estimate of needs, while spending on climate change adaptation and mitigation is around 11 percent of the lower bound of estimated need. For water and sanitation the amounts are much smaller, and official development assistance commitments are closer to the estimated costs.

Closing the funding gap: currency transaction tax—from great idea to practical policy

The funding gap in resources available to address the deprivations and challenges documented in this Report could be substantially narrowed by taking advantage of new opportunities. The prime candidate is a currency transaction tax. Argued for by the 1994 *HDR*, the idea is increasingly being accepted as a practical policy option. The recent financial crisis has revived interest in the proposal, underscoring its relevance and timeliness.

Today's foreign exchange settlement infrastructure is more organized, centralized and standardized, so the feasibility of implementing the tax is something new to highlight. It has high-level endorsement, including from the Leading Group on Innovative Financing, with some 63 countries, among them China, France, Germany, Japan and the United Kingdom. And the UN High-Level Advisory Group on Climate Change Financing recently proposed that 25–50 percent of the proceeds from such a tax be directed to climate change adaptation and mitigation in developing countries.

Our updated analysis shows that at a very minimal rate (0.005 percent) and without any additional administrative costs, the currency transaction tax could yield additional annual revenues of about $40 billion. Not many other options at the required scale could satisfy the new and additional funding needs that have been stressed in international debates.

A broader financial transaction tax also promises large revenue potential. Most G-20 countries have already implemented a financial transaction tax, and the International Monetary Fund (IMF) has confirmed the administrative feasibility of a broader tax. One version of the tax, a levy of 0.05 percent on domestic and international financial transactions, could raise an estimated $600–$700 billion.

Monetizing part of the IMF's surplus Special Drawing Rights has also attracted interest. This could raise up to $75 billion at little or no budgetary cost to contributing governments. The SDRs have the added appeal of acting as a monetary rebalancing instrument; demand is expected to come from emerging market economies looking to diversify their reserves.

Reforms for greater equity and voice

Bridging the gap that separates policy-makers, negotiators and decision-makers from the citizens most vulnerable to environmental degradation requires closing the accountability gap in global environmental governance. Accountability alone cannot meet the challenge, but it is fundamental for building a socially and environmentally effective global governance system that delivers for people.

We call for measures to improve equity and voice in access to financial flows directed

> At a minimal rate and without additional administrative costs, a currency transaction tax could yield annual revenues of $40 billion. Not many other options could satisfy the new and additional funding needs stressed in international debates

at supporting efforts to combat environmental degradation.

Private resources are critical, but because most of the financial flows into the energy sector, for example, come from private hands, the greater risks and lower returns of some regions in the eyes of private investors affect the patterns of flows. Without reform, access to financing will remain unevenly distributed across countries and, indeed, exacerbate existing inequalities. This underlines the importance of ensuring that flows of public investments are equitable and help create conditions to attract future private flows.

The implications are clear—principles of equity are needed to guide and encourage international financial flows. Support for institution building is needed so that developing countries can establish appropriate policies and incentives. The associated governance mechanisms for international public financing must allow for voice and social accountability.

Any truly transformational effort to scale up efforts to slow or halt climate change will require blending domestic and international, private and public, and grant and loan resources. To facilitate both equitable access and efficient use of international financial flows, this Report advocates empowering national stakeholders to blend climate finance at the country level. National climate funds can facilitate the operational blending and monitoring of domestic and international, private and public, and grant and loan resources. This is essential to ensure domestic accountability and positive distributional effects.

The Report proposes an emphasis on four country-level sets of tools to take this agenda forward:

- *Low-emission, climate-resilient strategies* —to align human development, equity and climate change goals.
- *Public-private partnerships*—to catalyse capital from businesses and households.
- *Climate deal-flow facilities*—to bring about equitable access to international public finance.
- *Coordinated implementation and monitoring, reporting and verification systems*—to bring about long-term, efficient results and accountability to local populations as well as partners.

Finally, we call for a high-profile, global Universal Energy Access Initiative with advocacy and awareness and dedicated support to developing clean energy at the country level. Such an initiative could kickstart efforts to shift from incremental to transformative change.

*   *   *

This Report casts light on the links between sustainability and equity and shows how human development can become more sustainable and more equitable. It reveals how environmental degradation hurts poor and vulnerable groups more than others. We propose a policy agenda that will redress these imbalances, framing a strategy for tackling current environmental problems in a way that promotes equity and human development. And we show practical ways to promote jointly these complementary goals, expanding people's choices while protecting our environment.

> Any truly transformational effort to scale up efforts to slow or halt climate change will require blending domestic and international, private and public, and grant and loan resources

CHAPTER 1

Why sustainability and equity?

The human development approach has enduring relevance for making sense of our world. Last year's *Human Development Report* (*HDR*) reaffirmed the concept of human development—emphasizing empowerment, equity and sustainability in expanding people's choices. It showed that these key aspects do not always coincide and highlighted challenges in addressing them. And it raised the need to promote empowerment, equity and sustainability so that they are mutually reinforcing.

That report also documented substantial progress over the past four decades. The Human Development Index (HDI) has risen dramatically since 1970—41 percent overall and 61 percent in low HDI countries—reflecting strong advances in health, education and incomes. Significant gains have been made in girls' primary and secondary education, for example. If these rates of progress are sustained, by 2050 more than three-quarters of the world's people will live in countries with an HDI similar to that of very high HDI countries today. There has also been progress in other dimensions: the share of countries that are democracies has risen from less than a third to three-fifths. The 2011 Arab Spring marked another leap forward, appearing to end decades of autocratic rule for some 100 million people.

But we cannot assume that average past rates of progress will continue: progress has been far from uniform across countries and over time. And in two key dimensions of human development, conditions have deteriorated. For environmental sustainability, evidence of devastating current and future impacts is mounting. And income inequality has worsened, while disparities in health and education remain significant.

These are the themes of this Report: the adverse human repercussions of environmental degradation, which causes disproportionate harm to poor and disadvantaged people, and the need to make greater equity part of the solution. Exploring patterns and implications, the Report sounds a bold call to action. In so doing, it identifies ways to break the pernicious link between environmental degradation and economic growth that has tainted much of the development experience of at least the past half-century and threatens future progress.

This vision aligns with that of international declarations on sustainable development —including those in Stockholm (1972), Rio de Janeiro (1992) and Johannesburg (2002)— which advanced the notion of three pillars of sustainable development: environmental, economic and social.[1] Intragenerational equity is part of the social pillar. Our call for prudence in managing the environment and basic natural resources springs from an emphasis on expanding opportunities for the most disadvantaged and from the need to consider the risks of catastrophic events.

We do not deal at length with broader issues of economic, financial and political sustainability, though we draw on some important lessons from those spheres. We can add more value by concentrating on a well defined set of issues, rather than attempting to cover related fields. The choice of scope is also driven by the urgency of addressing today's grave environmental threats.

In sum, this Report highlights the links between two closely related challenges to show how human development can become both more environmentally sustainable and more equitable.

*   *   *

This chapter sets the stage by reviewing the notion of limits to human development and two alternate paradigms of sustainability that fundamentally affect how we assess some of humanity's most pressing choices. We take a conservative stance because we cannot be certain of always finding technological fixes to the problems we create. Central to this approach is recognizing the inherent uncertainty associated with the future and the need to deal with risks responsibly to meet our obligations to current and future generations.

Are there limits to human development?

Most people around the world have seen major improvements in their lives over the last 40 years. But there are major constraints in our capacity to sustain these trends. If we deal decisively with these challenges, we could be on the cusp of an era of historic opportunities for expanded choices and freedoms. But if we fail to act, future generations may remember the early 21st century as the time when the doors to a better future closed for most of the world's people.

We care about environmental sustainability because of the fundamental injustice of one generation living at the expense of others. Poeple born today should not have a greater claim on Earth's resources than those born a hundred or a thousand years from now. We can do much to ensure that our use of the world's resources does not damage future opportunities—and we should.

Amartya Sen notes that "a fouled environment in which future generations are denied the presence of fresh air ... will remain foul even if future generations are so very rich."[2] The fundamental uncertainty about what people will value in the future means that we need to ensure equal freedom of choice, the lynchpin of the capability approach, in part by protecting the availability and diversity of natural resources.[3] Such resources are critical in allowing us to lead lives that we value and have reason to value.[4]

The early HDRs recognized the centrality of the environment. The first report warned of the continuing increase in environmental hazards, including health risks, from Earth's warming, damage to the ozone layer, industrial pollution and environmental disasters.[5]

The 1994 HDR asserted "there is no tension between human development and sustainable development. Both are based in the universalism of life claims."[6]

The 2010 HDR went further, emphasizing sustainability in reaffirming human development:[7]

> Human development is the expansion of people's freedoms to live long, healthy and creative lives; to advance other goals they have reason to value; and to engage actively in shaping development *equitably and sustainably on a shared planet*. People are both the beneficiaries and the drivers of human development, as individuals and in groups.

Sustainable development gained prominence with the 1987 publication of *Our Common Future*, the report of the UN World Commission on Environment and Development, headed by former Norwegian Prime Minister Gro Harlem Brundtland. The report produced what became the standard definition of sustainable development: "development that meets the needs of the present without compromising the ability of future generations to meet their own needs."[8] But the commission's work is relevant for much more. It differed from much subsequent work on sustainability in its emphasis on equity:

> Many problems of resource depletion and environmental stress arise from disparities in economic and political power. An industry may get away with unacceptable levels of water pollution because the people who bear the brunt of it are poor and unable to complain effectively. A forest may be destroyed by excessive felling because the people living there have no alternatives or because timber contractors generally have more influence than forest dwellers. Globally, wealthier nations are better placed financially and technologically to cope with the effects of climatic change. *Hence, our inability to promote the common interest in sustainable development is often a product of the relative neglect of economic and social justice within and amongst nations.*

The commission also voiced concerns that the world was reaching its natural limits to growth in economic activity. In 1972 a group of scientists commissioned by the Club of Rome published *The Limits to Growth*, predicting that at current rates of consumption growth, many natural resources would run out in the next century. Economists criticized this thesis for its disregard of price adjustments and technological change that would moderate rising demand for resources.[9] But the facts seemed to bear out some of their predictions —adjusted for inflation, oil prices rose fivefold between 1970 and 1985.[10]

Over the next two decades the perception of scarcity changed. Most commodity prices peaked in the mid-1980s, and by 1990 prices had fallen from their 1980s highs—57 percent for petroleum, 45 percent for coal and 19 percent for copper. Against this backdrop the belief that we were approaching a global resource constraint became less plausible—if resources were becoming scarce, prices should be rising not falling. By 1997 even the United Nations Economic and Social Council was referring to the Club of Rome report's predictions as "dogmatic," "unreliable" and "politically counterproductive."[11]

Now, the pendulum has swung back again. Concerns differ in some respects from those four decades ago. Today, the problems are more evident in the preservation of *renewable* natural resources, ranging from forests and fisheries to the air we breathe. But the message is clear: our development model is bumping up against concrete limits.

Competing paradigms

The idea that resource scarcity limits the world's development potential has a long history. In the late 18th century Malthus believed that limited land was an absolute constraint on food consumption and therefore on the population that could inhabit the Earth. Yet 200 years later, the world is home to seven times more people than when Malthus wrote.

In practice, technological improvements and substitution of abundant for scarce resources have allowed living standards to continue to rise over the past two centuries. The inflation-adjusted price of food is much lower today than it was 200—or even 50—years ago, and known reserves of many minerals are now substantially higher than in 1950.[12] With improved farming techniques, world food production has outstripped population growth. The Green Revolution doubled rice and wheat yields in Asia between the 1960s and 1990s through the introduction of high-yield plant varieties, better irrigation and the use of fertilizers and pesticides.[13] These increased yields were achieved, however, through means that were not always sustainable. Our concerns for more sustainable agricultural practices go hand in hand with our awareness of the roughly 1 billion people who are undernourished and face serious food insecurity.[14]

These observations have led some to posit that as the stock of nonrenewable resources is consumed, technological innovation and price signals will avert shortages that limit future development. As a resource becomes scarcer, rising relative prices mean higher potential profits for innovators and for the owners of assets that can be substituted for the diminished scarce resource. These forces can cut resource use substantially even as consumption grows. The Worldwatch Institute estimates that the production of one unit of output in the United States in 2000 required less than a fifth as much energy as it did in 1800.[15] This leads to a thesis known as *weak sustainability*, which focuses on total capital stock rather than on natural resource depletion.

Disputing this view, advocates of the *strong sustainability* thesis believe that some basic natural assets have no real substitutes and thus must be preserved.[16] These assets are fundamental not only to our capacity to produce goods and services but also to human life. Societies should strive to sustain the flow of services from natural capital over time because the accumulation of physical or other kinds of capital cannot compensate for Earth's warming, ozone layer depletion and major biodiversity losses.

While advocates of strong sustainability do not disregard the growing efficiency of resource use, they argue that history is not necessarily a good guide to the future. In the past some

The thesis of weak sustainability focuses on total capital stock rather than on natural resource depletion; that of strong sustainability focuses on the belief that some basic natural assets have no real substitutes and thus must be preserved constraints on natural capital may not have been binding, but today some types of natural capital are irreplaceable. No example illustrates this better than Earth's warming. There is overwhelming evidence that we are reaching an upper limit to our capacity to emit greenhouse gases without dire consequences. As one advocate of strong sustainability argues, we are moving from an "empty world" economy, where human-made capital was limiting and natural capital superabundant, to a "full world" economy, where the opposite is true.[17]

Beyond these debates, more recent thinking has emphasized the potential congruence of growth and environmental sustainability within the broader paradigm of a green economy.[18] This thinking diverges from the traditional discourse on sustainability by focusing on ways in which economic policies can engender sustainable production and consumption patterns with inclusive, pro-poor solutions that integrate environmental considerations into everyday economic decisions.[19] Our approach complements and enriches the green economy discourse, emphasizing people, the multiple dimensions of well-being and equity. Our concerns include—but go beyond —growth alone.

The critical role of uncertainty

Differences between strong and weak sustainability approaches go beyond whether financial savings can substitute for natural resource depletion. A key difference lies in the role of uncertainty.

How can we be sure of finding ways to offset the damage caused by current and future production and consumption? The answer is that we cannot be certain. Acknowledging this inherent uncertainty supports the strong sustainability thesis.

Consider biodiversity. Its instrumental benefits for people are well known: greater biodiversity increases the chances of finding cures for illnesses, developing high-yield crops and maintaining ecosystem goods and services such as water quality. We know that ecosystems are resilient—up to a point. Yet defining the threshold at which ecosystems break down is hard. An ecosystem might sustain piecemeal destruction for some time until an unknown threshold is breached such that it unravels.[20] These risks and unknown thresholds have led to real concerns about gambling with the planet (box 1.1).

Technological change is uncertain. Productivity growth accelerated after the Second World War, for example, then slowed between the 1970s and 1990s.[21] We can understand retroactively what drove accelerations and slowdowns, but it is very difficult to predict the future. Even more uncertainty surrounds the types of innovations that will emerge. History is replete with unfulfilled predictions of specific innovations—from all-purpose personal robots to mass-market space travel—and with the failure to anticipate other innovations, such as personal computers, the Internet and mobile communications.[22]

BOX 1.1

Environmental risk management—gambling with the planet

We are gambling with our planet through "games" in which private individuals reap the benefits while society bears the costs. A system that allows such outcomes is doomed to mismanage risk. As Nobel Prize–winning economist Joseph Stiglitz recently noted, "the bankers that put our economy at risk and the owners of energy companies that put our planet at risk may walk off with a mint. But *on average* and *almost certainly*, we as a society, like gamblers, will lose."

Perverse incentives provide investment banks and energy companies with hidden subsidies, like low liability caps, the prospect of bailouts, and the knowledge that taxpayers will shoulder the costs. Because these companies do not have to bear the full cost of any resulting crises, they may take excessive risks. Consider the 2010 BP Deepwater Horizon oil spill in the United States, for example, where the costs well exceeded the $75 million liability limit. And even where liability is limitless, loopholes exist. In Japan, for instance, the Nuclear Compensation Act excludes cases in which "the damage is caused by a grave natural disaster of exceptional character."

Rare events with huge consequences are of course difficult to predict. But we can no longer afford to turn a blind eye, notwithstanding uncertainties. These events are occurring more frequently. And because most greenhouse gases will remain in the atmosphere for centuries, we cannot wait until all uncertainties are resolved. The sooner we act, the better.

What level of risk will persuade people of the need to change their behaviour? Research in behavioural psychology and experimental economics yields sobering insights. In simulation exercises showing how groups of participants respond when asked to invest collectively in preventing climate change, too many players were free riding, that is, counting on the altruism of others. In scenarios where the probability of disastrous climate change was very low, almost no funds were pledged. But even when the probability was 90 percent, only about half of 30 study groups pledged sufficient funds.

The projected costs of averting climate change pale beside those of allowing change to continue unbridled. But precisely because cooperation is not guaranteed, even under high-probability scenarios, strong political and advocacy efforts are needed to elicit commitments.

As Joseph Stiglitz warns, the risks of inaction are too high: "If there were other planets to which we could move at low cost in the event of the almost certain outcome predicted by scientists, one could argue that this risk is worth taking. But there aren't, so it isn't."

Source: Stiglitz 2011; Milinksi and others 2008; Speth 2008.

Climate change debates have brought into sharp relief the relevance of uncertainty and risk for understanding the future.[23] Scientists have concluded that the probability of a disastrous systemwide collapse is not negligible. And since we cannot place a meaningful upper bound on the catastrophic losses from large temperature changes, we need to cut greenhouse gas emissions not only to mitigate the consequences known to result from their accumulation but also to protect ourselves against uncertain worst-case scenarios.[24]

It follows that weak and strong sustainability differ, more than anything, in their attitude towards risk. The question is not whether different types of natural and other forms of capital were substitutes in the past, but whether technological and institutional change will proceed at a pace and direction that ensure continuing improvements in human development.

The position we take depends also on the value we put on the well-being of future generations relative to that of current generations —in other words, on how we discount the future. From the perspective of capabilities, there is no justification to assume that the future will provide greater opportunities than the present or to place a lower value on the well-being of the present generation over future ones.[25]

Given the principles underlying the human development approach, the inclination to give equal weight to the well-being of all generations and the centrality of risk and uncertainty, our position leans towards that of strong sustainability.

Sustainability, equity and human development

Since the Brundtland Report, scholars have offered further definitions of sustainable development. One point of contention was the commission's reference to "needs," often interpreted to mean *basic* needs, which some believe is too narrow.

Economist Robert Solow offered an alternative definition in 1993, arguing that the duty of sustainability was "to bequeath to posterity not any particular thing but rather to endow them with whatever it takes to achieve a standard of living at least as good as our own and to look after their next generation similarly." Solow added, "We are not to consume humanity's capital, in the broadest sense," which is a succinct statement of the case for weak sustainability. Of course, just what "standard of living" refers to is an open question,[26] while what is "good" is also value dependent.

What we mean by sustainability

Most definitions of sustainable development capture the precept that the possibilities open to people tomorrow should not differ from those open today, but generally do not adequately capture sustainable *human* development. They do not refer to the expansion of choice, freedoms and capabilities intrinsic to human development. They do not recognize that some dimensions of well-being are incommensurable. And they do not consider risk.

Human development is the expansion of the freedoms and capabilities people have to lead lives they value and have reason to value. Freedoms and capabilities that enable us to lead meaningful lives go beyond satisfaction of essential needs. In recognizing that many ends are necessary for a good life and that these ends can be intrinsically valuable, freedoms and capabilities are also very different from living standards and consumption.[27] We can respect other species, independent of their contribution to our living standards, just as we can value natural beauty, regardless of its direct contribution to our material standard of living.

The human development approach recognizes that people have rights that are not affected by the arbitrariness of when they were born. Further, the rights in question refer not only to the capacity to sustain the same living standards but also to access the same opportunities. This limits the substitution that can occur across dimensions of well-being. Today's generation cannot ask future generations to breathe polluted air in exchange for a greater capacity to produce goods and services. That would restrict the freedom of future generations to choose clean air over more goods and services.

Since we cannot place a meaningful upper bound on the catastrophic losses from large temperature changes, we need to cut greenhouse gas emissions not only to mitigate the known consequences but also to protect against uncertain worst-case scenarios

A central concern of the human development approach is protecting the most disadvantaged groups. The most disadvantaged are not just the generations that are worse off on average. They are also those who would suffer most from the realizations of the adverse risks they face as a result of our activity. Thus, we are concerned not only with what happens on average or in the most likely scenario but also with what happens in less likely but still possible scenarios, particularly those that entail catastrophic risks.

Building on the work of Anand and Sen,[28] we define "sustainable human development" as "the expansion of the substantive freedoms of people today while making reasonable efforts to avoid seriously compromising those of future generations." Like the 1994 HDR, this definition emphasizes that the objective of development is to sustain the freedoms and capabilities that allow people to lead meaningful lives. Our definition of sustainable human development is normative: we seek the sustainability not just of any state of events but of those that expand substantive freedoms.

Therefore, inequitable development can never be sustainable human development.

This Report does not propose a unique measure of sustainable human development. Despite recent advances, measuring sustainability remains plagued by major data limitations (box 1.2). A perennial challenge is the disconnect among local, national and global measures—such as the distinction between whether a national economy is sustainable and its contribution to global sustainability. For example, attributing the damage from carbon dioxide to the economy that produces goods that have been exported for consumption ignores both who benefited from consuming the goods and services and the global nature of the damage.

Focusing too much on measurement can obscure some key but unquantifiable issues. These include the risks faced by different people and groups and the role of public deliberation in making policy choices and enabling a society to decide how to avoid seriously compromising future well-being.

What we mean by equity

Early ideas of equity postulated that individuals should be rewarded according to their contribution to society.[29] Used interchangeably with fairness, equity has come to refer primarily to distributive justice—that is, unjust inequalities between people.

Contemporary thinking on equity owes much to the work of US philosopher John Rawls, who argued that just outcomes are those that people would agree to under a "veil of ignorance"—that is, if they did not know what status they would occupy in society.[30] Rawls's idea of justice espoused basic liberties and procedural fairness and permitted inequalities only if they could reasonably be expected to be to everyone's advantage (and if reducing them would make everyone worse off).

The capability approach emerged from thinking about which inequalities are just or unjust. In a set of landmark lectures in 1979, Amartya Sen proposed that we think about equality in terms of capabilities. Equality is neither necessary nor sufficient for equity. Different individual abilities and preferences lead to

BOX 1.2

Measures of sustainability—a conceptual overview

The conceptual paradigm—weak sustainability or strong—has implications for how we measure and assess trends. Given the range of opinions on how to define sustainability, it is not surprising that a broadly acceptable quantitative measure is hard to pin down. Many measures have emerged in the literature. One recent study identified 37—some better known than others. Here we review those that are most in use.

Green national accounting adjusts such measures as gross domestic product or savings for environmental quality and resource depletion. Adjusted net savings, a measure of weak sustainability, adds education spending and subtracts for the depletion of energy, minerals and forests and for damage from carbon dioxide emissions and pollution. It is an aggregate measure of all capital in an economy—financial, physical, human and environmental. It implies that the different kinds of capital are perfect substitutes, so that financial savings can replace a loss of natural resources, for example.

Composite indices aggregate social, economic and environmental indicators into a single index. A great deal of innovative work has pursued this approach. Two examples capturing strong sustainability are the ecological footprint—a measure of the annual stress people put on the biosphere—and the environmental performance index.

None of the aggregate measures is perfect. For instance, some scholars take issue with adjusted net savings' valuing such nonmarket components as the damage from carbon dioxide emissions, while the ecological footprint has been criticized for neglecting biodiversity.

Informed by ongoing debates about measurement, we refer to the main composite measures alongside a dashboard that presents specific indicators to capture different aspects of sustainability (see statistical tables 6 and 7). The single indicators underline the importance of strong sustainability by exposing poor performance and deterioration on any front.

Source: Jha and Pereira 2011; Dasgupta 2007; Neumayer 2010a, 2010b.

different outcomes, even with identical opportunities and access to resources. Absolute levels of capabilities matter: inequality between millionaires and billionaires is less the focus than inequalities between the poor and the wealthy. And personal characteristics are also important: poor and disadvantaged groups, including people with mental or physical disabilities, need greater access to public goods and services to achieve equality of capabilities.

Despite conceptual differences, inequity and inequality in outcomes are closely linked in practice—because inequalities in outcomes are largely the product of unequal access to capabilities. A Malian can expect to live 32 fewer years on average than a Norwegian because the possibilities for people in Mali are far narrower on average than those for people in Norway. In this case, clearly the inequalities between Mali and Norway are also inequitable. Moreover, we can measure inequality in key outcomes, whereas we cannot readily observe the distribution of capabilities. So, in this Report we use inequality as a proxy for inequity, pointing out the exceptions where the relationship is not straightforward. We also consider inequality in human development—extending beyond income inequality to inequalities in access to health, education and broader political freedoms.

Why centre on equitable sustainability?

This Report concentrates on the links between sustainability and equity. The main issues are the adverse repercussions for human development of the lack of environmental sustainability, especially for those currently disadvantaged, and more positively, the intersections between greater sustainability and equity, as well as the potential for progressive reforms that promote both goals. We will argue that promoting human development entails addressing local, national and global sustainability and that this can—and should—be equitable and empowering.

We ensure that the aspirations of the world's poor for better lives are fully taken into account in moving towards greater environmental sustainability.[31] Expanding people's opportunities and choices is a major imperative of the human development approach. There may be trade-offs and difficult choices. But as we discuss below, the existence of these choices also implies a higher order moral imperative to consider how to build positive synergies that keep the present from being at odds with the future.

Concerns with sustainability and equity are similar in one fundamental sense: both are about distributive justice. Inequitable processes are unjust, whether across groups or generations. Inequalities are especially unjust when they systematically disadvantage specific groups of people, whether because of gender, race or birthplace, or when the gap is so great that acute poverty is high. The current generation's destroying the environment for future generations is no different from a present-day group's suppressing the aspirations of other groups for equal opportunities to jobs, health or education.

Anand and Sen made the case for jointly considering sustainability and equity more than a decade ago: "It would be a gross violation of the universalist principle," they argued, "if we were to be obsessed about *inter*generational equity without at the same seizing the problem of *intra*generational equity."[32] Yet many theories on sustainability view equity and the plight of the poor as separate and unrelated. Such thinking is incomplete and counterproductive. Thinking about policies to restore sustainability independent of policies to address inequalities between and within countries is equivalent to framing policies to address inequalities between groups (such as rural and urban) while disregarding the interrelationships with equity between other groups (such as poor and rich).

While we argue strongly for the need to consider sustainability and equity jointly, we do not claim that the two are the same. Sustainability is concerned with one type of equity—across people born in different times —as distinct from the distribution of outcomes, opportunities or capabilities *today*. If this were not the case, it would be meaningless to speak about the effect of equity on sustainability.

> Promoting human development entails addressing local, national and global sustainability; this can—and should —be equitable and empowering

The reasons to focus on the links between sustainability and equity are normative but also empirical. The empirics help us understand their links—how they reinforce each other in some cases—and the trade-offs that can arise, as we investigate in chapters 2 and 3.

Our focus of inquiry

This Report identifies ways to jointly advance sustainability and equity. Our line of inquiry supports the broader human development agenda, which seeks to understand the actions and strategies people can use to expand their freedoms and capabilities. While we recognize that many factors could impede or enhance the sustainability of human development, we limit our focus to environmental sustainability. We discuss what people, communities, societies and the world can do to ensure that processes respect distributive justice between and across generations while expanding capabilities wherever possible.

Pursuing sustainability and equity jointly does not require that they be mutually reinforcing. In many instances they will not be. But it compels us to identify positive synergies between the two and to give special consideration to the trade-offs.

Figure 1.1 illustrates this logic with examples of specific policies that typically improve or worsen sustainability and equity.[33] While we have sought to highlight likely outcomes, the implications are often context-specific, so the figure is not intended to be deterministic. Some examples:

- Expanded access to renewable energy and a global currency transaction tax to finance climate change mitigation and adaptation can advance both sustainability and equity (quadrant 1), as we will explore in chapters 4 and 5.
- Subsidies on gasoline consumption, still common in many countries, may set us back in both dimensions (quadrant 3) by favouring those who can afford a car while generating an incentive for excessive resource depletion. Countless cases of regressive, inequitable subsidies in agriculture, energy and water are also often associated with environmental damage.[34]
- Some policies may advance one objective but set back the other. Subsidizing coal in developing countries may promote growth but also contribute to higher greenhouse gas emissions. Such a policy could have positive effects on global equity but negative effects on sustainability (quadrant 4).
- The converse can also occur: policies can improve sustainability while worsening inequity (quadrant 2). For example, policies that limit access to common property resources such as forests may enhance sustainability by preserving the natural resource but can deprive poor groups of their primary source of livelihoods, though this is certainly not always the case.

We do not assume a positive empirical association between sustainability and equity. This association may well exist, and it requires investigation. Schematically, it can arise whenever most of the feasible alternatives fall in either quadrant 1 or 3 of figure 1.1. But it is also possible that most feasible alternatives fall in quadrant 2 or 4, which present trade-offs between sustainability and equity. And the pathways may be nonlinear. Such possibilities require explicit and careful consideration.

FIGURE 1.1

An illustration of policy synergies and trade-offs between equity and sustainability

This framework encourages special attention to identifying positive synergies between the two goals and to considering trade-offs.

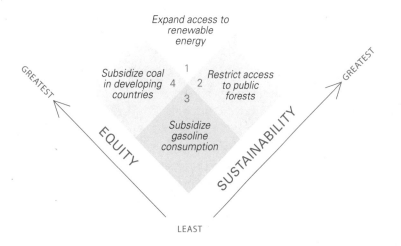

But we can go further. A trade-off between sustainability and equity is like a trade-off in the well-being of two disadvantaged groups. Because no trade-off is isolated from a society's structural and institutional conditions, as in the case of trade-offs between the claims of different groups, we must address the underlying constraints. So, our policy focus is aimed not only at finding positive synergies but also at identifying ways to build synergies. Our objective is to find solutions that fall in quadrant 1—solutions that are win-win-win (good for the environment while promoting equity and human development). We should prefer approaches in quadrant 1, whenever available, to those that fall in quadrant 2 or 3 but recognize that options in quadrant 1 may not always be available.[35]

*   *   *

The next chapter reviews how resource constraints and environmental thresholds impede human development and equity. We review the cross-national evidence of links among sustainability, equity and human development —and identify the challenges to meeting these goals successfully.

Patterns and trends in human development, equity and environmental indicators

This chapter reviews patterns and trends in human development, inequality and key environmental indicators. We present new evidence of the threats to progress posed by environmental degradation and inequalities within and across countries. The most disadvantaged bear and will continue to bear the consequences of environmental degradation, even if many contribute little to the underlying causes.

Progress and prospects

Progress in many aspects of human development has been substantial over the past 40 years, as the 2010 *Human Development Report* (*HDR*) showed. But income distribution has worsened, and environmental degradation threatens future prospects.

Progress in human development

Most people today live longer, are more educated and have more access to goods and services than ever before. Even in economically distressed countries, people's health and education have improved greatly. And progress has extended to expansions in people's power to select leaders, influence public decisions and share knowledge.

Witness the gains in our summary measure of development, the Human Development Index (HDI), a simple composite measure that includes health, schooling and income. The world's average HDI increased 18 percent between 1990 and 2010 (41 percent since 1970), reflecting large improvements in life expectancy, school enrolment, literacy and income.[1] Almost all countries benefited. Of the 135 countries in our sample for 1970–2010 (with 92 percent of the world's people), only three had a lower HDI in 2010 than in 1970. Poor countries are catching up with rich

countries on the HDI, convergence that paints a far more optimistic picture than do trends in income, where divergence continues.

But not all countries have seen rapid progress, and the variations are striking. People in Southern Africa and the former Soviet Union have endured times of regress, especially in health. And countries starting from the same position had markedly different experiences. China's per capita income grew an astounding 1,200 percent over the 40 years, but the Democratic Republic of the Congo's fell 80 percent. Advances in technical knowledge and globalization made progress more feasible for countries at all levels of development, but countries took advantage of the opportunities in different ways.

The 2010 *HDR* reviewed trends in empowerment—people's ability to exercise choices and to participate in, shape and benefit from household, community and national processes. For the Arab States the situation described last year—of few signs of in-depth democratization—has changed profoundly since late 2010 (box 2.1).

Has progress come at the cost of environmental degradation?

Not all sides of the story are positive. Income inequality has worsened, and production and consumption patterns, especially in rich countries, seem to be unsustainable.

To explore environmental trends, we need to decide which measure of environmental degradation to use. The conceptual challenges were considered in chapter 1. There are also data challenges, and some measures are available only for recent years. Box 2.2 discusses the important insights offered by leading aggregate sustainability measures. But to understand patterns and trends, we prefer to use specific indicators.[2]

BOX 2.1

Overcoming the democratic deficit—empowerment and the Arab Spring

Last year's *Human Development Report (HDR)* looked at the "democratic deficit" in the Arab States, seeking to understand why the region had demonstrated few signs of significant democratization.

Drawing on the *Arab Human Development Reports* since 2002, the 2010 global *HDR* pointed to the stark contrasts between actual practice and formal adherence to democracy, human rights and the rule of law. It emphasized that many democratic reforms in the region had been offset by countermeasures limiting citizen rights in other respects—including nearly unchecked concentration of power in the executive branch. Civil society, in turn, was weak: "Popular demand for democratic transformation and citizens' participation is a nascent and fragile development in the Arab countries," noted the 2009 *Arab Human Development Report* (p. 73).

Even so, in most of the Arab States long-term trends showed major progress in income, health and education, the Human Development Index (HDI) dimensions, since 1970. Five Arab States emerged among the top 10 performers—Oman, Saudi Arabia, Tunisia, Algeria and Morocco—while Libya was among the top 10 countries in nonincome HDI achievement. All these countries advanced due mainly to improvements in health and education.

Particularly striking were the changes in these countries relative to others at a similar HDI 40 years earlier. For instance, in 1970 Tunisia had a lower life expectancy than the Democratic Republic of the Congo and fewer children in school than Malawi. Yet by 2010 Tunisia was in the high HDI category, with an average life expectancy of 74 years and most children enrolled through secondary school.

The recent pro-democracy protests across the Arab States began in Tunisia and Egypt, driven in both cases by educated urban youth. Multiple and complex causes underlie any social phenomena, but the democratization movement can be considered a direct consequence of human development progress. Indeed, many analysts over the years—sociologists, political scientists and others both in and outside the region—have argued that popular demand for democracy and human rights is an integral part of broader modernization and development. As the first *Arab Human Development Report* affirmed in 2002 (p. 18): "Human development, by enhancing human capabilities, creates the ability to exercise freedom, and human rights, by providing the necessary framework, create the opportunity to exercise it. Freedom is both the guarantor and the goal of both human development and human rights."

In the long run people who have attained higher levels of education and who have experienced rising living standards are unwilling to tolerate continued autocratic rule. For example, health and education are often necessary for meaningful participation in public life. Progress in these areas often occurs through their extension to the disadvantaged and disenfranchised, and once extended, it is very hard for elites to exclude the broader population from civic and political rights. The transition in the former Soviet Union is an earlier example of this pattern.

But this progress must be placed within a broader context. Development has led to other contradictions, with rising but unfulfilled expectations often generating deep social frustrations. Inequality has increased while cellphones and Twitter™ have permitted more rapid transmission of ideas. Many analysts have pointed to high unemployment and underemployment among educated youth as a key factor driving political dissent in the region. Half the population in the Arab States is under 25, and youth unemployment rates are nearly double the global average. In Egypt an estimated 25 percent of college graduates cannot find full-time professional work—in Tunisia that figure rises to 30 percent.

Although the outcome of this year's political upheavals will not be clear for some time, the region has already profoundly changed. What was striking until recently was the juxtaposition of authoritarian rule and rising development achievement. In 2011 this "Arab democracy paradox" seemed to be coming to a sudden end, opening the door to a much fuller realization of people's freedoms and capabilities throughout the region.

Source: 2010 *HDR* (UNDP–HDRO 2010; see inside back cover for a list of *HDR*s); UNDP 2002, 2009; Kimenyi 2011.

We have drawn on a wealth of research and analysis to determine which indicators provide the best insights.

We start by looking at patterns of carbon dioxide emissions over time, a good if imperfect proxy for the environmental impacts of a country's economic activity on climate. Emissions per capita are much greater in very high HDI countries than in low, medium and high HDI countries combined, because of many more energy-intensive activities, such as driving cars, using air conditioning and relying on fossil fuel–based electricity.[3] Today, the average person in a very high HDI country accounts for more than four times the carbon dioxide emissions and about twice the emissions of the other important greenhouse gases (methane, nitrous oxide) as a person in a low, medium or high HDI country.[4] Compared with an average person living in a low HDI country, a person in a very high HDI country accounts for about 30 times the carbon dioxide emissions. For example, the average UK citizen accounts for as much greenhouse gas emissions in two months as a person in a low HDI country generates in a year. And the average Qatari —living in the country with the highest per capita greenhouse gas emissions—does so in only 10 days, although this figure reflects both consumption within the country and production that is consumed elsewhere, an issue we revisit below.

Of course, development has many dimensions. The HDI recognizes this by aggregating measures of three key dimensions— income, health and education. How do these

BOX 2.2

What can we learn from trends in aggregate measures of sustainability?

Of the aggregate measures of sustainability surveyed in box 1.2 in chapter 1, only two are available for a large number of countries over a reasonably long period: the World Bank's adjusted net savings and the Global Footprint Network's ecological footprint. What do these measures tell us?

Adjusted net savings is positive for all Human Development Index (HDI) groups, meaning that the world is (weakly) sustainable (see figure). The positive trend for low, medium and high HDI countries suggests that their sustainability has improved over time, while that of the very high HDI countries is declining over time.

However, as reviewed in chapter 1, the concept of weak sustainability underlying adjusted net savings has been criticized for not acknowledging that sustainability requires maintaining some natural capital. Adjusted net savings also involves some other controversial methodological choices. For example, valuing natural resources at market prices can overestimate the sustainability of an economy that produces them as the resources become scarcer and thus more expensive.

Further analysis—taking into account the uncertainty embodied in greenhouse gas emissions and their monetary valuation—shows that the number of countries considered unsustainable in 2005 would rise about two-thirds—from 15 to 25—if adjusted net savings used a more comprehensive measure of emissions that includes methane and nitrous oxide as well as carbon dioxide and acknowledged valuation uncertainties. In other words, adjusted net savings may be overestimated.

The ecological footprint, by contrast, shows that the world is increasingly exceeding its global capacity to provide resources and absorb wastes. If everyone in the world had the same consumption as people in very high HDI countries and with current technologies, we would need more than three Earths to withstand the pressure on the environment.

Source: Garcia and Pineda 2011; Stiglitz, Sen and Fitoussi 2009.

Adjusted net savings and ecological footprint show different results for sustainability trends over time

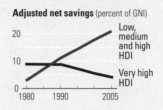

Adjusted net savings (percent of GNI)

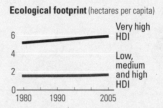

Ecological footprint (hectares per capita)

Source: HDRO calculations based on data from World Bank (2011b) and www.footprintnetwork.org.

The big message from the ecological footprint is that patterns of consumption and production are unsustainable at the global level and imbalanced regionally. And the situation is worsening, especially in very high HDI countries.

The ecological footprint estimates the amount of forest that would be required to absorb carbon dioxide emissions—though this is not the only method for sequestering emissions. It neglects other key aspects of the environment, including biodiversity, and such amenities as water quality. And it focuses on consumption, so that the consumer country rather than the producer country is responsible for the impact of imported natural resources.

One further issue is that most changes over time (both global and national) are driven by carbon dioxide emissions, and there is a strong correlation between the volume of carbon emissions and the value of the ecological footprint.

Another more recent measure is the environmental performance index, developed at Yale and Columbia Universities. This composite index uses 25 indicators to establish how close countries are to established environmental policy goals—a useful policy tool, built from a rich set of indicators and providing a broad definition of sustainability. But the measure's data intensity (requiring 25 indicators for more than 160 countries) inhibits construction of a time series for the analysis of trends in this Report.

dimensions interact with measures of environmental degradation?

The dimensions interact very differently with carbon dioxide emissions per capita: the association is positive and strong for income, still positive but weaker for the HDI and nonexistent for health and education (figure 2.1). This result is of course intuitive: activities that emit carbon dioxide into the atmosphere are those linked to the production and distribution of goods. Carbon dioxide is emitted by factories and trucks, not by learning and vaccinations. These results also show the nonlinear relationship between carbon dioxide emissions per capita and HDI components: there is practically no relation at low levels of human development, but a "tipping point" appears to be reached beyond which a strong positive correlation between carbon dioxide emissions per capita and income is observed.

The correlation between some key measures of sustainability and national levels of development are well known. Less well known, and emerging from our analysis, is that growth in carbon dioxide emissions per capita is related to the *speed* of development. Countries with faster HDI improvements also experience a faster increase in carbon dioxide emissions per capita (figure 2.2).[5] Changes over time—not the snapshot relationship, which reflects cumulative effects—are the best guide to what to expect as a result of development today.

The bottom line: recent progress in the HDI has come at the cost of global warming. In countries advancing fastest in the HDI, carbon dioxide emissions per capita also grew faster. But these environmental costs come from economic growth, not broader gains in HDI, and the relationship is not fixed. Some

FIGURE 2.1

The association with carbon dioxide emissions per capita is positive and strong for income, positive for the HDI and nonexistent for health and education

Carbon dioxide emissions per capita (tonnes)

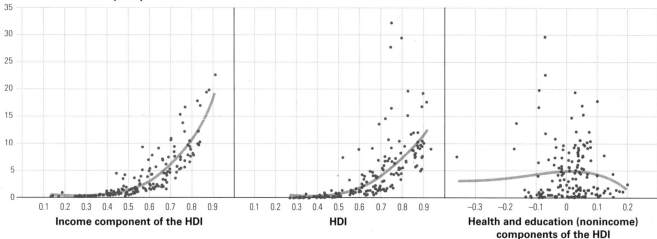

| Income component of the HDI | HDI | Health and education (nonincome) components of the HDI |

Note: Data are for 2007.

Source: HDRO calculations, based on data from the HDRO database.

countries have advanced in both the HDI and environmental sustainability (those in the lower right quadrants of figure 2.2)—an important point investigated below.

This relationship does not hold for all environmental indicators. Our analysis finds only a weak positive correlation between levels of the HDI and deforestation, for example. Why do carbon dioxide emissions per capita differ from other environmental threats?

Research shows that some environmental threats have increased with development and others have not. A seminal study points to an inverted-U relationship for air and water pollution, showing that environmental degradation worsens then improves as the level of development rises (a pattern known as the environmental Kuznets curve).[6] This can be explained in terms of the increasing responsiveness of governments to people's desire for

FIGURE 2.2

Countries with higher growth also experience faster increase in carbon dioxide emissions per capita

Change in carbon dioxide emissions per capita (tonnes)

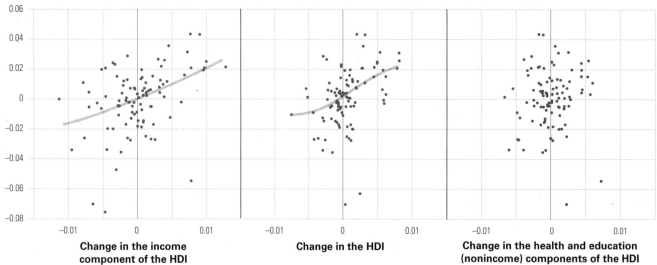

| Change in the income component of the HDI | Change in the HDI | Change in the health and education (nonincome) components of the HDI |

Note: Data are for 2007.

Source: HDRO calculations, based on data from the HDRO database.

clean and healthy environments as countries become richer. But with carbon dioxide emissions, the damage is global and harms mostly future generations, so even very rich countries have little to gain from reining in greenhouse gas emissions unless others act too.

These global patterns can be seen as a series of environmental transitions and related risks for people, set against overall HDI trends. In a twist on the traditional Kuznets story, the global evidence suggests that countries address direct household deprivations first (such as access to water and energy), then community deprivations (notably pollution) and finally deprivations with global effects and externalities (namely climate change).[7] Where the link between the environment and quality of life is direct, as with pollution, environmental achievements are often greater in developed countries; where the links are more diffuse, performance is much weaker. Figure 2.3 depicts three generalized findings:

- Environmental risk factors with an immediate impact on households—such as indoor air pollution, poor water and sanitation—are more severe at lower HDI levels and decline as the HDI rises. As we show in chapter 3, within countries these threats also tend to be concentrated among the multidimensionally poor.

- Environmental risks with community effects—such as urban air pollution—seem to worsen as the HDI rises from low levels and then begin to improve beyond a certain point.[8] This is the Kuznets part of the story.

- Environmental risk factors with global effects—such as greenhouse gas emissions tend to increase with the HDI, as shown empirically in figure 2.2.

Of course, the HDI itself is not the true driver of these transitions. Public policies are important too. Incomes and economic growth have an important explanatory role for emissions—but the relationship is not deterministic. For example, Norway's per capita carbon dioxide emissions (11 tonnes) are less than a third those of the United Arab Emirates (35 tonnes), although both have high incomes.[9] Patterns of natural resource use also

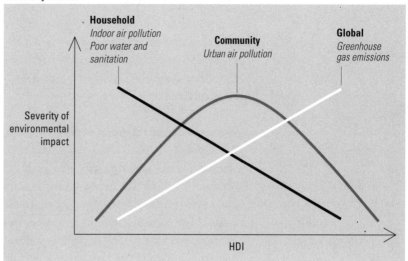

FIGURE 2.3

Patterns of risk change: environmental transitions and human development

Source: Based on Hughes, Kuhn and others (2011).

BOX 2.3
Consumption and human development

Runaway growth in consumption among the best-off people in the world is putting unprecedented pressure on the environment. The inequalities remain stark. Today, there are more than 900 cars per 1,000 people of driving age in the United States and more than 600 in Western Europe, but fewer than 10 in India. US households average more than two television sets, whereas in Liberia and Uganda fewer than 1 household in 10 has a television set. Domestic per capita water consumption in the very high Human Development Index (HDI) countries, at 425 litres a day, is more than six times that in the low HDI countries, where it averages 67 litres a day.

Consumption patterns are converging in some respects as people in many developing countries are consuming more luxury goods: China is poised to overtake the United States as the world's largest luxury consumer market. But even among very high HDI countries, consumption patterns vary. Consumption accounts for 79 percent of GDP in the United Kingdom and 34 percent in Singapore despite the countries' having nearly the same HDI. Among the explanations for these differences are demographic patterns and social and cultural norms, which affect savings practices, for example.

At the same time, the links with human development are often broken, as explored in the 1998 *Human Development Report*: new products often target richer consumers, discounting the needs of the poor in developing countries.

Education can be fundamentally important in tempering excessive consumption. Such efforts have been promoted by the UN General Assembly's declaration of the UN Decade of Education for Sustainable Development (2005–2014) and United Nations Educational, Scientific and Cultural Organization activities geared at encouraging sustainable consumption.

Source: Data from Morgan Stanley, as cited in *The Economist* 2008a; data from Bain and Company 2011, as cited in Reuters 2011; Heston, Summers and Aten 2009 (Penn World Table 6.3).

vary: Indonesia deforested nearly 20 percent a year between 1990 and 2008; the Philippines, with similar per capita income, reforested 15 percent over the same period.[10] And consumption patterns are also important (box 2.3). At the international level broader forces interact in a complex manner, changing patterns of risk—trade often allows countries to outsource the production of goods that degrade the environment, as we discuss below for deforestation. There are also outlier countries that have performed relatively well, as we show later using a broader framework of environmental risk.

Are there causal relations at play?

Did changes in sustainability come before or after changes in human development? Is there a causal relation? Are increasing inequality and environmental unsustainability causally related? For example, if wealthier groups and corporations have disproportionate political and economic power and benefit from activities that degrade the environment, they may obstruct measures that protect the environment. A counter-example is how the empowerment of women often goes hand in hand with greater protection of the environment.

Our analysis of sequencing finds that in the short run the effects go in both directions for the HDI, greenhouse gas emissions and pollution. In the long run, however, a rising HDI precedes a rise in greenhouse gas emissions, so while not conclusive, the evidence is consistent with a causal relationship where rising HDI—or at least the income component —implies higher greenhouse gas emissions in the future.

What about inequality? Using quasi-experimental methods, we explored the causal relationship between inequality (measured in terms of HDI and gender disparities) and sustainability. Although country differences in environmental performance are driven by multiple contextual and other factors, it is possible to establish causality where sources of what economists call "exogenous variation" can be identified.[11] We used climate-related shocks and changes in institutional arrangements, such as the year women received full electoral rights, as sources of exogenous variation. The results are striking.

- Poor sustainability performance—as measured by net forest depletion and especially air pollution—raised inequality in the HDI.[12]

- Higher levels of gender inequality (as measured by the Gender Inequality Index) led to lower levels of sustainability—a theme explored in chapter 3.[13]

These findings lend empirical weight to our argument that inequality is bad not just intrinsically but also for the environment. And weak environmental performance can worsen disparities in the HDI. We now examine these disparities in more detail.

Equity trends

To explore what has happened to equity over time we use a multidimensional approach that goes beyond incomes. This analysis builds on the innovation in the 2010 *HDR*, the Inequality-adjusted HDI (IHDI), which discounts human development achievements by the inequality in each dimension, and so the IHDI falls farther below the HDI as inequality rises.[14] The basic idea is intuitive. Schooling and longevity (like income) are necessary to lead fulfilling lives; therefore, we care about how they are distributed between those with more and those with less. Although incomplete, especially in the neglect of empowerment, the approach provides a fuller picture than a focus on income inequality alone.

This Report takes an important step forward by presenting trends in the IHDI since 1990 for 66 countries (see statistical table 3 for the 2011 values; *Technical note 2* explains the methodology).[15]

- Worsening income inequality has offset large improvements in health and education inequality, such that the aggregate loss in human development due to inequality sums to 24 percent.[16]

- The global trends conceal widening educational inequality in South Asia and deep health inequality in Africa.

- Latin America remains the most unequal region in income, but not in health and education.

- Sub-Saharan Africa has the greatest inequality in the HDI.

Narrowing health inequalities

Health affects people's capability to function and flourish. The evidence shows a positive correlation between health and socioeconomic status. This has led researchers to focus on income and social inequalities as determinants of health, with recent investigations using new household data to examine trends.[17]

Our analysis suggests that the rising longevity around the world—investigated in the 2010 *HDR*—has been associated with greater equity: health inequality, measured by life expectancy, declined across the board.[18] Very high HDI countries led the way, closely followed by improvements in East Asia and the Pacific and Latin America and the Caribbean, with the Arab States not far behind. Gains were most modest in Sub-Saharan Africa, from the lowest starting levels, due mainly to the HIV/AIDS pandemic, especially in Southern Africa, where adult HIV/AIDS prevalence rates still exceed 15 percent (figure 2.4).[19]

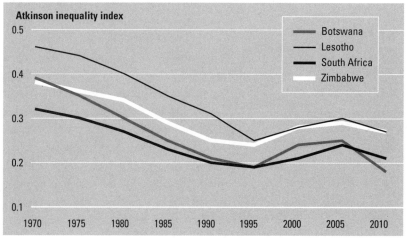

FIGURE 2.4

High HIV/AIDS prevalence rates in Southern Africa stall improvements in health inequality

Loss in the health component of the HDI due to inequality, 1970–2010

Note: See *Technical note 2* for definition of the Atkinson inequality index. Each observation represents a five-year average.
Source: HDRO calculations based on life expectancy data from the United Nations Department of Economic and Social Affairs, Population Division, Population Estimates and Projections Section, and Fuchs and Jayadev (2011).

Improving equity in education

Progress in expanding education opportunities has been substantial and widespread, reflecting improvements in the quantity of schooling and greater gender equity and access. Not only are more children going to school, more finish.[20]

As with health, trends in the distribution of education opportunities show narrowing inequalities around the world as overall enrolments and attainment rise. For example, a study of 29 developing countries and 13 developed countries found that the power of parents' education as a predictor of their children's schooling fell substantially in most countries over the last 50 years, indicating reduced intergenerational inequality in education.[21]

Our analysis of national trends in education inequality (measured by average years of schooling) since 1970 shows improvements in most countries. In contrast with trends in income inequality, education inequality declined most in Europe and Central Asia (almost 76 percent), followed by East Asia and the Pacific (52 percent) and Latin America and the Caribbean (48 percent).

Though rising average levels of education and health attainments have generally been accompanied by narrowing inequality, the effect is not automatic. Average attainments and inequality can move in different directions and at different speeds.[22] Education inequality worsened about 8 percent in South Asia, for instance, despite a massive average increase in education attainment of 180 percent.

Widening income disparities

Income inequality has deteriorated in most countries and regions—with some notable exceptions in Latin America and Sub-Saharan Africa. Some highlights:

- Detailed studies show a striking increase in the income share of the wealthiest groups in much of Europe, North America, Australia and New Zealand.[23] From 1990 to 2005 within-country income inequality, measured by the Atkinson inequality index, increased 23.3 percent in very high HDI countries.[24] The gap between the rich and the poor widened over the last two decades in more than three-quarters of Organisation for Economic Co-operation and Development countries and in many emerging market economies.[25]

- Income has also become more concentrated among top earners in China, India and South Africa.[26] In China, for example, the top quintile of income earners had 41 percent of total income in 2008, and the Gini coefficient for income inequality rose from 0.31 in 1981 to 0.42 in 2005.

Using the same Atkinson inequality index applied to health and education and the overall IHDI, our own analysis confirms this picture and finds that average country-level income inequality increased around 20 percent over 1990–2005. The worst deterioration was in Europe and Central Asia (more than 100 percent).

Over the last decade or so, much of Latin America and the Caribbean has bucked this trend: within-country inequality has been falling, especially in Argentina, Brazil, Honduras, Mexico and Peru, with some exceptions, including Jamaica.[27] Some trace Latin America's performance to the shrinking earnings gap between high- and low-skilled workers and to the increase in targeted social transfer payments.[28] The shrinking earnings gap follows expanding coverage in basic education in recent decades, but it may run into headwinds when the poor are turned away from university education because of the low quality of their primary and secondary schooling.

Why has declining inequality in health and education not been accompanied by improved income distribution? Increased access to education may be part of the story. The returns to basic education fall as more people gain access. Completion of primary school brought smaller income gains than before, while the relative value of education to those at the top of the distribution increased. This increase in the "skill premium" resulted from a combination of skill-biased technical change and changes in policy—though country institutions and policies strongly influenced country-level effects.[29]

We might also expect financial crises to affect trends in inequality. To what extent do crises increase income inequality? Does income inequality make crises more likely? Can government policy make a difference? This Report focuses on the effects of environmental shocks, but recent research on the causes and effects of financial crises offers some parallels (box 2.4).

Prospects—and environmental threats

The global HDI has risen strongly in recent decades, but what does the future hold? How might HDI values change for developed and developing countries through 2050? And how severely might environmental and inequality constraints affect that advance? Given inherent uncertainties, we compare three scenarios through 2050, produced by the University of Denver's Frederick S. Pardee Center for International Futures (figure 2.5).[30]

- A *base case* scenario, which assumes limited changes in inequality, environmental threats and risks, anticipates for 2050 a global HDI that is 19 percent higher than today's (44 percent higher for Sub-Saharan Africa). The increase is less than a simple extrapolation of past trends would yield because progress in the HDI tends to slow at very high levels.[31]

- The *environmental challenge* scenario envisions intensified environmental risks at the household (indoor solid fuel use), local (water and sanitation), urban and regional (outdoor air pollution) and global levels

BOX 2.4

Sustainability, crises and inequality

Background research commissioned for this Report considered income inequality and two types of economic crisis—banking crises and collapses in consumption or gross domestic product—over the century to 2010. The analysis focused on 25 countries—some experiencing the crisis, others not—14 in North America and Europe and 11 elsewhere.

Does inequality make crises more likely? There is some support for the hypothesis that a rise in inequality is associated with subsequent crises, but high inequality is not always linked to crisis. Rising inequality preceded crises in Sweden in 1991 and in Indonesia in 1997 but not in India in 1993. Where rising inequality did precede a crisis, it could be attributed to overconsumption among some groups or underconsumption among others and to the effects of such patterns on the broader economy.

Who bears the brunt of a crisis? For 31 banking crises for which inequality data are available, there are a few cases of rising overall inequality followed by crises and then a fall in inequality, notably the 2007 Icelandic crisis—but such cases do not predominate. Inequality rose in about 40 percent of the cases, fell in just over a quarter and showed no change in the remainder.

Overall, the analysis suggests no systematic relationship between crises and income inequality, even for countries simultaneously experiencing banking crisis and economic collapse. Inequality rose in the Republic of Korea, Malaysia and Singapore as a result of the 1997 Asian financial crises but remained steady in Indonesia. While data are not yet available to allow rigorous analysis of the effects of the 2008 financial crisis, some evidence affirms the lack of a clear pattern across countries—with inequality rising in some countries and falling in others.

The effects of inequality and of crisis also reflect policy responses. For example, following crises, compensatory transfers or progressive taxation can mitigate inequality, while cutting transfers to reduce budget deficits can do the opposite. Crises have often prompted institutional change, for instance the introduction of social security in the United States in the 1930s. Following the Nordic crises of the 1990s, the welfare state and fiscal provisions seem to have been a powerful moderating force on any increase in inequality.

Source: Atkinson and Morelli 2011.

(especially increasing impacts of climate change on agricultural production) and inequality and insecurity.[32] The global HDI in 2050 is 8 percent lower than in the base case and 12 percent lower for South Asia and Sub-Saharan Africa.

- Under an *environmental disaster* scenario most early 21st century gains have eroded by 2050 as biophysical and human systems are stressed by overuse of fossil fuels and falling water tables, glacial melting, progressive deforestation and land degradation, dramatic declines in biodiversity, greater frequency of extreme weather events, peaking production of oil and gas, increased civil conflict and other disruptions. The model does not exhaustively consider the potential for associated vicious feedback loops, which would exacerbate these trends. Under this scenario the global HDI in 2050 would be some 15 percent below the baseline scenario.

Both the environmental challenge and environmental disaster scenarios would lead to breaks in the pattern of convergence in human development across countries observed over the past 40 years. And longer term projections suggest that divergence would widen further after 2050.

This is illustrated by projections of cross-country inequality in the HDI, using the Atkinson inequality index, which has fallen more than two-thirds over the past 40 years, reflecting the convergence trends. Under the base case, inequality among countries is projected to continue to fall over the next 40 years. But under the disaster scenario, future convergence, as measured by changes in the Atkinson inequality index, would be on the order of only 24 percent by 2050, compared with 57 percent under the baseline (figure 2.6).

Threats to sustaining progress

Past patterns suggest that, in the absence of reform, the links between economic growth and rising greenhouse gas emissions could jeopardize the extraordinary progress in the HDI in recent decades. But climate change —with effects on temperatures, precipitation,

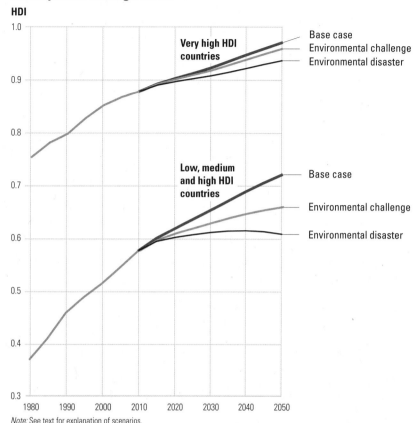

FIGURE 2.5

Scenarios projecting impacts of environmental risks on human development through 2050

Note: See text for explanation of scenarios.

Source: HDRO calculations based on data from the HDRO database and Hughes, Irfan and others (2011), who draw on forecasts from International Futures, Version 6.42.

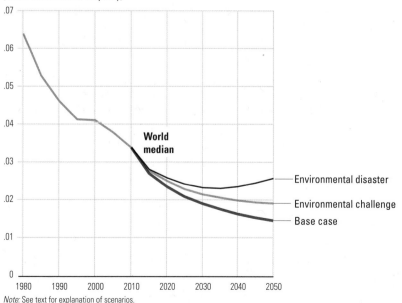

FIGURE 2.6

Scenarios projecting slowdown and reversals of convergence in human development due to environmental risks through 2050

Note: See text for explanation of scenarios.

Source: HDRO calculations based on data from the HDRO database and Hughes, Irfan and others (2011), who draw on forecasts from International Futures, Version 6.42.

sea levels and natural disasters—is not the only environmental problem.

Degraded land, forests and marine ecosystems pose chronic threats to well-being, while pollution has substantial costs that appear to rise and then fall with development levels. We discuss these threats in turn, then consider which countries have performed better than their regions and the world.

Climate change

Global temperatures now average 0.75°C higher than at the beginning of the 20th century, and the rate of change has accelerated (figure 2.7). The main cause is human activity, particularly burning fossil fuels, cutting forests

and manufacturing cement, which increase carbon dioxide emissions. Other greenhouse gases, such as those regulated by the Montreal Protocol, also pose serious threats. The 100-year global warming potential of nitrous oxide is nearly 300 times that of carbon dioxide and 25 times that of methane.[33] That climate change is caused by human activities is scientifically accepted,[34] though public awareness still lags, with less than two-thirds of the population worldwide aware of climate change and its causes (box 2.5).

Key drivers

Global carbon dioxide emissions have increased since 1970—248 percent in low, medium and high HDI countries and 42 percent in very high HDI countries. The global growth of 112 percent can be broken down into three drivers: population growth, rising consumption and carbon-intensive production.[35] Rising consumption (as reflected by GDP growth) has been the main driver, accounting for 91 percent of the change in emissions, while population growth contributed 79 percent. The contribution of carbon intensity, in contrast, was −70 percent, reflecting technological advances (table 2.1). In other words, the principal driver of increases in emissions is that more people are consuming more goods—even if production itself has become more efficient, on average.

Although the carbon efficiency of production (units of carbon to produce a unit of GDP) has improved 40 percent, total carbon dioxide emissions continue to rise. Average carbon dioxide emissions per capita have grown 17 percent over 1970–2007.

Patterns of carbon dioxide emissions vary widely across regions and stages of development. Some highlights:

- In very high HDI countries the carbon intensity of production has fallen 52 percent, but total emissions and emissions per capita have more than doubled and are 112 percent higher now than 40 years ago. Improvements in carbon efficiency have not kept up with economic growth.
- Emissions are more than 10 times higher in East Asia and the Pacific than in Sub-Saharan Africa.

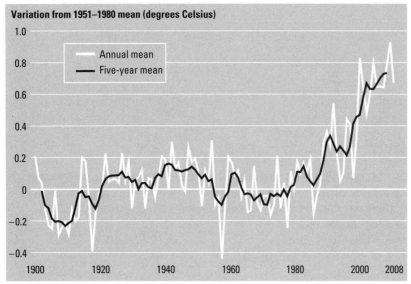

FIGURE 2.7

Average world temperatures have risen since 1900

Variation from 1951–1980 mean (degrees Celsius)

— Annual mean
— Five-year mean

Note: Calculated using average temperatures in 173 countries, weighted by average population in 1950–2008.
Source: HDRO calculations based on data from the University of Delaware.

TABLE 2.1

Growth in carbon dioxide emissions and its drivers, 1970–2007 (percent)

	Growth		Percentage share of total growth[a]		
	Per capita	Total	Population	GDP per capita	Carbon intensity
HDI group					
Very high	7	42	81	233	−213
High	3	73	94	116	−111
Medium	276	609	32	82	−15
Low	49	304	72	21	7
World	17	112	79	91	−70

a. Based on an accounting decomposition of the effects on carbon growth that simplifies the Kaya identity presented in Raupach and others (2007) from four drivers to three. Values may not sum to 100 percent because of rounding.
Source: HDRO calculations based on data from World Bank (2011b).

- Emissions per capita vary from a low of 0.04 tonnes in Burundi to a high of 53 tonnes in Qatar.

Trade enables countries to shift the carbon content of the goods they consume to the trading partners that produce them. The carbon dioxide emitted in the production of goods traded internationally increased by half from 1995 to 2005.[36] Several countries that have committed to cutting their own emissions are net carbon importers, including Germany and Japan, as are countries that have not signed or ratified global treaties, such as the United States.

While very high HDI countries account for the largest share of world carbon dioxide emissions, low, medium and high HDI countries account for more than three-fourths of the *growth* in carbon dioxide emissions since 1970. East Asia and the Pacific is the largest contributor by far to the increase in these emissions (45 percent), while Sub-Saharan Africa contributed only 3 percent, and Europe and Central Asia, 2 percent (figure 2.8). For methane and nitrous oxide, we have data for a shorter period, but here too, the contribution of the East Asia and the Pacific region is pronounced.

The stock of carbon dioxide trapped in the atmosphere is a product of historical emissions—"carbon is forever."[37] Today's concentrations are largely the accumulation of developed countries' past emissions. With about a sixth of the world's population, very high HDI countries emitted almost two-thirds (64 percent) of carbon dioxide emissions between 1850 and 2005.[38] Since 1850 about 30 percent of total accumulated emissions have come from the United States. The next highest emitters are China (9 percent), the Russian Federation (8 percent) and Germany (7 percent). Very high HDI countries have generated cumulatively more than nine times more carbon dioxide per capita than low, medium and high HDI countries combined —hence the Kyoto Protocol's "common but differentiated responsibilities" for addressing climate change, explored in detail below.

Repercussions for temperature, rainfall, sea level and disaster risk

Climate change affects not only temperature but also rainfall, sea level and natural disasters.

BOX 2.5
Are people aware of climate change and its causes?

Despite overwhelming scientific evidence of the seriousness of the climate change threat and growing evidence around the world that we are already experiencing many of the effects, public awareness remains limited. The Gallup World Poll, a representative survey carried out regularly in nearly 150 countries since 2007, reveals some major gaps in public knowledge of the seriousness of the problem, its causes and even its existence (see table).

Less than two-thirds of people in the world have heard of climate change. Awareness is associated with level of development. Some 92 percent of respondents in very high Human Development Index (HDI) countries reported at least some knowledge of climate change, compared with 52 percent in medium HDI countries and 40 percent in low HDI countries.

Perceptions of other environmental issues also differ. Overall, 69 percent of people are satisfied with water quality while 29 percent are not, and 76 percent of people are satisfied with air quality while 22 percent are not. Not surprising, there is wide disparity across countries. For example, only 2.5 percent of people are dissatisfied with water quality in Denmark, compared with 78 percent in the Democratic Republic of the Congo.

Public opinions on climate change (percent agreeing)

Country group	Aware of climate change (n = 147)	Climate change is a serious threat (n = 135)	Human activity causes climate change (n = 145)
Regions			
Arab States	42.1	28.7	30.3
East Asia and the Pacific	62.6	27.7	48.3
Europe and Central Asia	77.7	48.2	55.0
Latin America and the Caribbean	76.5	72.7	64.8
South Asia	38.0	31.3	26.9
Sub-Saharan Africa	43.4	35.5	30.6
HDI groups			
Very high	91.7	60.2	65.3
High	76.1	61.2	60.7
Medium	51.6	29.3	38.8
Low	40.2	32.8	26.7
World	60.0	39.7	44.5

Note: n refers to the number of countries surveyed. Data are population-weighted averages and refer to the most recent year available since 2007. For details on the Gallup sample and method, see https://worldview.gallup.com/content/methodology.aspx.

Source: HDRO calculations based on Gallup World Poll data (www.gallup.com/se/126848/worldview.aspx).

Temperature and precipitation

The past half century's most dramatic changes in temperature have been in the polar regions and at higher latitudes (map 2.1).[39] Does this mean that climate change harms high HDI countries more? Not necessarily. Countries with lower initial temperatures can better withstand temperature rises—whereas in climate-sensitive tropical areas a small rise in temperature can severely disrupt natural conditions, with adverse repercussions for water availability and crop productivity.[40]

In recent decades precipitation has fallen more than 2 millimetres (almost 3 percent)

FIGURE 2.8

Sources of greenhouse gas growth

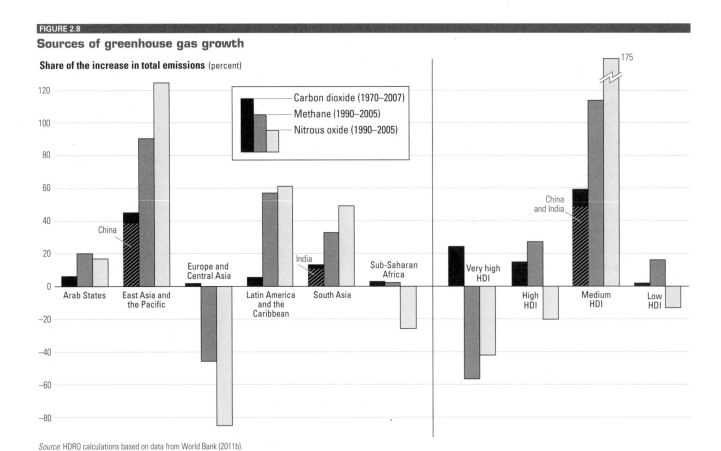

Share of the increase in total emissions (percent)

Legend:
- Carbon dioxide (1970–2007)
- Methane (1990–2005)
- Nitrous oxide (1990–2005)

Source: HDRO calculations based on data from World Bank (2011b).

MAP 2.1

Temperature changes are greatest in polar regions and higher latitudes

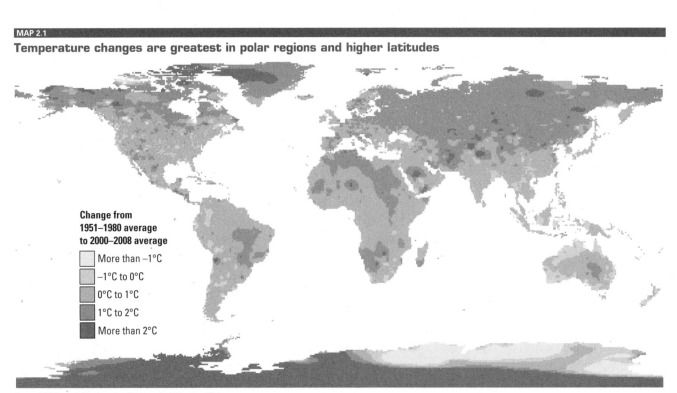

Change from 1951–1980 average to 2000–2008 average
- More than −1°C
- −1°C to 0°C
- 0°C to 1°C
- 1°C to 2°C
- More than 2°C

Source: HDRO calculations based on data from the University of Delaware.

from a 1951–1980 baseline. The largest decline has been in Sub-Saharan Africa (7 millimetres, or more than 7 percent) and in low HDI countries (4 millimetres, or more than 4 percent), followed by medium HDI countries (figure 2.9).[41] Low HDI countries have also experienced the sharpest increases in rainfall variability.

What to expect going forward? There is no scientific consensus on the net effects of climate change on precipitation, given different patterns around the world.[42] However, some broad regional trends emerge from the climate models. Africa is expected to see higher than average warming—with less rain in North Africa and the southern and western parts of the continent but more rain in East Africa. Western Europe is expected to become warmer and wetter, while the Mediterranean will experience less rainfall. In Asia the number of hot days will increase, and the number of cold days will decrease. In Latin America and the Caribbean temperatures are likely to rise while precipitation falls. Small island developing states are expected to have lower than average temperature increases, but they will likely be hard hit by changes in the sea level, as we see further below.[43]

Sea level rise

Since 1870 the average sea level has risen 20 centimetres, and the rate of change has accelerated. If this accelerated rate holds, the sea level will be 31 centimetres higher in 2100 than in 1990,[44] with devastating impacts, especially for small island developing states, which are particularly exposed (box 2.6, table 2.2). Many face high mitigation costs relative to income, and their vulnerability risks discouraging private investors, affecting their ability to adapt.[45]

These sea-related increases will affect all coastal regions. A half-metre sea level rise by 2050 would flood almost a million square kilometres—an area the size of France and Italy combined—and affect some 170 million people.[46]

The share of people likely to be affected is largest in very high HDI countries and small island developing states, but very high HDI

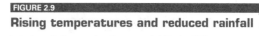

FIGURE 2.9

Rising temperatures and reduced rainfall

Levels and changes in climate variability by HDI group

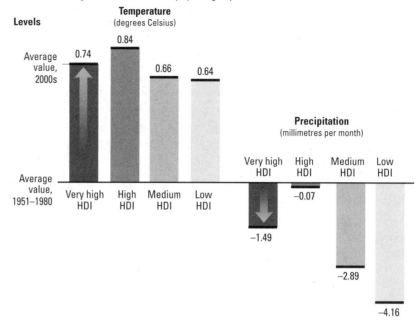

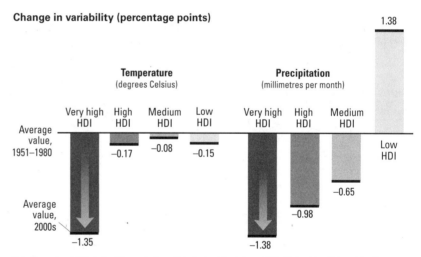

Change in variability (percentage points)

Note: Change in variability is the difference in the coefficients of variation between 1951–1980 and the 2000s, weighted by average population for 1950–2008.

Source: HDRO calculations based on data from the University of Delaware.

countries have the resources and technology to reduce the risk of losses. The Netherlands, with large, densely populated areas of low-lying land, has abated the risk of flooding and reclaimed inundated land with innovative technology and infrastructure investments.[47]

Among regions, the impact will be largest in East Asia and the Pacific, where more than 63 million people are likely to be affected (see table 2.2). The greatest economic impacts will be felt in East Asia and the Pacific and in medium HDI countries (both around

Impacts of climate change on small island developing states

Small island and low-lying coastal countries share similar challenges, including small populations, lack of resources, remoteness, susceptibility to natural disasters, dependence on international trade and vulnerability to global developments. Their temperatures are predicted to increase 1°–4°C by 2100 (relative to 1960–1990), with adverse effects on people, including displacement and poorer health.

Rising sea levels will displace people and inundate cultivable low-lying lands. Island countries with a low mean elevation—such as Tuvalu (1.83 metres), Kiribati (2.0 metres) and the Marshall Islands (2.13 metres)—are seriously threatened by the possibility of a 0.18–0.59 metre sea level rise by the end of 21st century. In low-elevation coastal zones the entire population of the Maldives and 85 percent of the population of the Bahamas are at risk.

Health effects may be severe as well. Kiribati can expect a 10 percent drop in rainfall by 2050—reducing fresh water 20 percent. Moreover, salt water intrusions are increasing due to sea level rise and frequent coastal flooding, further contaminating ground water wells, the primary fresh water source for its rapidly growing population. About 19 percent of potable water in Trinidad and Tobago following heavy rainfall tested positive for

cryptosporidium, a diarrhoea-causing parasite. Similarly, dengue fever has a clear association with rainfall and temperature in the Caribbean.

Small island developing states are vulnerable not only to climate change but also to natural disasters, including storm surges, floods, droughts, tsunamis and cyclones. Natural disasters are particularly frequent on small islands. Of the 10 countries suffering the greatest number of natural disasters per capita from 1970 to 2010, 6 were small island developing states. And a single disaster can cause huge economic losses. Hurricane Gilbert in 1988 cost Saint Lucia almost four times its GDP, while Hurricane Ivan in 2004 was responsible for losses in Grenada that were twice its GDP. The 2004 Indian Ocean tsunami that hit the Maldives killed more than 100 people and affected more than 27,000. By 2100, 90 percent of coral reefs that protect islands from ocean waves and storms could disappear, making natural disasters more likely still.

Constraints extend to data and statistics. We have improved coverage of the HDI in these states, from 23 last year to 32 out of 49 this year. These states have an average HDI of 0.617, compared with the global average of 0.649.

Source: www.sidsnet.org/2.html; Elisara 2008; UNDESA 2010a; Kelman and West 2009; Mimura and others 2007; Elbi and others 2006; Amarakoon and others 2008; Noy 2009; Heger, Julca and Paddison 2009; www.climate.gov.ki/Climate_change_effects_in_Kiribati.html; www.emdat.be/result-country-profile; http://pdf.wri.org/reefs_at_risk_revisited.pdf.

Projected impacts of a half-metre rise in sea level by 2050

Country group	Number of countries	Population likely to be affected by sea level rise (millions)	Share of total population likely to be affected (percent)
Regions			
Arab States	20	8.9	2.6
East Asia and the Pacific	22	63.1	3.3
Europe and Central Asia	17	4.4	1.2
Latin America and the Caribbean	31	7.0	1.3
South Asia	6	38.9	2.4
Sub-Saharan Africa	30	10.2	1.9
Small island developing states	35	1.7	3.4
HDI groups			
Very high	41	41.0	16.0
High	42	15.0	4.5
Medium	38	84.6	0.4
Low	32	30.8	9.4
World	153	171.4	2.7

Source: HDRO calculations based on data from Wheeler 2011.

2 percent of GDP). Low HDI countries, many landlocked, will lose proportionately less (0.5 percent).[48]

Natural disasters

Climate change is increasing the likelihood of extreme weather events, such as droughts, storms and floods. The average number of such

natural disasters more than doubled from 132 a year over 1980–1985 to 357 over 2005–2009.[49] Although it is hard to link any single disaster directly to climate change—given the inherent randomness in what generates these events—science links global warming to their increased incidence.[50] The frequency of high intensity tropical cyclones and associated precipitation is predicted to rise 20 percent by 2100.[51]

The growing incidence of reported natural disasters does not affect everyone equally—not only because the damage wrought by the average natural disaster may change but also because the capacity of societies to respond and protect themselves also varies.[52]

Most countries do not experience natural disasters, so patterns differ markedly by country and region. In recent years South Asia experienced the largest number, an average of almost six a year per country. Low HDI countries, while often vulnerable to drought, tend to have fewer disasters than medium HDI countries, partly because many are landlocked. Small island developing states are also highly exposed to natural disasters (see box 2.6).

These numbers, which are affected by extreme cases and may differ from the average, can reveal how societies are marked by most natural disasters and demonstrate their resilience. The good news is that the median costs of these events (whether number of deaths, people affected or economic losses) have fallen over the past four decades globally and for all HDI groups (table 2.3). Highlights include the significant drop in the median number of deaths due to natural disasters, with the steepest declines in low HDI countries (down almost 72 percent). Natural disasters afflict many more people and are much more costly in low and medium HDI countries than in high and very high HDI countries. Medium HDI countries are particularly affected: the typical natural disaster in a medium HDI country takes 11 percent more lives and affects nearly twice as many people as a typical natural disaster in a low HDI country. Economic losses have also declined over time as a share of income, though the estimates depend on underlying assumptions.

* * *

In sum, the poorest countries bear many of the costs of climate change, and the prospect of worsening global inequality is very real. Low HDI countries are experiencing the steepest declines in precipitation and the sharpest increases in its variability. Some of the largest temperature increases are in already-hot parts of developing countries. The frequency of natural disasters is highest in low and medium HDI countries, though the good news is that the human development cost of the typical natural disaster has declined. Sea level rise has the largest direct effects on coastal developed countries, which are often better prepared to deal with them, and on small island developing states, which are far more vulnerable.

Chronic environmental threats

Climate change is not the only environmental threat. Deforestation and overexploitation of soil and waterways can threaten long-term livelihoods, fresh water availability and essential renewable resources, such as fisheries. These problems sometimes reflect imbalances in

opportunities and power, as chapter 3 shows, and carry further implications such as loss of biodiversity (box 2.7).

Soil erosion, desertification and water scarcity

Agricultural output has doubled over the past 50 years, with only a 10 percent increase in cultivated land. But degradation of soil and water resources is increasing: soil erosion, reduced fertility and overgrazing are affecting as much as 40 percent of croplands.[53]

At the extreme, overexploitation can turn arable land into desert—though the overall extent of degradation is hard to quantify.[54] It affects an estimated 31 percent of total land area in low, medium and high HDI countries and about 51 percent in very high HDI countries. The lowest shares of severely and very severely degraded land in developing regions are in Latin America and the Caribbean and Europe and Central Asia, and the highest are in South Asia. Nonetheless the highest shares of people living on degraded land are in the Arab States (25 percent of the population) and Sub-Saharan Africa (22 percent) (see statistical table 7).

Water is vital for natural systems and human development. Irrigated lands produce two to three times as much as rainfed agriculture. Agriculture accounts for 70–85 percent of water use—and an estimated 20 percent of global grain production uses water unsustainably. And demand for water for food production is projected to double by 2050.[55]

Low HDI countries are experiencing the steepest declines in precipitation and the sharpest increases in its variability

TABLE 2.3

Disaster-related casualties and costs, median annual values by HDI group, 1971–1990 and 1991–2010

Country group	Deaths (per million people)		Affected population (per million people)		Cost (percent of GNI)	
	1971–1990	1991–2010	1971–1990	1991–2010	1971–1990	1991–2010
HDI group						
Very high	0.9	0.5	196	145	1.0	0.7
High	2.1	1.1	1,437	1,157	1.3	0.7
Medium	2.7	2.1	11,700	7,813	3.3	2.1
Low	6.9	1.9	12,385	4,102	7.6	2.8
World	2.1	1.3	3,232	1,822	1.7	1.0

Note: Values are for median impacts of climatological, hydrological and meteorological natural disasters.
Source: HDRO calculations based on Centre for Research on the Epidemiology of Disasters Emergency Events Database: International Disaster Database.

BOX 2.7

Biodiversity—the accelerating loss of our ecosystems

Healthy and resilient ecosystems—and the life-supporting services that they provide—depend on the biodiversity they contain. But rapid loss of biodiversity is accelerating globally, with serious declines experienced in the last decade in fresh water wetlands, sea ice habitats, salt marshes and coral reefs. The Convention on Biological Diversity's *Global Biodiversity Outlook 3* points to "multiple indications of continuing decline in biodiversity in all three of its main components—genes, species and ecosystems." According to the report, natural habitats in most parts of the world are shrinking, and nearly a quarter of plant species are estimated to be threatened with extinction.

Environmental scientists believe that we are witnessing what may be the fastest mass extinction of species, with about half the Earth's estimated 10 million species expected to disappear this century. The biggest cause of this loss is the conversion of natural areas to agriculture and urban development; other causes include the introduction of invasive alien species; overexploitation of natural resources; pollution; and, increasingly, the effects of climate change.

Some 10–30 percent of mammal, bird and amphibian species are threatened by extinction, with more in poorer countries. This partly reflects the location of "biodiversity hotspots" (areas with the richest and most threatened resources of animal and plant life) in tropical areas.

The impact of biodiversity loss on human development is severe in tropical developing countries, where poor communities rely heavily on natural resources. For example, wild foods are an important source of vitamins and minerals in the diets of many African communities. Use of wild foods can also reduce disease transmission in complex tropical ecosystems.

Source: Klein and others 2009; Myers and Knoll 2001; Rockström and others 2009; Roscher and others 2007; Secretariat of the Convention on Biological Diversity 2010.

FIGURE 2.10

Some regions deforest, others reforest and afforest

Forest cover shares and rates of change by region, 1990–2010 (millions of square kilometres)

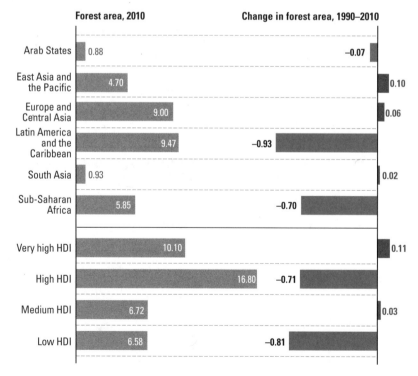

Source: HDRO calculations based on data from World Bank (2011b).

Water withdrawals have tripled over the last 50 years.[56] Pumping from aquifers exceeds natural replenishment, so water tables are falling. The main causes: destruction of wetlands, watersheds and natural water towers to make way for industrial and agricultural use. The 2006 *HDR* documented how power, poverty and inequality contribute to water scarcity.

Deforestation

One way the demands of development appear at odds with environmental sustainability is in the loss of forest cover. This has been occurring for a long time: Earth's forest cover today is only three-fifths of what it was in prehistoric times.[57] While deforestation has often been linked to development, trends today are associated more with underdevelopment.

The average forest share is similar in very high and low HDI countries (28–29 percent), and around 23 percent in medium HDI countries.[58] And while very high HDI countries have increased total forest cover about 1 percent since 1990, low HDI countries have averaged 11 percent loss and high HDI countries 4 percent loss, while medium HDI countries have had almost no change. Latin America and the Caribbean and Sub-Saharan Africa had the greatest loss, followed by the Arab States; the other regions have seen minor gains (figure 2.10).[59]

Seven developing countries (Bhutan, China, Costa Rica, Chile, El Salvador, India, and Viet Nam) have recently transitioned from deforesting to reforesting with support from domestic and international programmes. However, there are indications that some of these countries have, in effect, shifted deforestation to other developing countries, so that for every 100 hectares of reforestation they import the equivalent of 74 hectares in wood products.[60] Simulations suggest that the European Union transfers 75 of every 100 cubic metres of reduced timber harvest to developing countries, mainly to the tropics; Australia and New Zealand, 70 cubic metres; and the United States, 46 cubic metres.[61] Understanding trends in global forestation thus requires examining consumption and trade as well as production.[62] Switzerland, for example, consumes agricultural products equivalent to more than 150 percent of its cultivated land.[63]

A related concern is the rise of international "land grabs," as governments and corporations acquire large tracts in land-abundant and poorer countries (box 2.8).

Degradation of marine ecosystems

Fish are an important source of protein for hundreds of millions of people: on average, people eat 24 kilograms of fish a year in North America, 18.5 in Asia and 9.2 in Latin America and the Caribbean.[64] But fishing that exceeds the natural rate of regeneration, coupled with dredging, dumping, discharge of pollutants, coastal infrastructure and coastal tourism undermines the conditions required for healthy marine ecosystems, thereby threatening their sustainability.

The current annual fish catch of 145 million tonnes far exceeds the maximum annual sustainable yield of 80–100 million tonnes.[65] In 2008 the Food and Agriculture Organization estimated that 53 percent of known fish stocks were fully exploited, 28 percent were overexploited, 3 percent were depleted and only 15 percent were moderately exploited.[66] Although total output has not yet fallen, yields for some species, especially larger fish, have declined considerably since the 1980s.

Here again we see considerable disparity. Some 10 percent of fishing activities account for an estimated 90 percent of the total catch —mostly developed country fishers using capital-intensive methods such as technologically advanced fishing vessels with long-term storage facilities and mechanized trawls suitable for fishing in deep waters. Average annual production by fish farmers is 172 tonnes in Norway, 72 in Chile, 6 in China and 2 in India. Although 85 percent of people in the fish industry work in Asia, annual production in the region is 2.4 tonnes per ocean fisher, compared with amounts as high as 23.9 tonnes in developed regions such as Europe.[67] Large commercial fishing companies not only catch more fish but also engage in damaging practices, using high bycatch methods and bottom trawling.

BOX 2.8
Land grabbing—a growing phenomenon?

Private, government and public-private joint ventures, usually from capital-rich countries, are acquiring long-term leases or ownership rights to large portions of land (often more than 1,000 hectares) in developing countries. Economically powerful developing countries, such as China, India and Saudi Arabia, as well as developed countries, are joining the land grab. While sources differ, all suggest a recent acceleration, with estimates of more than 20–30 million hectares transacted between 2005 and mid-2009 and about 45 million hectares between 2008 and 2010. The rise in commodity prices appears to be motivating both government and private purchases.

Some see this phenomenon as an opportunity for long-awaited investments in agricultural modernization that will provide access to better technology, create more jobs for farmers and reduce poverty in rural areas. But others consider it a threat to local populations. A recent World Bank study supports the latter view, finding that expected benefits were not achieved. Several studies have reported human rights violations, with local populations forcibly displaced and access to local natural resources restricted. Hurt most were smallholders, indigenous people and women, who often lack formal title to the lands on which they live and farm. Environmental organizations have criticized negative impacts, including deforestation, loss of biodiversity and threats to wildlife.

Recent international initiatives seek to provide a regulatory framework to spread out the benefits and balance opportunities with risks. The challenge is to implement multilevel institutional arrangements, including effective local participation, to promote sustainability and equity in this major change in land use.

Source: Borras and Franco 2010; Deiniger and others 2011; IFAD 2011; Da Vià 2011.

Catch rates are still rising, most rapidly in some developing regions, despite government initiatives to reduce overfishing.[68] Rates more than quadrupled in East Asia and the Pacific, for example, between 1980 and 2005. Once again, this increase partly reflects high production for export to developed countries, where consumption per capita is greater.

Pollution

Recent studies suggest that pollution transitions may be more complex than those described by the environmental Kuznets curve, which asserts that pollution first rises and then falls with economic development.[69] For example, low-income cities have local, immediate and poverty-related environmental problems; middle-income cities have citywide problems related to rapid growth; and high-income cities experience the consequences of wealthy lifestyles.[70] So, while affluence reduces the "brown" pollution problems of low-income cities, such as poor water supply, sanitation and solid waste management, it replaces them with "green" ecological issues such as waste reduction, high emissions and inefficient transport systems.

Cities are at once sources of major pollution and opportunities for fostering sustainability. People in cities consume 60–80 percent of energy produced worldwide and account for roughly similar proportions of carbon emissions.[71] Cities can foster sustainability, especially when urban planning integrates environmental considerations. High population density fosters economies of scale and skill and enterprise specialization. These features make most infrastructure and public goods, such as water, sanitation and drainage, and public transportation systems, more cost efficient and provide more options for material reuse and recycling. It has been estimated that when a city doubles in population, the associated increase in infrastructure requirements is only 85 percent.[72] Per capita emissions in New York City are only 30 percent of the US average; the same holds for Rio de Janeiro and Brazil.[73] The average Manhattan resident accounts for 14,127 fewer pounds of carbon emissions annually than a suburban New Yorker, in part due to lower vehicle use.[74] The pattern appears in all US metropolitan areas.

But the downside of cities from waste generation and outdoor air pollution can be huge. Air pollution, which tends to be worse in urban areas, is a major cause of respiratory and cardiovascular diseases globally, while limited access to safe drinking water and proper sanitation accounts for 1.6 million deaths a year.[75] Urbanites also produce enormous quantities of waste, too often poorly managed. Areas near New Delhi and Kathmandu, for example, suffer from severe river pollution.[76] Some richer countries are exporting their waste to poorer countries, with harmful effects, despite the 1992 Basel Convention restricting such trade (box 2.9). Outdoor air pollution is generally worse in cities, as are related health effects (chapter 3). The high density of pollutants also increases cloud concentration, affecting precipitation.

High population density means that even small declines in per capita pollution emissions, water use or energy use can bring major absolute improvements. With around half the world's population living in urban areas,

Cities can foster sustainability, especially when urban planning integrates environmental considerations. High population density fosters economies of scale and skill and enterprise specialization, but the downside from waste generation and outdoor air pollution can be huge

these potential improvements present an enormous opportunity. The relationship between equity and the density of cities is complex. But more compact neighbourhoods and affordable transport systems can enhance equity by increasing accessibility, and some evidence suggests that higher density is correlated with less social segregation.

Natural disasters affecting cities can be especially devastating, as with Hurricane Katrina in New Orleans in the United States. Cities need investments in infrastructure and systems to manage these vulnerabilities. Rio de Janeiro uses sophisticated modelling techniques to predict natural disasters and take pre-emptive measures.

Global trends tell a more optimistic story. Pollution measurement has been a subject of vigorous debate, but outdoor concentrations of particulate matter suggest declines around the world over the past two decades.[77] Sub-Saharan Africa has seen more rapid decline, though from a higher level. In very high HDI countries pollution has fallen almost one-third. Even so, average concentrations of particulate matter in urban areas are 2.3 times higher in low, medium and high HDI countries than in very high HDI countries.[78] Richer countries have tougher air quality regulations and measures targeting air pollution, such as control systems on power plants and industrial facilities, catalytic converters on vehicles and cleaner fuels.[79]

*   *   *

This section on trends in key environmental indicators and their threats to human development has shown deterioration on several fronts, but not on all. Remarkable progress in curbing air pollution, for example, suggests that some dimensions of the environment can improve with development. Of greatest concern is that the poorest countries experience the most serious consequences of environmental degradation. The next chapter confirms that this pattern also holds within countries. We now explore how countries have broken these patterns to achieve sustainable and equitable progress in human development.

Hazardous waste and the Basel Convention

As public concern about hazardous waste mounted in developed countries in the 1970s and 1980s, many governments passed restrictive legislation. An unexpected result was a massive increase in exports of hazardous waste—including asbestos, mercury, ash, heavy metals, clinical waste and pesticides—to developing countries. Economic inequalities made the prospect of accepting hazardous waste attractive to some countries. In the 1980s a coalition of European and US companies offered Guinea-Bissau $600 million—about five times its gross national product—to accept shipments of toxic waste, an offer it ultimately refused because of international pressure.

The Basel Convention on the Control of Transboundary Movements of Hazardous Wastes and Their Disposal regulates such exports, requiring informed consent about the nature of the waste. Today, 175 countries are parties to the Basel Convention; the United States is among those that are not. A 1995 amendment prohibits all exports of hazardous waste, but it has not yet been ratified by the necessary three-quarters of participants. The convention recognizes the urgency of the problem, but an adequate international regulatory framework has not yet been established.

Exposure to hazardous waste in developing countries remains serious. In 2006 a Dutch company dumped 500 tonnes of toxic waste in 16 sites in Abidjan, contaminating the city's drinking water, soil and fisheries; killing at least 10 people; and affecting more than 100,000 people. Such cases reflect not only weaknesses in the Basel Convention but also the economic reality in many developing countries. The convention assumes that developing countries have the technical and administrative capacity to assess the risk of accepting waste shipments and the good governance necessary to resist monetary inducements, not always the case.

Electronic waste (e-waste), the fastest growing sector of global waste, is hazardous to human health and the environment. E-waste from China, India, Thailand, the United States and the European Union over 2004–2008 totalled 17 million tonnes a year; the United Nations Environment Programme estimates global e-waste at 20–50 million tonnes a year. Only a small share of e-waste is recycled. For example, in 2007 the United States recycled less than 20 percent of e-waste from obsolete televisions, cell phones and computer products. The rest was disposed in landfills, mostly in developing countries such as China, India and Nigeria. Nevertheless, e-waste recycling has become a dynamic economic sector, particularly in China and India, where recovering, repairing, and trading materials from discarded electronic devices provide an important livelihood for poor people. But the lead, mercury and cadmium in these products are highly toxic. While precautions can be taken, many people are unaware of the risks.

Source: Andrews 2009; Sonak, Sonak, and Giriyan 2008; Widmer and others 2005; Robinson 2009; UNEP/GRID-Europe 2005; GreenPeace 2009; UNEP and UNU 2009; www.epa.gov/international/toxics/ewaste.html; http://toxipedia.org/display/toxipedia/Electronic+Waste+%28E-Waste%29.

Success in promoting sustainable and equitable human development

How can we best interpret these contrasting patterns? Can we identify the better performing countries in human development, sustainability and equity? The task is difficult, not least because no single indicator captures sustainability well. But we illustrate a potentially useful approach to assessing joint progress towards these objectives and review a range of indicators that provide interesting insights into promising policy approaches. The findings synthesize much of the evidence we have accumulated so far and provide a bridge to the community and household analysis in the next chapter. We propose a method, identify some instances of positive synergies, where countries have promoted sustainable human development with equity, and discuss the main policy implications.

How can we identify positive synergies? Our framework reflects both local and global dimensions of sustainability that we highlighted in figure 2.3. The local aspects, which we will explore in greater depth in the next chapter, relate to the immediate human impacts of household-level deprivation in terms of access to water and indoor air pollution. These variables are gauged relative to regional medians of achievement. We need to account for regional differences—otherwise only very high HDI countries would be deemed successful, which would shed little light on the range of circumstances facing people around the world.

The global environmental aspects of sustainability—those that pose wide-ranging threats—are measured by greenhouse gas emissions, deforestation and water use, in a normative manner, each relative to global norms reflecting good practice. Following the same logic, we identify countries with a better record on the HDI and inequality than the median of their region. Applying this multidimensional filter enables us to identify a shortlist of countries with relatively better performance in responding to both localized and global environmental threats, as well as with respect to the HDI and equity. The results are illustrative, owing to patchy data and other issues relating to comparability. Nonetheless, for the indicators that we are able to assemble, they suggest some promising approaches that have the potential to promote relatively equitable and environmentally sustainable policy as well as human development more broadly.

Table 2.4 illustrates the application of the joint lens described above to identify countries that have performed better than the global

threshold (for global threats) and better than the regional median (for local impacts, HDI and HDI losses due to inequality).[80] A few countries perform well on at least four of the five environmental fronts considered. Costa Rica stands out for good performance on all five criteria. Germany and Sweden, two very high HDI countries, perform well in deforestation, water use, water access and indoor air pollution but less well in greenhouse gas emissions. The Philippines is an interesting case particularly with respect to afforestation, because the increase in forest area has been supported by community-based social forestry programs. Also, indoor air pollution in the Philippines is only 48 percent of the regional median, and broad access to schooling and healthcare offsets traditionally high income inequality. Box 2.10 highlights the experiences of Costa Rica and Sweden.

Of course, this picture is incomplete. Data limitations have already been hinted at. And, an obvious shortcoming, it does not include any indicators of political freedom and empowerment or performance on gender equality and women's empowerment (as captured by the GII, for example, which is explored in the next chapter). All four countries are democracies and do well relative to their HDI group in terms of gender equality.

Exploring trends over time also gives a more mixed picture. Of the four countries we identify here as relatively strong performers, only Germany and Sweden improved on all dimensions. Since the 1990s all countries on the list have reduced air pollution and maintained or improved the share of the population with access to water, and all but

Positive synergies in Sweden and Costa Rica

The performance of countries identified as doing well on environmental, human development and equity fronts can offer insights and development lessons. Here we focus on environmental performance in Sweden and Costa Rica.

Sweden is currently seventh in the Human Development Index (HDI), sixth best in human development loss due to inequality and first in the Gender Inequality Index. Its per capita emissions were the sixth lowest for very high HDI countries, and air pollution rates were the lowest for very high HDI countries and the fourth lowest globally. Sweden's performance appears to be rooted in its strong environmental awareness and a tradition of egalitarian and democratic policy. For example, the Committee for Research into the Preservation and Utilization of Natural Resources, established in 1957, worked to raise public awareness of environmental issues and served as a powerful pressure group. Other early clues include a 1969 survey indicating majority support for both slower economic growth to prevent environmental deterioration and for higher local taxes to fight water pollution, reflecting a willingness to pay for better environment quality. The right to common access is rooted deeply in the Swedish social psyche and in centuries-old customs. Contemporary awareness is reflected in Gallup Poll results showing that 96 percent of Swedes are aware of climate change and almost half regard it as a serious threat. Sweden's achievements in equity and education might translate into stronger political voice, partly explaining why popular environmental awareness and sensitivity are reflected in environmentally friendly policies.

Successive governments in Costa Rica have implemented policies and built institutions with environmental objectives in mind. In 1955 Costa Rica established the Institute for Tourism to protect the country's natural resources. But it was the forestry legislation of the late 1980s that really launched its environmental policy. The law defines the environmental services of forests as carbon sequestration, biodiversity protection, water flow regulation and scenery. It was also the foundation for introducing payments for environmental services as a financial mechanism to protect forests. By the mid-1990s environmental rights were enshrined in the Constitution, and Costa Rica had become a pioneer in selling carbon reduction credits (to Norway). Active participation by civil society, the population's pride in the country's beauty, biodiversity and natural resources, and investment opportunities related to sustainable practices in sectors such as tourism have also contributed.

Source: UNDP Costa Rica Country Office, Observatorio del Desarrollo and Universidad de Costa Rica 2011; Kristrom and Wibe 1997; Lundqvist 1972.

TABLE 2.4

Good performers on the environment, equity and human development, most recent year available

	Global threats			Local impacts		Equity and human development	
Country	Greenhouse gas emissions	Deforestation	Water use	Water access	Air pollution	HDI (percent of regional median)	Overall loss (percent of regional median)
Costa Rica	✔	✔	✔	✔	✔	104	77
Germany		✔	✔	✔	✔	103	91
Philippines	✔	✔		✔	✔	103	89
Sweden		✔	✔	✔	✔	102	70

Note: These countries all pass the criteria of absolute thresholds for global threats as defined in note 80, perform better than the median of their respective regional peers both in the human development and inequality dimensions and perform better than the regional median for local impacts.

the Philippines have reduced greenhouse gas emissions.[81] Multidimensional inequality also fell in these top countries except in Costa Rica, which nevertheless still has lower inequality than its regional median.[82]

Many developing countries also demonstrate successful, scalable, sectoral models for transition to a green economy. Some examples:[83]

- The city of Curitiba in Brazil has successfully implemented innovative approaches to urban planning, city management and transport to address the challenge of rapid population growth. The city now has the highest rate of public transport use in Brazil (45 percent of all journeys) and one of the country's lowest rates of air pollution.

- Kenya's Ministry of Energy adopted a feed-in tariff in 2008 to supply and diversify electricity generation sources, generate income and employment and reduce greenhouse gas emissions. The tariff covers biomass, geothermal, small hydroelectric, solar and wind power.

In sum, it is possible to identify countries that have promoted sustainable and equitable human development through a higher HDI, lower inequality and performance on a set of environmental indicators that reflect global sustainability and local threats. While data constraints preclude presenting a complete ranking of countries, we offer some illustrative results and suggest that the method offers a valuable means of demonstrating that countries in different regions, with very different structural characteristics and levels of development, can adopt policies consistent with more sustainable and equitable human development.

*   *   *

This chapter has considered key patterns and trends in human development and the environment and provided evidence of major cross-country disparities as well as new findings about positive synergies. In many cases the poorest countries bear the brunt of environmental deterioration, even though they contribute only a small share to the problem. But greater equality—both across and within countries—is consistent with better environmental performance.

The analysis underlines the potential pay-offs from development models that both promote equity and less lopsidedly favour economic growth, themes that we explore in subsequent chapters.

Tracing the effects— understanding the relations

We have seen major intersections between equity and the environment. In this chapter we focus on how environmental unsustainability affects people and how inequality mediates this relationship. We also draw attention to countries and groups that have broken the pattern, emphasizing transformations in gender roles and empowerment.

Poor and disadvantaged people suffer most from environmental degradation. That fact surprises no one. Almost every week the media report catastrophes that shatter lives in the poorest parts of the world—lives of people who already face major disadvantages.

While extreme events are disequalizing, so too are activities that harm the environment. Studies for the United States, for example, show that toxic waste facilities are located disproportionately in working class and minority neighbourhoods, harming health and education as well as property values.[1] Whether these outcomes arose because land and housing in those areas lost value after the facilities were built or because residents were less able to resist location decisions, it is clear that environmentally harmful practices accentuate racial and social inequalities. These location decisions do not happen only in market economies: in the former Soviet Union the Mayak nuclear facility was built in a region settled mostly by Muslim Tatar and Bashkir people and descendants of people repressed and exiled under Stalin.[2] This chapter aims to understand why and how these patterns come about today.

Which factors condition the relationship between environmental degradation and human development? Both the absolute level and the distribution of individual, household and community capabilities matter. Absolute deprivations can hurt the environment, and bad environmental conditions erode people's capabilities. Many examples illustrate these

links—educated girls have lower fertility rates, and more empowered communities suffer less pollution.

Through the lens of multidimensional poverty, this chapter first documents deprivations in the immediate environments of the poor and how such deprivations can intersect with adverse repercussions of climate change. Next the related environmental threats to people's health, education and livelihoods are explored, followed by how chronic disadvantage interacts with acute risks to make extreme events more disequalizing. The chapter closes with a focus on gender and power inequalities and on how greater equality in these areas can have positive effects on the environment, laying the ground for the investigation of policy options in the chapters that follow.

A poverty lens

A key theme of this Report is that the world's most disadvantaged people carry a "double burden." More vulnerable to environmental degradation, they must also cope with immediate environmental threats from indoor air pollution, dirty water and unimproved sanitation.[3] Our Multidimensional Poverty Index (MPI), introduced in the 2010 *Human Development Report* (*HDR*), gives us a closer look at these household-level deprivations (figure 3.1).

The MPI measures deficits in health, education and living standards, combining both the number of deprived people and the intensity of their deprivations. This year we explore the pervasiveness of environmental deprivations among the multidimensionally poor—focusing on the lack of improved cooking fuel, drinking water and sanitation—and the extent of their overlap at the household level, an innovation of the MPI.

These are absolute deprivations that both matter in themselves and are violations of basic

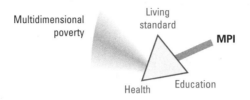

FIGURE 3.1

Multidimensional Poverty Index— a focus on the most deprived

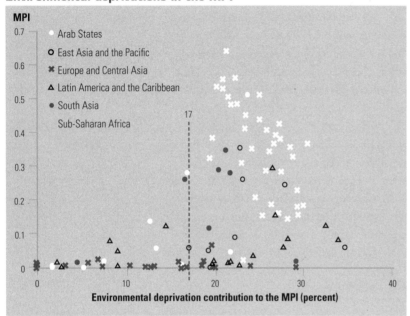

FIGURE 3.2

Environmental deprivations in the MPI

Note: The dashed line in the top panel denotes what the average contribution of environmental deprivations would be if their contribution to total poverty were equal to their weight in the MPI. Countries to the right have disproportionate environmental poverty, and countries to the left, less than expected. Survey years vary by country; see statistical table 5 for details.

Source: HDRO staff estimates based on data in statistical table 5.

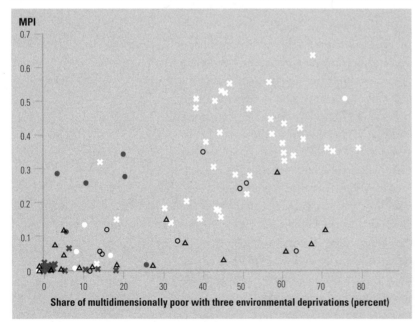

human rights. Ensuring access—including to modern cooking fuel, safe water and basic sanitation—also creates the potential to expand higher order capabilities, thereby enlarging people's choices and furthering human development. The lens of the MPI highlights joint deprivations in access.

Deprivations facing the poor

Multidimensional poverty is estimated for 109 countries (see statistical table 5),[4] and the results are striking.

- Globally, at least 6 in 10 people experience one environmental deprivation, and 4 in 10 experience two or more.[5] These deprivations are more acute among the multidimensionally poor. More than 9 in 10 face at least one deprivation: nearly 90 percent do not use modern cooking fuels, 80 percent lack adequate sanitation and 35 percent lack clean water.

- Most suffer overlapping deprivations: 8 in 10 poor people experience two or more environmental deficits, and 29 percent face all three.

- The rural poor are more afflicted. A striking 97 percent face at least one environmental deprivation, and about a third suffer all three. Comparable data for urban areas are 75 percent and 13 percent.

- State- and provincial-level MPIs show wide disparities in environmental deprivations. Within Haiti the proportion of people who are both multidimensionally poor and deprived of clean water in Aire Métropolitaine/Ouest is 19 percent, while in the Centre it is 70 percent. Similarly, in Senegal the proportion of people who are both multidimensionally poor and deprived in cooking fuel is about 4 percent in Dakar and about 88 percent in Kolda. And in India deprivations in sanitation among multidimensionally poor people range from 3.5 percent in Kerala to more than 70 percent in Bihar.

Environmental deprivations typically rise with the MPI, but the composition of multidimensional poverty varies, even for countries with similar poverty levels. Overall, environmental deprivations disproportionately contribute to multidimensional poverty, accounting for 20 percent of the MPI—above their 17 percent weight in the index (figure 3.2, top panel).[6] In rural areas the average is 22 percent of poverty, compared with 13 percent in urban areas. In Mongolia, Peru, Swaziland and Uganda such deprivations account for more than 30 percent of multidimensional poverty.

But there are some good performers as well, with lower shares of environmental deprivation.[7] In several Arab States (Jordan, Occupied Palestinian Territory, the Syrian Arab Republic and the United Arab Emirates) and European and Central Asian countries (Croatia, Estonia, Russian Federation and Ukraine) such deprivations are less than half their weight in the index. Brazil has also performed well.

Regional patterns show that environmental deprivations are most acute in Sub-Saharan Africa: 99 percent of the multidimensionally poor face at least one environmental deprivation, and nearly 60 percent face all three (figure 3.2, bottom panel). Environmental deprivations are also severe, if less pervasive, in South Asia: 97 percent of the poor suffer at least one deficit, and 18 percent face all three. By contrast, in Europe and Central Asia 39 percent of the poor have one or more environmental deprivations (excluding Tajikistan, where the poor population is large and the share with one deprivation or more is an unusually high 82 percent). Few have all three—just over 1 percent, excluding Tajikistan.

Deprivations are most widespread for access to cooking fuel (figure 3.3). In South Asia and Sub-Saharan Africa, the two poorest regions, more than 90 percent of the multidimensionally poor lack access to modern cooking fuel. More than 85 percent of poor people in both regions lack access to improved sanitation. In several Arab States water problems are paramount, affecting more than 60 percent of the multidimensionally poor.

The extent of environmental deprivation is also associated with the country's Human Development Index (HDI) value. More than 4 in 10 multidimensionally poor people in low

HDI countries face all three environmental deprivations. And these countries typically have above average environmental poverty— about 6 percentage points higher than if the environmental deprivations they face equalled their weight in the MPI. For example, 65 percent of the population in Madagascar lack access to clean water. The repercussions are extensive. Most schools in Madagascar have no running water for adequate hygiene and sanitation, so pupils fall sick regularly, missing classes and underperforming. Diarrhoea causes an estimated annual loss of 3.5 million school days in Madagascar.[8]

There is also good news, sometimes reflecting successful outreach by governments and nongovernmental organizations (NGOs). For example, South Asia stands out for having a relatively low share of its population (less than 15 percent) deprived in access to water.

Understanding the relations

To better understand environmental deprivations, we analysed the data holding poverty levels constant.[9] Countries were ordered by their share of multidimensionally poor people facing one or more environmental deprivations and the share facing all three. In both cases the share of the population with environmental deprivations rises with the MPI but with much variation around the trend (figure 3.4).

Countries above the trend line have higher than average environmental poverty, and those below perform better. The countries with the lowest shares of their population facing at least one deprivation are concentrated in the Arab States and Latin America and the Caribbean (7 of the top 10), while those with the lowest share of the population with all three are concentrated in South Asia (5 of the leading 10; table 3.1).

Brazil, Djibouti, Guyana, Morocco and Pakistan are in both top 10 lists. They perform well in having a low share of the population with at least one environmental deprivation and with all three.

Some examples:
- The Brazilian government has been expanding access to water and sanitation for several decades, investing in water

FIGURE 3.3

Environmental deprivations are greatest for access to modern cooking fuel

Share of multidimensionally poor with environmental deprivations, by region (percent)

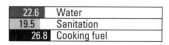

Europe and Central Asia

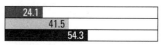

Latin America and the Caribbean

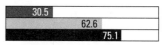

East Asia and the Pacific

South Asia

Sub-Saharan Africa

Note: Survey years vary by country; see statistical table 5 for details. Data are not shown for the Arab States because low poverty levels render the results potentially unreliable.
Source: Calculated based on data in statistical table 5.

FIGURE 3.4

The share of the population with environmental deprivations rises with the MPI but with much variation around the trend

Share of multidimensionally poor with at least one deprivation (percent)

Share of multidimensionally poor with three deprivations (percent)

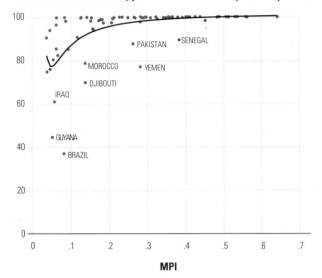
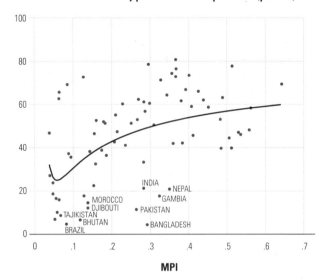

Note: Survey years vary by country; see statistical table 5 for details. The figures depict deviations from the trend for the regression exercises described in the text.

Source: HDRO calculations based on data in statistical table 5.

TABLE 3.1

Ten countries with the lowest share of environmental deprivations among the multidimensionally poor, most recent year available for 2000–2010

Lowest share of multidimensionally poor with at least one deprivation	Lowest share of multidimensionally poor with all three deprivations
Brazil	Bangladesh
Guyana	**Pakistan**
Djibouti	Gambia
Yemen	Nepal
Iraq	India
Morocco	Bhutan
Pakistan	**Djibouti**
Senegal	**Brazil**
Colombia	**Morocco**
Angola	**Guyana**

Note: Countries in bold are on both lists.

Source: HDRO calculations based on data in statistical table 5.

supply and using cross-subsidies to benefit low-income households.[10] Innovation has also been important. Brasilia has developed condominial sewerage systems that use narrow pipes installed at shallow depths instead of more expensive conventional construction.[11] Almost all Brazilian households (98 percent) use liquefied petroleum gas (LPG) fuel, thanks to policies beginning in the late 1960s for

a national LPG delivery system and cross-subsidies for LPG through taxes on other fuels.[12]

- In Bangladesh only 4 percent of the multidimensionally poor lack access to clean water, thanks to the country's thousands of hand tubewells. But there are caveats. Coverage rates include access to a public standpipe, and wait times can be long. Dhaka has only one public tap for every 500 slum dwellers.[13] Moreover, arsenic levels exceed World Health Organization (WHO) recommendations in about a third of hand tubewells, jeopardizing the health of tens of millions of Bangladeshis.[14]

- The Djibouti government made water and sanitation a priority in the mid-1990s.[15] Reforms included priority funding and new construction.[16] More than 8 in 10 Djibouti households use modern sources of cooking fuel, though use of wood and charcoal is now reportedly rising because of higher kerosene costs.[17]

- In Nepal water access is also fairly high among the multidimensionally poor (around 78 percent). This has been attributed to the lead role local communities and women, empowered through NGOs, have played in planning, designing and implementing small subprojects for water supply, sanitation, health and hygiene.[18]

The worst performers by share of the multidimensionally poor with environmental deprivations are located across several regions, with Sub-Saharan African countries featuring prominently. Among the countries performing relatively poorly in this respect, weak institutional capacity emerges as one explanation. Some examples:

- The share of Peru's population with access to water and sanitation is among the lowest in Latin America.[19] Institutional capacity, planning and quality control have impeded progress.[20] Low rural electrification rates mean that more than 80 percent of rural households rely on fuelwood for cooking. The availability of modern fuel is limited in many rural areas because of poor transportation networks and high upfront costs.[21]

- In Mongolia large rural–urban disparities in access to clean water and sanitation are exacerbated by weak institutional capacity and lack of investment. In theory the government gives priority to the water needs of the poor, but in practice lack of regulations has resulted in price structures that provide water at low cost to business and industry while disregarding the poor. Per litre, rural consumers and small businesses pay 84 times more for clean water than do industrial and mining companies.[22]

The MPI sheds light on the patterns of environmental deprivations facing households (box 3.1). It shows the prevalence of overlapping deprivations but also, more optimistically, highlights countries that have done relatively well, including through programmes we explore in the next chapter. In addition to how countries perform relative to each other, this year we also explore how some have fared over time.

These findings should be interpreted with care, however. Last year's *HDR* recognized several limitations of the MPI as a measurement tool. The datasets cover different years, limiting comparability. In some cases the surveys may not reflect recent improvements. Additional caveats apply to the analysis here. The three environmental deprivations were selected as the best comparable measures across countries, but other environmental threats may be equally or more acute at the local or national level. Flooding may be a more pressing concern for poor households in Bangladesh, for example, than access to water.

And it is important to underline that good performance (or bad) with respect to these specific indicators is not necessarily indicative of environmental degradation more broadly. Some countries, such as Syria, have a very low MPI (and low contribution of environmental deprivation) but still face pressing environmental stresses relating to water availability, land deterioration and agricultural productivity. And, as we explore in chapter 4, addressing household-level deprivations needs to be done in a way that minimizes environmental degradation more broadly.

Chapter 2 argues that as countries develop, the nature and severity of their environmental problems tend to evolve. The types of direct environmental threats experienced at the individual and household levels—those we explore here—tend to be more severe and widespread in countries at low HDI levels, and they are experienced even more acutely by the poor. We have also highlighted a double burden of the multidimensionally poor: that they may be more exposed not only to these localized, household-level threats but also to environmental degradation writ large.

We investigate this pattern further by looking at the relationship between the MPI and changes in climate. For 130 nationally defined administrative regions in 15 countries, we are able to compare area-specific MPIs with changes in temperature and precipitation —the "anomalies" discussed in chapter 2 (see map 2.1). The results are thought provoking.

- In our sample, on average, temperature was 0.5°C higher in 2000–2008 than in 1951–1980, while rainfall increased nearly 9 millimetres (4.6 millimetres, if we exclude some extreme changes in Indonesia). The temperature rose in 106 of 110 cases, and rainfall rose in nearly 85 cases (80 percent).

- Overall, a strong positive association emerges between MPI levels and warming,

The MPI sheds light on the patterns of environmental deprivations facing households, showing the prevalence of overlapping deprivations but also, more optimistically, highlighting countries that have done relatively well

BOX 3.1
Trends in multidimensional poverty

Our concern with equity leads us to focus on the most disadvantaged. This year we use the Multidimensional Poverty Index (MPI) to reveal trends in the multiple deprivations that batter poor people at the same time for seven countries—Bolivia, Colombia, Jordan, Kenya, Lesotho, Madagascar and Nigeria—and find that poverty declined in all of them (see figure). The decline was fastest in absolute terms in Bolivia, Nigeria and Lesotho, while annualized percentage reductions were greater in Bolivia, Colombia and Jordan, where low poverty means that small reductions translate into large relative declines.

Capturing reductions in both the incidence and intensity of poverty is one of the MPI's key strengths, creating useful incentives to reduce both the number of people in poverty and the number of deprivations that they jointly face. The index thus overcomes a well known problem associated with traditional ("headcount only") poverty measures, which can lead to a focus on moving people from just below to just above the poverty line.

In our seven countries poverty has fallen by reducing both the number of multidimensionally poor people and the intensity of their poverty. Madagascar's improvement, for example, was driven mainly by reducing poverty intensity, while in the other countries the biggest change was in the number of poor people.

Reduction in the MPI and in the multidimensional poverty headcount and intensity in seven countries, various years
(average annual percent change)

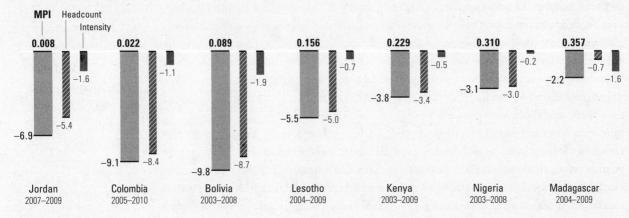

Note: Values in bold are MPI levels for the most recent year available. *Headcount* refers to the percentage of the population that is multidimensionally poor; *intensity* refers to the average percentage of deprivations experienced by people in multidimensional poverty.
Source: Alkire and others forthcoming.

Underlying the overall drops in poverty, different patterns emerge. For example, multidimensional poverty fell at a similar rate in Kenya and Nigeria, but Kenya's progress was driven by improvements across all standard of living indicators, whereas Nigeria progressed most in water, sanitation and child mortality. Poverty reduction was widely distributed across Kenya. In Nigeria, by contrast, poverty worsened in the northeast, the poorest region, while the south saw the most substantial reduction.

Source: Alkire, Roche and Santos forthcoming; Demographic and Health Surveys (www.measuredhs.com).

suggesting that localities that have had the largest increases in temperature tend to be poorer than those that have had smaller changes.[23]

But for rainfall there is no strong pattern,[24] and within countries, overall tendencies mask considerable variation. Nonetheless, the relationship is consistent with research exploring the effects of climate change on income poverty.[25] Further study is needed to extend this work to a multidimensional setting.

Where poverty and the effects of climate change intersect to constrain possibilities, the poor are especially vulnerable. But more generally, disadvantaged people and groups face particular threats from environmental degradation because their coping options are more limited. We go on to examine particular ways in which environmental degradation threatens human development and how it may harm already deprived groups the most.

Environmental threats to people's well-being

To better understand the channels through which environmental degradation impedes and damages capabilities, especially those of poor and disadvantaged groups, we look at adverse effects on health, education, livelihoods and other aspects of well-being, including choices on how to spend time, where to live and freedom from conflict.

Harming health

This section reviews the adverse health impacts of indoor and outdoor air pollution, dirty water and unimproved sanitation, and climate change. Environmental degradation affects people's health through impacts on physical and social environments as well as through the knowledge, assets and behaviours of individuals and households. Interactions between dimensions of disadvantage also affect health—for instance, health risks are greatest where water and sanitation are inadequate. Our analysis of multidimensional poverty suggests that such deprivations often coincide with deaths due to environmental causes: 6 of the 10 countries with the highest rates of death attributable to environmental causes are among the 10 countries with the highest MPI (figure 3.5).[26] The economic costs of the health impacts of environmental factors, including malnutrition, are also large. The World Bank recently estimated them at close to 6 percent of GDP in Ghana and more than 4 percent in Pakistan. Adding the longer term effects on education and income boosts the annual cost for each country to as much as 9 percent of GDP.[27]

The WHO's study of the global burden of disease underlines the importance of environmental factors. Unsafe water, inadequate sanitation and insufficient hygiene are among the top 10 leading causes of disease worldwide. Each year at least 3 million children under age 5 die from environment-related diseases, including acute respiratory infection and diarrhoea more than the entire under-five population of Austria, Belgium, the Netherlands, Portugal and Switzerland combined.[28] And in low HDI countries about 14 percent of the disease burden has environmental causes, notably indoor air pollution.

Indoor air pollution

Half the people in the world still use traditional biomass for heating and cooking. In low HDI countries 94 percent of the multidimensionally poor rely on such fuels, producing smoke

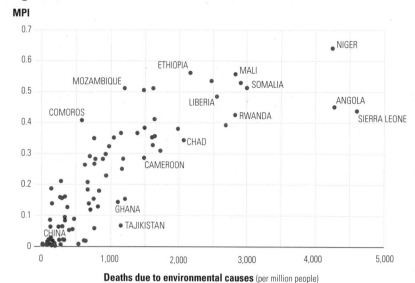

FIGURE 3.5

Deaths attributable to environmental risks are associated with high MPI levels

Note: Excludes very high HDI countries. Survey years vary by country; see statistical table 5 for details.
Source: Calculations based on data from statistical table 5 and Prüss-Üstün and others 2008.

associated with acute respiratory infections, lung cancer, reduced lung function, carbon monoxide poisoning and immune system impairment. Indoor smoke from solid fuel is linked to some 2 million deaths a year. About 36 percent of these deaths are in low HDI countries, with a further 28 percent in China and 25 percent in India.[29] Deaths related to indoor air pollution are concentrated among the rural poor, who rely on coal for cooking and heating. The uptake of modern cooking fuel has been faster in urban areas—in China, for instance, 82 percent of urban households use gas.[30]

Indoor pollution kills 11 times more people in low HDI countries than in other countries and 20 times more people than in very high HDI countries. It accounts for 5.4 percent of the disease burden in low HDI countries—as much as 10 percent in Afghanistan, the country most afflicted in absolute terms.[31]

Women and children in rural areas, who spend more time in houses that use fuelwood, suffer most.[32] Burning wood contributes to deforestation, which in turn forces households to burn dung and crop residues instead, intensifying the exposure to indoor air pollution because these fires require constant tending and their smoke is more toxic.[33]

Background research shows that deaths related to indoor air pollution are strongly related to the national MPI,[34] showing how deprivations in cooking fuel contribute to multidimensional poverty and to the ill health of the poor. Poor households know that burning wood irritates the eyes and damages the respiratory system. An older Bhutanese woman observed that burning wood caused eye problems and coughs for many elderly women in her village.[35] In India Rabiya Khatun of Bihar commented: "We have always used twigs and branches from nearby trees as cooking fuel. Everyone here does that. It burns our eyes, but it has to be done"; in West Bengal Faizul Haque observed that his wife, who is not yet 30, has been "sick for the last few years . . . she is hardly able to breathe, because of all the fumes."[36]

Improved stoves, better ventilation and clean fuel are expected to reduce indoor pollution and mitigate health risks, alongside efforts to expand access to modern energy sources, as we explore in the next chapter.

Outdoor air pollution

Long-term exposure to outdoor air pollution causes respiratory disorders, immune system damage and carbon monoxide poisoning, among other deleterious effects.[37] In Mexico City studies have found a significant impact from outdoor pollution on the mortality of the high-risk population,[38] and in Linfen, China, and Norilsk, Russian Federation, industries produce levels of air pollution that seriously threaten the health of their populations.[39] Disadvantaged groups are both more exposed and more vulnerable to the effects: in Hong Kong Special Administrative Region of China and Shanghai mortality due to outdoor air pollution is higher among the economically disadvantaged and the least educated.[40]

The pattern holds across the globe. In England half of municipal incinerators are in the most deprived tenth of municipalities.[41] People in the poorest households and ethnic minorities are most likely to breathe polluted air, while areas with the highest rate of car ownership enjoy the cleanest air.[42] In Rijnmond, Netherlands, poorer and minority households endure more air pollution and live closer to waste disposal sites.[43] In Kassel, Germany, the air is more polluted in neighbourhoods where the foreign-born population lives.[44] And French communities with higher proportions of immigrants host more industrial and nuclear waste sites, incinerators and waste management facilities.[45]

The good news, as reviewed in chapter 2, is that air pollution is declining, though on average it remains much higher in cities in poorer countries. China again emerges as an important case: rising energy consumption, based largely on coal and other solid fuels, and vehicle pollution have taken a toll on air quality (box 3.2).

BOX 3.2

Air pollution and its health consequences in China

Outdoor air pollution is high in China, especially in urban areas and the north. A recent official environmental assessment finds that almost one city in five does not meet government standards; far more would likely fail to reach World Health Organization (WHO) air quality standards. Outdoor air pollution is associated with some 300,000 deaths and 20 million cases of respiratory illness in China each year, with estimated health costs of about 3 percent of GDP annually.

Among the many sources of outdoor air pollution in China are residential and industrial coal combustion and motor vehicle exhaust. About 70 percent of the country's electricity is generated from coal, most of it high in sulphur. High sulphur dioxide emissions contribute to smog and acid rain, which affect more than half of China's cities.

Outdoor air pollution patterns suggest major challenges, particularly in cities. Vehicle emissions may be the fastest growing source of urban air pollution, with China's Environmental Protection Agency estimating that vehicles account for 70 percent of sulphur in the air. With rising incomes and better roads, the country has seen its vehicular fleet jump 20 percent a year since 1990. And since in 2009 only 3 percent of people in China owned a car, the trend is likely to continue. In Beijing more than 1,000 new cars are added to the total each day.

Air pollution in China has caused a dramatic rise in asthma. From 1990 to 2000 its prevalence among urban children rose 64 percent, affecting almost 2 percent of children. In Chongqing, one of the country's fastest growing cities, nearly 5 percent of children under age 14 suffered from asthma in 2000.

China's efforts to reduce outdoor air pollution are closely integrated with its policies aimed at climate change, energy efficiency and renewable energy use. In 2000 the government began requiring lead-free petrol, which reduced the lead content of urban air, and has made developing new clean energy vehicles the priority of the country's auto industry for the next five years. The country has pledged to reduce energy consumption and carbon emissions 18 percent per unit of industrial value added by 2015 and to increase consumption of non–fossil fuel energy to 15 percent by 2020, up from the current 8 percent, which should also reduce outdoor air pollution.

Source: China National People's Congress 2011; Fang and Chan 2008; Liu and Raven 2010: 8329; Millman, Tang and Perera 2008; Watts 2006, 2011; Zhan and others 2010.

Dirty water and unimproved sanitation

Lack of adequate sanitation and clean water compromises the life chances of many people, mainly in poorer countries. In medium HDI countries half the people lack access to improved sanitation, and one in eight lacks access to improved water. In low HDI countries the figures are 65 percent for sanitation and 38 percent for water. Nearly 4 in 10 people worldwide lack sanitary toilets, but as many as 8 in 10 of the multidimensionally poor do. Urban and rural disparities are large: less than half the rural population had improved sanitation facilities in 2008, compared with almost three-quarters of the urban population.[46]

These deprivations exact a high toll on health. For children under age 5 environmental factors account for more than a third of the global disease burden.[47] Diarrhoeal diseases account for some 2 million deaths of children under age 5 each year, and the most recent estimates indicate that improved sanitation and drinking water could save 2.2 million children a year, or some 5,500 a day.[48] Half of all malnutrition is attributable to environmental factors, particularly poor water, sanitation and hygiene.[49] Malnutrition from these causes is responsible for some 70,000 child deaths a year, while underweight children are more vulnerable to infectious disease and less likely to recover fully when they do fall sick.[50] Childhood malnourishment also impairs cognitive development and education performance, reducing opportunities over a lifetime.

Inadequate water and sanitation are linked to an even broader array of health problems, as the 2006 *HDR* exposed. Today, billions of people are affected by parasitic diseases: 1.5 billion with *ascaris*, 740 million with hookworm, 200 million with schistosomiasis and 40–70 million with liverfluke. Many millions are likely affected by tropical enteropathy, an intestinal disease caused by faecal bacteria that reduces nutrient absorption. These infections as well as hepatitis, typhoid and polio can be avoided through safe excreta disposal and other hygienic behaviours, as we discuss in chapter 4. Beyond the human costs, the financial repercussions are large. For instance, the economic costs of poor sanitation and hygiene in Cambodia (7.2 percent of GDP), Indonesia (2.3 percent), the Philippines (1.5 percent) and Viet Nam (1.3 percent) in 2007 amounted to around $9 billion (in 2005 prices) or 2 percent of their combined GDP.[51] And access to basic

sanitation services is especially important for women, not only for the health gains[52] but also for privacy, time savings and reduced risk of sexual violence.[53]

Climate change

The health risks posed by climate change are immense and diverse—from increased risks of extreme weather events to salinization of land and fresh water from rising sea levels and the changing dynamics of infectious disease caused by higher temperatures. Higher temperatures will broaden the spread and increase the transmission rates of vector- and rodent-borne diseases, expanding endemic areas for malaria, tick-borne encephalitis and dengue fever.[54] Estimates suggest that 260–320 million more people will be affected by malaria by 2080.[55] And many more will be at risk of contracting dengue fever.[56] A recent study of 19 African countries found that weather variations increased the prevalence of diarrhoea, acute respiratory infections and undernutrition in children under age 5.

Heat stress will rise with temperatures, and more people will die from heatstroke—particularly urban residents and people with respiratory conditions. The incidence of diarrhoea will also rise with temperatures.[57] By 2050 sea level rise, droughts, heat waves, floods and rainfall variation could increase the number of malnourished children by 25 million. Land and ecosystem degradation will also add to malnutrition.[58] These projections are based on a business-as-usual scenario. More sustainable behaviours and practices, outlined in chapter 4, could deflect these trajectories in positive ways.

Indigenous peoples may be especially susceptible to the adverse health effects of environmental degradation. In northern Australia, for example, higher temperatures and more frequent heat waves will assail indigenous peoples in remote areas, where cardiovascular and respiratory disease rates are already high. The health effects may be especially severe where indigenous peoples' connection to ecosystems —as a place of ancestry, identity, language, livelihood and community—is a key determinant of health.[59]

> Indigenous peoples may be especially susceptible to the adverse health effects of environmental degradation

Impeding education

As highlighted in the 2010 *HDR*, the expansion of primary education is one of the great successes of the past 40 years. The share of children attending school rose from 57 percent to 85 percent, with near universal enrolment in many parts of the world. Yet gaps remain. Nearly 3 in 10 children of primary school age in low HDI countries are not enrolled in school.[60] And a range of other constraints, some related to environmental factors, persist.

Electricity access can improve schooling. Better lighting allows for more study time, and electricity at home and school increases the time children and adults spend reading and keeps children in school longer.[61] In northwestern Madagascar electricity made it easier for girls to do their homework and for their mothers to help them in the evening after household tasks were done.[62] In Bangladesh the time children spent in school was correlated with access to electricity, even after controlling for family wealth (landholdings).[63] And in Viet Nam communes connected to the electric grid between 2002 and 2005 saw school enrolment increase 17 percent for boys and 15 percent for girls.[64]

Having access to electricity and other modern fuels can reduce the time spent collecting biomass fuel.[65] In Malawi children often collect fuelwood and other resources, and their likelihood of attending school falls as time allocated to this work rises.[66] In rural Ethiopia the probability of schooling as the main activity, especially for boys, falls as the time to reach a water source rises.[67]

A negative relationship was found between children's resource collection and their likelihood of attending school, though not the performance of those attending school. In Kenya's Central Province district of Kiambu, fuelwood collection averages more than 4 hours a day, ranging from half an hour to 10 hours.[68] Girls were more likely to combine resource collection and schooling.

In the Indian states of Andhra Pradesh, Gujarat, Rajasthan and Maharashtra, for example, the United Nations Children's Fund and others are providing solar-powered lamps to schools and women's literacy groups to promote education for girls. In the words of 13-year-old Manasha, "When there is no light, we go to bed very early after dinner and get up early. Now at night I can study."[69] Interventions to improve access to electricity are explored in chapter 4.

Endangering livelihoods

Environmental degradation can endanger the livelihoods of the millions of people around the world who depend directly on environmental resources for work. About 1.3 billion people, or 40 percent of the economically active people worldwide, work in agriculture, fishing, forestry, and hunting or gathering. Almost 6 in 10 of the economically active people engaged in these activities live in low HDI countries, while just 3 percent live in very high HDI countries. In Bhutan, Burkina Faso and Nepal, 92 percent of economically active people depend directly on natural resources for their livelihoods; less than 1 percent do in Bahrain, Qatar, Singapore and Slovenia.[70]

The rural poor depend overwhelmingly on natural resources for their income.[71] Even those who do not normally engage in natural resource–related activity may do so during times of hardship.[72] The effects of environmental degradation on crop production, fish supply, extraction of forest goods, and hunting and gathering vary, hurting some groups more than others. How it affects people depends on whether they are net producers or consumers of natural resources and whether they produce for subsistence or the market (and how readily they can shift between the two). Women in poor countries engage disproportionately in subsistence farming and water collection, exposing them more to adverse repercussions.[73]

Indigenous peoples deserve special mention (box 3.3). While they make up about 5 percent of the world's people,[74] they own, occupy or use (generally by customary rights) up to 22 percent of the world's land, which holds 80 percent of the planet's biodiversity.[75] Indigenous peoples and communities legally own around 11 percent of global forests,[76] and an estimated 60 million of them depend totally on forest resources for their livelihoods.[77] They often live in ecosystems particularly vulnerable

> Environmental degradation can endanger the livelihoods of the millions of people around the world who depend directly on environmental resources for work

to the effects of climate change, such as small island developing states, arctic regions, on the coast or at high altitude, and depend on fishing, hunting and farming to survive.[78]

We turn now to the differentiated impacts of environmental trends on people engaged in agriculture, forestry and fishing.

Threatening agriculture

Agriculture is the main source of livelihood for most of the world's poor.[79] The natural environment delivers support functions to agricultural production, such as regulating the nutrient and water cycles. And as agriculture intensifies to meet the food needs of growing populations, healthy ecosystems remain an important foundation. Environmental degradation thus threatens livelihoods and food security. Among the many complex interactions, the focus here is on the effects of land degradation, water stress and climate change.

Land degradation reduces arable land and crop yields and increases the frequency of flooding. Specifically:

- Loss of fertile topsoil is reducing land productivity, with estimated yield losses as high as 50 percent in the most adverse scenarios.[80] Sub-Saharan Africa (especially Angola, Gabon and Swaziland) and East Asia and the Pacific (especially China, Indonesia, Malaysia and Myanmar) are hit hardest.
- Drylands, home to about a third of the world's population, are threatened by desertification.[81] Some areas are especially vulnerable, such as Sub-Saharan Africa's drylands, where adaptive capacity is low.[82] Other parts of the world have also been affected. Land degradation in northern China's Minqin County led to the abandonment of more than 80 percent of its farmland.[83]

By 2025 water scarcity is expected to affect more than 1.8 billion people.[84] Field research suggests that the direct impacts of water depletion on crop cultivation can be worse for poor farmers. For example, in rural Mexico poor farmers without the capital to adapt to falling water tables cannot buy more drought-resistant seeds or piped water. And government

BOX 3.3

Indigenous peoples, land rights and livelihoods

Unusual weather patterns and storms hurt indigenous communities that rely on natural resources for their livelihoods. In northern Canada global warming has shortened the period when sea-ice access routes to hunting areas are open, reducing food security and safety among the Inuit in Nunavik, Quebec, and in Nunatsiavut, Labrador. In Peru freak cold spells have increased, with temperatures falling to an unprecedented −35°C in the high Andes. In 2004, 50 children and up to 70 percent of livestock died, and as many as 13,000 people became severely ill.

Indigenous peoples' relationship with their lands often has cultural and spiritual dimensions, which land management practices can disrupt. As outsiders increasingly seek indigenous peoples' lands for conservation and resource extraction, decisions are being made about the use of these lands without meaningful participation by the affected peoples. Indigenous communities may want to keep their environment and resources intact, leading to tension and conflict.

As chapter 4 shows, governments are increasingly recognizing the special nature of indigenous peoples' relationships with their land and environment. In 2004 the Canadian Supreme Court recognized the government's obligation to honour the environment-related rights of two native tribes in British Columbia. Most Latin American constitutions include a provision governing indigenous peoples' lands, territories and natural resources. The 2009 Bolivian constitution recognizes the rights of indigenous peoples to their original communal lands, guaranteeing the use and improvement of sustainable natural resources—in line with an alternative vision of development (vivir bien) that seeks the spiritual and collective well-being of people as well as greater harmony with nature.

Source: Furgal and Seguin 2006; Simms, Maldonado and Reid 2006; World Bank 2008c; Colchester 2010; Green, King and Morrison 2009; Manus 2006; Aguilar and others 2010.

financing programmes do not help the poor when the technical requirements and matching contributions are too onerous.[85]

The effects of climate change on farmer livelihoods vary with the crop, region and season. Researchers have studied the relation between climate change and crop and pasture yields using simulation models, statistical studies and hedonic approaches. Some results suggest that moderate temperature increases (no more than 2°C) might benefit yields in the short run in temperate regions but will have adverse effects in tropical and semiarid regions. Globally, maize production has decreased 3.8 percent and wheat production 5.1 percent since 1980 due to climate change, with considerable regional variation (and some countries even benefitting from a changing climate). For rice and soy, countries benefitting and losing largely balanced out.[86] Projections through 2030 suggest that maize and wheat production in Southern Africa will fall sharply, while rice yields are expected to be positively affected by climate change.[87] Rainfed maize yields are predicted to increase in China's northeast but to fall in its southern regions. Across the world the biophysical impacts of climate change on both irrigated and rainfed crops are likely to be negative by 2050.[88]

The variability of effects underlines the need for detailed, local analysis. So does the variability in household production and consumption patterns, access to resources, poverty levels and ability to cope.[89] For instance, agriculture is the most common source of work for rural women in most developing regions, yet they have less access than men to assets, inputs and complementary services. Disparities in landholdings are particularly acute—just 20 percent of landholders in developing countries are women, and their landholdings are smaller than those of men.[90]

Food production must rise to meet the demands of growing populations, but the combined environmental effects of land degradation, water scarcity and climate change will restrict supply. Adverse environmental factors are expected to drive up world food prices in real terms 30–50 percent in the coming decades and increase price volatility.[91] Income poverty and malnutrition could worsen if the prices of key staples rise—as vividly demonstrated during the 2007–2008 food price spike.[92] The poor spend a large share of their income on staple foods, and to survive, they sacrifice nutrition and eat less.[93]

The effects of food price hikes depend on household consumption and production. People in urban areas and nonfarm rural households, who are net food consumers, tend to be relatively worse off. But the research results are mixed:

- One modelling exercise covering 15 countries found that the effects on income poverty depend on a household's location and whether it engages in agriculture.[94] Price hikes were predicted to hurt nonagricultural households most, with 20–50 percent falling into poverty in parts of Africa and Asia. But households specializing in agriculture benefit, and many in Latin America and the Caribbean and elsewhere in Asia are lifted from poverty.
- Another recent study of nine countries (Bolivia, Cambodia, Madagascar, Malawi, Nicaragua, Pakistan, Peru, Viet Nam and Zambia) found that rising food prices increased income poverty overall, even if rural food producers did better.[95] Similarly, food price hikes increased the incidence and intensity of poverty in Indonesia, the Philippines and Thailand.[96]

Because different types of environmental change have different effects on land, labour and food production, it is important to examine the joint effects. In India climate change could lead to a sharp drop in land productivity for some 17 percent of farmers, through the effect on cereal prices, but effects on consumption would be muted, as most rural households derive their income largely from wage employment. Costs would fall disproportionally on the poor in urban areas, who would pay more for food, and on wage earners and net consumers of food in rural areas.[97]

Pressuring forests

Around 350 million people living in or near forests depend on forest wood and nonwood resources for subsistence and income.[98] Many people in developing countries rely on forests for fuelwood: in Asia and the Pacific more than 70 percent of wood removed from forests is for fuel; in Africa the share may be as high as 90 percent.[99]

Women are responsible for most fuelwood collection in many parts of the world. Though global data are lacking on the number of women working in forestry, evidence suggests that women, with fewer occupational options and less mobility, rely on forests more than men do.[100]

Forest resources also generate income, through employment and the sale of goods and services. Nonwood forest products—such as food, fuel for cooking and heating, animal fodder, wild game, medicinal herbs and shelter—provide local communities with subsistence and marketable goods. They also provide cash to pay for school, medicine, equipment, supplies and food.

Poor people typically depend more on forests for cash and noncash incomes—and as safety nets.[101] A review of case studies of rural communities living in or on the fringes of tropical forests found that poor households derived more than a fourth of their incomes from forest resources, compared with 17 percent for nonpoor households.[102] Some examples:

- In Arunachal Pradesh, India, poor households depended on community forests for basic survival, and households that had less land and less education and that were farther from markets depended more on forest products.[103]

- In southern Ethiopia forest income kept a fifth of the population above the poverty line, reducing income inequality some 15 percent.[104]

- In Viet Nam forest products provided rural households with a safety net when other sources of income failed. People stricken by illness and health shocks were more likely than others to extract forest products.[105]

It follows that poor people are more vulnerable to forest degradation and exclusion.[106] In South Asia households relying on fuel collection responded to reduced access by increasing collection time, purchasing fuelwood and cooking less often. Wealthier households, by contrast, shifted to alternative fuels.[107]

Damaging fisheries

An estimated 45 million people directly engage in capture fisheries or aquaculture, at least 6 million of them women.[108] More than 95 percent of small-scale fishers and post-harvest workers live in developing countries and face precarious living and working conditions. Countries most at risk from overfishing and climate change are also among those relying most on fish for dietary protein, livelihoods and exports.[109]

More than 80 percent of the world's poor fishers are in South and Southeast Asia. But two-thirds of the countries whose capture fisheries are most vulnerable to climate change are in tropical Africa.[110]

Climate change is predicted to reduce fishery resources in the Pacific Islands by as much as half by 2100 and to drastically reduce mangrove forests and coral reefs.[111] Research commissioned by the United Nations Development Programme Pacific Centre emphasizes the centrality of fishing to livelihoods in the Pacific region for both subsistence and cash.[112] Rising sea temperatures will adversely affect more men, who typically engage in deep-ocean fisheries and commercial fishing, while coastal erosion will hurt more women, who typically gather invertebrates closer to the shore.

How people respond to the impacts of climate change on fisheries is likely to vary. In Kenya, for example, even with catch declines of up to 50 percent, subsistence fishers from poor households and with less diverse income sources were more likely to continue fishing than were fishers from households with more assets and diversified livelihoods.[113]

But not all the expected effects are negative. For countries near the Equator fresh water aquaculture of fish such as tilapia may benefit from greater fresh water availability and higher temperatures.[114] And ocean warming and the retreat of sea ice at high latitudes are predicted to increase the potential catch in the long term —with the greatest benefits likely to accrue in Alaska, Greenland, Norway and the Russian Federation.[115]

*   *   *

People can adjust their production and consumption strategies to environmental conditions—for instance, they may grow crops more suited to poorer soils or warmer temperatures or eat food that requires less cooking and thus uses less fuelwood. People often react to environmental degradation by pursuing alternative livelihood strategies in the same area or by moving.[116] We now consider other adverse repercussions on well-being.

Other adverse repercussions

Environmental degradation has additional, interacting repercussions on disadvantaged groups. Here, we explore the links with time use, migration and conflict. Environmental stress can increase the difficulties in making a living from natural resources—forcing people to go farther to collect them, to work more to obtain a similar livelihood or even to migrate. In some cases environmental stresses have been linked with greater likelihood of conflict.[117]

Time use

For people who lack access to modern fuels and safe water, collecting fuelwood and water takes

> Countries most at risk from overfishing and climate change are also among those relying most on fish for dietary protein, livelihoods and exports

considerable time. Nearly half the households in low HDI countries, mostly in Sub-Saharan Africa, spend more than 30 minutes a day collecting water. The burden is especially high in rural areas. Trips average 82 minutes in Somalia, 71 minutes in Mauritania and 65 minutes in Yemen.[118]

Widespread environmental stress increases time burdens for households, with adverse implications for their well-being. Time-use surveys illuminate this burden, showing how tasks are allocated within households and how they can be affected by environmental degradation.[119] Studies in India have found that fuelwood collection time has increased markedly in recent decades: in Kumaon, Uttar Pradesh, women and children travelled on average 1.6 hours and 1.6 kilometres to collect wood in the early 1970s and 3–4 hours and 4.5 kilometres in the 1990s.[120]

Women and children have primary responsibility for fetching wood and water. A recent study of seven low HDI countries found that 56–86 percent of rural women fetched water, compared with 8–40 percent of rural men.[121] In rural Malawi, for instance, women spend more than eight times what men do fetching wood and water, and girls spend about three times what boys do on these chores (table 3.2).

Collecting fuelwood and water has been linked in women to spinal damage, complications during pregnancy and maternal mortality.[122] The demands on time can also have a high opportunity cost in forgone schooling or leisure time for children and labour market activity for adults. In rural Pakistan, for example, difficult access to water increases women's total work burden and reduces the time they devote to market-oriented activities.[123]

Thus, the gains from secure and sustainable access to these resources and more modern alternatives could be large. In Sierra Leone improved access to water and electricity reduced domestic work time about 10 hours a week.[124] A study in the 1990s found that if all households in the Mbale district of Eastern Uganda had secure access to water and fuel—living 400 metres or less from potable water and no more than 30 minutes from a fuelwood source—they would gain more than 900 hours a year.[125] And a recent study estimated that 63 percent of the economic benefits from reaching the Millennium Development Goal target for water supply would come from time savings.[126]

Migration

Environmental stress can also drive people to relocate, especially where families and communities are deprived in multiple dimensions and see better opportunities elsewhere. It is difficult to quantify how many people move due to environmental stresses, because other factors also constrain people's freedoms.

Some prominent estimates have been very high—the 1994 Almeria Statement observed that 135 million people might be at risk of displacement due to desertification.[127] And the Stern Review suggested that 200 million people might be displaced by 2050.[128] But other estimates are far lower. The UN High Commissioner for Refugees found that 24 million people had been displaced by floods, famine and other environmental factors.[129] A recent detailed estimate suggests that temperature and rainfall variation drove some 2.35 million people in Sub-Saharan Africa to move between 1960 and 2000.[130]

As argued in the 2009 *HDR*, expanding people's opportunities to choose where they live is an important way to expand their freedoms. Mobility can be associated with improved income-earning opportunities and better opportunities for children. The problems, of course, are that a degraded environment constrains choices—especially for those whose livelihoods depend on a healthy

---

TABLE 3.2

Average time per week spent fetching wood and water, rural areas of selected Sub-Saharan African countries (hours)

Gender and ratio	Guinea (2002–03)	Madagascar (2001)	Malawi (2004)	Sierra Leone (2003–04)
Women	5.7	4.7	9.1	7.3
Men	2.3	4.1	1.1	4.5
Girls	4.1	5.1	4.3	7.7
Boys	4.0	4.7	1.4	7.1
Women/men	2.5	1.1	8.3	1.6
Girls/boys	1.0	1.1	3.1	1.1

Source: HDRO calculations based on data from Bardasi and Wodon (2009) (Guinea); Blackden and Wodon (2006) (Madagascar); Beegle and Wodon (2006) (Malawi); and Wodon and Ying (2010) (Sierra Leone).

environment—and that legal constraints on movement make migration riskier.[131]

Conflict

Finally, climate change and limited natural resources have been linked to an increased likelihood of conflict, one of the most pernicious threats to human development. They may also undermine the prospects for peace. Most resource-related conflicts are domestic, but increasing scarcity of land, water and energy could spark international strife. An estimated 40 percent of civil wars over the past 60 years are associated with natural resources, and since 1990 at least 18 violent conflicts have been fuelled by the exploitation of natural resources and other environmental factors.[132] Some cross-country evidence is illustrative. For example, greater variability in rainfall increases the risk of civil conflict, particularly in Sub-Saharan Africa, where a 1°C rise in temperature is associated with a greater than 10 percent increase in the likelihood of civil war the same year.[133]

Recent episodes support the link. Competition over land contributed to postelection violence in Kenya in 2008 and to tensions leading to the 1994 genocide in Rwanda. Water, land and desertification are major factors in the war in Darfur, Sudan. In Afghanistan conflict and the environment are caught up in a vicious cycle—environmental degradation fuels conflict, and conflict degrades the environment.[134] Policy responses, when they are badly designed or fail to consider all parties' interests, can also exacerbate the risk of conflict.

Global and local resource scarcity may be key causes of conflict—a well known early study highlights the interplay between environmental degradation, population growth and unequal resource distributions in stirring up strife.[135] And countries with high dependence on primary commodity exports may be at increased risk—an abundance of resources is a powerful incentive for conflict.[136]

But natural resources are rarely, if ever, the sole driver of violent conflict. They are threat multipliers that interact with other risks and vulnerabilities.[137] The evidence does not suggest that there are direct links between

environmental scarcity and conflict but that resource scarcity has to be embedded in the context of the broader political economy: separating the processes and elements associated with environmental conflict from the structures within which they are embedded is "both difficult and a distortion of reality."[138]

Disequalizing effects of extreme events

People living in urban slums in low and medium HDI countries face the greatest risk from extreme weather events and rising sea levels, caused by a combination of high exposure and inadequate protective infrastructure and services.[139] By 2050, with a projected 0.5 metre rise in sea level, Bangladesh is likely to lose about 11 percent of its land, affecting an estimated 15 million people.[140] Over the same period rising sea levels could displace more than 14 million Egyptians as increased salinization of the Nile reduces the irrigated land available for agriculture.[141]

The United Nations estimates that 29 percent of the world's slum dwellers live in low HDI countries—with an additional 24 percent in China and 15 percent in India (both medium HDI countries).[142] Vulnerable groups in megacities are particularly exposed to natural disasters, because of both their precarious living conditions and the absence of public services and formal social security systems. But, as shown below, some substitution with social capital, which builds resilience, can reduce risk.

Our own analysis suggests that a 10 percent increase in the number of people affected by an extreme weather event typically reduces a country's HDI by almost 2 percent, with particularly strong effects on the income component of HDI and in medium HDI countries. In some countries poorer regions suffer most. In Ha Giang Province, Viet Nam, one of the country's poorest regions and home to 22 ethnic minorities, irregular rainfall, massive flooding and unpredictable storms have submerged land and crops, drowned livestock and destroyed infrastructure.[143] In Mexico natural disasters, particularly droughts and floods, set

People living in urban slums in low and medium HDI countries face the greatest risk from extreme weather events and rising sea levels, caused by a combination of high exposure and inadequate protective infrastructure and services the HDI back in affected municipalities by about two years and increased extreme poverty almost 4 percentage points.[144]

The risk of injury and death from floods, high winds and landslides has been systematically higher among children, women and the elderly, especially the poor. In Bangladesh poorer groups tend to live closer to rivers and thus face a greater risk of flooding.[145] Local case studies of a 1991 Bangladeshi cyclone, the 2003 European heat wave and the 2004 Asian tsunami affirm the greater vulnerability of women and children, as does broader cross-country evidence. Sri Lanka's tsunami killed nearly 1 in 5 displaced women and almost 1 in 3 displaced children under age 5—more than two times and four times the mortality of displaced men (about 1 in 12), respectively.[146] And in rural India the mortality differential between girls and boys increases during droughts.[147]

The strikingly unequal gender effects of natural disasters suggest that inequality in exposure and sensitivity to risk—as well as disparities in access to resources, capabilities and opportunities—overlap and systematically disadvantage some groups. In 141 countries over 22 years, higher female mortality from natural disasters and their aftermaths cannot be explained by biology and physiology.[148] And major catastrophes, as approximated by the number of people killed relative to population size, have more severe impacts than smaller disasters on women's life expectancy relative to that of men.

The explanations lie in social norms and roles and, more generally, in the socioeconomic status of women in the specific context. The higher women's socioeconomic status (measured by such factors as freedom of choice of employment, nondiscrimination at work and equal rights to marriage and education), the smaller the gender-differentiated impacts on life expectancy. In other words, it is the socially constructed vulnerability of women that leads to the higher mortality rates due to natural disasters.[149] Along similar lines, countries that focused on female education suffered far fewer losses from extreme weather events than less progressive countries with equivalent income and weather conditions.[150]

The risks and impacts are largest overall in developing countries—but the patterns of structural disadvantage are not confined to them. Witness Hurricane Katrina in the United States. New Orleans's poorest districts, composed mainly of black communities, bore the brunt of the 2005 hurricane—three-quarters of people in flooded neighbourhoods were black.[151] In the 2003 European heat wave, more women than men died, as did more elderly people than young people.

Shocks can have longer term adverse effects that extend beyond the destruction of life and immediate damage to health and livelihoods. Children may suffer disproportionately from weather shocks through the lasting effects of reduced schooling and malnourishment. In response to transitory income shocks, families without assets or other income opportunities, such as wage labour, may pull children out of school. The perceived *risk* of income loss contributes in its own right. Further, schooling infrastructure may be affected, and teachers may be injured or killed.[152] The relationship is not always straightforward, however. In Mexico, high-impact disasters were linked to increased school attendance and reduced dropout rates for primary school, and in Mozambique, to better school performance,[153] possibly because the opportunity cost of sending children to school fell along with market wages.

Weather shocks can also affect child health, notably through increases in malnutrition. One study in Zimbabwe found that children who were exposed to shocks (civil war and the 1982–1984 drought) at ages 12–24 months completed 0.85 grade of schooling less and were on average 3.4 centimetres shorter than those who were not. This stunting was shown to reduce lifetime earnings by 14 percent.[154] In Nicaragua infant malnutrition more than tripled among households most exposed to rainfall during Hurricane Mitch.[155] And Bangladesh experienced a resurgence of child poverty after 2000 in the low-lying coastal regions of the country most vulnerable to flooding.[156]

In Viet Nam evidence suggests that household responses vary by type of shock. Households exposed frequently to shocks such as drought or moderate flooding learn to

> The strikingly unequal gender effects of natural disasters suggest that inequality in exposure and sensitivity to risk —as well as disparities in access to resources, capabilities and opportunities—overlap and systematically disadvantage some groups

adapt.[157] But survey analysis suggests no adaptation to less frequent storms and hurricanes —hurricanes can halve consumption in households near large cities, especially since disaster relief largely neglects those areas.

Disempowerment and environmental degradation

Inequality, as manifested in unequal access to resources and decision-making, can harm human development and the environment. We assess the implications of gender disparities, focusing on reproductive health and participation in decision-making. We then focus on empowerment as a driver of environmental challenges to inform the policy discussions in chapters 4 and 5.

Gender equality

Women's economic opportunities and empowerment remain severely constrained. Access to reproductive healthcare has been improving in most regions, but not fast enough to achieve Millennium Development Goal 5 (to improve maternal health).[158] Indicators under the target of universal access to reproductive healthcare include the adolescent birth rate, antenatal care and unmet need for family planning.

Last year's *HDR* introduced the Gender Inequality Index (GII) for 138 countries. This year it covers 145 countries, and our updated estimates confirm that the largest losses due to gender inequality are in Sub-Saharan Africa, followed by South Asia and the Arab States. In Sub-Saharan Africa the biggest losses arise from gender disparities in education and from high maternal mortality and adolescent fertility rates. In South Asia women lag behind men in each dimension of the GII, most notably in education, national parliamentary representation and labour force participation. Women in Arab States are affected by unequal labour force participation (around half the global average) and low educational attainment. All the low HDI countries have high gender inequality across multiple dimensions. Of the 34 low HDI countries included in the 2011 GII, all but four also have a GII score in the worst quartile. By contrast, only one very high HDI

country and one high HDI country included in the GII perform as badly.

We focus on two intersections between gender equity and environmental sustainability: reproductive choice and participation in decision-making. Contraceptive prevalence and the ability to make reproductive choices carry ramifications for the environment and for women's empowerment. And, as we show, women's political empowerment is not only intrinsically important, but it also has consequences for proenvironment policy and practice.

Reproductive choice

Poor reproductive health is a major contributor to gender inequality around the world. Lack of access to reproductive health services results in debilitating outcomes for women and children—and to fatalities in excess of those caused by the most devastating natural disasters. An estimated 48 million women give birth without skilled assistance, and 2 million give birth alone. An estimated 150,000 women and 1.6 million children die each year between the onset of labour and 48 hours after birth.[159]

For the bottom 20 countries in the GII the population-weighted maternal mortality ratio averages about 327 deaths per 100,000 live births, and the adolescent fertility rate averages 95 births per 1,000 women ages 15–19, both roughly double the global averages of 157 deaths and 49 births. In these countries contraceptive use is low, averaging only 46.4 percent. More broadly, an estimated 215 million women in developing countries have unmet need for family planning.[160]

Every country, developed or developing, that offers women a full range of reproductive health options has fertility rates at or below replacement.[161] Cuba, Iran, Mauritius, Thailand and Tunisia have fertility rates of less than two births per woman.[162] And Addis Ababa's is also less than two births per woman, while Ethiopia's rural fertility rate remains above six. In much of rural Bangladesh, despite widespread poverty, fertility is now at the replacement rate.[163] And family sizes have fallen as rapidly in Iran as they have in China, but without government limits on family size.[164]

Women's ability to make reproductive choices carries ramifications for the environment and for women's empowerment, and women's political empowerment has consequences for proenvironment policy and practice

As table 2.1 in chapter 2 illustrates, population growth seriously strains the limits of world resources. A range of studies suggest that lower population growth could offset at least some of the higher greenhouse gas emissions associated with rising incomes. One early estimate was that by 2020 carbon dioxide emissions would be about 15 percent lower than they would be without family planning.[165] A more recent study of 34 developed and developing countries with 61 percent of the world's population finds that halving 2010's population growth could provide 16–29 percent of the carbon dioxide emissions reductions needed by 2050 and 37–41 percent needed by the end of the century to avoid dangerous climate change.[166] Another study estimated that meeting unmet need for family planning would avert 53 million unintended pregnancies a year and cut carbon emissions by 34 gigatonnes, or about 17 percent of the world's current yearly total, as of 2050.[167] The environmental pay-offs are thus clearly enormous, over and above the benefits to women's empowerment.

Gender inequality and contraceptive prevalence are closely linked (figure 3.6). Where women have greater standing, as in Japan, the Netherlands and Norway, most couples use some form of contraception. But where gender inequality is high, as in Mali, Mauritania and Sierra Leone, contraceptive prevalence is below 10 percent. Data collected between 2000 and 2009 show that fewer than 3 in 10 women of reproductive age in low HDI countries use modern contraception, compared with 88 percent in Norway and 84 percent in the United Kingdom.

Further analysis highlights the importance of national HDI levels, especially education and health achievements, in explaining the relationship between gender inequality and contraceptive prevalence. However, the same does not apply for income—if we control for income alone, gender inequality and contraceptive prevalence continue to be strongly linked. This underlines the importance of investments in health and education in furthering reproductive health choices.

The reported unmet demand for family planning is very low in Chad, the Democratic Republic of the Congo and Niger (below 5 percent), alongside very high average fertility.[168] This can happen because of cultural or religious objections by women, their husbands or other family members; a lack of knowledge of contraceptive methods or fear of their side effects; or preference for larger families.[169] Low unmet need can be associated with low contraceptive prevalence at low levels of development (where fertility preferences are high) and with high contraceptive prevalence at high levels of development (where fertility preferences are low). This means that family planning programmes must go beyond supplying contraception at affordable prices to raising awareness of its use and health effects and addressing the structural constraints facing poor women (see chapter 4). Some studies link fertility decisions to deforestation and difficult access to water, which require women and children to spend more time collecting fuelwood and water.[170]

Unmet need is often high—more than 30 percent of people in some countries, including Haiti, Liberia, Mali and Uganda, would like to use family planning but do not.[171] Multidimensional poverty is correlated with unmet need for contraception. The incidence of people living in households with unmet family planning needs is always higher among

FIGURE 3.6

Gender equality and contraceptive prevalence are closely linked

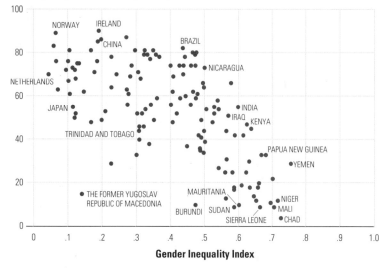

Contraceptive prevalence rate (percent)

Note: Contraceptive prevalence rates are for the most recent year available from the World Health Organization for each country during 2000–2008; see statistical table 4 for details. The Gender Inequality Index is for 2011.

Source: HDRO calculations based on data from the World Health Organization.

the multidimensionally poor (figure 3.7). In Bolivia 27 percent of the multidimensionally poor have unmet need for family planning, more than twice the share among the nonpoor (12 percent), and in Ethiopia unmet need among the multidimensionally poor (29 percent) is almost three times the share among the nonpoor (11 percent).

Fertility is also affected by women's education. A recent study covering more than 90 percent of the world's people found that women who have never gone to school average 4.5 children, those with even a few years of primary school average just 3, and those with one or two years of secondary school average 1.9. And when women enter the workforce, start businesses or inherit assets, their desire for a large family also tends to diminish.[172]

The principles and routes—removing barriers to the use of family planning and rights-based population policies—are not new. They were directly envisioned by conferees in Cairo in 1994 and committed to by nearly all governments. Chapter 4 argues that progress has been too slow and highlights some promising avenues to consider.

Women's participation in decision-making

Gender inequalities are also reflected in women's low participation in national and local political fora. This has ramifications for sustainability if, as some research suggests, women express more concern for the environment, support more proenvironmental policy and vote for proenvironmental leaders.

- Countries with higher female parliamentary representation are more likely to set aside protected land areas, as a study of 25 developed and 65 developing countries reveals.[173]
- Countries with higher female parliamentary representation are more likely to ratify international environmental treaties, according to a study of 130 countries with about 92 percent of the world's people.[174]
- Of the 49 countries that reduced carbon dioxide emissions between 1990 and 2007, 14 were very high HDI countries, 10 of which had higher than average female parliamentary representation.

FIGURE 3.7

Unmet contraceptive need is higher among the multidimensionally poor

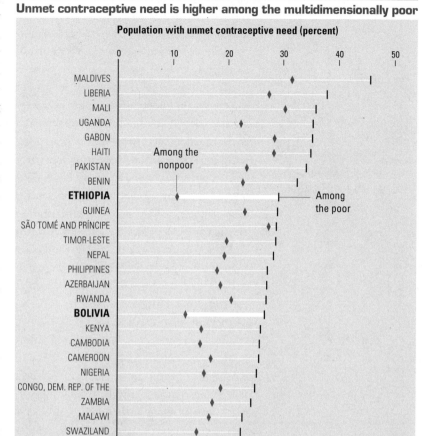

Note: Data are for most recent year available during 2000–2010 and are based on the Demographic and Health Survey second definition of unmet need (DHS 2008).

Source: Calculated based on data on MPI from statistical table 5 and from Demographic and Health Surveys.

But women continue to be underrepresented in national parliaments, on average occupying only 19 percent of seats and accounting for just 18 percent of ministers.[175] Higher positions are even more elusive: only 7 of 150 elected heads of state and only 11 of 192 heads of government are women. The situation is similar in local government.[176]

Other evidence suggests that gender empowerment and environmental awareness may be related. The number of women's and environmental NGOs per capita was negatively correlated with deforestation in a study of 61 countries between 1990 and 2005. That may be partly because of women's incentives to avert the negative effects of deforestation on their workload, income and health.[177] In developed countries survey data show that women are more likely than men to engage in environmentally sensitive behaviours, such as recycling, conserving water and avoiding environmentally harmful products.[178]

But the relationship, far from straightforward, varies with development. As we saw in box 2.5 in chapter 2, analysis of Gallup World Poll data on environmental attitudes suggests that concerns about environmental problems are not very high. On average, the attitudes of men and women differ little,[179] but some variation appears across HDI groups (table 3.3). In very high HDI countries women express more concern for environmental issues (climate change, water and air quality) than do men, while men express more concern in low HDI countries. The medium and high HDI countries (and most developing regions) fall in between.

While overall levels of education influence attitudes, the ratio of the share of women to men in secondary and tertiary education does not. The implication: women's greater concern for the environment in rich countries is not a function of their having more education, nor is the converse true in very poor countries.

Some evidence suggests that women's involvement is associated with better local environmental management. Yet women's mere presence in institutions is not enough to overcome entrenched disparities—additional changes and flexibility in institutional forms are needed to ensure that women can participate effectively in decision-making. In some cases including women and other marginal groups is perceived as a way of maintaining the status quo rather than achieving any specific outcomes or questioning inequalities.[180]

What matters, then, is not simply women's presence but the nature of their participation. Consider forestry management (box 3.4). A recently published study of community forestry institutions in India and Nepal found that women's proportional strength in forest management committees affects the effectiveness of their participation.[181] The more women on the management committee, the greater is the likelihood that they will attend committee meetings, speak up and become office holders.

The arguments here are not new. But they point to an important part of a reform package to address inequality and environmental degradation—with major expansions of women's freedoms.

Power inequalities

As a critical dimension of people's freedoms, empowerment is an important end in itself. But disempowerment and power imbalances add to environmental challenges. We build on the 2010 *HDR,* where we addressed several components of empowerment: agency, political freedoms, civil liberties and accountability. Box 2.1 in chapter 2 already highlighted some recent changes. Here we focus on the political arena—on national and local governments, accountability and democracy, and civil society.

> Disempowerment and power imbalances add to environmental challenges

TABLE 3.3

Attitudes towards the environment, by gender, low and very high HDI countries, 2010 (percent, unless otherwise noted)

Attitude	Low HDI countries			Very high HDI countries		
	Male	Female	Difference (percentage points)	Male	Female	Difference (percentage points)
Climate change is a serious threat	47.76	46.05	1.71	27.18	31.46	4.29
Dissatisfied with:						
Air quality	22.81	21.27	1.55	17.95	21.36	3.41
Water quality	50.48	47.32	3.16	13.56	16.28	2.72
Government environmental policy	54.82	52.12	2.70	46.36	48.38	2.02
Government emissions policy	61.46	49.16	12.30	53.13	60.83	7.70

Source: HDRO calculations based on data from Gallup World Poll (http://worldview.gallup.com).

History, power relations and context all affect the links between democracy and environmental public goods. State activity can usefully be seen as a continuum from "oligarchic, extractive, exploitive and divisive" to "inclusive, innovative, accountable, responsive and effective at mediating distributional conflict."[182] Where state activity falls along the continuum is determined by the underlying social contract—historically shaped interactions between political and economic elites and other social groups—as manifest in formal and informal institutions. As economic processes, both state action and capitalism are often weak in sustaining the environment —capitalism, intrinsically so, given the short time horizon of most firms and the importance of externalities. The state, despite its role in providing public goods and managing externalities, can often be limited by short political and electoral time horizons. These factors can interact with political and social structures to have harmful effects on the environment, especially where the adverse impacts affect mainly disempowered groups.

Studies have shown that democracies are typically more accountable to voters and more likely to allow civil liberties, enabling people to be more informed on environmental problems (thanks to a free press), to organize and to express concerns. At the national level the extent of democracy has been associated with environmental quality.[183] But even in democratic systems, the people and groups most adversely affected are those who are less well-off and less empowered. Policy priorities may not reflect their interests and needs. In many countries and contexts power inequalities affect environmental outcomes, mediated through political and social institutions.

State-level evidence across the United States suggests that greater inequality in power (measured by lower voter participation and educational attainment and weaker fiscal policies) leads to weaker environmental policies and more environmental degradation.[184] Cross-country evidence supports this view. In 180 countries variables such as literacy, political rights and civil liberties improve environmental quality in high- and low-income

Women's participation in community forest management

Participation of women in community decision-making is important for resource conservation and regeneration, particularly for community forest management. However, preexisting and structural gender inequalities (in income, assets and political endowments) often weaken women's ability to participate. Even in communities where women are not formally excluded from decision-making bodies, their ability to participate in policy-making may be limited by social inequalities. Requiring female representation on committees and ensuring that women are consulted are necessary but insufficient conditions—ultimately the issue is one of challenging and changing power relations.

In villages where women are not actively involved in decision-making, they are more adversely affected by forest management decisions such as forest closures than in communities where they are more involved.

Prior equality is not necessary for women to assert themselves in committee meetings. In fact, women from disadvantaged households are more outspoken in public forums than women from better-off households, a finding attributable to their opportunity to gain more if decisions go in their favour. This outcome was found to be more likely where a large number of women were present or where women had already been exposed to women's empowerment programmes. Other studies affirm that allowing women to participate, even in a limited role, changes cultural perceptions as to women's capacity to make decisions, in turn prompting the formation of other initiatives and cooperatives for women, allowing them to become more active outside the home.

Source: Agarwal 2001, 2009; see also Tole (2010), Gupte (2004) and Timsina (2003).

countries[185] and positively influence clean water and improved sanitation.[186]

New cross-national analyses of more than 100 countries commissioned for this Report confirmed the strong correlation between proxies for the distribution of power and environmental quality.[187] Empowerment is linked with access to improved water, less land degradation and fewer deaths due to indoor and outdoor air pollution and dirty water. And empowerment variables are even more important than income in explaining many key dimensions of environmental quality, including access to improved water, deaths due to pollution and mortality in children under age 5. The implication is that while powerful economic interests can distort policies, societies can do much to limit that power.

Investigations of environmental data over time for a large number of countries have found this relation to hold. Most studies focus on pollution, a public bad from which the state is expected to protect its population.[188] The general finding is that literacy and political rights are associated with less air and water pollution. A recent contribution highlights the importance of long-term democracy in lowering sulphur and carbon dioxide emissions.[189] This makes sense: it takes time for democracy to yield tangible instrumental gains. Other work in more than 100 countries links a higher level of democracy to less deforestation, less land degradation and less air and water pollution.[190]

Various studies suggest that democracy increases the likelihood of state commitment to goals to address climate change, transboundary air pollution and river management, if not policy implementation. But while democracies tend to be more committed to positive outcomes for climate change, the relationship is not very strong—given that the benefits are perceived to be external and beyond the time horizon of current voters (and politicians).[191] This widens the gaps between words and deeds.

Even within democracies, political institutions vary widely. Some are centralized, and others decentralized. Likewise, political representation is affected by the role of political parties, the existence of quotas for particular groups, the duration of electoral cycles and other factors. Some countries have a strong independent agency charged with protecting the environment; others may have only a weak line ministry. The strength of labour unions contributes to lower environmental air quality; the strength of green parties has the opposite effect.[192]

Civil society groups can organize and exert real impact on the decisions of policy-makers, offsetting the often disproportionate influence of powerful economic interests and lobbies. The possibility of developing this "countervailing power"[193] depends on whether institutions in a society allow for open and free participation. As Sweden's environmental policies show, strong democratic participation can translate into policies that reflect popular concern. But such concerns may be countervailed by other vested interests—as reported for the Russian Federation in the problems civil society faces in mobilizing public support around greening

industry.[194] Where civil society is active, it has been shown to bring about significant change:

- A recent study modelling environmental NGO impact in a framework of interest group participation and influence in 104 countries found that the number of environmental advocacy groups in a country had a statistically significant negative relation with the lead content in gasoline.[195]
- A study using cross-country panel data for 1977–1988 found a statistically significant negative relation between the number of environmental NGOs and air pollution levels and weaker relations between democracy and pollution and between literacy rates and pollution.[196]

Civil society, in turn, can thrive only with popular support. Where civil society groups are active, power imbalances can be overcome. In the 1990s activists in poor, racial minority neighbourhoods in Chicago, United States, succeeded in getting the national Environmental Protection Agency to act against illegal waste dumping in their communities. Community policing programmes were established, and city regulations and enforcement of illegal dumping were also strengthened, including new harsher penalties.[197] Civil society groups in a range of contexts have successfully opposed activities likely to be a detriment to the environment and the livelihoods of people who directly rely on it.

*　　　*　　　*

We have outlined the ways environmental deprivations and environmental degradation can constrain choices—showing how they seriously jeopardize health, education, livelihoods and other aspects of well-being and at times worsen prevailing inequalities. We have also suggested that greater equality between men and women and within populations may have transformative potential in advancing sustainability. We go on to explore this possibility and promising approaches and policies.

Greater equality between men and women and within populations may have transformative potential in advancing environmental sustainability

CHAPTER 4

Positive synergies—winning strategies for the environment, equity and human development

In facing the challenges laid out in chapters 2 and 3, a host of governments, civil society, private sector and development actors have sought to integrate environmental and equity concerns and promote human development —win-win-win strategies. An example at the global level is the 1987 Montreal Protocol, which bans ozone-depleting chemicals, thereby benefiting sustainability (through protection of the ozone layer), equity (through technology transfer to developing countries) and human development (through positive impacts on health).[1]

This chapter showcases local and national strategies to address environmental deprivations and build resilience, thereby demonstrating positive synergies. An important backdrop to this discussion is the need for healthy ecosystems and the services they provide, especially for the poor. Ecosystems build the foundation for water quality, food security, flood protection and natural climate regulation.[2]

Scaling up successful community and local initiatives is a prime focus. Key elements at the national level are policies that bring together social, economic and environmental concerns; coordination mechanisms aligned with budget frameworks; a culture of innovation; and strong institutions, alongside mechanisms that ensure accountability. Some countries have overcome siloed arrangements through medium-term plans that allow cross-sectoral coordination across government agencies and with development partners. Senior core ministries—such as finance and planning— are often critical, as are line agencies, especially working with other ministries. In Malawi the Ministry of Agriculture helped create demand for measures to reduce poverty and protect the environment, and in Rwanda the Ministry of State, Lands and the Environment garnered presidential and cabinet support for

integrating environmental concerns into the country's Economic Development and Poverty Strategy. And crucial at the local level are strong institutions, particularly those that pay attention to disadvantaged groups and promote community management.

The policy agenda is vast. This Report cannot do it full justice or cover all the challenges raised in the preceding chapters. Several recent global reports provide important details.[3] The value added here is in identifying win-win-win strategies that successfully address the world's social, economic and environmental challenges by managing, or even bypassing, trade-offs so that the approaches are good not only for the environment but also for equity and human development more broadly. This effort provides concrete experience and important motivation for the forward-looking final chapter.

Scaling up to address environmental deprivations and build resilience

We begin by highlighting promising win-win-win routes in energy and in water and sanitation.

Energy

Energy is central to a range of services supporting human development, from modern medical care, transportation, information and communications to lighting, heating, cooking and mechanical power for agriculture. Equitable and sustainable development requires making energy available for all, controlling emissions and shifting to new and cleaner energy sources.

Addressing energy deprivations

Some 1.5 billion people, more than one in five, lack access to electricity, and 2.6 billion cook

FIGURE 4.1

Large regional differences in the share of multidimensionally poor people lacking electricity

Percent

0.4	Europe and Central Asia
3.3	East Asia and the Pacific
11.1	Latin America and the Caribbean
27.7	South Asia
62.3	Sub-Saharan Africa

Note: Excludes very high HDI countries.
Source: HDRO staff calculations based on data from the Oxford Poverty and Human Development Initiative.

with wood, straw, charcoal or dung.[4] Major energy inequalities persist across regions, countries, gender and classes. Acknowledging that energy distribution cannot be considered apart from political and social exclusion,[5] the 65th United Nations General Assembly proclaimed 2012 as the International Year of Sustainable Energy for All.[6]

One multidimensionally poor person in three (32 percent) lacks electricity, and there is a strong regional pattern to this deprivation (figure 4.1). More than 60 percent of the multidimensionally poor in Sub-Saharan Africa lack electricity, compared with less than 1 percent in Europe and Central Asia. Progress in electrification has been slow in Africa. Electricity generation capacity per person in Sub-Saharan Africa today is similar to levels in the 1980s but just a tenth that in South and East Asia. And rural electrification has stagnated at below 10 percent—while growing to 50 percent for developing countries as a whole.[7]

Electrification can reduce poverty by increasing productivity, employment and time spent in school and reducing environmental pressures. For instance, in South Africa electrification is associated with a 13 percent greater likelihood of women participating in the labour market,[8] while in Viet Nam it increased income, consumption and schooling outcomes.[9] Bhutanese villagers attest enthusiastically to the difference electricity makes in their lives, citing the ability to work in the evenings and cook without wood, which reduced respiratory problems and time spent fetching fuel.[10]

Expanding energy access and mitigating climate change can be presented as trade-offs. For instance, the World Bank's recent $3.75 billion loan to South Africa to build one of the world's largest coal-fired plants will expand access, but the project raised concerns about greenhouse gas emissions and environmental degradation as well as carbon lock-in when the longevity of infrastructure prolongs the use of obsolete technologies.[11]

But the prospect of win-win-win options enables us to go beyond trade-offs. Recent *World Energy Outlook* estimates indicate that providing everyone with basic modern energy services would increase carbon dioxide emissions only 0.8 percent by 2030.[12] Off-grid and decentralized options are important and technically feasible. While difficult to quantify, the number of rural households already served by renewable energy is estimated in the tens of millions, through such schemes as micro-hydropower in villages and county-scale mini-grids, an important source of energy in Brazil, China and India.[13]

There have been some successes in extending energy access to the poor, including through decentralized energy systems. The challenge is to make such innovations happen at a scale and speed that will improve the lives of poor women and men now and in the future.[14] Governments can do more to support entrepreneurship and capital acquisition for alternative energy startups.[15] As Latvia and other countries have shown, the right legal framework can boost growth in the nonrenewable energy sector and limit emissions from traditional energy sources.

Increasing efficiency is important too. And innovations are proceeding, from improved stoves—which have reduced fuelwood requirements some 40 percent in parts of Kenya and dramatically cut pollution levels and improved child health in Guatemala[16]—to more energy-efficient buildings—which can reduce heating and cooling loads.[17]

Making energy cleaner

Any long-run strategy for broadening energy access must include actions to promote cleaner energy.[18] There are encouraging signs. By 2010 more than 100 countries—up from 55 in 2005 —had enacted some policy target or promotion policy for renewable energy, including all 27 EU members. Many countries specify a target share of renewables in electricity production, typically 5–30 percent, but within a range of 2 percent to 90 percent.

In several countries renewables constitute a rapidly growing share of total energy supply. The share is 44 percent of energy in Sweden, one of the better performers identified in chapter 2. As of 2008 Brazil produced almost 85 percent of its electricity from renewables, and Austria 62 percent. And hydropower accounts for close to 70 percent of electricity generated in Sub-Saharan Africa (excluding South Africa).[19]

According to the Renewable Energy Policy Network for the 21st Century, global energy supply reached a tipping point in 2010, as renewables accounted for a quarter of global power capacity and delivered almost a fifth of electricity supply[20] (see statistical table 6). Virtually every renewable technology has seen consistently strong growth. Some highlights:

- *Wind*. Despite the 2008 global economic crisis, new wind power installations reached a record 38 gigawatts in 2009, a 41 percent increase over 2008 and equivalent to nearly a quarter of total global installations.
- *Solar*. Grid-connected solar photovoltaic systems have grown at an annual average of 60 percent over the past decade, increasing 100-fold since 2000, with major expansions in the Czech Republic, Germany and Spain. Unit prices have declined sharply—some dropping 50–60 percent, to less than $2 a watt. Generous feed-in tariffs are one reason. An estimated 3 million households in rural areas get power from small solar photovoltaic systems, and an estimated 70 million households worldwide have solar hot water heating.

Since 2004 global renewable energy capacity for many technologies has grown 4–60 percent a year, spurred by new technology, high and volatile oil prices, climate change concerns, and local, national and global policy developments.[21]

Developing countries are adopting renewable energy and now have more than half of global renewable power capacity. China leads the world in several indicators of market growth, including wind power capacity and biomass power, while India stands fifth in wind and is fast expanding such rural renewables as biogas and solar. Brazil produces much of the world's sugar-derived ethanol and is adding new biomass and wind power plants.

The continuing roll-out of renewable energy sources will require large private investments, but corruption and lack of regulation can slow the momentum. A recent Transparency International study, for example, reported that almost 70 percent of potential energy investors in North Africa consider regulatory risk, including corruption, a serious impediment to investment.[22] Technical limitations must also be overcome. For example, intermittency raises capital costs for wind and solar power and requires supplementation by other sources. Improved storage technologies are also needed.

Currently, more than 90 percent of clean energy investments are in the G-20 countries.[23] To expand equity and sustainability in clean energy globally, concerted efforts are needed to improve conditions in other countries that would enable future investments.[24] In the next chapter we call for addressing perverse incentives and market distortions, reducing risks and increasing rewards, and increasing accountability in global environmental governance. Beyond facilitating greater access and lowering emissions, clean energy can create new industries and jobs. Installing 1 megawatt of wind turbine capacity creates an estimated 0.7–2.8 times the permanent employment of a comparable natural gas combined-cycle power plant; installing 1 megawatt of solar capacity creates up to 11 times more.[25] An estimated 3 million people worldwide already work in renewable energy industries, about half of them in biofuels.[26]

Reining in global emissions

Policies to cut emissions nationally entail both potential advantages and concerns about equity and capacity.

Table 4.1 lists illustrative policy instruments to cut carbon dioxide emissions and their key equity effects. Typically, instruments must be combined to deal with the broad range of market failures.

Pricing can powerfully affect behaviour. An obvious candidate is the reduction of fossil fuel subsidies, which are expensive (amounting to about $312 billion in 2009 in 37 developing countries)[27] and encourage consumption. The Organisation for Economic Co-operation and Development estimates that phasing out the subsidies could free fiscal resources and reduce global greenhouse gas emissions 10 percent by

> Developing countries are adopting renewable energy and now have more than half of global renewable power capacity

2050—more than 20 percent in oil-exporting countries.[28] Similarly, subsidized electricity prices for agriculture often encourage greater groundwater extraction, risking over-exploitation.[29] These types of perverse subsidies favour medium and large producers over smaller farmers because smaller farmers rarely pump water and instead use wheels, surface water or rainfall.[30]

TABLE 4.1

Key equity aspects of a menu of instruments to reduce carbon dioxide emissions

Policy instrument	Examples	Key equity aspects	Other considerations
Cap-and-trade permits	• EU trading scheme	• If permits are given away, this favours incumbent firms and does not raise revenue	• Potentially high monitoring and enforcement costs • Carbon permit prices can be volatile.
Emissions targets	• Voluntary targets of European Union, Indonesia and the Russian Federation to reduce emissions	• Depends on pattern of consumption and production	• If electricity is generated with fossil fuels, targets will cause prices to rise • Poor people spend a larger proportion of their income on energy
Taxes or charges	• Fuel and coal taxes • Motor vehicle taxes	• Depends on pattern of consumption and production	• Fiscal revenue potentially as high as 1–3 percent of GDP in Organisation for Economic Co-operation and Development countries by 2020[a]
Subsidies for renewables	• Hybrid cars • Subsidies for electric vehicles	• Depends on purchase patterns, but unlikely to be progressive; could be targeted (means tested)	• Potentially expensive; more than $7,000 per vehicle in Belgium, Canada, China, the Netherlands, the United Kingdom and the United States
Subsidy cuts	• Fossil fuels • Electricity for irrigation	• Eliminating subsidies would create substantial fiscal and environmental benefits	• Fossil fuel subsidies cost around $558 billion in 2008 and $312 billion in 2009 • Complete phase-out by 2020 could reduce emissions 20 percent in non-European countries, the Russian Federation and the Arab States
Performance standards	• Limits on car emissions • Energy efficiency standards	• May raise costs and limit access of the poor	• Does not allow firms to reduce emissions at the lowest possible cost
Technology standards	• Building and zoning codes	• Care needed to avoid cost increases that are prohibitive for the poor	• Importance of appropriate technology
Better information	• Public awareness campaign • Emission and energy use disclosure requirements	• Ensure outreach and accessibility to disadvantaged groups	• Group identity of users matters

a. At $50 per tonne of carbon dioxide equivalent greenhouse gas emissions.

Source: Based on OECD (2010c).

But the optimal policy here, as elsewhere, depends on context. Careful investigation and targeted compensation are needed where the affected goods and services account for a large share of family spending. Redistribution can be implemented through social transfers or, if the tax base is broad enough, through tax cuts for the poor. To compensate for lower oil subsidies, Indonesia implemented a cash transfer scheme in late 2005 targeting 15.5 million poor and near-poor households (some 28 percent of the population). To offset higher energy prices, Mexico supplemented its conditional cash transfer programme in 2007. And Iran replaced oil-based subsidies on fuel, food and other essentials with a transitional monthly $40 cash grant to 90 percent of the population in 2010, leading to a drop of 4.5 percent in gas consumption and 28 percent in diesel consumption.[31]

Several large developing countries have committed to deep carbon cuts. For example, in 2009 China set a goal of lowering carbon intensity 40–45 percent from 2005 levels over the next decade, later announced further short-term targets and is supporting renewable energy through subsidies, targets and tax incentives.[32] In 2010 India announced voluntary targeted reductions of 20–25 percent in carbon intensity.

These new commitments are important steps in the transition to a lower carbon economy. As we saw in table 2.1 in chapter 2, falling carbon intensity of production globally lowered total emissions growth between 1970 and 2007 well below what it would have been otherwise.

But the announcements must be put in perspective. Reduced carbon intensity can run alongside rising greenhouse gas emissions if economic growth continues apace. Despite increased energy efficiency, US emissions have continued to grow—more than 7 percent from 1990 to 2009.[33] China was already reducing carbon intensity at 1.4 percent a year over 1970–2007, but rapid economic growth meant that total emissions still grew 5.9 percent a year. The new target would more than double the rate of carbon intensity reduction to 3.8 percent a year, but again that does not mean that China's total emissions will decline. In fact, if China's economic growth through

2020 exceeds 3.9 percent (as predicted), its total emissions would continue to rise; if the economy continues to grow at the 9.2 percent annual rate of the past decade, total emissions would increase 2.8 percent a year.

Other countries have committed to reducing absolute emissions. Indonesia has announced a target of reducing carbon dioxide emissions 26 percent.[34] Similarly, the European Union, as part of its 20/20/20 plan to be met by 2020, committed to cutting greenhouse gas emissions 20 percent from 1990 levels, increasing renewable energy use 20 percent and reducing energy consumption 20 percent through improved energy efficiency.[35]

*　　　*　　　*

In sum, expanding access to modern energy for all and developing renewable energy sources are gaining traction, but involving the state, donors and international organizations is critical for investing in research and development and reducing disparities within and across countries. Moreover, strong efforts are needed to include the poor: if current trends continue, more people will lack access to modern energy in 2030 than today.[36]

Water access, water security and sanitation

Chapter 3 told of the devastating impacts of lack of access to potable water. Addressing this inequity calls for managing water resources differently to serve a growing world population. Water security, defined as a country's ability to secure enough clean water to meet needs for household uses, irrigation, hydropower and other ends, has win-win-win possibilities. In poorer countries the greatest needs are for household and agricultural uses. While the two uses are closely linked, particularly for rural communities, the policy implications differ.

Household water

A first step in increasing access to potable water is recognizing equal rights to water, regardless of ability to pay. Right-to-water legislation exists in 15 countries in Latin America, 13 in Sub-Saharan Africa, 4 in South Asia, 2 in East Asia and the Pacific and 2 in the Arab States.[37] In July 2010 the UN General Assembly recognized the right to water and sanitation and acknowledged that clean drinking water and improved sanitation are integral to the realization of all human rights. In all countries, improving access to these facilities can be a key driver in poverty reduction.

And there is cause for optimism. Innovative approaches are under way in many countries.[38] Some highlights:

- *Providing affordable access.* Small-scale, needs-driven technologies can provide households with low-cost potable water. In Cameroon cheap biosand filters, developed in South Africa, are used to make water safe to drink.[39] In India the international nongovernmental organization (NGO) Water for People partnered with a local university to develop simple, locally manufactured filters that remove arsenic from the water at public wellheads in West Bengal.[40] Governments have the obligation to connect their populations to modern waterworks through public, private or civil society service provision, but encouraging these types of local innovations can relieve water deprivation even before larger water infrastructure projects can be implemented.
- *Supporting local communities.* Small grants can support local community efforts to manage water resources. The United Nations Development Programme's Community Water Initiative and other small grant programmes have worked with governments in Guatemala, Kenya, Mauritania and Tanzania to support community water projects.[41]

Agricultural water

Agricultural water problems range from lack of access to overexploitation. But again there is cause for optimism—in efficiency gains and real-cost pricing that moves away from often regressive subsidies. Even in a water-abundant country such as the United States farmers use 15 percent less water now than 30 years ago to grow 70 percent more food; the country has doubled its water productivity since 1980.[42]

Expanding access to modern energy for all and developing renewable energy sources are gaining traction, but involving the state, donors and international organizations is critical for reducing disparities

Recognizing the problems of overexploitation of water and the need to ensure equitable access has led to promising new schemes. Several countries in the Arab States have water user associations that now operate and manage irrigation systems, establishing service levels and charges. In Yemen water-saving technologies and regulatory systems are designed in consultation with users to ensure that the technologies meet farmers' needs and that regulatory systems are equitable. And in Egypt pilot programmes have reduced public subsidies; increased the efficiency of water use, operations and maintenance; and reduced pollution.[43]

Analysis of the distributional impacts of water investments is important. For example, irrigation investments can buffer weather shocks to smooth consumption over time, but the effects can be uneven. Recent analysis of large irrigation dams in India found that people living downstream were likely to benefit, while those living upstream were likely to lose.[44]

Healthy, intact ecosystems, such as forest headwaters, are vital for sustaining the flow and quality of water for human use. An estimated one-third of the world's largest cities depend on intact protected forest areas for their water supply.[45] In Venezuela water from 18 national parks meets the fresh water needs of 19 million people, or 83 percent of the urban population, and about 20 percent of irrigated lands depend on protected areas for water.[46] This is also critical for rural areas. Indonesia's Lore Lindu National Park provides water for irrigation and fish to support rural livelihoods.

Sanitation

Almost half the people in developing countries lack access to basic sanitation services.[47] Expanding access can improve health directly and productivity indirectly and, as discussed in chapter 3, contributes to human dignity, self-respect and physical safety, particularly for women. Our own analysis confirms that better access to safe water and sanitation are also positively associated with women's health outcomes relative to men—in other words, women benefit disproportionately

from access to safe water and sanitation, all else equal.

Several innovative approaches have provided small-scale access to sanitation:
- Manaus, Brazil, recently used a $5 million grant to connect 15,000 mainly poor households to a modern sewage system, by subsidizing services to poor households that otherwise could not afford the service. To encourage take-up, the project worked to raise awareness of the benefits, since the failure of even a small number of households to adopt modern sewage systems can result in contamination of water sources.[48]
- SaniMarts (Sanitation Markets) in eastern Nepal help households buy materials to construct or upgrade latrines. Piloted in Southern India, SaniMarts are local shops staffed by trained sanitation promoters who sell latrine construction materials at affordable prices.[49]
- The Sanitation Marketing Pilot Project in Cambodia sought to enhance the adoption of latrines in the provinces of Kandal and Svay Rieng by demonstrating that selling them could be a profitable business enterprise. The "easy latrine" was sold as a complete package that households could easily install themselves. The commercial viability of the product led private businesses to invest their own resources to address demand.[50]

Despite some regional successes, most such programmes have not been scaled up, largely because they lack strong local leadership or interest, because skills are weak and because monitoring and evaluation are insufficient.[51] One exception is an initiative known as the Global Scaling up Rural Sanitation Project, supported by the World Bank in rural India, Indonesia and Tanzania, which has reached an estimated 8.2 million people over four years. Its success is traceable, at least in part, to better performance monitoring, which shifts the focus to outcomes.[52]

While most approaches focus on supply, Community-led Total Sanitation targets demand (box 4.1). Along with increasing the use of toilets, other behavioural interventions,

> Better access to safe water and sanitation can improve health directly and productivity indirectly and contributes to human dignity, self-respect and physical safety, particularly for women

such as promoting hand washing,[53] are reducing faecal bacterial contamination in Africa and Asia.

* * *

In sum, greater public policy efforts are needed to increase investments in water and sanitation to improve access. Current patterns of natural resource exploitation are creating huge environmental hardships for the poor, who are often excluded from even minimal levels of service. Access can be increased by building on the successes of a range of countries, many at the local and community levels, and by involving national governments and development partners.

Averting degradation

We turn now to three keys to reducing degradation pressures: expanding reproductive choice, supporting community management of natural resources and conserving biodiversity while promoting equity.

Expanding reproductive choice

Reproductive rights, including access to reproductive health services, are a precondition for women's health and empowerment and essential to the enjoyment of other fundamental rights. They form a foundation for satisfying relationships, harmonious family life and opportunities for a better future. Moreover, they are important for achieving international development goals, including the Millennium Development Goals. Important in themselves, fully realized reproductive rights can also have positive spillover effects on the environment if they slow population growth and reduce environmental pressures.

Recent projections put the world's population at 9.3 billion by 2050 and 10 billion by 2100, assuming that fertility in all countries converges to replacement levels.[54] However, calculations also suggest that simply addressing unmet family planning need in 100 countries could shift global fertility below replacement levels, putting the world on a path to an earlier peak in population and then a gradual decline.[55] This can be done through initiatives

BOX 4.1
From subsidy to self-respect—the revolution of Community-led Total Sanitation

Chapter 3 reviewed how faecal-related infections, now rare in richer countries, are stubbornly endemic in others. Some 2.6 billion people lack sanitary toilets, and 1.1 billion people defecate in the open.

That the Millennium Development Goal for sanitation is the farthest off track results partly from a failed reliance on hardware subsidies. The top-down approach, with subsidized standard designs and materials, has provided inadequate toilets that cost too much, delivered them to people who are not the most poor, achieved only partial coverage and use, and engendered dependence.

Community-led Total Sanitation (CLTS) turns all this on its head. There is no hardware subsidy, no standard design, no targeting the poor from outside. Collective action is key. Pioneered by Kamal Kar and the Village Education Resource Centre in partnership with WaterAid in Bangladesh in 2000, CLTS teaches communities to map and inspect their defecation areas, calculate how much they deposit and identify pathways between excreta and mouth. It helps communities "face the shit" (the crude local word is always used). Disgust, dignity and self-respect trigger self-help through digging pits and adopting hygienic behaviours. With follow-up encouragement, community members also address equity. Children and schools are often involved.

Sustainability is enhanced by social pressures to end open defecation. There are challenges, and few communities have done away with it completely. Sandy pit walls can collapse —and floods devastate—but households and communities have bounced back and moved themselves up the sanitation ladder, installing better, more durable toilets.

Where governments and communities have endorsed CLTS and enabled quality training and well led campaigns, outcomes have been remarkable. In Himachal Pradesh, India, the number of people in rural areas who had toilets rose from 2.4 million in 2006 to 5.6 million in 2010 out of a total population of 6 million. CLTS has spread to more than 40 countries: more than 10 million people in Africa and Asia already live in open defecation–free communities, and many more have benefited from toilets. In some countries CLTS is making the sanitation Millennium Development Goal look not just achievable but surpassable.

In a 2007 *British Medical Journal* poll sanitation was voted the most important medical advance of the past 150 years. And CLTS won the journal's competition in 2011 for the idea most likely to have the greatest impact on healthcare by 2020. The quality of training, facilitation and follow-up are all critical as CLTS is scaled up. CLTS expansion could reduce the suffering and enhance the health, dignity and well-being of hundreds of millions of deprived people.

Source: Chambers 2009; Mehta and Movik 2011.

that empower women and increase their access to contraceptives and other reproductive health services.

It follows that greater worldwide availability and adoption of reproductive health and family planning services raise the prospect of a win-win-win for sustainability, equity and human development. Of course the environmental gains depend on carbon footprints at the individual level. For instance, an average citizen in Australia or the United States accounts for as much carbon dioxide emissions in two days as an average citizen of Malawi or Rwanda in a year. Reproductive health and family planning are critical in Malawi and

Rwanda—where women still have an average of five children—but will not significantly reduce carbon dioxide emissions. By contrast, innovative programmes such as Family PACT in California, which reimburses physicians for providing reproductive healthcare to low-income women and prevents almost 100,000 unintended births each year, not only improve the lives and health of women and their families but also reduce the future carbon footprint by some 156 million tonnes a year.[56]

Reproductive rights include choosing the number, timing and spacing of one's children and having the information and means to do so. A rights-based approach means addressing demand—by informing, educating and empowering—and ensuring access to the supply of reproductive health services. Many reproductive choice initiatives are under way worldwide—though most focus more on the supply side.[57]

The incremental infrastructure requirements of reproductive services are typically modest because service delivery can often piggyback on other health programmes. Several initiatives exploit synergies among population, health and environment programmes at the community level. These include a United States Agency for International Development pilot programme in Nepal covering some 14,000 community forest user groups[58] and the PATH Foundation's Integrated Population and Coastal Resource Management Initiative in the Philippines, which show how to bring reproductive health services into existing community-run programmes. Cambodia and Uganda have similar initiatives.[59] ProPeten, an organization devoted to preventing deforestation in Guatemala, augmented its deforestation prevention initiatives with an integrated approach to population, health and environment that was associated with a decline in average fertility in the region from 6.8 births per woman to 4.3 over a decade.[60]

Better management and more effective targeting of resources often bring large gains, even in resource-poor areas. A local sustained leadership development programme for health workers in Aswan, Egypt, led to more frequent prenatal and childcare visits by health workers, with large benefits in reduced maternal mortality.[61]

A number of governments have reformed policy frameworks and programmes to improve reproductive health. In Bangladesh the fertility rate fell from 6.6 births per woman in 1975 to 2.4 in 2009, a huge drop attributed to the introduction of a major policy initiative in 1976 that emphasized population and family planning as integral to national development. Measures included community outreach and subsidies to make contraceptives more easily available, efforts to influence social norms through discussions with the community (religious leaders, teachers, NGOs), education of both men and women and development of reproductive health research and training activities.[62]

In many cases partnerships across different groups and with a range of service providers have brought gains. In three rural districts and two urban slums in Kenya, poor families were given vouchers to pay for reproductive health and gender-based violence recovery services.[63] In Viet Nam a long-term collaboration of the government, provincial health institutions and several NGOs has led to dramatic improvements in the quality of reproductive health services, provision of new services and establishment of a sustainable clinical training network in reproductive health.[64]

Similarly, in Iran efforts to introduce reproductive health services began in the late 1980s, when rapid population growth was recognized as an obstacle to development. Today, nearly 80 percent of married women use contraception[65]—the country also has a maternal mortality ratio that is less than 8 percent of that in South Africa, which has a similar per capita income. In 2009 Mongolia endorsed a national strategy for reproductive health, included the services in the mid-term budget framework and committed to fully funding contraceptive supply by 2015. Lao PDR's Ministry of Health implemented a community-based distribution model for providing family planning services in three poor southern provinces. The programme sharply increased contraceptive prevalence, in some

Greater worldwide availability and adoption of reproductive health and family planning services raise the prospect of a win-win-win for sustainability, equity and human development regions from less than 1 percent in 2006 to over 60 percent in 2009.[66]

Several initiatives show encouraging evidence of the effect of raising awareness of reproductive healthcare. ProPeten sponsored a radio soap opera to disseminate information on the environment, gender issues and reproductive health.[67] Using the extensive mobile phone networks now common in developing countries—more than 76 percent of the world's population[68] and more than 1 billion women in low- and middle-income countries currently have access[69]—multiple initiatives, including the Mobile Alliance for Maternal Action, provide customized health information to expectant and new mothers in Bangladesh, India and South Africa.[70] These approaches have enormous potential, though their widespread effectiveness has yet to be demonstrated.

Concerted government efforts are needed to achieve universal access to reproductive healthcare, which yields rich dividends in lower fertility rates and better health and education outcomes. Bangladesh's success suggests that the bottleneck is not resources but priorities and political will. The incremental infrastructure requirements are low, but just increasing provision is not enough. Information and training are needed to boost uptake of these programmes in ways that respect tradition and social mores. Community-based programmes have great potential, as do new forms of communications and connectivity.

Supporting community management of natural resources

Support is growing for community management of natural resources as an alternative to centralized control, especially where communities depend on local natural resources and ecosystems for their livelihoods. Increasing interest in reforestation in countries as diverse as Costa Rica, Estonia and India reflects the potential for success.[71]

While participatory management of common resources has been widely embraced as a promising concept, a detailed review commissioned for this Report shows that the reality is more nuanced.[72] Local structural factors affect who benefits from community management. The distribution of wealth (including land tenure rights) and knowledge and participation in decision-making are especially important. For example, when influential stakeholders benefit from a common resource, they might invest heavily in restricting access, thus enhancing sustainability but at a cost to equity. As we discuss below, evidence suggests that more equal and socially cohesive communities are more likely to organize and agree on how to deal with collective action problems.[73]

A major threat to equity is women's exclusion from decision-making. With no community voice, women are often excluded from the benefits of common resources while bearing a disproportionate share of the costs, as in some parts of India.[74] For example, deciding to close forests without considering women's needs can deprive women of fuelwood, increase the time they spend finding alternative sources of fuelwood and fodder and reduce their income from livestock products. More generally, our analysis suggests a causal link between our Gender Inequality Index and deforestation in more than 100 countries between 1990 and 2010. And as chapter 3 notes, empirical evidence stresses the importance of the nature and extent of women's participation in management decisions.[75]

One of the most successful and equitable models of community management of natural resources is the community-conserved area —land or water protected by legal or other means and owned and managed by a community. Around 11 percent of the world's forests are known to be under community ownership or administration,[76] but this is likely a severe underestimate.[77] Community-conserved areas help ensure equitable access to resources, sustain human development through essential ecosystem services and maintain ecosystem integrity.

Locally managed marine areas—areas of near-shore waters and their associated coastal and marine resources—also provide win-win solutions. Pacific Island communities, such as Fiji, have dozens of such areas where island communities have long practiced traditional management systems that include

> As an alternative to centralized control, community-conserved areas help ensure equitable access to resources, sustain human development through essential ecosystem services and maintain ecosystem integrity

BOX 4.2
Culture, norms and environmental protection

The values and beliefs that shape people's relationships with their natural environment are central to environmental sustainability, as are accumulated traditional knowledge and community practices of environmental management. The environmental management skills of local people may include multiuse strategies of appropriation, small-scale production with little surplus and low energy use, and a variety of custodial approaches to land and natural resources that avoid waste and resource depletion.

Case studies suggest that traditional values can protect natural resources. Over three decades in the Zambezi Valley of Zimbabwe, for instance, forests considered sacred lost less than half the cover of those that were not. In Ghana conservative traditions and practices led to the designation of sacred areas and to periodic restrictions on farming, harvesting and fishing. Local knowledge also informs natural disaster responses. Chile reported only 8 fisher victims out of an estimated population of about 80,000 following the February 2010 tsunami, thanks mostly to lessons from previous tsunamis passed down through elders' stories and neighbours' evacuation alerts.

Though such knowledge is often downplayed and overlooked, traditional values have also informed policy. In Andavadoaka, a small fishing village in Madagascar, the community initiated a sustainable octopus fishing initiative that inspired other villages and became the country's first locally managed marine area, involving 24 villages. And in Afghanistan the government is drawing on elements of long-standing *mirab* systems—in which locally elected leaders manage water rights—in creating water use associations.

Source: Byers and others 2001; Marín and others 2010; Thomas and Ahmad 2009; Sarfo-Mensah and Oduro 2007; UN 2008.

seasonal fishing bans and temporary no-take areas. Community-conserved marine areas provide enormous value to local communities in the forms of fish protein and sustainable livelihoods.[78]

Communities can manage natural resources using a variety of mechanisms, including payments for ecosystem services and community-conserved areas. Cultural or traditional norms emerge as important (box 4.2). Success requires broad stakeholder inclusion in returns—from the resources themselves as well as from their management. Local processes and national commitment are also important. Sweden's experience in the 1960s, reviewed in box 2.10 in chapter 2, shows that national environmental protection mandates can support community management.

Where the livelihoods of multiple stakeholders are closely tied to natural resources, community-based management is susceptible to conflict. As discussed in chapter 3, scarcity of natural resources and environmental stresses can contribute to the eruption and escalation of conflict. In some cases public policies exacerbate the sources of conflict, especially when policies worsen horizontal inequality[79] or negatively affect people living within particular ecosystems. In some cases—including Costa Rica and the Philippines—greater decentralization and comanagement of natural resources have helped alleviate tensions.

Conserving biodiversity while promoting equity

In recent years perceived trade-offs between preserving livelihoods and maintaining biodiversity have been replaced by a clearer understanding of the potential synergies. For instance, preserving natural ecosystems and biodiversity can help secure livelihoods, food, water and health. Many countries (including Botswana, Brazil and Namibia) and international organizations (including the United Nations Development Programme) are calling for investments to preserve biodiversity for its potential development benefits. One instrument is to assign and enforce protected area status to ecosystems, putting in place measures to avert or reverse land degradation and ecotourism. Ecotourism in particular is a promising route to protecting biodiversity while enhancing livelihood opportunities for the local community. The primary challenge is to ensure equitable participation, including by women.[80]

A recent survey found that nature-based tourism is one of several conservation mechanisms that can reduce poverty.[81] In Namibia, for example, an ecotourism programme has protected nearly 3 million hectares of land and marine areas housing great biodiversity. Especially important for equity, the programme has improved livelihoods immensely. And with roughly 29 percent of the wealth generated by these protected areas going to labour and another 5 percent to traditional agriculture, the programme shows the potential of protected areas to reduce poverty as well.[82] Similarly, an initiative to conserve biodiversity at the level of landholders in the island state of Vanuatu led to the establishment of 20 conservation sites, which reduced poaching and enhanced fishstocks and incomes for local communities. And in Ecuador the government entered into an agreement with the United Nations Development Programme in 2010 to establish an international trust fund to protect Yasuní National Park, an area rich in biodiversity and home to the indigenous Tagaeri and Taromenane people, from oil drilling. Though too early to assess the results, the initiative offers a model for preserving such ecosystems through developed country compensation of poorer countries.[83]

Another example of promoting livelihoods while maintaining biodiversity is agroforestry, which entails an integrated approach of combining trees, shrubs and plants with crops and livestock to create more diverse, productive, profitable, healthy and sustainable land-use systems. Agro-forestry production can be seen in the Yungas region on the eastern slope of Peru's Central Andes, among an indigenous community of around 32,000 inhabitants. This enables the community to conserve genetically important species while providing for a range of nutritional, medicinal and commercial purposes.[84]

Integrated conservation and development projects aim to conserve biodiversity while promoting rural development. For example, in Nepal's western Terai Complex communities reduce pressures on natural forests by focusing on biodiversity-friendly and sustainable land and resource use practices. Such projects ensure that communities, particularly women and the poor, have viable alternatives for income, while reducing pressures on natural ecosystems.[85]

Addressing climate change— risks and realities

Finally in this review of promising approaches, we consider two key policy directions to offset the impacts of climate change on people: equitable and adaptive disaster responses and innovative social protection.

Equitable and adaptive disaster responses

As chapters 2 and 3 show, natural disasters are disequalizing, reflecting economic and power relations at the local, national and global levels. But planning and targeted responses can reduce the disparities. Two promising avenues are community-based disaster risk mapping

and progressive distribution of reconstructed public assets.

Experience has led to a shift from top-down models of disaster recovery to decentralized approaches. Community-based disaster risk programmes are generally better than centralized programmes at tapping local knowledge of capacities and constraints for emergency relief and longer term recovery and reconstruction. Local organizations are also often better able to reach remote and restricted areas—as demonstrated in Aceh, Indonesia, and Sri Lanka, where periods of armed conflict made it difficult for international aid workers to operate.[86] Some attention is needed to avoid depending exclusively on local organizations, which could intensify disparities and exclusion.

Community-led vulnerability and resource mapping has demonstrated effectiveness:[87]

- In Mount Vernon, one of the poorest communities in Jamaica, community-led disaster mapping highlighted flooding problems and led to agreement on the need for footbridges.

- A community-led mapping of women's access to resources and services in Jinja, Uganda, identified corrupt land distribution and denial of women's rights to land as impediments to women's access. Grassroots leaders responded by setting up savings clubs and rotating loan schemes, which improved women's access to land titles and helped them develop their property.

Community involvement can be enormously empowering for poorer communities, as shown by disaster training programmes in 176 districts in the 17 most hazard-prone Indian states. Female master trainers reached out to women in their communities and served as role models. Engaging women in community risk-mapping involved them in decision-making, giving them greater voice and control over their lives. In the words of Mitali Goswami of Ngoan District in Assam, "We feel very useful and are filled with pride when we see ourselves fulfilling our responsibilities towards the family and community."[88]

Poor rural communities are disproportionately affected by ecosystem degradation and disproportionately benefit from their protection and restoration. Sometimes the most efficient and equitable ways to avoid and mitigate disasters are to manage, restore and protect the ecosystems that buffer the community. For example, villages with healthy mangroves, coral reefs and lowland forests were better protected from the 2004 tsunami in India, Indonesia, Malaysia and Sri Lanka.[89]

Structural inequalities are often embedded in patterns of infrastructure and social investments and reflected in the outcomes. Rebuilding after environmental disasters can address past biases and other factors that perpetuate poverty and inequality. When Northern California was recovering from the 1989 Loma Pietra earthquake, the community opposed rebuilding the freeway along the original route, which divided neighbourhoods and exposed them to vehicular pollution. The freeway was rerouted through nearby industrial land, and agreements were reached to promote local hiring and contracting on reconstruction.[90]

Innovative social protection

Growing evidence shows that social protection programmes—assistance and transfers to enhance the capacity of poor and vulnerable people to escape poverty and manage risks and shocks—can help families maintain stable consumption and meet broader distributive goals.[91] As many as 1 billion people in developing countries live in households that receive some form of social transfer.[92]

Table 4.2 shows four types of social protection measures that, appropriately combined, can promote both equity and environmental objectives. We highlight both the potential benefits and the challenges of targeted cash transfers, employment schemes, weather-based crop insurance and asset transfers.

Social protection programmes can help people access modern energy sources, clean water and adequate sanitation. A recent study illuminates the impacts of cash transfers to poor households under Mexico's Oportunidades programme that go beyond the well studied effects on health and education. The transfers have affected both short-run spending on energy services and long-run spending on new appliances (refrigerators, gas stoves). They have enabled families to switch from wood or charcoal to the cleaner, more expensive electricity and liquefied petroleum gas.[93]

Countries should consider more integrated approaches to social protection—approaches that address environmental sustainability, equity and human development. A recent survey of social protection, disaster risk reduction and climate change adaptation schemes in South Asia revealed that few countries integrate such programmes. Of the 124 programmes surveyed, just 16 percent combined all three elements.[94] One example is South Africa's Working for Water, part of an Expanded Public Works Programme launched in 2004. The project, the first of its kind to include an environmental component, increased stream flows and water availability, improved land productivity and biodiversity in some ecologically sensitive areas and inspired

TABLE 4.2

Social protection for adaptation and disaster risk reduction: benefits and challenges

Programme and example	Benefits	Challenges
Targeted cash transfers Ethiopia: Productive Safety Net Programme	• Targets the most vulnerable • Stabilizes consumption • Allows adaptive risk-taking and investment • Enhances flexibility to cope with climate shocks	• Ensuring adequate size and predictability of transfers • Reducing risk through long-term focus • Demonstrating the economic case for cash transfers associated with climate shocks • Using socioeconomic vulnerability indices for targeting
Employment schemes India: Mahatma Gandhi National Rural Employment Guarantee Act	• Provides 100 days of employment on demand in rural areas • Constructs infrastructure, including projects that enhance community resilience against climate change impacts • Provides a guaranteed income to combat seasonal variations in income	• Ensuring adequate benefits • Accountability and transparency • Increasing awareness to ensure high participation • Controlling costs and avoiding the risk of exclusion
Weather-based crop insurance Government of Malawi and partners: weather-indexed crop insurance for groundnut production	• Guards against risk-taking associated with insurance • Frees up assets for investment in adaptive capacity • Can be linked to trends and projections for climate change • Supports adaptive flexibility	• Targeting marginal farmers • Tackling differentiated gender impacts • Keeping premiums affordable for the poor • Subsidizing capital costs • Integrating climate projections into financial risk assessment • Establishing guarantee mechanisms for reinsurance
Asset transfers Bangladesh: Reducing Vulnerability to Climate Change project	• Targets the most vulnerable • Can be integrated into livelihood programmes	• Ensuring provision commensurate with the threats faced • Ensuring local appropriateness of assets • Integrating changing natural environmental stresses in asset selection

Source: Adapted from Davies and others in OECD (2009).

similar initiatives for wetlands, coastal areas and waste management.[95] When reviews of the first phase (2004–2009) found that public works programmes were too short and wages too low to substantially reduce poverty, the government set a new minimum wage for the next phase of the programme.

Public works programmes need to provide options for women and for people unable to work. South Africa's Working for Water has quotas for women (60 percent) and for people with disabilities (2 percent).[96] In India women and members of scheduled castes and scheduled tribes account for (an overlapping) 50 percent of participants in the National Rural Employment Guarantee Act.

Involving the community in designing and managing adaptive social protection programmes is important. A review of the India National Rural Employment Guarantee Act illustrates how villagers have been empowered to identify projects and negotiate with local authorities.[97] How widespread participation in governance and decision-making contributes to strong and accountable institutions and equitable outcomes is discussed further in the following chapter.

Ultimately, how adaptive social protection is implemented turns largely on political preferences for equity and the environment and on how well society is mobilized behind programmes for building long-term resilience as part of social protection and poverty reduction.

*   *   *

This review of promising approaches provides strong grounds for optimism. It is possible to identify and implement strategies that improve both sustainability and equity—strategies that fall in quadrant 1 of figure 1.1 in chapter 1—to address many of the challenges outlined in chapters 2 and 3. And we have seen successes in such approaches around the world, with tangible benefits for poor and disadvantaged people and the environment. But such outcomes are not automatic. More concerted efforts are needed to integrate equity into policy and programme design and engage people in discussions and decisions that affect their lives. Such approaches must be resourced appropriately, in ways that ensure a progressive distribution of responsibilities. It is to these challenges that we turn in chapter 5.

> We have seen successes around the world with strategies that improve both sustainability and equity

CHAPTER 5

Rising to the policy challenges

This Report has focused on the large disparities across people, groups and countries—disparities that coexist with and worsen environmental degradation and loss of ecosystem services that the world's poor depend on. Yes, the challenges are massive. But in several respects conditions today are more conducive to progress than ever. Global public awareness is higher, and the new calls for democracy sweeping parts of the world augur well for reform.

Taking the debate further entails bold thinking, especially on the eve of the 2012 UN Conference on Sustainable Development (Rio+20). This Report advances a new vision for promoting human development through the joint lens of sustainability and equity. For that vision to become a reality, institutions must be strengthened, capacities enhanced, policies reformed and democratic governance fortified.

The vision calls for an expansive rethinking of the role of the state and communities —and their capacity to identify and exploit emerging opportunities. Building on the insights of Amartya Sen and the key principles of the human development approach, this vision stresses an approach to sustainability and equity rooted in inclusion, participation and reasoned public debate, while recognizing diverse values, conditions and objectives.

Beyond the Millennium Development Goals the world needs a post-2015 development framework that reflects equity and sustainability: Rio+20 stands out as a great opportunity to reach a shared understanding about how to move forward.

This chapter proposes key reforms at the national and global levels:

- At the national level it stresses the need to bring equity to the forefront of policy and programme design, and the potential

multiplier effects of greater empowerment in the legal and political arenas.
- At the global level it calls for greater resources to be devoted to pressing environmental threats and for more equitable representation of disadvantaged countries and groups in accessing finance.

Concerted actions can bring equity and sustainability closer to the centre of human development. Too often development plans invoke unnecessary trade-offs—sacrificing a healthy environment or equitable distribution of wealth for the sake of economic growth. Implicit is the notion that one aim is a luxury, less important than the other. Power imbalances and political constraints loom large. And too often the plans are incomplete, not designed to promote equity. But policies can maximize the synergies among healthy communities, healthy economies and a healthy environment.

The chapter reinforces the central contention of this Report: that integrating the approaches to sustainability and equity can produce innovative solutions and concrete guidelines to promote human development.

Business-as-usual is neither equitable nor sustainable

The conventional focus on maximizing growth has been associated with a model that ignores the environmental impacts and externalities of economic activity. This is true in a command and control system (the former Soviet Union), in a liberalizing socialist economy (China in the 1990s) and in fairly free market economies (Australia and the United States over much of the 20th century). Especially since the Second World War, accelerations in economic growth have been carbon-intensive, and economic regulation has been scaled back. As chapter 2 shows, untrammelled growth without regard for the environment has brought the world to the point where the concentration of carbon dioxide in the atmosphere already exceeds 350 parts per million and is heading to levels that risk multiple catastrophes.

In the face of daunting environmental challenges that endanger prospects for continuing progress in human development, concerted global action too often falls far short of what is needed. This chapter reviews the scale of the challenges and points to a fundamental contradiction: business-as-usual is neither sustainable nor equitable, but attempts to move forward are beset by political economy constraints. It proposes key principles for countries to promote change and then addresses key elements at the global level.

Worsening environmental degradation could soon break the 40-year pattern of convergence in human development across countries. Consider the potential trade-offs between economic costs and environmental damage given today's technology and carbon intensity of production. Simulations for this report suggest that if no country or region is prepared to bear a loss of more than 1 percent in total future income, or more than 5 percent of its income in any five-year period, carbon dioxide levels will trigger a temperature increase of 3°C above preindustrial levels by 2100.[1] But a temperature rise above the 2°C threshold would be catastrophic for many developing countries,[2] as chapter 2 describes. So, we highlight the potential outcomes of alternative paths and a framework to induce global cooperation. Systematic thinking about how to share the costs of adjustment and promote greener growth is critical, alongside concerted public action to support innovations in technology and enhance voice and accountability.

A fundamental rethinking of the conventional growth model is well under way. The 2008 global financial crisis and its aftermath reinforced the growing consensus that deregulation went too far and that the pendulum should swing back.[3] Indeed, compounding the economic failures of conventional policies are the other costs they can introduce —such as greater inequality and environmental degradation. As chapter 1 argues, lessons from the recent financial crisis can be applied to the potential effects of climate change (see box 1.1). More active public policy is critical, not least because development must be decoupled from carbon emissions and the true value of ecosystem services should be incorporated into national development plans. The good news is that there is growing recognition, or rediscovery, of industrial policy—of proactive policies and interventions to restructure an economy towards more dynamic activities—even at such institutions as the World Bank, long a proponent of free market approaches.[4]

Overcoming pervasive market imperfections requires, among other things, internalizing the externalities in decision-making and in some cases creating markets where none exist —as for some ecosystem services. Because of the costs and risks created by greenhouse gas emissions, the loss of ecosystem services due to environmental degradation and underinvestment in innovations, more support should go to promoting innovative renewable energy technologies. If firms underestimate the long-term benefits of investing in new technologies or if they cannot appropriate the benefits, they will invest less than is optimal socially and globally.

As chapter 4 shows, well designed, well implemented incentives can elicit change. For example, Japan's 2009 buy-back system for residential rooftop photovoltaics promoted investment and provided incentives for customers to reduce electricity use. Similarly, tax incentives have encouraged renewable energy investments in Canada, Denmark, India, Sweden and the United States.[5] But price-based incentives, especially for scarce resources, need careful calibration to avoid impoverishing or excluding already disadvantaged groups.

A key constraint to public action on environmental problems is lack of awareness. About a third of the world's people seem unaware of climate change, and only about half consider it a serious threat or know that it is caused at least partly by human activity (see box 2.5 in chapter 2). But even with raised awareness, serious political constraints would remain—in other words, our collective failure to act also reflects the complexity of the politics and the power

Worsening environmental degradation could soon break the 40-year pattern of convergence in human development across countries of groups opposing change. Chapters 2 and 3 show how many countries and communities most affected by climate change lack power and influence. So understanding these constraints is a vital first step in framing strategies with a real chance of meaningful change.

As chapter 4 discusses, national planning processes are critical, but capacity constraints and siloed approaches can limit effectiveness. In the western Balkan countries, for example, a major barrier impeding implementation of climate change mitigation policies is the lack of national coordination mechanisms.[6]

It is clear that equity issues go well beyond developed versus developing countries—and beyond mitigation costs alone—to the burden of adjustment. Procedural justice requires that all parties be able to participate effectively[7] —some of the groups that lobby nationally, including those pushing for more equitable policies for women and indigenous peoples, also merit a voice on the global stage. Similarly, global environmental finance and governance mechanisms must be informed by principles of equity and fair representation that go beyond country governments.

Rethinking our development model—levers for change

The required transformations involve a progressive approach that integrates the pillars of sustainable human development. Due consideration must be given to differences in country contexts: one-size-fits-all thinking is rarely effective when formulating policy or implementing programmes. Proposed here are two major avenues to guide such efforts—one is the integration of equity concerns into policy and programme design and evaluation, the other is empowerment in the legal and political arenas. For each avenue the chapter sets forth basic principles and highlights the experiences of selected countries.

Integrating equity concerns into green economy policies
The need to integrate equity concerns more fully into environmental policy is a major theme of this Report. Conventional

assessments are often silent on the winners and losers of a policy or programme.[8] But distributional aspects require explicit consideration because effects on the poor or the rich might differ from average effects—and sometimes from intended outcomes. It is important to consider differences between the rich and the poor, between men and women, among indigenous peoples and across regions. Such considerations are consistent with the stated objectives of green economy policies, but they warrant a sharper focus in practice.

Integrating distributional aspects into cost–benefit analysis has long been recognized as important[9] but has rarely been practiced, resulting in neglect of equity in project and policy analysis. In the absence of transfers, policies and projects that pass cost–benefit tests might not make everyone better off— and might even reduce the welfare of some groups (box 5.1). But appropriately valuing environmental and resilience-promoting benefits is difficult. This is true especially of the ecosystems for which the value of services is not fully known.

The distributional analysis of economic policy reforms has advanced in the past decade —examining effects on the well-being of different groups, especially the poor and vulnerable. The World Bank has supported many such analyses, though sometimes the timing is too late to inform decision-making or policy-makers fail to adequately incorporate the results of such assessments.[10] And distributional analyses still tend to be restricted to income, using conventional economic tools and focusing on such transmission mechanisms as prices and employment. Because such analyses can miss important parts of the picture, we propose that the approach be expanded and deepened.

Key principles
Environmental regulations and subsidies can affect people's capabilities as individuals, family members, workers, entrepreneurs and farmers (figure 5.1). Policy can affect people's endowments, opportunities and agency—and through them the distribution of a range of assets.

> Equity issues go well beyond developed versus developing countries— and beyond mitigation costs alone—to the burden of adjustment

FIGURE 5.1

Integrating equity into policy design

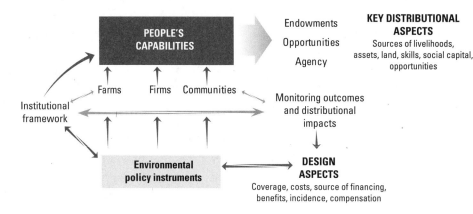

Both vertical and horizontal equity are important. Vertical equity looks at the treatment of individuals across the distribution—for example, how a tax on gasoline would affect people at the bottom of the distribution differently from those at the top. Horizontal equity relates to differences across groups or areas.

BOX 5.1

Distributional impacts of policies to cut pollution

Current discussions often raise concerns that policies to reduce pollution can be regressive, but rarely is systematic impact analysis brought to bear. The type of analysis needed can be illustrated for a carbon permit system such as cap-and-trade—which raises the price of products that use fossil fuels intensively, such as electricity. It draws attention to first- and second-round effects:

1. Everyone faces real income losses, but the effect is regressive if low-income households spend a higher fraction of their income on these goods.
2. If technologies are capital-intensive, a mandate to abate pollution can induce firms to substitute capital for polluting inputs, depressing demand for labour and relative wages. Low-income households receive a larger share of their income from wages, so they may again be more affected.
3. Unemployment may be concentrated among certain regions, industries and groups, such as coal miners. When the industry shrinks, workers with industry-specific human capital lose that investment, while premiums go to skilled workers in renewables and other energy-efficient technologies.

These effects raise important empirical questions to be investigated case by case. Research in Organisation for Economic Co-operation and Development (OECD) countries points to few truly "green" skills and suggests that most green jobs resemble familiar occupations. This is good news for displaced workers in developed countries, but it warrants investigation elsewhere.

Low-skilled workers are more likely to be displaced by carbon taxes. In OECD countries these workers stay unemployed for longer after job losses than do higher skilled workers and are less likely to find employment that pays as well. So, governments need to watch out for adversely affected groups when implementing environmental regulations, particularly when regulations will affect already disadvantaged groups. Policies must include redistributive and backstop mechanisms to avoid these problems.

Source: Fullerton 2011.

Key priorities for integrating equity into green economy policy design include:

- *Mainstreaming the nonincome dimensions of well-being.* Building on the Multidimensional Poverty Index could broaden understanding of disadvantage and highlight the impacts of policy changes across all dimensions of deprivation. For instance, higher charges for water could reduce access, harming health, while more expensive kerosene could push households back to using biomass for cooking, bad for health and the environment.
- *Understanding direct and indirect effects.* Direct effects can be followed by a second round of indirect changes (see box 5.1).
- *Considering compensation mechanisms.* Countries with well developed tax-and-transfer systems can use income tax schedules or social benefits to offset negative effects. For example, South Africa provides an income tax deduction for communal and private landowners who set aside land with high biodiversity value and manage it as a protected area.[11] But where such systems are less feasible, alternative compensation or exemptions are needed.
- Understanding the risk of extreme events. However small the probability, it is essential to consider the huge adverse consequences of extreme weather events, especially for the most vulnerable—and to reduce the risks.[12] Such analysis may reveal that investing in land use planning and ecosystems can be a cost-effective buffer for

vulnerable groups against climate risks, as demonstrated by mangrove restoration in Viet Nam.[13]

So, rather than accept or reject an individual policy, it is important to consider a range of designs and to determine which can improve outcomes for equity. There are always constraints in data, analysis, capacity and time, so flexibility is needed in meeting the main goals.

Stakeholder analysis is critical. Political economy factors and the influence of various actors can affect both design and implementation of policy. For instance, the oil industry in the United States spent almost $1.5 billion on federal lobbying in 2010.[14] And in Tanzania the proposed reform of charcoal production, trade and use highlights the needs and influence of dealer-transporter-wholesaler networks.[15] Policy design and implementation must address such influences and their likely impacts.

Institutional arrangements must guard against rent-seeking and official corruption— and more than this, against distortions of scientific facts, breaches of principles of fair representation and false claims about the green credentials of consumer products.[16] Countries need industrial policies that support inclusive green growth while being mindful of the pitfalls and challenges of state promotion of selected types of economic activity. The features of a new industrial policy are relevant for policies to reduce the carbon intensity of development—limited incentives to new activities, automatic sunset provisions (so that the subsidies are temporary) and clear benchmarks for success. This requires the right institutions, a political champion and systematic deliberations that engage the private sector.[17]

Country experience

More countries are using distributional analysis to inform environmental policy design. South Africa's plans to introduce environmental taxes as part of its fiscal reforms were informed by stakeholder analyses of likely quantitative and qualitative effects.[18] Viet Nam announced new taxes following impact assessments simulating price and sectoral effects.[19]

Policies to drive structural change, such as pollution pricing, will inevitably have winners and losers. Some companies will claim unfair adverse impacts. Policy measures to respond to such concerns, such as exemptions and compensation, can be costly, and the distributional impacts need to be understood. Alternatives, such as more effective consultations and public communications, should also be contemplated.[20]

Consumption and production profiles can shape distributional effects. Two examples from the energy sector:

- Ghana's electricity sector was draining the government budget. In 2002 public utility company deficits approached 11 percent of government spending, or 4 percent of GDP. Distributional analysis found that subsidies benefited mainly middle-class urban customers: only 7 percent of the rural poor used electric light. The lack of rural electrification in the poorest northern regions warranted reducing subsidies, raising public awareness of energy efficiency and increasing efforts to improve market efficiency.[21]

- In Lao PDR, which experienced rapid expansion of access to modern energy services after the late 1980s, key equity aspects were incorporated in programme design. A "power to the poor" component provides interest-free credits to connect poor households to the grid, benefiting female-headed households in particular. Local communities and rural households also receive support for electricity use for income-generating activities.[22]

While some insights can be drawn from such interventions, the effects are always context-specific and require local analysis.

Data constraints can limit understanding. The joint analysis of human development and equity impacts requires individual and household information, as well as qualitative data, to build statistical capacity. This underlines the importance of continuing to improve disaggregated data, especially in developing countries.

Ex ante assessments need to be followed by results monitoring. In rural Bangladesh home solar power systems were estimated to displace kerosene use equivalent to 4 percent of total annual carbon emissions.[23] Surveys showed that solar subsidies—amounting to almost $400 million and allocated through a private microcredit agency—were progressive when accurately targeted, because the bottom two income groups spent about three times more on kerosene than the top two. Benefits also included better lighting, good for children's education, and reduced indoor air pollution, with benefits for health.

Empowering people to bring about change

This Report argues for empowerment to bring about greater equity and environmental benefits—and as an important outcome in itself. What does this mean in practice? Consider two spheres where enhancing voice and representation has important links to sustainability—the legal, with enabling institutions and rights to a clean and safe environment, and the political, with more participation and accountability.

A clean and safe environment— a right, not a privilege

That all people, born and yet to be born, have the right to a clean and safe environment is a powerful idea, grounded in the framework in chapter 1. Despite the slow progress in securing such rights globally,[24] constitutions in at least 120 countries address environmental norms or the state's obligation to prevent environmental harm.[25] And many countries without explicit environmental rights interpret general constitutional provisions for personal rights as including a fundamental right to a clean, safe and healthy environment. That right derives from people's rights to bodily health and integrity and to enjoyment of the natural world.

Amartya Sen, Martha Nussbaum and others have noted a close relationship between the capabilities approach and rights-based approaches to human development.[26] But unlike the idea of freedom or capability in itself, an acknowledged human right also incorporates corresponding obligations. Notwithstanding such obligations, human rights

are not equivalent to legal rights, although they can motivate legislation and thus provide the basis for legal action. Some rights are procedural—as with the right to information discussed below—and must encompass both opportunity and process aspects.[27]

Constitutionally recognizing equal rights to a healthy environment promotes equity because such access is no longer limited to those who can afford it.[28] And embodying such rights in the legal framework can influence government priorities and resource allocations.

Growing country experience

Many EU countries recognize fundamental environmental rights as a matter of natural law—as inherent universal rights. In the United Kingdom the Human Rights Act includes the right to a healthy environment.[29] And although the European Convention on Human Rights does not mention environmental rights, it establishes that serious environmental damage may violate the right to respect for private life and family life.[30] Sweden recognizes the right of public access through its constitutional "Don't disturb; don't destroy" policy: people have the right to roam freely in the countryside as long as they do not inconvenience others.[31]

Kenya's 2010 Constitution grants the right to a clean environment and requires the government to maintain its natural resources.[32] At least 31 other African countries express environmental rights in their constitutions, and some—such as Ethiopia and Namibia—also stress that economic development should not harm the environment.[33]

The enforceability of environmental rights in Africa is largely untested, however, except in South Africa. Some countries have structural impediments. In Cameroon citizens do not have the right to appeal to the country's constitutional council, which limits enforceability.[34] And in Namibia environmental rights can be enforced only by someone with a private interest, barring claims in the public interest.[35]

Several Latin American countries, including Chile, Costa Rica, Ecuador and Peru, have enforceable environmental rights. The Chilean Supreme Court voided a government-issued timber licence because it had been approved without sufficient evidence of environmental viability, thus violating the right of all Chileans—not just those directly affected—to live free of environmental contamination.[36]

Many Latin American constitutions recognize environmental rights for indigenous peoples.[37] Paraguay guarantees that the state will defend them against habitat degradation and environmental contamination.[38] In Guyana environmental rights exist alongside recognition of the rights of indigenous peoples.[39] Bolivia's proposed Law of Mother Nature takes this recognition a step further, giving the natural world equal rights with people. The proposal is heavily influenced by a resurgent indigenous Andean spiritual world view that places the environment and the earth deity Pachamama at the centre of life.[40]

Among Asian countries India is notable for allowing aggrieved individuals to challenge state action or inaction related to the environment.[41] The Indian judiciary has broadly interpreted environmental rights in the constitution to protect public health as well. For example, environmental advocates successfully argued that environmental laws obliged the government to reduce air pollution in New Delhi in the interests of public health, resulting in an order mandating conversion of city buses from diesel to compressed natural gas.[42]

Bhutan has pioneered placing environmental conservation at the centre of its development strategy, reflecting traditional norms and culture.[43] Article 5 of the 2008 Constitution emphasizes the responsibility of all Bhutanese to protect the environment, conserve its biodiversity and prevent ecological degradation. It also stipulates that at least 60 percent of the country remain forested in perpetuity.

Even if rights provide only what Immanuel Kant called imperfect obligations, they can still empower groups and individuals to take public action to protect their environment. As Amartya Sen wrote, "because of the importance of communication, advocacy, exposure and informed public discussion, human rights can have influence without necessarily depending on coercive legislation."[44] Indeed, procedural human rights linked to environmental protection often receive more attention than substantive environmental rights.[45]

Enabling institutions

Alongside legal recognition of equal rights to a healthy, well functioning environment, enabling institutions are needed, including a fair and independent judiciary and the right to information from governments. For example:

- In the United States conservation groups have used information on emissions levels to bring public nuisance actions against private companies.[46]
- One Million Acts of Green, launched by Cisco in partnership with the Canadian Broadcasting Corporation and Green-Nexxus in Canada in 2008, uses television, Facebook®, Twitter™ and other Internet resources to engage Canadians in conversations on environmental issues and encourage "green acts." The initiative elicited nearly 2 million green acts within a year.[47]

An institutional context conducive to civil liberties is a necessary backdrop. But recent Gallup data suggest that a majority of the people in close to half of nearly 140 countries surveyed lack confidence in their judicial system and courts.[48] This underlines the importance of implementing broader reforms and improving the context for enforcing rights.

Rights to government information are spreading. At least 49 national constitutions recognize them, and at least 80 legislatures have enacted right-to-information laws. South Africa's 1996 Constitution guarantees all "the right of access to any information held by the state and held by another person that is required for the exercise or protection of any rights." In Argentina, Canada, France, India, Israel and the Republic of Korea higher courts have held that constitutional guarantees of free expression implicitly recognize a constitutional right of access to information.[49]

But legislation is just a first step. Implementation and enforcement are equally critical. Civil society organizations are important for implementation by helping citizens understand and use legal rights of access to

> Alongside legal recognition of equal rights to a healthy, well functioning environment, enabling institutions are needed, including a fair and independent judiciary and the right to information from governments

information, by training public officials in information disclosure and by monitoring implementation. In Bulgaria a nongovernmental organization, the Access to Information Programme, provided legal assistance and disseminated information to the wider public about the right-to-information law and the scope of citizens' rights.[50]

Information disclosure is very important to environmental protection and citizen empowerment. Ensuring that polluters disclose information on emissions and discharges can reduce violations and complement regulation. British Columbia's public disclosure strategy had a larger impact on emissions and compliance than the sanctions traditionally imposed by Canada's Ministry of the Environment. Stricter standards and larger penalties were also influential—suggesting that both information and regulation can reduce emissions.[51] And in China programmes to rate and publicly disclose companies' environmental performance have prompted facilities to reduce air and water pollution, improving firms' market competitiveness and relationships with communities and other stakeholders.[52] The Czech Republic, Egypt, Indonesia and Mexico recorded similar results with the new mandated Pollutant Release and Transfer Registers.[53]

The international community is increasingly recognizing a right of access to environmental information.[54] This in turn supports a broad interpretation of national constitutional rights to information.

The complex cross-sectoral challenges of sustainable human development have a long time horizon and require long-term commitments.[55] Changing decisions, mobilizing investment and developing new strategic plans can take years if not decades. This may involve major institutional reforms to mainstream environmental considerations in government planning. The government of Rwanda recognized the need to integrate environmental and natural resource management plans into the country's development strategy. Its Environmental Management Authority works closely with the national and local governments as well as civil society to promote sustainable development and the right to live in a clean and productive environment by requiring that all sectors of society manage the environment efficiently and use natural resources rationally.[56]

Participation and accountability

Process freedoms, which enable people to advance goals that matter to them, are central to human development and—as discussed in last year's *HDR*—have both intrinsic and instrumental value. Major disparities in power are reflected in unsustainable outcomes, but the converse is that greater empowerment can bring about positive environmental change equitably, as chapter 3 argues. Democracy is important, but to enable civil society and foster popular access to information, national institutions need to be accountable and inclusive—especially with respect to women and other affected groups.

Forums to facilitate participation

A prerequisite for participation is open, transparent and inclusive deliberative processes. Consider energy. As work commissioned for this Report demonstrates, most energy decisions are made behind closed doors and rarely in democratic fora.[57] Because of concerns for commercial confidentiality or geostrategic sensitivities about energy supplies, the public has participated little in negotiating energy policy decisions. "Consultations" can provide limited or incomplete information, neglect equity and impact assessments, and fail to report results effectively. Even where public participation or comment is formally invited, its role is often to legitimize prior policy choices and decisions, not to shape them.[58] In Australia, for example, cases have demonstrated a lack of open exchanges among local government, polluting industries and local communities and a failure to inform citizens of the risks of living and working near toxic sites.[59]

Where governments are responsive to popular concerns, change is more likely. In the United States, for example, 23 states allow citizens to petition for a direct vote on a policy initiative, a mechanism that some states have used to adopt environmental and energy policies (such as Washington in 2006).[60] Some groups have pursued accountability of

> Democracy is important, but to enable civil society and foster popular access to information, national institutions need to be accountable and inclusive— especially with respect to women and other affected groups

private corporations in emissions and climate change.[61] But such concerns may be offset by other vested interests—as reported for the Russian Federation in the problems civil society faced in mobilizing public support around greening industry.[62] And where civil society is active, as chapter 3 shows, it can bring about positive outcomes.

An active press raises awareness and facilitates public participation. In Rwanda the government launched radio and television promotions highlighting national environmental issues and targeting all levels of society. Media coverage increased support from the Environmental Management Agency and other government ministries to jointly explore ways to integrate environmental concerns into planning and to enhance cooperation for environmental protection.[63]

For climate change and other global environmental problems, procedural justice implies an equal opportunity for all countries to affect the direction and content of international negotiations. But weak capacity often means that few developing country governments are represented, let alone able to represent their citizens' interests adequately in arenas with high demands for legal and scientific expertise. Although 194 countries attended the UN Climate Change Conference in Copenhagen in 2010, only a powerful handful negotiated the terms of the Copenhagen Accord. In international summits the top five polluting countries usually field more than three times the delegates of the five countries most affected by climate change.[64]

The news is not all bad, however. Governance of the Climate Investment Funds is already moving towards more equitable voice and participation—with an equal number of representatives from donor and developing country governments on the governing committees for each of the trust funds and with decisions made by consensus. The Climate Investment Funds have also institutionalized formal observer roles for civil society, the private sector and in some cases indigenous peoples, while making the role of observers more meaningful by enabling them to suggest agenda items and contribute to discussions.[65]

The United Nations Collaborative Programme on Reducing Emissions from Deforestation and Forest Degradation in Developing Countries goes even farther, since its board, which decides on strategic directions and budget allocations, includes representatives of indigenous peoples and civil society as full members, not just as observers.[66]

Still, barriers to effective participation persist in many national and local contexts. Some groups, such as women, have traditionally been excluded from governance institutions. But here again, there have been changes, with documented results not only on equity but on sustainable management of environmental resources.[67] For example, in Europe local authorities in jurisdictions with the highest recycling rates had a higher than average percentage of female managers.[68] And extensive fieldwork in India has documented that active participation by women in community forest management significantly improved forest protection.[69]

Community management

Chapter 4 illustrates the growing recognition of the benefits of community management of natural resources. To ensure that such approaches do not exclude poor people, women, the elderly and other marginalized groups, governments and other organizations that sponsor community-based projects need to involve all groups in decision-making and implementation. For example, initiatives to mentor community forest groups in Nepal sensitized them to issues of equity and participation, ultimately increasing the participation and influence of women and the poor.[70]

Where women and other marginalized groups are included in community decision-making, the benefits can be substantial. For example, Bhutanese community forests have the dual purpose of engaging locals in managing forests and regulating access to forest resources for sustainable livelihood activities. Enabling access to fuelwood, which benefits women more than men, is one benefit of this approach. Household surveys of Bhutanese communities have found that poorer households and female-headed households were

> For climate change and other global environmental problems, procedural justice implies an equal opportunity for all countries to affect international negotiations, but weak capacity often means that few developing country governments are represented

usually assigned a larger share of trees than richer households, and women were able to collect more fuelwood from community forests.[71]

*   *   *

In sum, implementing a joint equity–sustainability approach at the national level involves integrating equity into policy and programme design and evaluation, bolstering empowerment through legal rights and corresponding institutions, and promoting greater participation and accountability.

Financing investment and the reform agenda

Policy debates about sustainability raise major questions about investment and financing, particularly on how much is needed, who should have access and who should be responsible for financing what.

Development finance constrains the equitable transition to a global green economy in two ways. First, it falls far short of global requirements. Second, countries and sectors have unequal access, so they do not always receive the financing they need to address environmental deprivations; the poorest countries often miss out.

Global capital markets, with some $178 trillion in financial assets, have the size and depth to step up to the challenge.[72] Over the medium to long term, and with sufficient public sector support, the United Nations Environment Programme estimates that private investment in clean energy technologies could reach $450 billion by 2012 and $600 billion by 2020.[73] The Global Environment Facility's experience suggests that private investment can be substantial: public funding for climate mitigation has leveraged private investment by 7 to 1 or more.[74] This leveraging requires public efforts to catalyse investment flows, by developing an appropriate investment environment and building local capacity.

These issues are covered in depth in a recent UNDP report that highlights policies for building developing country capacity to mobilize the public and private investment flows needed to finance the transition towards a low-emission,

climate-resilient society.[75] Medium-term plans, budgets and investments can be a foundation for consolidating good intentions and providing cross-sectoral mechanisms for effective coordination across donors and government agencies.

Lively debates about the future of official development assistance continue. While recognizing the growing importance of private flows and the likelihood that aid will shrink as a share of development finance for most countries, rich countries must not shirk their responsibilities. Strong equity arguments warrant substantial transfers of resources from rich countries to poor to meet equity goals and guarantee equal access to financing. And strong economic arguments support measures to solve global collective action problems, such as climate change.

Where does the world stand?
Although evidence on global needs[76] and official aid commitments and disbursements is patchy and magnitudes are uncertain, the overall picture is clear. Development assistance reaches only 1.6 percent of even the lower bound estimate of needs for low-carbon energy and around 11 percent for climate change (figure 5.2). These numbers are slightly better for water and sanitation, where aid commitments are more than twice the lower estimate of needs and close to 20 percent of the upper estimate.

Access to financing is uneven and generally correlated with a country's level of development. Many resources go to the countries developing fastest. Low-income countries account for a third of the 161 countries receiving Global Environment Facility allocations, but they receive only 25 percent of the funding (and least developed countries, only 9 percent).[77] In 2010, under the Climate Investment Funds, Mexico and Turkey accounted for about half the approved project funding in clean technology.[78] Evidence also suggests that the resources have been allocated less equally over time.[79]

What development assistance can do
Official development assistance is a vital source of external finance for many developing countries. Recent years have seen much progress in increasing the quality and quantity of official aid, which rose some 23 percent from 2005 to 2009.

But the contributions still do not meet the world's development challenges. The $129 billion committed in 2010 was 76 percent of the estimated cost of achieving the Millennium Development Goals—and not all aid goes to achieving the goals.[80] Rich countries have consistently failed to meet their stated pledges, including that of the G-8 at Gleneagles in 2005 (to increase aid by $50 billion a year by 2010), the European Union (to increase aid from 0.43 percent of gross national income to 0.56 percent) and the United Nations (the long-standing target of 0.7 percent of gross national income).

Developed countries have pledged $100 billion a year by 2020 to finance climate change mitigation and adaptation in developing countries. It is unclear, however, whether the funding would really be additional—one concern is that current aid will simply be diverted to meet the new targets.[81]

Access to energy and climate change investments

As this Report has already noted, providing clean energy to the 1.5 billion people who lack electricity and the 2.6 billion who rely on traditional biomass for cooking is a major win-win-win. Clean energy offers the potential to alleviate poverty, reduce health impacts from indoor air pollution and drive social and economic development, while mitigating energy's impact on the climate.

FIGURE 5.2

Official development assistance falls far short of needs

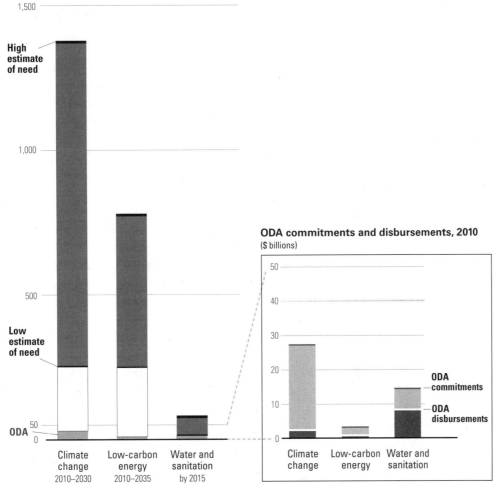

Estimated future needs and existing official development assistance (ODA)

Annual expenditures ($ billions)

Source: Based on data from IEA (2010), UN Water (2010a), UNDESA (2010a) and OECD Development Database on Aid Activities: CRS online.

International financial institutions have overseen sweeping reforms of the energy sector in many parts of the world, with a view to opening markets and guaranteeing equitable access to funds. And countries have positioned themselves to mobilize and attract private investments to the energy sector. But policymakers have yet to steer energy finance towards tackling energy poverty[82] or climate change on a larger scale, especially in places less attractive to the private sector.

Redirecting energy finance will require greater political will and exceptional leadership. Moreover, addressing energy poverty needs to stay at the head of the agenda because doing so is central to maintaining public support and development assistance for achieving the Millennium Development Goals and beyond.

A key dimension of climate policy discussions relates to the size, direction and source of financing. The World Bank recently outlined the difficulties in tracking such investments, including limited and inconsistent information in reporting systems, the ambiguous purpose of some flows, the confidential nature of some transactions and double counting.[83] Costing is difficult, in both theory and practice, and the scope of the estimates differs along with the methods. Underlying assumptions matter—especially those regarding the discount rate. So do assumed consumption and production elasticities to changing prices. With these caveats in mind, we review the available evidence and find:

- Recent estimates of the investments needed to reduce the concentration of greenhouse gases (mitigation costs) range widely, from 0.2 percent of annual global GDP to 1.2 percent by 2030.[84]
- Estimating adaptation costs is even harder, and it is difficult to distinguish them from related development investments. This Report's updated estimates of annual investment requirements for adaptation are of the order of $105 billion,[85] within the $49–$171 billion range proposed by the United Nations Framework Convention on Climate Change by 2030. Other estimates, which account for the costs of adapting to

the impact of climate change on ecosystems, are two to three times higher.[86]

- Estimates of total annual mitigation and adaptation costs to address climate change by 2030 range from $249 billion to $1,371 billion. Why the large difference? Because the costs of integrating renewable energies are context- and site-specific and thus difficult to estimate globally.

The amounts needed are clearly large, if uncertain. But they are below current spending on defence, on recent financial sector bailouts and on perverse subsidies, indicating the scope for reassessing priorities. In 2009 global military expenditure neared 3 percent of world GDP, while some countries spent much more, including the United States (4.7 percent of GDP) and the Russian Federation (4.3 percent of GDP).[87] The bailouts in the wake of the recent financial crisis were close to $700 billion in the United States under the Troubled Asset Relief Program, while EU commitments were close to $1 trillion (about 6 percent of annual GDP in both cases).

As the previous chapter shows, there is enormous scope for reducing environmentally harmful subsidies. Uzbekistan, for example, spends over 10 times more on fossil fuel consumption subsidies than on health (32 percent of GDP, compared with 2.5 percent), while Iran spends 20 percent of GDP on fossil fuel consumption subsidies, compared with less than 5 percent on education.[88]

Are developed countries meeting the financing commitment implied by their "common but differentiated responsibilities" under the Framework Convention on Climate Change? No. Almost $32 billion has been pledged for climate change actions (about 19 percent of total official development assistance).[89] But the pledges fall well short of estimated needs, and disbursements fall well short of pledges: most of the "new and additional" funds pledged at the 2009 UN Climate Change Conference in Copenhagen have not been delivered, and less than 8 percent of pledges for climate change were disbursed in 2010. Governments have yet to agree how to track spending or determine whether funding is truly additional—accurate monitoring requires an aid baseline.

Though large, the amounts needed to address climate change are below current spending on defence, on recent financial sector bailouts and on perverse subsidies, indicating the scope for reassessing priorities

Some 24 special climate change funds already exist, ranging from international sources of funding such as the Hatoyama Initiative (which has received 48 percent of total pledges to date—35 percent from public sources and 13 percent from private sources) to national trust funds that can receive donor funds, such as the Indonesia Climate Change Trust Fund (0.06 percent of pledges). The funds differ in structure and include both bilateral and multilateral arrangements, making reliable monitoring of spending very difficult.

Given this fragmentation, climate finance must incorporate the lessons of aid delivery to improve how assistance is organized and delivered. The 2005 Paris Declaration on Aid Effectiveness and the 2008 Accra Agenda for Action agreed on principles to promote country ownership, aid alignment and harmonization, results, and mutual accountability. The 2007 Bali Action Plan shows how these principles can be incorporated into climate change finance. This state of affairs does not imply that there should be one global superfund, which is neither feasible nor desirable, but it did show the scope for reducing complexity and enhancing access and transparency. Equally important is avoiding parallelism in funding, as far as possible, instead integrating provisions for climate change in national planning and budgets.

Water supply and sanitation

How much will it cost to meet the Millennium Development Goal targets for safe drinking water and basic sanitation? Assessments depend on baseline and demographic assumptions and on whether they include maintenance costs and use low-technology options. Moreover, definitions of "water supply" and "basic sanitation" differ, and consistent data are often lacking.

The 2010 *Global Annual Assessment of Sanitation and Drinking Water (GLAAS)* estimates for achieving the Millennium Development Goal water and sanitation targets, which take several earlier cost estimates into account, range from $6.7 billion to $75 billion a year.[90] Much more would be needed to achieve universal access.

The amounts now being spent from domestic and international sources are much lower. For 20 developing countries reporting drinking water and sanitation expenditures, *GLAAS 2010* estimates median government domestic spending at $65 million in 2008 (0.48 percent of GDP). For 2009, the most recent year with data, aid commitments totalled $14.3 billion and disbursements $7.8 billion.

Investor belief that the water and sanitation sector in developing countries is a high-risk, low-return investment makes market-based financing difficult to mobilize. And while reforms in governance, institutions and tariffs are critical to the sector's financial sustainability, innovative schemes are bridging the financing gaps in the interim (box 5.2).[91]

Again, greater efforts are needed. Government clearly is important, but reliance on financial aid is high, covering much national spending on sanitation and drinking-water —in some countries, near 90 percent. And even with cost-effective innovative approaches, as in community sanitation, public commitment is too low. Refocusing assistance is called for, alongside mobilizing more domestic and private resources for scaling up investments. Although the gap in aid allocations between high HDI and low HDI countries is smaller for water and sanitation than for low-carbon energy, the disparities are still large. Part of the constraint relates to capacity, though more predictable donor funding would help.[92]

BOX 5.2
Innovative financing schemes for water and sanitation

A review of financing schemes to promote investment in water and sanitation reveals some promising new avenues. Some schemes supported by donors encourage private investment. Indonesia's Master Meter Scheme uses microcredit to connect the urban poor to water, and the Coca-Cola Company and the United States Agency for International Development sponsored the installation of locally made rope pumps in Zinder, Niger. In Kenya an innovative combination of commercial finance (through a microcredit institution) and a subsidy that ties public funding to achieving specified goals has improved water supply and connected poor households to piped water.

Other financing schemes include blended grants and repayable financing (as funded by the World Bank in Senegal and the European Investment Bank in Mozambique), revolving funds for water and sanitation (as funded by the World Bank, Denmark and Finland in Viet Nam and by UFUNDIKO, a small nongovernmental organization, in Tanzania) and pooled funds (as in Tamil Nadu, India), which disbursed bond-issue funds to municipalities as subloans. Market-based finance is also becoming more common. For instance, several US cities and Johannesburg, South Africa, have used municipal bonds to fund water infrastructure.

Source: Nelson 2011; Coca-Cola Company 2010; World Bank 2010a; International Water and Sanitation Centre and Netherlands Water Partnership (2009); OECD 2010c.

Social protection

Estimates put global allocations to social protection at a sizeable 17 percent of GDP.[93] But much of this spending bypasses the most disadvantaged groups. High-income countries spend on average nearly 20 percent of GDP, while low-income countries spend around 4 percent.[94] Clearly, there is enormous scope for increasing the coverage of social protection schemes in the poorest countries, as part of national and global efforts. It makes sense, then, to take these needs into account in discussions on financing the sustainability and equity agenda.

Setting a social protection floor—a set of essential social transfers, in cash and in kind, to provide a minimum income and secure livelihood—is promising. Such programmes need not be expensive. Brazil's Bolsa Familia and Mexico's Oportunidades cost their governments about 0.4 percent of GDP and cover about a fifth of their populations. India's Mahatma Gandhi National Rural Employment Guarantee Act cost about 0.5 percent of GDP in 2009 and benefited 45 million households, about a tenth of the labour force.[95] For several African and Asian countries the International Labour Organization (ILO) estimated in 2008 that a scheme guaranteeing workers 100 days of employment a year could cost less than 1 percent of GDP on average.[96]

The ILO estimates that less than 2 percent of global GDP would provide all the world's poor with a minimum package of social benefits and services—defined as access to basic healthcare, basic education and basic income transfers in case of need.[97] Broadening the scope to include adaptation to climate change by bolstering local resilience and supporting livelihood diversification strategies would cost more.[98] Based on admittedly heroic assumptions, this could increase the cost to a still manageable 2.5 percent of global GDP.[99]

* * *

In sum, the financing challenges loom large, but there is cause for optimism. The priorities for governments around the world are clear:

- Ensure that appropriate institutional and regulatory features are in place to enable scaling up private investments, especially in poorer countries, which have largely missed out on private finance.
- Have all governments re-examine their spending priorities so that sustainability and equity objectives are well reflected in budget allocations.
- Mobilize additional resources to narrow the large gaps in addressing the environmental deprivations facing billions of poor people around the world and to solve the major global collective action problem presented by climate change.
- Ensure that national and community partners have the capability to define policies and budgets and implement programmes that promote and support sustainability, equity and inclusiveness.

Innovations at the global level

Environmental sustainability and equity challenges have major implications at the global level, including for financing and governance, the two key areas addressed here.

Innovative new sources to meet the financing gap

As outlined above, massive new investments are needed to avoid business-as-usual trajectories, but sufficient funding has not been forthcoming, especially for poor countries. And the fiscal outlook is difficult. Many government budgets are under pressure in the wake of the 2008 global financial crisis and given longer term structural problems, while climate change is intensifying the development challenges facing poor countries. Domestic commitments are important, though the scale of the investments needed suggests that more international public funds will be required to attract large additional private funds. It follows that innovative sources of financing are vital, alongside stronger commitments and concrete actions from developed countries.

The prime candidate to close the financing gap is a currency transaction tax. Originally proposed and promoted in the 1994 *Human Development Report* (*HDR*), the idea is increasingly being accepted as a practical

> The prime candidate to close the financing gap is a currency transaction tax

policy option. What is new today is its greater feasibility. The infrastructure for global real-time settlements, introduced after the most recent global financial crisis, makes it straightforward to implement. The foreign exchange settlement infrastructure is now more organized, centralized and standardized (box 5.3). Recent innovations—notably real-time gross settlement and measures to reduce settlement risk—mean that existing systems now capture individual transactions.

The tax can be a simple proportional levy on individual foreign exchange transactions assessed on foreign exchange dealers and collected through existing financial clearing or settlement systems. Because the financial infrastructure is now in place, a currency transaction tax can be implemented relatively quickly and easily. The tax has high-level endorsement from the Leading Group on Innovative Financing for Development.[100] Belgium and France already have legislative frameworks in place for instituting a currency transaction tax. And Brazil, Chile, Japan, Norway and Spain have started to move in that direction. The tax also enjoys broader support from nongovernmental stakeholders, such as the Bill and Melinda Gates Foundation and the Citizen's Coalition for Economic Justice.

Such a tax could address a major anomaly in the financial sector: many of its transactions are not taxed.[101] That, along with the large scale of financial activity, makes a strong case for a small levy on foreign exchange transactions to fund global public goods, such as mitigating and adapting to climate change in poor countries. The incidence of the tax would be progressive, as the countries with larger currency transactions tend to be more developed. The allocation of revenues should also be progressive, as discussed below. Distributional issues, such as a potential minimum tax threshold, need to be considered, so as not to unduly burden individual remittance transfers. Such details need to be examined during design and monitoring.

The tax could also substantially reduce the macroeconomic volatility caused by the high volume of short-term speculative funds flowing through world financial markets.

Appropriately designed and monitored, the tax would allow those who benefit most from globalization to help those who benefit least—and help finance the global public goods that can sustain globalization.

The tax rate should not impose too heavy a burden but should reduce speculative flows. Estimates of revenue generation depend on, among other things, assumptions about the effect of the tax on trading volumes. In updated analysis prepared for this Report, the North–South Institute estimates that a tax of 0.005 percent would yield around $40 billion a year.[102] The revenue potential is thus huge. The Center for Global Development estimates donor spending on global public goods at around $11.7 billion in 2009. The bulk of the spending is on UN peacekeeping; excluding this important function lowers global public good expenditure to about $2.7 billion.[103] The currency transaction tax would mobilize nearly 15 times as much each year. Even a unilateral currency transaction tax (limited to the Euro) could mobilize $4.2–$9.3 billion in additional financing. Clearly, then, a currency transaction tax could, even under very

BOX 5.3

The currency transaction tax: newfound feasibility

Today, there are many ways to trade foreign currency in the wholesale market: on an exchange, online, through a human or electronic broker or by phone or fax. But there are just two ways to make the payments to settle a deal. One is by sending both payments to a continuous linked settlement bank, which matches and exchanges them simultaneously. The other is by sending them to the Society for Worldwide Interbank Financial Communication (SWIFT), where they are matched and then forwarded to the correspondent banks in the two currency-issuing countries. These two highly organized clearing and settlement systems are the core infrastructure of today's foreign exchange industry. They keep detailed records of nearly every foreign exchange transaction around the world.

How would a tax work? SWIFT keeps itemized records of the details of global foreign exchange trading activity in the world's frequently traded currencies as it clears or settles foreign exchange transactions. A copy of the transaction details would be sent to the usual tax authority or its agent. The authority would calculate the tax due from each trader and add it to a running tally. Traders would pay their currency transaction tax obligations to the tax authority periodically.

Incentive and compliance issues are surmountable. It is unlikely that trading banks would opt out of SWIFT's communications platform to avoid paying the tax. Doing so would cost more than the tax. Further, there are only a few large traders in the wholesale market for foreign exchange, so they could easily be audited for tax purposes. There would be no intrusion on individual privacy, because the currency tax would be assessed on the large banks, investment funds and corporations participating in the wholesale foreign exchange market.

Source: Schmidt and Bhushan 2011.

conservative assumptions, dramatically scale up global public good expenditure.

This is also an occasion to reconsider a broader financial transaction tax. The International Monetary Fund (IMF) recently pointed out that many G-20 countries have already implemented some form of financial transaction tax.[104] While the revenue potential depends on the tax's design and the response of traders, a broad-based, low-rate financial transactions tax of 0.01–0.05 percent could generate nearly €200 billion a year at the European level and $650 billion at the global level.[105] Other estimates suggest that in the United States alone the tax could raise more than 1 percent of GDP (about $150 billion in 2011), even with very substantial reductions in trading volume.[106]

Taxes on currency and financial transactions would not have prevented the recent financial crisis, which originated in the United States and spread to the rest of the world. But in addition to the revenue potential, such taxes are tools for discouraging the short-term reckless behaviour that drove the global economy into crisis.

Transaction taxes need not be the only instrument to close the financing gap. Using the IMF's Special Drawing Rights (SDRs) for innovative financing and climate change adaptation is another avenue worth exploring.[107] Monetizing part of the IMF's surplus could raise up to $75 billion at little or no budgetary cost for contributing governments.[108] IMF analysis of the possible role of SDRs as seed finance for a new global green fund suggests that issuing additional SDRs and other reserve assets could mobilize $100 billion a year by 2020. The SDRs have the added appeal of acting as a monetary rebalancing instrument; demand is expected to come from emerging market economies looking to diversify their reserve holdings. Because the SDR is not a sovereign currency, it would not be subject to the currency transaction tax, thus avoiding double taxation.

Several public and private sources could also be tapped to close the financing gap. Already, innovative financing instruments—such as the Clean Technology Fund and the Strategic Climate Fund—are blending funding from multilateral development banks, governments, climate finance instruments and the

private sector. They have raised an additional $3.7 billion for development and can leverage substantial additional funds.[109] Considerable private funding has also been leveraged.

Ensuring equity and voice in governing and in access to finance

Bridging the gap separating policy-makers, negotiators and decision-makers from the people most vulnerable to environmental degradation requires closing the accountability gap in global environmental governance. Accountability alone cannot meet the challenge, but it is fundamental for building a socially and environmentally effective global governance system that delivers for people.

Private resources are critical, but because most financial flows into the energy sector, for example, are private, the greater risks and lower returns of some regions of the world affect the patterns of flows. In the absence of reform, access to financing across countries will remain unevenly distributed, and indeed add to existing inequalities.[110] This underlines the importance of ensuring that flows of public investments are equitable and create conditions to attract future private flows.

Failing to ensure equitable access to climate finance would also constrain the capacity of industries to capitalize on low-cost opportunities to improve efficiency and reduce greenhouse gas emissions cost-effectively. The building sector, for example, could not take advantage of cost-effective energy efficiency improvements. This is particularly important over the next 5–10 years as low-income countries invest in long-lived power generation and urban infrastructure. Limited access to climate financing would lock these countries into high-emission development paths, constraining the world's capacity to limit increases in global temperature.

The implications are clear. Principles of equity should guide and encourage international financial flows. Support for institution building should help developing countries establish appropriate policies and incentives. And the associated governance mechanisms for international public financing must allow for voice and social accountability.

Any truly transformational effort to scale up climate change mitigation and adaptation will require blending resources—domestic and international, private and public, and grant and loan. To facilitate both equitable access and efficient use of international financial flows, this Report advocates empowering national stakeholders to blend climate finance at the country level.

Bringing about long-term, efficient results and accountability to local populations and partners will require four sets of tools (figure 5.3):

- Low-emission, climate-resilient strategies —to align human development, equity and climate change goals.
- Public-private partnerships—to catalyse capital from businesses and households.
- Climate deal-flow facilities—for equitable access to international public finance.
- Coordinated implementation and monitoring, reporting and verification systems.

Most climate control activities today are discrete and incremental mitigation or adaptation projects. But broader strategic approaches are also needed. Low-emission, climate-resilient development strategies could prove a critical institutional innovation for incorporating equity and climate change into development planning. Involving all stakeholders, such strategies can help manage uncertainty by identifying development trajectories resilient to a range of climate outcomes. These strategies can incorporate priorities for win-win mitigation and adaptation initiatives. And they can assess the policy changes and capacity development required to implement them.[111] A comprehensive strategy to attract investments in green and equitable development must come to grips with the large distortions in energy markets—in favourable tax treatment, regulatory privileges and legacy monopolies. The investment climate can be improved by reducing risks (say, through greater policy predictability or guarantee instruments) and increasing rewards (say, through tax credits).[112]

Strategies need to involve municipalities: since cities account for the majority of greenhouse gas emissions, actions by subnational governments will be key to reining in temperature change. This calls for coordinated

planning and robust collaboration with a variety of traditional and new development actors, including national and regional technical centres of expertise, the private sector, communities and civil society organizations.

A second key institutional innovation could be market-making public-private partnerships. These partnerships aim at market transformation and apply to both climate change mitigation (renewable energy technologies, energy efficiency appliances and the like) and adaptation (weather indices, climate-resilient agricultural commodities, climate-resilient buildings and the like). They would build on recent experience but go beyond traditional service delivery and infrastructure to bring together the potentially diverging interests of a wide range of stakeholders and blend various sources of finance. The public policies and measures underlying such partnerships will need to provide incentives and support to improve the risk and reward profile of climate investments, consistent with national development goals.

The third set of tools involves establishing climate deal-flow facilities to help national and subnational project proponents assemble bankable projects and tap international public climate finance. Carbon finance, as in the Clean Development Mechanism, has shown that limited capacity to prepare bankable projects can be a major barrier to catalysing private climate finance in many locations. Similarly, the complexity of application and reporting requirements for international public funds makes it difficult to determine eligibility and appropriateness, posing obstacles to use, monitoring and evaluation. So, the climate deal-flow facilities should enhance the capacity of countries to gain access to international sources of both private and public finance.

The fourth set of tools in the proposed framework for equitable and efficient climate finance addresses the need for coordinated implementation and reporting. Climate finance on a scale sufficient to rein in temperature changes to 2°C demands unprecedented efforts to implement, monitor, verify and report—over several decades, with multiple actors, diverse sets of actions and a variety of

FIGURE 5.3

Key elements in transforming climate financing efforts

Low-emission, climate-resilient development strategies

Market-making public-private partnerships

Climate deal-flow facility

Implementation and reporting instruments

Source: Adapted from Glemarec and others 2010.

financing sources. National climate funds can facilitate the operational blending and monitoring of domestic and international, private and public, and grant and loan resources—essential to ensuring domestic accountability and positive distributional effects.

Enabling universal access to energy

Central to moving to universal access in energy is addressing the barriers to investing in clean energy. While potentially earning an attractive return, most technologies for renewable energy and energy efficiency require substantial upfront investment. Even if offset by lower operational costs, these upfront capital costs can be prohibitive. The financial constraints that businesses and consumers face are often more severe than those implied by national discount rates or long-term interest rates. And they are usually compounded by behavioural, technical, regulatory or administrative barriers. Take wind power: no country will attract private investment if independent power producers face barriers in access to grids, uncertain licensing processes, limited local expertise or lack of long-term price guarantees.

Achieving universal energy access requires a response strategy on multiple levels from various partners—here again, there is no one-size-fits-all solution. National and local governments must set the stage for other players ranging from civil society and the private sector at the national and subnational levels to global finance and energy companies.

It is time to launch a high-profile global initiative for universal access to energy in developing countries. It could have two parts: first, a global advocacy and awareness-raising campaign; second, investments on the ground through dedicated support to sectoral approaches in clean energy. Together, they can kick-start a shift from incremental to transformative change.

A global campaign to promote a participatory and informed initiative, key in both donor and developing countries, can harness existing capacities for advocacy, analysis, planning, knowledge management and communications.

The time is right for such a campaign. The UN General Assembly has designated 2012 as the International Year of Sustainable Energy For All while the Rio+20 conference will provide a unique opportunity to define a global approach for universal access to energy, bringing together the energy, green economy and climate agendas. This global approach can then be developed through regional and national energy dialogues.

Complementing the campaign, support to developing countries for climate-resilient development strategies could identify barriers, benefits and impacts for disadvantaged groups—and create favourable investment conditions. Major market failures heighten the importance of public policies to attract private finance. Such policies can improve clean energy investment risk-reward profiles by reducing risks (stable regulatory context, local supply of expertise, streamlined administrative arrangements, guarantee instruments and the like) and by increasing rewards (premium prices, tax credits and the like). For example, a commercially unattractive renewable energy investment could become profitable by guaranteeing independent power producers access to the grid and a price premium.

Support from the Universal Energy Access Initiative could include assistance for determining priority energy access technologies, ideally in the context of formulating a low-emission, climate-resilient strategy; identifying key barriers to technology diffusion; selecting an appropriate mix of policy instruments to remove barriers; and accessing funding options to deploy the selected mix of policies.

*   *   *

This Report calls for a new vision that jointly considers equity and environmental sustainability. It elaborates ways to attain synergies between the two objectives that are crucial for shaping our understanding of how to move forward and guide policy. Taking up this challenge will expand choices for people today and in the future—the hallmark of human development.

> It is time to launch a high-profile global initiative for universal access to energy in developing countries

Notes

Chapter 1

1. UN 2002, 2010.
2. Sen 2003: 330.
3. Weikard (1999) as cited in Scholtes (2011).
4. Scholtes 2011.
5. 1990 *HDR*: 38 (UNDP–HDRO 1990; see inside back cover for a list of *HDR*s).
6. 1994 *HDR*: 19 (UNDP–HDRO 1994; see inside back cover for a list of *HDR*s).
7. 2010 *HDR*: 2; emphasis added (UNDP–HDRO 2010; see inside back cover for a list of *HDR*s).
8. WCED 1987: 57–59; emphasis added.
9. Solow 1973.
10. USEIA 2008.
11. Commission on Sustainable Development 1997, paragraph 12.
12. Baumol, Litan and Schramm 2007.
13. FAO 1996.
14. UNDESA 2011a.
15. Brown and others 2001.
16. On strong sustainability, see Barbier, Markandya and Pearce (1990) and Ross (2009).
17. Daly 2005.
18. UNEP 2011; OECD 2010a.
19. UNDESA 2011a.
20. Perrings and Pearce 1994; Barbier, Burgess and Folke 1994.
21. See Nordhaus (2004), who estimates a slowdown of 0.86 percent a year.
22. Babbage 2010.
23. See Weitzman (2009a), Stern and Taylor (2007), IPCC (1997), and Dietz and Neumayer (2007).
24. Weitzman 2009b.
25. This stands in contrast to the Stern Review's proposal of a long-term discount rate of 1–2 percent (Stern 2007), itself much lower than commonly used rates of 4–5 percent.
26. Solow 1993: 168.
27. Economists have defined sustainability in terms of living standards, consumption or utility. Consumption-based definitions are favoured by advocates of weak sustainability, such as Dasgupta and Heal (1974), Hartwick (1977) and Solow (1974). Utility-based definitions, such as that offered by Neumayer (2010a), consider a path to be sustainable if people become progressively more efficient at attaining greater utility.
28. Anand and Sen 1994, 2000; Sen 2010.
29. The concept originated in the work of Adams (1965), Homans (1961) and Blau (1964).
30. Rawls 1971.
31. The priority of poverty eradication in the search for sustainable development has been reaffirmed in several UN declarations, including the 1992 Rio Declaration on Environment and Development (UN 1992), the resolution on the Programme for the Further Implementation of Agenda 21 (UN 1997) and the 2002 Johannesburg Declaration (UN 2002).
32. Anand and Sen (2000: 2,038), emphasis in original.
33. Of course, some policies can be neutral in impacts, but these are omitted for simplicity.
34. See Brown (2003).
35. A caveat arises for solutions not in quadrant 1 because major improvements in one dimension cause small deteriorations in the other. Would any solution that improves both dimensions slightly be preferred? It can be argued that a policy that improves both dimensions should be preferred only if it benefits groups that are objectively worse off. In other words, a policy that enhances sustainability but worsens equity should be preferred only if the most disadvantaged future generations that will benefit from the change would have been worse off than the poorest today.

Chapter 2

1. 2010 *HDR*: chapter 2 (UNDP–HDRO 2010; see inside back cover for a list of *HDR*s).
2. On this issue, see UNECE (2011) for a recent review.
3. The ratio of per capita greenhouse gas emissions in very high to those in low, medium and high HDI countries was 3.7 in 1990 and 3.3 in 2005. Underlying the small drop in the ratio, total greenhouse gas emissions have grown much faster in developing countries, partly because of their faster population growth.
4. The differences are 4.4 times for carbon dioxide emissions, 1.3 times for methane and 2.1 times for nitrous oxide.
5. The strong correlations between both the levels and changes in environmental impacts and the HDI also suggest that the link between these two phenomena has not changed much over time. This contrasts, for example, with life expectancy and income, where levels but not changes are correlated, indicating changes over time in the underlying processes. See 2010 *HDR* (UNDP–HDRO 2010; see inside back cover for a list of *HDR*s) and Georgiadis, Pineda and Rodríguez (2010).
6. Grossman and Krueger 1995.
7. Hughes, Kuhn and others 2011.
8. Grossman and Kruger (1995) suggested a peak, in most cases, before a country reached a per capita income of $8,000 (in 1985 dollars). Other studies have identified different thresholds.
9. See statistical table 6. Gross national income (GNI) per capita data are from the World Bank (http://data.worldbank.org/indicator/NY.GNP.PCAP.PP.CD).
10. See statistical table 6.
11. An exogenous variable is independent of the state of other variables in a causal model—that is, its value is determined by factors outside the causal system examined (Wooldridge 2003).
12. Doubling net forest depletion as a percentage of GNI increases overall inequality 2 percent (or 0.42 percentage point), while doubling particulate emission damage as a percentage of GNI increases overall inequality by a massive 26 percent (or 5.6 percentage points).
13. The number of years since women received the formal right to vote and the contraceptive prevalence rate are instruments for the Gender Inequality Index (GII). In particular, a 10 percent increase in gender inequality (measured by the GII) leads to a 1.13 point (or 150 percent) increase in net forest depletion as a percentage of GNI. For details on the method and results, see Fuchs and Kehayova (2011).
14. The IHDI is a measure of the average level of human development in a society once inequality is taken into account. It captures the HDI of the average person in society, which is less than the aggregate HDI when there is inequality in the distribution of health, education and income. Under perfect equality, the HDI and IHDI are equal; the greater the difference between the two, the greater the inequality. See Alkire and Foster (2010).
15. As we reviewed in last year's report, global inequality across people is an important measure, but most studies are limited to income. Almost all agree that inequality is high, though there is no consensus on recent trends (Anand and Segal 2008). Sala-i-Martin (2006), providing estimates for 1970–2000 by integrating the income distributions of 138 countries, found that mean per capita incomes had risen, but inequality had not. Other studies—such as Milanovic (2009)—concluded the opposite. Still others—such as Bourguignon and Morrisson (2002)—found no change.
16. Pradhan, Sahn and Younger 2003.
17. O'Donnell and others 2008.
18. This is consistent with earlier studies (for example, Neumayer 2003 and Becker, Philipson and Soares 2003). Becker, Philipson and Soares monetize life expectancy and create a measure of "full" income—which rose 140 percent in developed countries from 1965 to 1995 and 192 percent in developing countries.
19. 2010 *HDR*: 32 (UNDP–HDRO 2010; see inside back cover for a list of *HDR*s). Other studies have highlighted similar points; see, for example, McGillivray (2011).
20. According to the 2010 *HDR* (UNDP–HDRO 2010; see inside back cover for a list of *HDR*s), primary completion rates have risen from 84 percent in 1991 to 94 percent today. Expected years of schooling have also risen—from 9 years in 1980 to 11 years today.
21. Hertz and others 2007.
22. For example, in a study over 1960–1995, Checchi (2001) found that inequality in years of schooling

remained almost constant at low levels in Organisation for Economic Co-operation and Development countries, despite increases in average education attainment.

23 Atkinson, Piketty and Saez 2011.

24 HDRO calculations based on data from Milanovic (2011). We include a group of 29 developed countries for which we have income inequality observations for 1990, 1995, 2000 and 2005.

25 OECD 2011a.

26 OECD 2010a.

27 HDRO calculations based on data from Milanovic (2011) and Lopez-Calva and Lustig (2010: 10).

28 Lopez-Calva and Lustig 2010.

29 OECD 2010a.

30 Hughes, Irfan and others 2011.

31 Not only does the logarithmic term on income contribute mechanically to such slowing, so does the inevitable slowing of rising years of formal education, of advances in life expectancy in better off countries, and of convergence of low- and middle-income countries as their health and education gaps with rich countries narrow.

32 Environmental risks are modeled with the Environmental Risks Scenario, developed by Hughes, Irfan and others (2011). Inequality and insecurity factors are modeled with the Security First Scenario, developed by the United Nations Environment Programme (UNEP 2007). This involves socioeconomic and environmental stresses, economic and personal insecurity, significant domestic and global inequality, high levels of protectionism, barriers to migration, and more militarism and conflict.

33 Global warming potential measures the relative radioactive effect of a given substance. For the latest estimates, see IPCC (2007: chapter 2).

34 Of the scientists publishing most actively in the field, 98 percent support the idea that climate change is caused by human activity (Anderegg and others 2010). While some studies have pointed to mistakes in the Intergovernmental Panel on Climate Change reports (Khilyuk and Chilingar 2006; Church and others 2008), none has seriously questioned its key conclusions.

35 Raupach and others 2007.

36 Aichele and Felbermayr 2010; Grether and Mathys 2009.

37 Carbon dioxide can remain in the atmosphere for thousands of years, unlike methane, which lasts about 12 years, and nitrous oxide, which lasts about 114 years. See Archer and Brovkin (2008) and IPCC (2007).

38 See the Climate Analysis Indicators Tool of the World Resources Institute (http://cait.wri.org).

39 Areas above the 45th parallel north and below the 45th parallel south experienced a 2.66°C increase in average temperature for November–April during the 2000s over that during 1951–1980; areas between the coordinates saw a 0.66°C increase.

40 Cooper 2008.

41 Very high HDI countries had a more than 2 percent decline in precipitation.

42 For example, estimates show that rainfall is very likely (90 percent probability) to increase in high latitude areas and likely (66 percent probability) to fall in most subtropical regions and to increase in variability in equatorial areas (IPCC 2007; Dore 2005).

43 Christensen and others 2007.

44 The Intergovernmental Panel on Climate Change (IPCC 2007) projects increases of 0.18–0.59 metre under six scenarios, while other studies suggest that the increase could be as much as 2 metres. Ice thinning is expected to ultimately break up ice shelves, which is likely to accelerate sea level rise (Gregory and Huybrechts 2006; Jevrejeva and others 2006; Thomas and others 2004).

45 Anthoff 2010.

46 Wheeler 2011.

47 Vankoningsveld and others 2008.

48 Dasgupta and others 2009.

49 These figures refer to climatological, hydrological and meteorological natural disasters, as estimated from the Centre for Research on the Epidemiology of Disasters Emergency Events Database: International Disaster Database. An event is classified as a disaster if it meets at least one of the following criteria: 10 or more people died, 100 or more people were affected, a state of emergency was declared or international assistance was requested. But data may not be fully consistent across countries. Population growth increases the number of people affected and thus the number of the events classified as disasters. See also Neumayer and Barthel (2011) on the effects of awareness and reporting bias.

50 IPCC 2007. Changes in atmospheric moisture affect moisture absorption capacity, leading to a greater probability of intense precipitation and associated natural disasters.

51 Knutson and others 2010.

52 The numbers could also reflect people's greater exposure to natural hazards (for example, settlement in previously uninhabited areas) and increased vulnerability.

53 Wood, Sebastian and Scherr 2000.

54 Two UN bodies—the Food and Agriculture Organization and the Secretariat of the United Nations Convention to Combat Desertification—produce estimates, but their approach has been criticized in academic circles; see Veron, Paruelo and Oesterheld (2006).

55 Hanasaki and others (2008); UNEP (2009).

56 World Water Assessment Programme 2009.

57 Ball 2001.

58 These shares are the total land area–weighted average for each HDI group.

59 Estimates differ by method and data coverage: assessments based on satellite images in 2002 indicate 23 percent lower deforestation rates than those reported in FAO (2001). Source data from official or informal institutions are often inaccurate and incomplete, and detailed information is lacking on forest composition, maturity, disturbance, canopy cover and quality. See Grainger (2010). Some countries, such as Brazil, have made major achievements in reducing deforestation (www.undp.org/latinamerica/biodiversity-superpower/).

60 See Meyfroidt, Rudel and Lambin (2010). Bhutan and El Salvador have reportedly used more land abroad than they have reforested within their boundaries.

61 Gan and McCarl 2007.

62 Mayer and others 2005, 2006.

63 Würtenberger, Koellner and Binder 2005.

64 In 2007 annual average per capita consumption was 28.7 kilograms in developed countries and 9.5 kilograms in least developed countries (FAO 2010a).

65 Data on current catch are from FAO Fisheries and Aquaculture Information and Statistics Service 2009; sustainable yield is from FAO (2005).

66 FAO 2010a.

67 FAO 2010a.

68 For instance, Peru's introduction of individual fishing rights over its anchovy fishery, the *anchoveta*, is cited as key to improving the sustainability of its fishing stock (Fréon and others 2008; Schreiber forthcoming).

69 Grossman and Krueger 1995.

70 McGranahan and others 2001.

71 OECD 2010b.

72 Bettencourt and others 2007.

73 Dodman 2009.

74 Lehrer 2010.

75 See www.unesco.org/water/wwap/facts_figures/basic_needs.shtml.

76 Tachamo and others 2009; Pepper 2007.

77 Urban pollution is defined as suspended particulates less than 10 microns in diameter (PM10), expressed in micrograms per cubic metre (World Bank 2011a).

78 Calculations are based on urban population-weighted averages.

79 See UNDESA (2006).

80 The thresholds for greenhouse gases are total accumulated emissions over the next 50 years likely to keep temperature change within 2°C (1,678 gigatonnes), no deforestation and global fresh water withdrawals of 5,000 cubic kilometres a year, which we expressed in per capita terms for our analysis. There is considerable uncertainty and estimated variance around these thresholds in the scientific community. For more information on global environmental thresholds, see, for example Rockström and others (2009) and Meinshausen and others (2009). Greenhouse gas emissions combine 2005–2007 averages for carbon dioxide and 2005 data, the latest available, for methane, nitrous oxide and other greenhouse gases. Forest data from 2000 and 2010 are used to calculate deforestation. Total water withdrawals are based on averages from the 2000s, and data on improved water access are for 2008. Data on air pollution are averages over 2006–2008. Thresholds for the local impacts are regional medians. See statistical table 6 for data sources.

81 The earliest observation from the 1990s and latest from the 2000s were used to calculate changes over time.

82 However, Costa Rica is among the few countries in Latin America that has experienced an increase in income inequality during the last decade despite the growth boom that preceded the global economic crisis of 2008. Inequality in health and education fell over the same period.

83 UNEP 2010.

Chapter 3

1 Ash and others 2010; Brulle and Pellow 2006; Pastor 2007; Sze and London 2008; United Church of Christ 1987.

2 When the plant exploded in 1957, nearby ethnic Russians were evacuated and resettled, but the Tatar people were left to suffer the effects of contamination (Agyeman, Ogneva-Himmelberger and Campbell 2009).

3 The shares of the population with access to an improved water source and improved sanitation are Millennium Development Goal indicators relating to environmental sustainability (goal 7). A household is considered deprived if it relies on dung, wood or charcoal for cooking; if it lacks access to clean drinking water (or if the water is more than 30 minutes away); and if it lacks improved sanitation (or shares it with other households). See Alkire and Santos (2010).

4 Since last year's *HDR*, these estimates were updated for 19 countries and presented for the first time for an additional 5. Countries with MPI data include 11 in the Arab States, 9 in East Asia and the Pacific, 23 in Europe and Central Asia, 18 in Latin America and the Caribbean, 5 in South Asia and 37 in Sub-Saharan Africa. There are 103 countries that have complete data on environmental deprivations—the descriptive analysis focuses on these countries. Data for the Arab States are not given because low poverty levels render the results potentially unreliable.

5 These aggregates are for the 2000s; the survey dates span 2000–2010. Population data correspond to each country's survey year here and in the following analysis.

6 The MPI reflects deprivations across three dimensions, each weighted equally, and 10 indicators. For more details, see *Technical note 4*.

7 However, low poverty may conceal poverty that exists subnationally. In Ghana, for instance, poverty is 10 times higher in Greater Accra than in Northern Ghana, and other countries also exhibit sharp area-based differences. And in Europe and Central Asia, groups such as Roma are likely to be much more deprived than national poverty measures would suggest.

8 UNICEF Madagascar Water Sanitation and Hygiene 2007.

9 The exercise was also carried out with controls for HDI group and regional fixed effects, but they were not jointly significant and thus were dropped. The total sample consisted of 73 country-year observations. Fifty-two country-year observations were not included in the exercise: those whose poverty was based on lower or upper bounds (see Alkire and Santos 2010), those missing an environmental indicator and those whose MPI value was less than 0.032 because the small number of poor people in these countries (less than 8.5 percent) makes the results potentially unreliable. The 30 countries missing nonenvironmental indicators were retained, but the analysis controlled for their absence.

10 De Oliveira 2008.

11 Hall and Lobina 2008.

12 Da Costa, Cohen and Schaeffer 2007; De Oliveira and Laan 2010.

13 UN Habitat 2003

14 Milton and others 2010; UNICEF 2010; Argos and others 2010.

15 UNDP Water Governance Programme 2010.

16 UNDP Water Governance Programme 2010.

17 IMF 2004; statistical table 5; see also Djibouti on the Austro-Arab Chamber of Commerce's Arab Countries Profile (www.aacc.at).

18 See IDA at work: Nepal (http://go.worldbank.org/TXVG8IJ8L0).

19 Peru Ministry of Housing, Construction and Santiation 2006.

20 IADB 2008.

21 Meier and others 2010.

22 World Water Assessment Programme 2006.

23 The Spearman correlation is .6 for temperature anomalies (1951–1980, compared with 2000–2008). When we consider only those statistically significant changes, which could be interpreted as suggestive of climate change, the result is nearly unchanged.

24 A weak negative correlation disappears altogether when we exclude Indonesia from the sample and when we consider only statistically significant changes over time for the full sample.

25 For a recent review, see Skoufias, Rabassa and Olivieri (2011).

26 Environmental risk factors include indoor smoke from solid fuel use; outdoor air pollution; inadequate water, sanitation and hygiene; solar ultraviolet radiation; climate change; lead; mercury; occupational carcinogens; occupational airborne particulates; and second-hand smoke (Prüss-Üstün and others 2008).

27 World Bank 2008a.

28 Prüss-Üstün and others 2008.

29 Prüss-Üstün and others 2008. Estimates are based on 2004 WHO country health statistics. The use of solid fuels is a reliable indicator of exposure to indoor air pollution, but over time, as improved stoves and decent ventilation come into widespread use, the two will not be as closely correlated.

30 Between 1990 and 2005 the percentage of urban households with access to gas increased from 19 percent to 82 percent (Vennemo and others 2009).

31 Data based on 2004 WHO burden of disease data.

32 Smith, Mehta and Maeusezahl-Feuz 2004.

33 Shandra, Shandra and London 2008.

34 Correlation = .82, $p < .05$.

35 Fieldwork by the Oxford Poverty and Human Development Initiative (www.ophi.org.uk/policy/multidimensional-poverty-index/mpi-case-studies/).

36 Fieldwork by Indrajit Roy (www.ophi.org.uk/policy/multidimensional-poverty-index/mpi-case-studies/).

37 Kjellstrom and others 2006.

38 Riojas-Rodríguez and others 2006.

39 Blacksmith Institute 2007.

40 On Hong Kong Special Administrative Region, China, see Wong and others (2008, 2010); on Shanghai, see Kan and others (2008), as cited in HEI (2010).

41 Friends of the Earth 2004.

42 Mitchell and Dorling 2003; Brainard and others 2002.

43 Kruize and Bouwman 2004.

44 Kockler 2005.

45 Viel and others 2010; Laurian 2008.

46 UN Water 2010a. Data are from Prüss-Üstün and others (2008).

47 Prüss-Üstün and Corvalán 2006.

48 UN Water 2010a. Data are from Prüss-Üstün and others (2008).

49 Prüss-Üstün and Corvalán 2006.

50 Prüss-Üstün and others 2008.

51 World Bank 2008b.

52 UN Water 2010a.

53 For example, sexual violence can result when women have to relieve themselves in the open after nightfall (UN Water 2006).

54 Costello and others 2009.

55 Lindsay and Martens 1998.

56 Hales and others 2002.

57 Checkley and others 2000, 2004; Speelmon and others 2000; Lama and others 2004.

58 Nelson and others 2009.

59 Green, King and Morrison 2009; Galloway McLean 2010. King, Smith and Gracey (2009) review the literature.

60 2010 *HDR*: statistical table 13 (UNDP–HDRO 2010; see inside back cover for a list of *HDR*s).

61 Independent Evaluation Group 2008.

62 Daka and Ballet 2011.

63 Khandker and others 2009a.

64 Khandker and others 2009b.

65 Flora and Findis 2007.

66 Nankhuni and Findeis 2004.

67 Senbet 2010.

68 Ndiritu and Nyangena 2010.

69 Walker 2010.

70 FAO (2010b) data. "Economically active population" refers to the number of people constituting the labour supply and refers to all employed and unemployed people (including those seeking work for the first time).

71 World Resources Institute 2005. Aside from small-scale agriculture, the collection of wild foods, materials and medicines are the main sources of environmental income.

72 Pattanayak and Sills 2001.

73 Vincent 2011; UNFPA 2009.

74 IWGIA 2008.

75 Sobrevila 2008.

76 Sobrevila 2008.

77 World Bank 2008c.

78 Galloway McLean 2010.

79 Hertel and Rosch 2010. For a review, see Nellemann and others (2009).

80 Nellemann and others 2009.

81 Millennium Ecosystem Assessment 2005.

82 Fraser and others 2010.

83 Yonghuan and others 2007.

84 2007/2008 *HDR* (UNDP–HDRO 2008; see inside back cover for a list of *HDR*s).

85 World Bank 2009.

86 Lobell, Schlenker and Costa-Roberts 2011.

87 Lobell and others 2008.

88 Nelson and others 2010.

89 Thornton and others 2009.

90 The Food and Agriculture Organization estimates that if gender access to productive resources were equal, yields would increase 20–30 percent and agricultural output would rise 2.5–4 percent on average (FAO 2010b: 5).

91 Nellemann and others 2009.

92 FAO 2010b.

93 Ulimwengu and Ramadan 2009.

94 Hortol, Burko and Loboll 2010.

95 Ivanic and Martin 2008.

96 Cranfield, Preckel and Hertel 2007.

97 Jacoby, Rabassa and Skoufias forthcoming.

98 See www.fao.org/forestry/28811/en/.

99 FAO 2011.

100 Agarwal 2010b: 37; FAO 2010b: 16.

101 Mayers 2007.

102 Vedeld and others 2004: meta-study examining 54 case studies (33 in Africa).

103 Mitra and Mishra 2011.

104 Yemiru and others 2010.

105 Based on surveys covering 2002–2008 (Volker and Waible 2010). Similar findings are reached by Pattanayak and Sills (2001) for Brazil and McSweeney (2004) and Takasaki, Barham and Coomes (2004) for Honduras.

106 Agarwal 2010b.

107 Arnold, Kohlin and Persson 2006.

108 FAO 2010a.

109 Allison and others 2009.

110 Allison and others 2005. See also Allison and others (2009).

111 Secretariat of the Pacific Community 2011.

112 AUSAid and UNDP Pacific Centre 2008.

113 Cinner, Daw and McClanahan (2009), a small scale study of 434 households, from 9 coastal villages, from which there were 141 fishers.

114 Secretariat of the Pacific Community 2011.

115 Cheung and others 2009.

116 Iftikhar 2003. Afifi and Warner 2008; Boano, Zetter and Morris 2008.

117 See, for instance, Miguel, Satyanath and Sergenti (2004), Hendrix and Glaser (2005), Boano, Zetter and Morris (2008) and Burke and others (2010).

118 Calculated on the basis of Demographic and Health Survey and Multiple Indicator Cluster Survey data, most recent year available since 2000.

119 These surveys are available for only a small number of countries because they are expensive and difficult to conduct. The questionnaires differ, so the resulting data are illustrative rather than strictly comparable.

120 Agarwal 2010b: 36, table 2.1.

121 Koolwal and Van de Walle 2010.

122 Kramarae and Spender 2000.

123 Ilahi and Grimard 2000.

124 Wodon and Ying 2010.

125 Blackden and Wodon 2006.

126 To estimate the economic benefits of improvements in water supply, Hutton, Haller and Bartram (2006) assume that expanding access to water supply would save 30 minutes for each household per day.

127 See www.sidym2006.com/eng/eng_doc_interes.asp.

128 Boano and others 2008.

129 UNHCR 2002: 12.

130 Marchiori and others 2011.

131 2009 HDR: chapter 4 (UNDP–HDRO 2009; see inside back cover for a list of HDRs).

132 UNEP 2009.

133 Miguel and others 2004; Hendrix and Glaser 2005; Raleigh and Urdal 2008; Fiola 2009; Burke and others 2010.

134 Evans 2010.

135 Homer-Dixon 1994.

136 Collier 2006.

137 Evans 2008; Collier 2007.

138 Boano and others 2008: 22.

139 Bartlett 2008.

140 Wheeler 2011.

141 Boano and others 2008.

142 UN HABITAT Global Urban Indicators database (www.unhabitat.org/stats/). Slum households are defined as lacking in any of the following elements: access to improved water, access to improved sanitation, secure tenure, durable housing or sufficient living area.

143 Asia Summit on Climate Change and Indigenous Peoples 2009; see also the Asia Summit on Climate Change and Indigenous People (www.tebtebba.org/index.php?option=com_content&view=article&id=47&Itemid=58).

144 Rodriguez-Oreggia and others 2010.

145 Brouwer, Akter and Brander 2007.

146 Nishikiori and others 2006. Oxfam International's 2005 report on the 2004 Asian tsunami's impact on women finds a similar pattern for floods.

147 Rose 1999.

148 Neumayer and Plumper 2007.

149 Neumayer and Plumper 2007.

150 Blankespoor and others 2010.

151 The probability of dying as a result of Hurricane Katrina was higher for people who were black and poor (Price 2008; 2007/2008 HDR: 81, box 2.3 [UNDP–HDRO 2008; see inside back cover for a list of HDRs]).

152 Baez, de la Fuente and Santos 2010.

153 Seballos and others 2011.

154 Alderman, Hoddinott and Kinsey (2006). Jensen (2000) found similar results in Côte d'Ivoire.

155 Baez and Santos (2007).

156 Alkire and Roche forthcoming.

157 Christiaensen, Do and Trung 2010.

158 UN 2010.

159 See the Mobile Alliance for Maternal Action (www.mobilemamaalliance.org/issue.html).

160 Engelman 2011.

161 Engelman 2009: 5.

162 UNDESA 2011b.

163 We note, however, that even after the large decline in fertility during the 1970s and 1980s, population-related problems in Bangladesh remain serious, and a sense of complacency has led to less rigorous policy implementation and programme performance in recent years (Khan and Khan 2010).

164 Potts and Marsh 2010: p. 5.

165 United States National Academy of Sciences 1992: 26.

166 O'Neill and others 2010.

167 Wire 2009.

168 Of 6.2 births per woman for Chad, 4.4 for the Democratic Republic of Congo and 7.1 for Niger; see statistical table 4.

169 Mills, Bos and Suzuki 2010.

170 Filmer and Pritchett (2002) find a partial correlation between indicators of fuelwood scarcity and fertility in Pakistan, and Biddlecom, Axinn and Barber (2005) link poorer environmental quality and a greater reliance on public natural resources with higher fertility in Western Chitwan Valley, Nepal. National data for Nepal, however, indicate that environmental scarcity is associated with less demand for children (Loughran and Pritchett 1997).

171 Based on the most recent Demographic and Health Survey data (www.measuredhs.com/accesssurveys/).

172 Engelman 2009.

173 Nugent and Shandra 2009. However, why this result came about was not clear.

174 Norgaard and York 2005.

175 See www.ipu.org/wmn-e/world.htm (accessed 14 July 2011). See statistical table 4 for country and regional data.

176 UNDESA 2010b.

177 Shandra, Shandra and London 2008.

178 Gallup World Poll data (www.gallup.com/se/126848/worldview.aspx) for the most recent year available since 2007.

179 Differences between men and women are significant for perceived severity of climate change and government environmental efforts (at the 95 percent level) and for air quality and emissions policy (99 percent level) but not for satisfaction with water quality.

180 Arora-Jonsson 2011.

181 Agarwal 2009.

182 Walton 2010: 36.

183 Gallagher and Thacker 2008; Bernauer and Koubi 2009.

184 Boyce and others 1999.

185 Torras and Boyce 1998.

186 Torras 2006. Power is assessed using the Gini index, political rights and civil liberties, literacy rate, higher education, population density, Internet user density and female representation in government.

187 The principal components method was used to create an index of power equality using data on income inequality, adult literacy, Internet access, political rights and civil liberties, and political stability. The results are similar to those of Boyce and Torras (2002).

188 All these studies tend to test a variety of outcomes and to use a variety of datasets and specifications.

189 Gallagher and Thacker 2008; see also Torras and Boyce 1998.

190 Li and Reuveny 2006.

191 Neumayer 2002. Battig and Bernauer (2009) found similar results for 1990–2004 in 185 countries: democracy had a positive effect on political commitment to climate change mitigation, but the effects on policy outcomes—emissions levels and trends—were ambiguous.

192 Bernauer and Koubi 2009.

193 The term "countervailing power" was coined by Galbraith (1952).

194 Crotty and Rodgers forthcoming.

195 Fredrikkson and others 2005.

196 Specifically, the results suggest that a 10 percent increase in the strength of NGOs (measured by number of environmental NGOs per capita) lowers sulphur dioxide levels 5.1–9.3 percent, smoke 5.7 percent and heavy particulates 0.8–1.5 percent. Additional estimates suggest an even greater impact after controlling for potential endogeneity and measurement error (Binder and Neumayer 2005).

197 Pellow 2004.

Chapter 4

1 Barrett 2009.

2 Ervin and others 2010.

3 UNDESA 2009; OECD 2010c; IEA 2010; UN Rio Preparatory Committee Meeting 2011 publications (www.uncsd2012.org/rio20/index.php?page=view&type=13&nr=28&menu=24).

4 REN21 2010: 47.

5 Newell, Phillips and Mulvaney 2011.

6 UN 2011.

7 Bernard 2010: 1–2.

8 Dinkelman 2008.

9 Khandker and others 2009b.

10 www.ophi.org.uk/policy/multidimensional-poverty-index/mpi-case-studies/.

11 Zacune 2011.

12 This is compared with the New Policies Scenario, which takes into account countries' broad policy commitments and plans, even where not yet implemented. Under this scenario, through 2035, carbon dioxide emissions rise over 21 percent relative to 2008. Fossil fuels—mainly coal and natural gas—remain dominant in this scenario, but their share of total generation drops from 68 percent to 55 percent, as nuclear and renewable sources expand and the amount of carbon dioxide emitted per unit of electricity generated falls by a third (see IEA and others 2010).

13 Renewable Energy Policy Network for the 21st Century 2011.

14 Under the New Policies Scenario world primary energy demand increases some 36 percent between 2008 and 2035, or 1.2 percent a year. More than 80 percent of electricity demand is from non–Organisation for Economic Co-operation and Development (OECD) countries (IEA and others 2010: 4 and 8).

15 OECD 2010c.

16 On Kenya, Okello (2005); on Guatemala, Bruce and others (2004).

17 AGECC 2010.

18 Renewable Energy Policy Network for the 21st Century 2010.

19 Eberhard and others 2008.

20 Around 80 percent of renewable power generated in 2010 came from hydropower, which also accounted for around a third of new renewable capacity added between 2010 and 2011. Renewable Energy Policy Network for the 21st Century 2010.

21 Geothermal power grew at an annual rate of 4 percent, ethanol production 23 percent, wind power 27 percent and solar photovoltaic 60 percent (Renewable Energy Policy Network for the 21st Century 2011: figure 2).

22 Transparency International 2011.

23 The Pew Charitable Trusts 2010.

24 Glemarec 2011.

25 Kammen, Kapadia and Fripp 2004.

26 Renewable Energy Policy Network for the 21st Century 2010: 9.

27 IEA, UNDP and UNIDO 2010.

28 Burniaux and Chateau 2011.

29 Badiani and Jessoe 2011.

30 World Bank 2009.

31 On Indonesia, Kojima and Bacon (2006); on Iran, Global Subsidies Initiative (2011).

32 Norton Rose Group 2011.

33 United States Environmental Protection Agency 2011. Emissions fell about 6 percent in 2008–2009, due mainly to the economic recession, which led to fuel switching as the price of coal rose and the price of natural gas fell.

34 India Prime Minister's Council on Climate Change 2008; Stern and Taylor 2010.

35 ec.europa.eu/clima/policies/package/index_en.htm.

36 IEA, UNDP and UNIDO 2010.

37 See www.righttowater.info/progress-so-far/. Such legislation exists also in Kazakhstan and in four Western European countries.

38 Leonhardt 2011.

39 Klopfenstein and others 2011.

40 Sarkar and others 2010.

41 See www.undp.org/water/community-water-initiative.shtml.

42 Fishman 2011.

43 World Bank 2007.

44 Duflo and Pande 2007.

45 Dudley and Stolton 2003.

46 Mulongoy and Gidda 2008.

47 www.unicef.org/wash/.

48 Inter-American Development Bank 2010.

49 Nepal Water for Health 2004.

50 Baker and others 2011.

51 Roseinweig 2008.

52 World Bank 2011a.

53 See Perez and others (2011); www.stanford.edu/group/jennadavis/index.html; Lwin Oo 2010; Wilkinson, Moilwa and Taylor 2004.

54 UNDESA 2010b.

55 Engelman 2011.

56 Potts and Marsh 2010.

57 www.unfpa.org/stronger_voices.

58 www.ehproject.org/phe/adra-nepalfinal.html.

59 www.ehproject.org/phe/phe.html.

60 Grandia 2005; Guatemala Instituto Nacional de Estadistica 1999, 2009.

61 Mansour, Mansour and Swesy 2010.

62 Bangladesh Ministry of Health and Family Welfare 2004; UNDESA 2009.

63 Kenya National Coordinating Agency for Population and Development 2008.

64 www.pathfind.org/site/PageServer?pagename=Programs_Vietnam_Projects_HIV_RH_Integration.

65 Roudi 2009.

66 UNFPA 2010.

67 Lopez Carr and Grandia 2011.

68 ITU 2011.

69 The GSMA Development Fund, the Cherie Blaire Foundation for Women and Vital Wave Consulting 2010.

70 www.mobilemamaalliance.org/opportunity.html.

71 For example, Costa Rica went from a deforestation rate of 0.8 percent a year between 1990 and 2000 to a reforestation rate of 0.9 percent in the subsequent decade, and India increased its reforestation rate from of 0.2 percent a year between 1990 and 2000 to 0.5 percent a year between 2000 and 2010 (FAO 2011).

72 Nagendra 2011.

73 Ostrom 1992.

74 Agarwal 2001; Gupte 2004.

75 Agarwal 2010a.

76 Molnar and others 2004.

77 Corrigan and Granziera 2010.

78 UNDP, UNEP, World Bank and WRI 2005.

79 http://us.macmillan.com/horizontalinequalities andconflict.

80 Leisher and others 2010.

81 Leisher and others 2010.

82 UNDP and GEF 2010.

83 Baud and others 2011; Martin 2011.

84 Ervin and others 2010.

85 Ervin and others 2010.

86 Roper, Utz and Harvey 2006.

87 Gupta and Leung 2011.

88 Government of India and UNDP Disaster Risk Management Programme 2008.

89 Chung and others 2002.

90 Duval-Diop and Rose 2008.

91 See Grosh and others (2008) and Tucker (2010).

92 UKaid–DFID 2011.

93 Fuchs 2011.

94 See Arnall and others (2010).

95 Lieuw-Kie-Song 2009.

96 South Africa Department of Environmental Affairs and UNEP 2011.

97 UNDP 2011c.

Chapter 5

1 Frankel and Bosetti 2011.

2 IPCC 2007.

3 Chang and Grabel 2004; Rodrik 2006.

4 See Aghion (2009); Rodrik (2005); Lin 2010.

5 IPCC 2011.

6 UNDP 2011a.

7 Grasso 2004.

8 Even if the importance of distributional aspects is increasingly recognized; see, for example, OECD (2010a).

9 Atkinson and Stiglitz 1980.

10 Oxfam International 2007.

11 Cadman and others 2010.

12 Weitzman 2009a, 2009b; Torras 2011.

13 http://go.worldbank.org/5JP4U774N0.

14 See www.opensecrets.org/influence/index.php.

15 World Bank 2010c.

16 Transparency International 2011.

17 Rodrik, Subramanian and Trebbi 2004; Iyigun and Rodrik 2004.

18 Speck 2010.

19 Willenbockel 2011.

20 OECD 2010c.

21 Ghana Ministry of Energy and World Bank 2004.

22 World Bank 2008b.

23 Wang and others 2011.

24 Gearty 2010. No such right has been recognized in the Universal Declaration of Human Rights or the International Covenant on Economic, Social and Cultural Rights.

25 Earthjustice 2004, 2008. Debate over the recognition of environmental human rights is ongoing within the human rights community. Some argue that recognizing a third generation of rights (one in which the protection of humans is not the central focus) would devalue the concept of human rights and divert attention from the need to implement existing civil, political, economic and social rights fully. Others assert the inherent value of recognizing a right to have the environment protected. See Boyle (2010).

26 Fukuda-Parr 2007; Nussbaum 1998, 2006; Sen 2009; Vizard, Fukuda-Parr and Elson 2011.

27 Sen 2009

28 Boyce 2011.

29 However, the legislation preserves Parliament's discretion to authorize any interference with environmental rights: May (2006).

30 See Pedersen (2008).

31 See the Swedish Environment Protection Agency (www.naturvardsverket.se/en/In-English/Start/Enjoying-nature/The-right-of-public-access/).

32 Every person has the right to a clean and healthy environment, which includes the right to have the environment protected for the benefit of present and future generations through legislative and other measures (Constitution of Kenya 2010, Chapter 5, Part 2). Since 1972 more than half of UN member states have added constitutional guarantees concerning the environment (Earthjustice 2007).

33 Article 44 of the 1994 Constitution of the Federal Democratic Republic of Ethiopia says that "government shall endeavor to ensure that all Ethiopians live in a clean and healthy environment" and Article 92 that "the design and implementation of programmes and of development shall not damage or destroy the environment."

34 Constitution of the Republic of Cameroon 1996, Article 47(2).

35 Constitution of the Republic of Namibia 1990, Article 25(2).

36 Bruch, Coker and VanArsdale 2007.

37 Costa Rica, El Salvador and Honduras do not recognize environmental rights for indigenous peoples, and the constitutions of Guatemala, Panama, Paraguay and Peru refer to land but not natural resources (Aguilar and others 2010).

38 Political Constitution of 1992, Republic of Paraguay, Article 66.

39 According to the Constitution of the Co-operative Republic of Guyana Act 1980: "The state shall protect the environment for the benefits of present and future generations" (Article 149J.2); "Everyone has a right to an environment that is not harmful to his or her health or well-being" (Aricle 149J.1); and "Indigenous Peoples shall have the right to the protection and promulgation of their languages, cultural heritage and way of life" (Article 149G).

40 Vidal 2011.

41 May 2006. Other countries whose national courts have explicitly recognized the enforceability of such rights include Argentina, Columbia, Costa Rica and Portugal.

42 Jackson and Rosencranz 2003.

43 UNDP Bhutan 2008.

44 Sen 2006.

45 Shelton 2010.

46 American Electric Power Co. v. Connecticut, 10-174. For discussion, see New York Times (2011).

47 Biggar and Middleton 2010.

48 Fifty percent or more of people in 61 of 137 countries surveyed do not have confidence in the judicial system and the courts (https://worldview.gallup.com).

49 See Constitutional Protections of the Right to Information (http://right2info.org).

50 Puddephatt 2009.

51 Foulon, Lanoie and Laplante 2002.

52 Jin, Wang and Wheeler 2010.

53 Wang and others 2002; Bennear and Olmstead (2006) also confirmed this in the context of water utility suppliers in Massachusetts (United States) over 1990–2003.

54 For example, the 1998 United Nations Economic Commission for Europe Convention on Access to Information, Public Participation in Decision-Making and Access to Justice in Environmental Matters (Aarhus Convention) and the Inter-American Strategy for the Promotion of Public Participation in Decision Making for Sustainable Development.

55 UNEP 2007, chapter 8.

56 See www.rema.gov.rw.

57 Newell and others 2011.

58 Newell and others 2011.

59 Lloyd-Smith and Bell 2003.

60 Byrne and others 2007.

61 Newell 2008.

62 Crotty and Rodgers forthcoming.

63 UNDP–UNEP Poverty-Environment Initiative 2008.

64 Transparency International calculations based on the Conference of Parties documentation, pollution data from 2006 (UN Stats Division 2010) and Climate Risk Index 2010 by Germanwatch (Transparency International 2011).

65 Ballesteros and others 2009.

66 www.un-redd.org/Home/tabid/565/Default.aspx.

67 In Eastern Cameroon, for example, a United Nations Development Programme (UNDP) initiative gave the Baka people access to video cameras to document how climate change is damaging the forests where they live, and the resulting documentary was used in advocacy work at the 2009 Global Indigenous Summit on Climate Change (UNDP 2010).

68 Buckingham 2010.

69 Agarwal (2009, 2010b) found that the overall forest condition was significantly higher where executive committees had more than two women than where they had two women or fewer and that the higher the percentage of women on the executive committee, the lower the percentage of degraded forest area.

70 Schreckenberg and Luttrell (2009).

71 Buffum, Lawrence and Temphel 2010.

72 Glemarec 2011.

73 Bloomberg New Energy Finance and UNEP 2010.

74 Kim and others 2009.

75 Glemarec 2011.

76 The global estimated needs exclude payments for ecosystem services. See Glemarec (2011).

77 For the Global Environment Facility over 2007–2010 China attracted 12 percent of funds approved, India 10 percent and the Russian Federation 6 percent. But China and India have a per capita allocation of only $0.10 and $0.09, far below the median of $0.43, while the Russian Federation receives $0.51. See www.gefonline.org.

78 See CIF 2011.

79 GEF 2009.

80 OECD 2011a; www.oecd.org/document/35/0, 3746,en_2649_34447_47515235_1_1_1,00.html. Percentage calculated based on UN Millennium Project (2005) table 7.

81 There is not even a consensus on a working definition of new and additional finance. The European Commission has requested that all EU member states declare their own working definitions, with the goal of having a common and unified definition by 2013. See Bird, Brown and Schalatek (2011).

82 Sanchez 2010.

83 World Bank 2010b.

84 At the lower end is the United Nations Framework Convention on Climate Change estimate of about $200 billion in additional financial flows by 2030. The McKinsey & Company (2009) estimate of $800 billion to stabilize carbon dioxide at 450 parts per million is in the middle of the range. The numbers reported by the Stern Review ranged from $600 billion to $1,200 billion a year, depending on the emission targets (see UNDESA 2009). A recent Intergovernmental Panel on Climate Change (2011) report estimated the annual infrastructure and technology investment costs of moving to a low greenhouse gas economy at $136–$510 billion a year for the next decade and at $149–$718 billion a year for 2021–2030. The higher cost scenario would stabilize atmospheric carbon dioxide concentration at 450 parts per million.

85 This is an update of the $86 billion figure, equivalent to 0.2 percent of Organisation for Economic Co-operation and Development (OECD) GDP, in UNDP–HDRO 2007/08, using the latest information available.

86 Parry, Lowe and Hanson 2009.

87 Stockholm International Peace Research Institute 2010.

88 See IEA (2010); calculations based on UNESCO Institute for Statistics (www.uis.unesco.org) and World Bank 2011b.

89 Climate Funds Update 2011 (www.climatefundsupdate .org/graphs-statistics/pledged-deposited-disbursed).

90 Not all these estimates can be broken out separately into water and sanitation, but those that can range from $4.5 billion to $13 billion for water and from $2.2 billion to $17 billion for sanitation (Fonesca and Cardone 2005).

91 On innovative financing, see OECD (2010c).

92 See UN Water 2010a.

93 ILO 2010.

94 Although worldwide nearly 40 percent of the working-age population is legally covered by contributory old-age pension schemes, only 26 percent have effective coverage. And while 75 percent of people over age 64 receive some kind of pension in high-income countries, less than 20 percent do in low-income countries, with a median of just over 7 percent (see ILO 2010).

95 OECD 2010b.

96 The ILO (2008) estimates the cost would not exceed 0.5 percent of GDP in Bangladesh, Cameroon, Guinea, India, Pakistan, Senegal and Viet Nam, for example; while for Burkina Faso, Ethiopia, Kenya, Nepal and Tanzania the costs are 0.7–0.8 percent of GDP.

97 See Cichon and Hagemejer (2006).

98 "Adaptive social protection" is a term coined by researchers at the Institute of Development Studies, Sussex, to bring together thinking about social protection, disaster risk reduction and climate change adaptation (Davies, Oswald and Mitchell 2009).

99 Our calculations indicate that an additional $15–$28 billion is needed to incorporate adaptation into the Millennium Development Goals. Calculations based on Frankhauser and Schmidt-Traub (2010) and the UN Millennium Project: Estimated Costs of meeting the Millennium Development Goals in all countries (www.unmillenniumproject.org/reports/ costs_benefits2.htm) (table 7).

100 Leading Group on Innovative Financing for Development 2010.

101 Griffith-Jones, Ocampo and Stiglitz 2010.

102 This estimate is slightly higher than Schmidt's (2008) estimate for a tax of 0.005 percent of $34 billion a year.

103 Other areas included are the Extractive Industries Transparency Initiative, Consultative Group on Agriculture, 3ie Evaluation Initiative, Global Environment Facility, UN Adaptation Fund, advanced market commitments, Montreal Protocol, International Finance Facility for Immunisation, Climate Investment Funds and International Monetary Fund surveillance. See Birdsall and Leo (2011).

104 IMF 2010.

105 European Parliament Committee on Economic and Monetary Affairs 2011.

106 Baker 2011.

107 SDR surpluses occur when a country's holdings exceed allocations. The largest SDR surplus countries include the United States, China, Japan, Libya, Saudi Arabia, Kuwait and Botswana.

108 Birdsall and Leo (2011). Willing governments would use a small portion of their SDR allocation to capitalize a third-party financing entity that would offer bonds on international capital markets backed by SDR reserves.

109 Climate Funds Update 2011 (www.climatefundsupdate .org/graphs-statistics/pledged-deposited-disbursed).

110 Newell and others 2011.

111 UNDP, and others, have developed a series of methodologies to assist such efforts: see www.undp.org/ climatestrategies.

112 Glemarec 2011.

References

Adams, J. S. 1965. "Inequity in Social Exchange." *Advances in Experimental Social Psychology* 62: 335–43.

Afifi, T., and K. Warner. 2008. *The Impact of Environmental Degradation on Migration Flows across Countries.* Working Paper 5. United Nations University, Institute for Environment and Human Security, Bonn, Germany.

Agarwal, B. 2001. "Participatory Exclusions, Community Forestry and Gender: An Analysis for South Asia and a Conceptual Framework." *World Development* 29 (10): 1623–48.

———. 2009. "Gender and Forest Conservation: The Impact of Women's Participation in Community Forest Governance." *Ecological Economics* 68 (11): 2785–99.

———. 2010a. "Does Women's Proportional Strength Affect Their Participation? Governing Local Forests in South Asia." *World Development* 38 (1): 98–112.

———. 2010b. *Gender and Green Governance: The Political Economy of Women's Presence within and beyond Community Forestry.* Oxford, UK: Oxford University Press.

AGECC (The Secretary-General's Advisory Group on Energy and Climate Change). 2010. *Energy for a Sustainable Future: Summary Report and Recommendations.* New York: United Nations.

Aghion, P. 2009. "Some Thoughts on Industrial Policy and Growth." Working Paper 2009-09. Sciences Po, Observatoire Français des Conjonctures Economiques, Paris. www.ofce.sciences-po.fr/pdf/dtravail/WP2009-09.pdf. Accessed 30 May 2011.

Aguilar, G., S. Lafoss, H. Rojas, and R. Steward. 2010. "South/North Exchange of 2009: The Constitutional Recognition of Indigenous Peoples in Latin America." *Pace International Law Review Online Companion* 2 (2): 44–96.

Agyeman, J., Y. Ogneva-Himmelberger, and C. Campbell. 2009. "Introduction." In *Environmental Justice and Sustainability in the Former Soviet Union*, eds. Agyeman, J. and Y. Ogneva-Himmelberger. Cambridge, MA: MIT Press.

Aichele, R., and G. Felbermayr. 2010. "Kyoto and the Carbon Content of Trade." Climate Change Economics Discussion Paper 10-2010. Hohenheim University, Hohenheim, Germany.

Alderman, H., J. Hoddinott, and B. Kinsey. 2006. "Long Term Consequences of Early Childhood Malnutrition." *Oxford Economic Papers* 58: 450–74.

Alkire, S. and J. Foster. 2010. "Designing the Inequality-Adjusted Human Development Index (IHDI)." Human Development Research Paper 2010/28. UNDP–HDRO, New York. http://hdr.undp.org/en/reports/global/hdr2010/papers/HDRP_2010_28.pdf. Accessed 18 May 2011.

———. 2011. "Counting and Multidimensional Poverty Measurement." *Journal of Public Economics* 95 (7–8): 476–87.

Alkire, S., and J. M. Roche. Forthcoming. "Beyond Headcount: Measures That Reflect the Breadth and Components of Child Poverty." In *Global Changes in Child Poverty at the End of the 20th Century*, eds. Alberto Minujin and Shailen Nandy. Bristol, UK: The Policy Press.

Alkire, S., J. M. Roche, and M. E. Santos. Forthcoming. "Multidimensional Poverty Index: An In-Depth Analysis of the New Country Results, Changes over Time and Geographical and Ethnical Decompositions." Working Paper. University of Oxford, Oxford Poverty and Human Development Initiative, Oxford, UK.

Alkire, S., and M. E. Santos. 2010. "Acute Multidimensional Poverty: A New Index for Developing Countries." Human Development Research Paper 2010/11. United Nations Development Programme, New York. http://hdr.undp.org/en/reports/global/hdr2010/papers/HDRP_2010_11.pdf. Accessed 5 June 2011.

Allison, E.H., W. N. Adger, M.-C. Badjeck, K. Brown, D. Conway, N. K. Dulvy, A. Halls, A. Perry, and J. D. Reynolds. 2005. "Effects of Climate Change on the Sustainability of Capture and Enhancement Fisheries Important to the Poor: Analysis of the Vulnerability and Adaptability of Fisherfolk Living in Poverty." Final Technical Report. UK Department for International Development, Fisheries Management Science Programme, London.

Allison, E. H., M. Badjeck, W. Adger, K. Brown, D. Conway, A. Halls, G. Pilling, J. Reynolds, N. Andrew, and N. Dulvy. 2009. "Vulnerability of National Economies to the Impacts of Climate Change on Fisheries." *Fish and Fisheries* 10 (2): 173–96.

Amarakoon, D., A. Chen, S. Rawlins, and D. D. Chadee, M. Taylor and R. Stennett. 2008. "Dengue Epidemics in the Caribbean Temperature Indices to Gauge the Potential for Onset of Dengue." *Mitigation Adaptation Strategies for Global Change* 13 (4): 341–57.

Amon, B., V. Kryvoruchko, T. Amon, and S. Zechmeister-Boltenstern. 2006. "Methane, Nitrous Oxide and Ammonia Emissions during Storage and after Application of Dairy Cattle Slurry and Influence of Slurry Treatment." *Agriculture, Ecosystems and Environment* 112 (2–3): 153–62.

Anand, S., and P. Segal. 2008. "What Do We Know about Global Income Inequality?" *Journal of Economic Literature* 46: 57–94.

Anand, S., and A. Sen. 1994. "Human Development Index: Methodology and Measurement." HDRO Occasional Papers. UNDP–HDRO, New York.

———. 2000. "Human Development and Economic Sustainability." *World Development* 28 (12): 2029–49.

Anderegg, W. R., J. W. Prall, J. Harold, and S. H. Schneider. 2010. "Expert Credibility in Climate Change." *Proceedings of the National Academy of Sciences of the United States of America* 107 (27): 12107–09.

Andrews, A. 2009. "Beyond the Ban: Can the Basel Convention Adequately Safeguard the Interests of the World's Poor in the International Trade of Hazardous Waste?" *Law Environment and Development Journal* 5(2): 169–84.

Anthoff, D. 2010. "The Economic Impact of Substantial Sea Level Rise." *Mitigation and Adaptation Strategies for Global Change* 15: 321–35.

Archer, D., and V. Brovkin. 2008. "The Millennial Atmospheric Lifetime of Anthropogenic CO2." *Climatic Change* 90: 283–97.

Argos, M., T. Kalra, P. J. Rathouz, Y. Chen, B. Pierce, F. Parvez, T. Islam, A. Ahmed, M. Rakibuz-Zaman, R. Hasan, G. Sarwar, V. Slavkovich, A. van Geen, J. Graziano, and H. Ahsan. 2010. "Arsenic Exposure from Drinking Water, and All-Cause and Chronic-Disease Mortalities in Bangladesh (HEALS): A Prospective Cohort Study." *Lancet* 376 (9737): 252–58.

Arnall, A., K. Oswald, M. Davies, T. Mitchell, and C. Coirolo. 2010. "Adaptive Social Protection: Mapping the Evidence and Policy Context in the Agriculture Sector in South Asia." Working Paper 345. Institute of Development Studies, Brighton, UK.

Arnold, J. E. M., G. Kohlin, and R. Persson. 2006. "Woodfuels, Livelihoods, and Policy Interventions: Changing Perspectives." *World Development* 34 (3): 596–611.

Arora-Jonsson, S. 2011. "Virtue and Vulnerability: Discourses on Women, Gender and Climate Change." *Global Environmental Change* 21 (2): 744–51.

Ash, M., J. K. Boyce, G. Chang, and H. Scharber. 2010. "Is Environmental Justice Good for White Folks?" University of Massachusetts, Political Economy Research Institute, Amherst, MA. http://works.bepress.com/james_boyce/33. Accessed 19 May 19 2011.

Asia Summit on Climate Change and Indigenous Peoples. 2009. "Report of the Summit." Tebtebba Indigenous Peoples' International Centre for Policy Research and Education, 24–27 February, Bali, Indonesia.

Atkinson, A. B., and S. Morelli. 2011. "Economic Crises and Inequality." Human Development Research Paper 6. UNDP–HDRO, New York.

Atkinson, A. B., T. Piketty, and E. Saez, 2011. "Top Incomes in the Long Run History." *Journal of Economic Literature* 49 (1): 3–71.

Atkinson, A. B., and J. E. Stiglitz. 1980. *Lectures in Public Economics.* New York: McGraw-Hill.

AusAID (Australian Agency for International Development) and UNDP (United Nations Development Programme) Pacific Center. 2008. *The Gendered Dimension of Disaster-Risk Management and Adaptation to Climate Change: Stories from the Pacific.* Suva, Fiji. www.undppc.org.fj/_resources/article/files/UNDP%20PC%20Climate%20Change.pdf. Accessed 14 July 2011.

Babbage. 2010. "Helping Hands." Babbage (blog), *The Economist,* 27 May. www.economist.com/blogs/babbage/2010/05/techview_robot_every_home. Accessed 10 May 2011.

Badiani, R., and K. Jessoe, 2011. "Elections at What Cost? The Impact of Electricity Subsidies on Groundwater Extraction and Agricultural Production." UC Davis Working Paper. University of California–Davis, Department of Agriculture and Resource Economics, Berkley, CA. http://areweb.berkeley.edu/documents/seminar/JessoeDraft.pdf. Accessed 20 June 2011.

Baez, J. E., de la Fuente, A., and I. V. Santos. 2010. *Do Natural Disasters Affect Human Capital? An Assessment Based on Existing Empirical Evidence.* Discussion Paper 5164. Institute for the Study of Labor, Bonn, Germany.

Baez, J. E., and I. V. Santos. 2007. "Children's Vulnerability to Weather Shocks: A Natural Disaster as a Natural Experiment." Working Paper. World Bank, Washington, DC.

Bain & Company. 2011. "Bain & Company Predicts Eight Percent Growth in Global Luxury Goods Sales in 2011; Five-to-Six Percent Annual Growth through 2014." Press Release, 3 May 2011. www.reuters.com/article/2011/05/03/idUS167455+03-May-2011+BW20110503. Accessed 14 July 2011.

Baker, D. 2011. "The Deficit-Reducing Potential of a Financial Speculation Tax." Issue Brief. Center for Economic and Policy Research, Washington, DC. www.cepr.net/documents/publications/fst-2011-01.pdf. Accessed 1 June 2011.

Baker T., M. Roberts, B. Cole, and C. Jacks. 2011. "The Sanitation Marketing Pilot Project: End of Project Report." Water and Sanitation Program, Washington, DC.

Ball, J. B. 2001. "Global Forest Resources: History and Dynamics." In *The Forests Handbook. Vol. 1,* ed. J. Evans. Oxford, UK: Blackwell Science.

Ballesteros, A., S. Nakhooda, J. Werksman, and K. Hurlburt. 2010. *Power, Responsibility, and Accountability: Re-Thinking the Legitimacy of Institutions for Climate Finance.* Washington, DC: World Resources Institute. www.wri.org/publication/power-responsibility-accountability. Accessed 1 August 2011.

Bangladesh Ministry of Health and Family Welfare. 2004. *Bangladesh Population Policy.* Dhaka. www.dgfp.gov.bd/population_policy_eng.pdf. Accessed 15 July 2011.

Barbier, E. B., J. Burgess, and C. Folke. 1994. *Paradise Lost? The Ecological Economics of Biodiversity.* London: Earthscan.

Barbier, E. B., A. Markandya, and D. W. Pearce. 1990. "Sustainable Agricultural Development and Project Appraisal." *European Review of Agricultural Economics* 17 (2): 181–96.

Bardasi, E., and Q. Wodon. 2009. "Working Long Hours and Having No Choice: Time Poverty in Guinea." Policy Research Working Paper 4961. World Bank, Washington, DC.

Barrett, S. 2009. "Rethinking Global Climate Change Governance." *Economics* 3 (5). www.economics-ejournal.org/economics/journalarticles/2009-5. Accessed 15 July 2011.

Bartlett, S. 2008. "Climate Change and Urban Children: Impacts and Implications for Adaptation in Low- and Middle-Income Countries." *Environment and Urbanization* 20 (2): 501–19.

Bättig, M. B., and T. Bernauer. 2009. "National Institutions and Global Public Goods: Are Democracies More Cooperative in Climate Change Policy?" *International Organization* 63 (2): 281–308.

Baud, M., F. de Castro, and B. Hogenboom. 2011. "Environmental Governance in Latin America: Towards an Integrative Research Agenda." *European Review of Latin American and Caribbean Studies* 90: 79–88.

Baumol, W. J., R. E. Litan, and C. J. Schramm. 2007. *Good Capitalism, Bad Capitalism, and the Economics of Growth and Prosperity.* New Haven, CT: Yale University Press.

Becker, G. S., T. J. Philipson, and R. R. Soares. 2003. "The Quantity and Quality of Life and the Evolution of World Inequality." *American Economic Review* 95 (1): 277–79.

Beegle, K., and Q. Wodon. 2006. "Labor Shortages Despite Under-Employment. Seasonality in Time Use in Malawi." In *Gender, Time Use, and Poverty in Sub-Saharan Africa,* eds. M. Blackden and Q. Wodon. Working Paper. World Bank, Washington, DC. http://mpra.ub.uni-muenchen.de/11083/. Accessed 26 April 2011.

Bennear, L. S., and S. M. Olmstead. 2006. "The Impacts of the "Right to Know": Information Disclosure and the Violation of Drinking Water Standards." *Journal of Economic Literature.* http://cbey.research.yale.edu/uploads/File/olmstead.pdf. Accessed 3 May 2011.

Bernard, T. 2010. "Impact Analysis of Rural Electrification Projects in Sub-Saharan Africa." *World Bank Research Observer.* September. http://wbro.oxfordjournals.org/content/early/2010/09/01/wbro.lkq008.abstract. Accessed 5 July 2011.

Bernauer, T., and V. Koubi. 2009. "Political Determinants of Environmental Quality." *Ecological Economics* 68 (5): 1355–65.

Bettencourt, L. M. A., J. Lobo, D. Helbing, and C. Kühnert, G. B. West. 2007. "Growth, Innovation, Scaling and the Pace of Life in Cities." *Proceedings of the National Academy of Sciences of the United States of America* 104 (17): 7301–06.

Biddlecom, A. E., W. G. Axinn, and J. S. Barber. 2005. "Environmental Effects of Family Size Preferences and Subsequent Reproductive Behavior in Nepal." *Population and Environment* 26 (3): 183–206.

Biggar, J., and C. Middleton. 2010. "Broadband and Network Environmentalism." *Telecommunications Journal of Australia* 60 (1): 9.1–9.17.

Binder, S., and E. Neumayer. 2005. "Environmental Pressure Group Strength and Air Pollution: An Empirical Analysis." *Ecological Economics* 55: 527–38.

Bird, N., J. Brown, and L. Schalatek. 2011. "Design Challenges for the Green Climate Fund." Climate Finance Policy Brief 4. Heinrich Boell Foundation and Overseas Development Institute, Berlin and London. www.odi.org.uk/resources/download/5256.pdf. Accessed 15 May 2011.

Birdsall, N., and B. Leo. 2011. "Find Me the Money: Financing Climate and Other Global Public Goods." Working Paper 248. Center for Global Development, Washington, DC.

Blackden, C. M., and Wodon, Q., eds. 2006. *Gender, Time Use and Poverty in Sub-Saharan Africa.* Working Paper 73. World Bank, Washington, DC http://siteresources.worldbank.org/INTAFRREGTOPGENDER/Resources/gender_time_use_pov.pdf. Accessed 15 April 2011.

Blacksmith Institute. 2007. *The World's Worst Polluted Places.: The Top Ten of the Dirty Thirty.* New York: The Blacksmith Institute. www.blacksmithinstitute.org/wwpp2007/finalReport2007.pdf. Accessed 15 July 2011.

Blankespoor, B., S. Dasgupta, B. Laplante, and D. Wheeler. 2010. "The Economics of Adaptation to Extreme Weather Events in Developing Countries." Working Paper 199. Center for Global Development, Washington, DC.

Blau, P. 1964. *Exchange and Power in Social Life.* New York: Wiley.

Bloomberg New Energy Finance and UNEP (United Nations Environment Programme). 2010. *Global Trends in Sustainable Energy Investment 2010: Analysis of Trends and Issues in the Financing of Renewable Energy and Energy Efficiency.* Nairobi: United Nations Environment Programme.

Boano, C., R. Zetter, and T. Morris. 2008. "Environmentally Displaced People: Understanding the Linkages between Environmental Change, Livelihoods and Forced Migration." Forced Migration Policy Briefing 1. University of Oxford Refugee Studies Centre, Oxford Department of International Development, Oxford, UK.

Borras, S., and J. Franco. 2010. *Towards a Broader View of the Politics of Global Land Grab: Rethinking Land Issues, Reframing Resistance.* Initiatives in Critical Agrarian Studies Working Paper Series 1. www.tni.org/sites/www.tni.org/files/Borras%20Franco%20Politics%20of%20Land%20Grab%20v3.pdf. Accessed 20 June 2011.

Bourguignon, F., and C. Morrisson. 2002. "Inequality among World Citizens: 1820–1992." *American Economic Review* 92: 727–44.

Boyce, J. K. 2011. "The-Environment as our-Common-Heritage." Triple Crisis (blog), 10 February. http://triplecrisis.com/the-environment-as-our-common-heritage/. Accessed 20 May 2011.

Boyce, J. K., A. R. Klemer, P. H. Templet, and C. E. Willis. 1999. "Power Distribution, the Environment, and Public Health: A state-level analysis." *Ecological Economics* 29: 127–40.

Boyce, J. K., and M. Torras. 2002. "Rethinking the Environmental Kuznets Curve" in *The Political Economy of the Environment*, ed. J. K. Boyce. Northampton, MA: Edward Elgar.

Boyle, A. 2010. "Human Rights and the Environment: A Reassessment." United Nations Environment Programme, New York.

Brainard, J. S., A. P. Jones, I. J. Bateman, and A. A. Lovett, and P. J. Fallon. 2002. "Modelling Environmental Equity: Access to Air Quality in Birmingham, England." *Environment and Planning* A 34: 695–716.

Brouwer, R., S. Akter, and L. Brander. 2007. "Socioeconomic Vulnerability and Adaptation to Environmental Risk: A Case Study of Climate Change and Flooding in Bangladesh." Poverty Reduction and Environmental Management Working Paper 06/01. Institute for Environmental Studies, Amsterdam.

Brown, L. 2003. *Plan B: Rescuing a Planet under Stress and a Civilization in Trouble*. New York and London : W.W. Norton & Company.

Brown, L., C. Flavin, H. French, J. N. Abramovitz, S. Dunn, G. Gardner, L. Mastny, A. Mattoon, D. Roodman, P. Sampat, M. O. Sheehan, and L. Starke. 2001. *State of the World 2001: A Worldwatch Institute Report on Progress towards a Sustainable Society*. New York and London: W. W. Norton and Company.

Bruce, C. J. McCracken, R. Albalak, M. Schei, K. R. Smith, V. Lopez, and C. West. 2004. "Impact of Improved Stoves, House Construction and Child Location on Levels of Indoor Air Pollution Exposure in Young Guatemalan Children." *Journal of Exposure Analysis and Environmental Epidemiology* 14: S26–S33.

Bruch, C., W. Coker, and C. VanArsdale. 2007. *Constitutional Environmental Law: Giving Force to Fundamental Principles in Africa*. Washington, DC: Environmental Law Institute.

Brulle, R. J., and D. N. Pellow. 2006. "Environmental Justice: Human Health and Environmental Inequalities." *Annual Review of Public Health* 27: 3.1–3.22

Buckingham, S. 2010. "Call in the Women." *Nature* 468: 502.

Buffum, B., A. Lawrence, and K. J. Temphel. 2010. "Equity in Community Forests in Bhutan." *International Forestry Review* 12 (3): 187–99.

Burke, M., J. Dykema, D. Lobell, E. Miguel, and S. Satyanath. 2010. "Climate and Civil War: Is the Relationship Robust?" Working Paper 16440. National Bureau of Economic Research, Cambridge, MA. www.nber.org/papers/w16440. Accessed 25 May 2011.

Burniaux, J. M., and J. Chateau. 2011. "Mitigation Potential of Removing Fossil Fuel Subsidies: A General Equilibrium Assessment." Economics Department Working Paper 853. Paris: Organisation for Economic Co-operation and Development.

Byers, B. A., R. N. Cunliffe, and A. T. Hudak. 2001. "Linking the Conservation of Culture and Nature: A Case Study of Sacred Forests in Zimbabwe." *Human Ecology* 29 (2): 187–218.

Byrne, J., K. Hughes, W. Rickerson, and L. Kurdgelashvili. 2007. "American Policy Conflict in the Greenhouse: Divergent Trends in Federal, Regional, State, and Local Green Energy and Climate Change Policy." *Energy Policy* 35 (9): 4555–73.

Cadman, M., C. Petersen, A. Driver, N. Sekhran, K. Maze, and S. Munzhedzi. 2010. *Biodiversity for Development: South Africa's Landscape Approach to Conserving Biodiversity and Promoting Ecosystem Resilience*. Pretoria: South African National Biodiversity Institute.

Chambers, R. 2009. "Going to Scale with Community-led Total Sanitation: Reflections on Experience, Issues and Ways Forward." IDS Practice Paper 2009–1. Institute of Development Studies, Brighton, UK.

Chang, H. J., and I. Grabel. 2004. "Reclaiming Development from the Washington Consensus." *Journal of Post Keynesian Economics* 27 (2): 273–91. www.jstor.org/stable/4538924. Accessed 20 April 2011.

Changa, S. E., M. Eeri, B. J. Adams, J. Alder, P. R. Berke, R. Chuenpagdee, S. Ghosh, and C. Wabnitz. 2006. "Coastal Ecosystems and Tsunami Protection after the December 2004 Indian Ocean Tsunami." *Earthquake Spectra* 22 (S3): 863–87.

Checchi, D. 2001. "Education, Inequality and Income Inequality." STICERD Distributional Analysis Research Programme Papers 52. Suntory and Toyota International Centres for Economics and Related Disciplines, London School of Economics, London, UK.

Checkley W., L. D. Epstein, R. H. Gilman, D. Figueroa, R. I. Cama, J. A. Patz, and R. E. Black. 2000. "Effects of *El Niño* and Ambient Temperature on Hospital Admissions for Diarrhoeal Diseases in Peruvian Children." *The Lancet* 355 (9202): 442–50.

Checkley, W., R. H. Gilman, R. E. Black, L. D. Epstein, L. Cabrera, C. R. Sterling, and L. H. Moulton. 2004. "Effect of Water and Sanitation on Childhood Health in a Poor Peruvian Peri-urban Community." *The Lancet* 363 (9403): 112–18.

Cheung, W. L., V. W. Y. Lam, J. L. Sarmiento, K. Kearney, R. Watson, D. Zeller, and D. Pauly. 2009. "Large-Scale Redistribution of Maximum Fisheries Catch Potential in the Global Ocean under Climate Change." *Global Change Biology* 16 (1): 24–35.

China National People's Congress. 2011. *12th Five-Year Plan*. Beijing.

Chinoko, T. C., S. S. Jagtap, and O. Nwofor. 2009. "West African Monsoon: Is the August Break "Breaking" in the Eastern Humid Zone of Southern Nigeria?" *Climatic Change* 103 (3–4): 555–70.

Christensen, J. H., B. Hewitson, A. Busuioc, A. Chen, X. Gao, I. Held, R. Jones, R. K. Kolli, W.-T. K., R. Laprise, V. M. Rueda, L. Mearns, C. G. Menéndez, J. Räisänen, A. Rinke, A. Sarr, and P. Whetton. 2007. "Regional Climate Projections." *Climate Change 2007: The Physical Science Basis*, eds. S. Solomon, D. Qin, M. Manning, Z. Chen, M. Marquis, K. B. Averyt, M. Tignor, and H. L. Miller. Contribution of Working Group I to the Fourth Assessment Report of the Intergovernmental Panel on Climate Change. Cambridge, UK and New York: Cambridge University Press.

Christiaensen, T. T. L., Q. T. Do, and L. D. Trung. 2010. "Natural Disasters and Household Welfare: Evidence from Vietnam." Policy Research Working Paper 5491. World Bank, Washington, DC.

Chung, E. C., V. Ramanathan, and J. T. Kiehl. 2002. "Effects of the South Asian Absorbing Haze on the Northeast Monsoon and Surface: Air Heat Exchange." *Journal of Climate* 15 (17): 2462–76.

Church, J. A., N. J. White, J. R. Hunter, and Kurt Lambeck. 2008. "Briefing a Post-IPCC AR4 Update on Sea-level Rise." The Antarctic Climate and Ecosystems Cooperative Research Centre, Hobart, Australia.

Cichon, M., and K. Hagemejer. 2006. "Social Security for All: Investing in Global Social and Economic Development: A Consultation." Issues in Social Protection Discussion Paper 16. International Labour Organization, Geneva.

Cinner, J. E., T. Daw, and T. R. McClanahan. 2009. "Socioeconomic Factors that Affect Artisanal Fishers' Readiness to Exit a Declining Fishery." *Conservation Biology* 23 (1): 124–30.

Climate Investment Funds. 2011. "The Clean Technology Fund (CTF) Disbursement Report." Washington, DC: Climate Investment Funds. www.climateinvestmentfunds.org/cif/sites/climateinvestmentfunds.org/files/Disbursement%20Report%20-%20CTF%20Dec%202010.pdf. Accessed 19 August 2011.

The Coca-Cola Company. 2010. "Rain Increases Access to Water Resources in Niger." News Release, 2 June 2010. www.thecoca-colacompany.com/citizenship/news_rain.html. Accessed 20 May 2011.

Colchester, Marcus. 2010. "Free, Prior and Informed Consent: Making FPIC Work for Forests and Peoples." Research Paper 11. The Forests Dialogue, New Haven, CT.

Collier, P. 2006. "Economic Causes of Civil Conflict and their Implications for Policy." International Network for Economics and Conflict. http://users.ox.ac.uk/~econpco/research/pdfs/EconomicCausesofCivilConflict-ImplicationsforPolicy.pdf. Accessed 15 June 2011.

———. 2007. *The Bottom Billion: Why the Poorest Countries Are Failing and What Can Be Done about It*. New York and London: Oxford University Press.

Commission on Sustainable Development. 1997. *Global Change and Sustainable Development: Critical Trends*. New York: United Nations Economic and Social Council. www.un.org/esa/documents/ecosoc/cn17/1997/ecn171997-3.htm. Accessed 14 June 2011.

Cooper, R. 2008. "The Case for Charges on Greenhouse Gas Emissions." Discussion Paper 08-10. Harvard Project on International Climate Agreements, Cambridge, MA.

Corrigan, C., and A. Granziera. 2010. *A Handbook for the Indigenous and Community Conserved Areas Registry*. Cambridge, UK: United Nations Environment Programme and World Conservation Monitoring Center. www.unep-wcmc.org/medialibrary/2010/09/13/f2ef7b9b/ICCA%20Handbook%201.2%20English.pdf. Accessed 29 May 2011.

Costello, A., M. Abbas, A. Allen, S. Ball, S. Bell, R. Bellamy, S. Friel, N. Groce, A. Johnson, M. Kett,

M. Lee, C. Levy, M. Maslin, D. McCoy, B. McGuire, H. Montgomery, D. Napier, C. Pagel, J. Patel, J. A. Puppim de Oliveira, N. Redclift, H. Rees, D. Rogger, J. Scott, J. Stephenson, J. Twigg, J. Wolff, and C. Patterson. 2009. "Managing the Health Effects of Climate Change." *The Lancet* 373: 1697–1723.

Cranfield, J. A. L., P. V. Preckel, and T. W. Hertel. 2007. "Poverty Analysis Using an International Cross-Country Demand System." Policy Research Working Paper 4285. World Bank, Washington, DC.

Crotty, J., and P. Rodgers. Forthcoming. "Sustainable Development in the Russian Federation: The Limits of Greening within Industrial Firms." www.business. salford.ac.uk/research/marketing-strategy/projects/environmental-sustainability-in-russian-federation/docs/The%20Limits%20of%20Greening%20in%20 Russian%20Firms.pdf. Accessed 15 July 2011.

Da Costa, M. M., C. Cohen, and R. Schaeffer. 2007. "Social Features of Energy Production and Use in Brazil: Goals for a Sustainable Energy Future." *Natural Resources Forum* 31: 11–20.

Da Vià, E. 2011. "The Politics of 'Win-Win' Narratives: Land Grab as Development Opportunity." Paper presented at the University of Sussex: Institute of Development Studies Conference on Global Land Grabbing, 6–8 April, Sussex, UK.

Daka, K. R., and J. Ballet. 2011. "Children's Education and Home Electrification: A Case Study in Northwestern Madagascar." *Energy Policy* 39 (5): 2866–74.

Daly, H. 2005. "Economics in a Full World." Policy Issue Briefs: Economic Growth and Development. United States Society for Ecological Economics, Burlington, VT.

Dasgupta, P. 1995. "Population, Poverty, and the Local Environment." *Scientific American* 272 (2): 26–31.

———. 2007. "Commentary: The Stern Review's Economics of Climate Change." *National Institute Economic Review* 199: 4–7.

Dasgupta, P., and G. Heal. 1974. "The Optimal Depletion of Exhaustible Resources." *Review of Economic Studies* 41 (Symposium on the Economics of Exhaustible Resources): 3–28.

Dasgupta, S., B. Laplante, C. Meisner, D. Wheeler, and J. Yan. 2009. "The Impact of Sea Level Rise on Developing Countries: A Comparative Analysis." *Climatic Change* 93: 379–88.

Davies, M., K. Oswald, and T. Mitchell. 2009. "Climate Change Adaptation, Disaster Risk Reduction and Social Protection." In *Promoting Pro-Poor Growth: Social Protection*, ed., Organisation for Economic Co-operation and Development. Paris: Organisation for Economic Co-operation and Development.

De Oliveira, A. 2008. "Private Provision of Water Service in Brazil: Impacts and Affordability." MPRA Paper 11149. University Library of Munich, Germany.

De Oliveira, A., and T. Laan. 2010. "Lessons Learned from Brazil's Experience with Fossil Fuel Subsidies and their Reform." International Institute for Sustainable Development, Geneva. www.hedon.info/docs/IISD_GSI_lessons_brazil_fuel_subsidies.pdf. Accessed 20 May 2011.

Deiniger, K., D. Beyerlee, J. Lindsay, A. Norton, H. Selod, and M. Stickler. 2011. *Rising Global Interest in Farmland: Can it Yield Sustainable and Equitable Benefits?* Washington, DC: World Bank. http://siteresources.worldbank.org/INTARD/Resources/ESW_Sept7_final_final.pdf. Accessed 10 June 2011.

DFID (UK Department for International Development). 2011. "Cash Transfers." Evidence Paper. London. www.dfid.gov.uk/r4d/PDF/Articles/Evidence_Paper-FINAL-CLEARAcknowledgement.pdf. Accessed May 1 2011.

Dietz, S., and Neumayer, E. 2007. "Weak and Strong Sustainability in the SEEA: Concepts and Measurement." *Ecological Economics* 61 (4): 617–26.

Dinkelman, T. 2008. "The Effects of Rural Electrification on Employment: New Evidence from South Africa." Working Paper 1255. Princeton University, Woodrow Wilson School of Public and International Affairs, Research Program in Development Studies, Princeton, NJ.

Dodman, D. 2009." Urban Density and Climate Change." Analytical Review of the Interaction between Urban Growth Trends and Environmental Changes Paper 1. United Nations Population Fund, New York.

Dore, M. H. I. 2005. "Climate Change and Changes in Global Precipitation Patterns: What Do We Know?" *Environment International* 31 (8): 1167–81.

Dudley, N., and S. Stolton, eds. 2003. *Running Pure: The Importance of Forest Protected Areas to Drinking Water.* World Bank/WWF Alliance for Forest Conservation and Sustainable Use, Washington, DC.

Duflo, E., and R. Pande. 2007. "Dams." *Quarterly Journal of Economics* 122 (2): 601–46.

Duval-Diop, D., and K. Rose. 2008. *Delivering Equitable Development to a Recovering Louisiana: A State Policy Guide for 2008 and Beyond.* New Orleans, LA: Policy Link and Louisiana Disaster Recovery Foundation. www.policylink.org/atf/cf/%7B97c6d565-bb43-406d-a6d5-eca3bbf35af0%7D/DELIVERINGEQUITABLERECOVERY-LOUISIANA_FINAL.PDF. Accessed 15 June 2011.

Dye, C. 2008. "Health and Urban Living." *Science* 319 (5864): 766–69.

Earthjustice. 2004. "Human Rights and the Environment." Issue paper presented at the 60th Session of the United Nations Commission on Human Rights, 15 March–23 April, Geneva. www.earthjustice.org/library/references/2004UNreport.pdf. Accessed 29 April 2011.

———. 2007. "Environmental Rights Report 2007: Human Rights and the Environment." Oakland, CA. http://earthjustice.org/sites/default/files/library/references/2007-environmental-rights-report.pdf. Accessed 20 May 2011.

———. 2008. "Environmental Rights Report 2008: Human Rights and the Environment." Oakland, CA. http://earthjustice.org/sites/default/files/library/reports/2008-environmental-rights-report.pdf. Accessed 20 May 2011.

Eberhard, A., V. Foster, C. Briceño-Garmendia, F. Ouedraogo D. Camos, and M. Shkaratan. 2008. "Underpowered: The State of the Power Sector in Sub-Saharan Africa." Summary of Africa Infrastructure Country Diagnostic Background Paper 6. World Bank, Washington, DC.

Ebi, K. 2008. "Adaptation Cost for Climate Change-Related Cases of Diarrheal Diseases, Malnutrition, and Malaria in 2030." *Globalization and Health* 4 (9).

The Economist. 2008. "A Global Love Affair: A Special Report on Cars in Emerging Markets." 13 November. www.economist.com/node/12544933/print. Accessed 24 June 2011.

El Araby, M. 2002. "Urban Growth and Environmental Degradation: The Case of Cairo, Egypt." *Cities* 19 (6): 389–400.

Elbi, K. L., N. D. Lewis, and C. Corvalan. 2006. "Climate Variability and Change and Their Potential Health Effects in Small Islands States: Information for Adaptation Planning in Health Sector." *Environmental health Perspectives* 114 (12): 1957–63.

Elisara, F. M. 2008. "Effects of Climate Change on Indigenous Peoples: A Pacific Presentation." Paper presented at the International Expert Group Meeting on Indigenous Peoples and Climate Change, 2–4 April, Darwin, Australia. www.un.org/esa/socdev/unpfii/documents/EGM_cs08_Elisara.doc. Accessed 11 May 2011.

Engelman, R. 2009. "Population and Sustainability: Can We Avoid Limiting the Number of People." *Scientific American,* 10 June.

———. 2011. "An End to Population Growth: Why Family Planning is Key to a Sustainable Future." *Solutions for a Sustainable and Desirable Future* 2 (3). www.thesolutionsjournal.com/node/919. Accessed 15 July 2011.

Ervin, J., N. Sekhran, A. Dinu. S. Gidda, M. Vergeichik, and J. Mee. 2010. *Protected Areas for the 21st Century: Lessons from UNDP/GEF's Portfolio.* New York: United Nations Development Programme.

European Communities. 2010. *European Commission, Annual Environment Policy Review.* http://ec.europa.eu/environment/policyreview.htm. Accessed 12 May 2011.

European Parliament Committee on Economic and Monetary Affairs. 2011. "Report on Innovative Financing at Global and European Level." European Parliament, Committee on Economic and Monetary Affairs. Brussels. www.europarl.europa.eu/sides/getDoc.do?type=REPORT&reference=A7-2011-0036&language=EN. Accessed 15 May 2011.

Evans, A. 2010. "Resource Scarcity, Climate Change and the Risk of Violent Conflict." Background paper for *World Development Report 2011.* World Bank, Washington, DC. http://siteresources.worldbank.org/EXTWDR2011/Resources/6406082-1283882418764/WDR_Background_Paper_Evans.pdf. Accessed 15 July 2011.

Evans, G. 2008. "Conflict Potential in a World of Climate Change." Address to Bucerius Summer School on Global Governance 2008, 29 August, Berlin.

Fang, M., and C. K. Chan. 2008. "Managing Air Quality in a Rapidly Developing Nation: China." *Atmospheric Environment* 43 (1): 79–86.

FAO (Food and Agriculture Organization). 1996. *Lessons from the Green Revolution: Towards a New Green Revolution.* World Food Summit Technical Paper. Rome. www.fao.org/docrep/003/w2612e/w2612e06a.htm#. Accessed 5 July 2011.

———. 2001. *State of the World's Forests*. Rome. www.fao.org/docrep/003/y0900e/y0900e00.htm. Accessed 5 June 2011.

———. 2005. *Review of the State of World Marine Fishery Resources*. Technical Paper 457. Rome. ftp://ftp.fao.org/docrep/fao/007/y5852e/Y5852E00.pdf. Accessed 12 June 2011.

———. 2010a. *The State of the World Fisheries and Aquaculture*. Rome.

———. 2010b. *The State of Food and Agriculture 2010–2011*. Rome. www.fao.org/docrep/013/i2050e/i2050e.pdf. Accessed 9 July 2011.

———. 2011. *The State of the World's Forests*. Rome. www.fao.org/docrep/013/i2000e/i2000e00.pdf. Accessed 30 April 2011.

Filmer, D., and L. Pritchett. 2002. "Environmental Degradation and the Demand for Children: Searching for the Vicious Circle in Pakistan." *Environment and Development Economics* 7: 123–46.

Fiola, N. 2009. "Where More is Too Much: The Effect of Rainfall Shocks on Economic Growth and Civil Conflict." www.nathanfiala.com/When%20More%20is%20Too%20Much.pdf. Accessed 10 June 2011.

Fishman, C. 2011. *The Big Thirst*. New York: Free Press.

Flora, J. N., and J. L. Findis. 2007. "Natural Resource Collection Work and Children's Schooling in Malawi." *Agricultural Economics* 31 (2–3): 123–34.

Fonesca, C., and R. Cardone. 2005. "Analysis of Cost Estimates and Funding Available for Achieving the MDG Targets for Water and Sanitation." Background report for WELL Briefing Note 9. Water, Engineering and Development Center, Loughborough University, London School of Hygiene and Tropical Medicine and IRC International Water and Sanitation Center, Leicestershire, London and Delft, the Netherlands. www.lboro.ac.uk/well/resources/Publications/Briefing%20Notes/BN9%20Fonseca.pdf. Accessed 20 July 2011.

Foulon, J., P. Lanoie, B. Laplante. 2002. "Incentives for Pollution Control: Regulation or Information?" *Journal of Environmental Economics and Management* 44(1): 169–87.

Frankel, J., and V. Bosetti. 2011. "Sustainable Cooperation in Global Climate Policy: Specific Formulas and Emission Targets to Build on Copenhagen and Cancun." Human Development Research Paper 7. UNDP–HDRO, New York.

Frankhauser, S., and G. Schmidt-Traub. 2010. "From Adaptation to Climate-Resilient Development: The Costs of Climate-Proofing the Millennium Development Goals in Africa." Policy Paper. Centre for Climate Change Economics and Policy Grantham Research Institute on Climate Change and the Environment in collaboration with the Africa Progress Panel. www.cccep.ac.uk/Publications/Policy/docs/PPFankhauseretal_costs-climate-proofing.pdf. Accessed 20 July 2011.

Fraser E. D. G., M. Termansen, K. Hubacek, A. J. Dougill, J. Sendzimir, and C. Quinn. 2010. *Assessing Vulnerability to Climate Change in Dryland Livelihood Systems: Conceptual Challenges and Interdisciplinary Solutions*. Centre for Climate Change Economics

and Policy Working Paper 24. University of Leeds, UK. www.cccep.ac.uk/Publications/Working%20Papers/Papers/20-29/WP24_dryland-livelihood-systems.pdf. Accessed 27 June 27.

Fredriksson, P. G., E. Neumayer, R. Damania, S. Gates. 2005. "Environmentalism, Democracy, and Pollution Control." *Journal of Environmental Economics and Management* 49 (2): 343–65.

Fréon, P., M. Bouchon, C. Mullon, C. Garcia, and M. Ñiquen. 2008. "Interdecadal Variability of Anchoveta Abundance and Overcapacity of the Fishery in Peru." *Progress in Oceanography* 79: 401–12.

Friends of the Earth. 2004. "Incinerators and Deprivation." Briefing. London

Fuchs, A. 2011. "Conditional Cash Transfer Schemes and Households' Energy Responses in Mexico," UC Berkeley Working Paper. University of California–Berkeley, CA.

Fuchs, A., and A. Jayadev. 2011. *Creating an Inequality Adjusted HDI Panel*. UNDP-HDRO Working Paper. United Nations Development Programme, New York.

Fuchs, A., and V. Kehayova. 2011. "Identifying Causal Relations between Inequality in Human Development and Sustainability: Use of Quasi-Experimental Design." Internal Research. UNDP–HDRO, New York.

Fukuda-Parr, S. 2007. "Human Rights and Human Development." Economic Rights Working Paper 4. University of Connecticut, Human Rights Institute, Storrs, CT.

Fullerton, D. 2011. "Six Distributional Effects of Environmental Policy." Working Paper 16703. National Bureau of Economic Research, Cambridge, MA.

Furgal, C., and J. Seguin. 2006. "Climate Change, Health, and Vulnerability in Canadian Northern Aboriginal Communities." *Environmental Health Perspective* 114 (12): 1964–70.

Galbraith, J. K. 1952. *American Capitalism: The Concept of Countervailing Power*. Boston: Houghton Mifflin.

———.1954. *The Great Crash, 1929*. New York: Houghton Mifflin.

Gallagher K., and S. Thacker. 2008. *Democracy, Income, and Environmental Quality*. Working Paper 164. University of Massachusetts, Amherst, Political Economy Research Institute, Amherst, MA.

Galloway McLean, K. 2010. *Advance Guard: Climate Change Impacts, Adaptation, Mitigation and Indigenous Peoples—A Compendium of Case Studies*. Darwin, Australia: United Nations University Traditional Knowledge Initiative.

Gan, J., and McCarl, B. A. 2007. "Measuring Transnational Leakage of Forest Conservation." *Ecological Economics* 64 (2): 423–32.

Garcia, C., and J. Pineda. 2011. "Measuring the Sustainability of Countries: An Uncertainty and Sensitivity Analysis of the Adjusted Net Savings Measure." Human Development Research Paper 12. UNDP–HDRO, New York.

Gearty, C. 2010. "Do Human Rights Help or Hinder Environmental Protection." *Journal of Human Rights and the Environment* 1 (1): 7–22.

Georgioadis, G., J. Pineda, and F. Rodriguez. 2010. "Has the Preston Curve Broken Down?" Human Development Research Paper 2010/32. United Nations Development Programme, New York. http://hdr.undp.org/en/reports/global/hdr2010/papers/HDRP_2010_32.pdf. Accessed 15 March 2011.

Ghana Ministry of Energy and World Bank. 2004. "Ghana Poverty and Social Impact Analysis Electricity Tariffs: Phase I." World Bank, Africa Region, Environmentally and Socially Sustainable Development Department, Washington, DC. http://siteresources.worldbank.org/INTPSIA/Resources/490023-1120841262639/psia_ghana_electricity.pdf. Accessed 30 May 2011.

Glemarec, Y. 2011. *Catalysing Climate Finance: A Guidebook on Policy and Financing Options to Support Green, Low-Emission and Climate-Resilient Development*. New York: United Nations Development Programme.

Glemarec, Y., O. Weissbein, and H. Bayraktar. 2010. "Human Development in a Changing Climate: A Framework for Climate Finance." Discussion Paper. United Nations Development Programme, New York.

Global Environment Facility. 2009. "Midterm Review of the Resource Allocation Framework." Evaluation Report 47. United Nations Development Programme, Global Environment Fund, Evaluation Office, New York. www.thegef.org/gef/sites/thegef.org/files/documents/RAF_MTR-Report_0.pdf. Accessed 15 July 2011.

Global Subsidies Initiative. 2011. *Subsidy Watch* 42. www.globalsubsidies.org/files/assets/subsidy_watch/sw42_feb_11.pdf. Accessed 28 June 2011.

Grainger, A. 2010. "Uncertainty in the Construction of Global Knowledge of Tropical Forests." *Progress in Physical Geography* 34 (6): 811–44.

Grandia, L. 2005. "Appreciating the Complexity and Dignity of People's Lives: Integrating Population-Health-Environment Research in Peten, Guatemala." *Focus on Population, Environment and Security* 10.

Grasso, M. 2004. "A Normative Framework of Justice in Climate Change." Working Paper Series 79. University of Milan, Department of Economics, Italy. http://dipeco.economia.unimib.it/repec/pdf/mibwpaper79.pdf. Accessed 25 May 2011.

Green, D., U. King, and J. Morrison. 2009. "Disproportionate Burdens: The Multidimensional Impacts of Climate Change on the Health of Indigenous Australians." *Medical Journal of Australia* 190 (1): 4–5.

GreenPeace. 2009. "Where Does E-Waste End Up?" www.greenpeace.org/international/en/campaigns/toxics/electronics/the-e-waste-problem/where-does-e-waste-end-up/. Accessed 10 July 2011.

Gregory, J. M., P. Huybrechts, S. C. B. Raper. 2004. "Climatology: Threatened Loss of the Greenland Ice Sheet." *Nature* 428 (6983): 616.

Gregory, J., and P. Huybrechts 2006. "Ice-Sheet Contribution to Future Sea-Level Change." *Philosophical Transactions of the Royal Society of London A* 364: 1709–31.

Grether, J.-M., and N. Mathys. 2009. "Is the World's Economic Centre of Gravity Already in Asia?" *Area* 42 (1): 47–50.

Griffith-Jones, S., J. A. Ocampo, and J. E. Stiglitz. 2010. *Time for a Visible Hand: Lessons from the 2008 World Financial Crisis.* New York: Oxford University Press.

Grosh, M., C. del Ninno, E. Tesliuc, and A. Ouerghi. 2008. *For Protection and Promotion: The Design and Implementation of Effective Safety Nets.* Washington, DC: World Bank.

Grossman, G., and A. Krueger. 1995. "Economic Growth and the Environment." *Quarterly Journal of Economics* 110 (2): 353–77.

The GSMA Development Fund, the Cherie Blaire Foundation for Women and Vital Wave Consulting. 2010. *Women and Mobile: A Global Opportunity: A Study on the Mobile Phone Gender Gap in Low and Middle-Income Countries.* London: GSM Association.

Guatemala, Instituto Nacional de Estadistica. 1999. *Encuesta Nacional de Salud Materno Infantil 1998-1999.* Calverton, Md.: Macro International.

———. 2009. *Informe Preliminar: ENSMI 2008/2009.* Guatemala City: Guatemala Ministerio de Salud Pública y Asistencia Social.

Gupta, S. And I. Leung. 2011. "Turning Good Practice into Institutional Mechanisms: Investing in Grassroots Women's Leadership to Scale Up Local Implementation of the Hyogo Framework for Action." An in-depth study for the HFA Mid-Term Review. United Nations Strategy for Disaster Reduction, Geneva.

Gupte, M. 2004. "Participation in a Gendered Environment: The Case of Community Forestry in India." *Human Ecology* 32 (3): 365–82.

Hales, S., N. de Wet, J. Maindonald, and A. Woodward. 2002. "Potential Effect of Population and Climate Changes on Global Distribution of Dengue Fever: An Empirical Model." *The Lancet* 360 (9336): 830–34.

Hall, D., and E. Lobina. 2008. *Sewerage Works: Public Investment in Sewerage Saves Lives.* Greenwich, UK: University of Greenwich, Public Services International Research Unit. www.psiru.org/reports/2008-03-W-sewers.pdf. Accessed 3 May 2011.

Hanasaki, N., S. Kanae, T. Oki, Masuda, K. Motoya, N. Shirakawa, Y. Shen, and K. Tanaka. 2008. "An Integrated Model for the Assessment of Global Water Resources Part 1: Model Description and Input Meteorological Forcing." *Hydrology and Earth System Sciences* 12 (4): 1007–37.

Hartwick, J. M. 1977. "Intergenerational Equity and Investing of Rents from Exhaustible Resources." *American Economic Review* 67 (5): 972–74.

The Health Effects Institute (HEI). 2010. *Outdoor Air Pollution and Health in the Developing Countries of Asia: A Comprehensive Review.* Special Report 18. Boston, MA: HEI International Scientific Oversight Committee.

Heger, M., A. Julca, and O. Paddison. 2009. "Vulnerability in Small-Island Economies: The Impact of "Natural" Disasters in the Caribbean." In *Vulnerability in Developing Countries*, eds. W. Naude, A. U. Santos-Paulino, and M. McGillivray. New York: United Nations University.

Hendrix, C., and S. M. Glaser. 2005. "Trends and Triggers: Climate Change and Civil Conflict in Sub-Saharan Africa." *Political Geography* 26 (6): 695–715.

Hertel, T. W., M. Burke, and D. Lobell. 2010. "The Poverty Implications of Climate-Induced Crop Yield Changes by 2030." *Global Environmental Change* 20 (4): 577–85.

Hertel, T. W., and S. Rosch. 2010. "Climate Change, Agriculture and Poverty." *Applied Economic Perspectives and Policy* 32 (3): 355–85.

Hertz, T., T. Jayasundera, P. Pirano, S. Selcuk, N. Smith, and A. Verashchagina. 2007. "The Inheritance of Educational Inequality: International Comparisons and Fifty-Year Trends." *The B.E. Journal of Economic Analysis and Policy* 7 (2): 1–48.

Heston, A., R. Summers, and B. Aten. 2009. "Penn World Table Version 6.3." University of Pennsylvania, Center for International Comparisons of Production, Income and Prices, Philadelphia, PA.

Homans, G. C. 1961. *Social Behavior: Its Elementary Forms.* New York: Harcourt, Brace & World.

Homer-Dixon, T. 1994. *Environment, Scarcities and Violent Conflict: Evidence from Cases.* Toronto, Canada: University of Toronto.

Hughes, B., M. Irfan, J. Moyer, D. Rothman, and J. Solórzano. 2011. "Forecasting the Impacts of Environmental Constraints on Human Development." Human Development Research Paper 8. UNDP–HDRO, New York.

Hughes, B., R. Kuhn, C. Mosca Peterson, D. Rothman, and J. Solórzano. 2011. *Improving Global Health: Third Volume of Patterns of Potential Human Progress.* Boulder, CO: Paradigm Publishers.

Hutton, G., L. Haller, and J. Bartram. 2006. "Economic and Health Effects of Increasing Coverage of Low Cost Water and Sanitation Interventions." Occasional Paper 2006/33. UNDP–HDRO, New York.

IADB (Inter-American Development Bank). 2008. "Improved Access to Water and Sanitation Services in Small Municipios." Donors Memorandum PE-M1049. Inter-American Development Bank, Washington, DC. http://idbdocs.iadb.org/wsdocs/getdocument.aspx?docnum=1645546. Accessed 5 May 2011.

———. 2010. "Brazilian City of Manaus Expands Access to Sanitation for Low-Income Families with Help from Spain." News Release, 28 May. www.iadb.org/en/news/news-releases/2010-05-28/manaus-extends-low-income-sanitation,7200.html. Accessed 15 May 2011.

IEA (International Energy Agency). 2008. *World Energy Outlook.* Paris: Organisation for Economic Co-operation and Development.

———. 2010. *World Energy Outlook.* Paris: Organisation for Economic Co-operation and Development.

IEA (International Energy Agency), UNDP (United Nations Development Programme) and UNIDO (United Nations Industrial Development Orgnization). 2010. *Energy Poverty: How to Make Modern Access Universal?* Special early excerpt of *World Energy Outlook 2010* for the UN General Assembly. Paris: International Energy Agency.

IFAD (International Fund for Agricultural Development). 2011. *Rural Poverty Report 2011.* Rome. www.ifad.org/rpr2011/report/e/rpr2011.pdf. Accessed 10 June 2011.

Iftikhar, U. A. 2003. "Population, Poverty and Environment." Background Paper. International Union for Conservation of Nature Pakistan Programme, Northern Area Strategy for Sustainable Development. http://cmsdata.iucn.org/downloads/bp_po_pov_env.pdf. Accessed 15 July 2011.

Ilahi, N., and F. Grimard. 2000. "Public Infrastructure and Private Costs: Water Supply and Time Allocation of Women in Rural Pakistan." *Economic Development and Cultural Change* 49 (1): 45–75.

ILO (International Labour Organization). 2006. *Social Security for All: Investing in Global Social and Economic Development.* Discussion Paper 16. Geneva: International Labour Office.

———. 2008. *Can Low-Income Countries Afford Basic Social Security?* Social Security Policy Briefings Paper 3. Geneva: International Labour Office. www.ilo.org/public/libdoc/ilo/2008/108B09_73_engl.pdf. Accessed 3 May 2011.

———. 2010. "Employment and Social Protection Policies from Crisis to Recovery and Beyond: A Review of Experience." Report to the G20 Labour and Employment Ministers Meeting, 20–21 April, Washington, DC. www.ilo.org/public/libdoc/jobcrisis/download/g20_report_employment_and_social_protection_policies.pdf. Accessed 14 July 2011.

IMF (International Monetary Fund). 2004. "Djibouti: Poverty Reduction Strategy Paper." IMF Country Report 04/152. International Monetary Fund, Washington, DC. www.imf.org/external/pubs/ft/scr/2004/cr04152.pdf. Accessed 10 May 2011.

———. 2010. "A Fair and Substantial Contribution by the Financial Sector: Final Report for the G20." International Monetary Fund, Washington, DC. www.imf.org/external/np/g20/pdf/062710b.pdf. Accessed 5 June 2011.

Independent Evaluation Group. 2008. *The Welfare Impact of Rural Electrification: A Reassessment of the Costs and Benefits.* IEG Impact Evaluation. Washington DC: World Bank.

India, Government of, and UNDP (United Nations Development Programme) Disaster Risk Management Programme. 2008. *Women as Equal Partners Gender Dimensions of Disaster Risk Management Programme Compliation of Good Practices.* Delhi: United Nations Development Programme India.

India Prime Minister's Council on Climate Change. 2008. *National Action Plan on Climate Change.* New Delhi. http://pmindia.nic.in/Pg01-52.pdf. Accessed 1 July 2011.

International Water and Sanitation Centre and Netherlands Water Partnership. 2009. *Smart Finance Solutions: Examples of Innovative Financial Mechanisms for Water and Sanitation.* Amsterdam: KIT Publishers. www.irc.nl/redir/content/download/142154/446902/file/Smart_Finance_Solutions.pdf. Accessed 15 July 2011.

IPCC (Intergovernmental Panel on Climate Change). 1997. *The Regional Impacts of Climate Change: An Assessment of Vulnerability*, eds. R. T. Watson, M. C. Zinyowera, R. H. Moss, and D. J. Dokken. Cambridge, UK: Cambridge University Press.

———. 2007. *Fourth Assessment Report: Climate Change 2007: Synthesis Report.* Contribution of Working Groups

I, II and III to the Fourth Assessment Report of the Intergovernmental Panel on Climate Change. Geneva, Switzerland.

———. 2011. "Summary for Policymakers." In *IPCC Special Report on Renewable Energy Sources and Climate Change Mitigation*, ed. O. Edenhofer, R. Pichs-Madruga, Y. Sokona, and K. Seyboth. Cambridge, UK and New York: Cambridge University Press.

ITU (International Telecommunications Union). 2011. *World Telecommunication/ICT Indicators Database*. Geneva: International Telecommunications Union.

Ivanic, M., and W. Martin. 2008. "Implications of Higher Global Food Prices for Poverty in Low-Income Countries." Policy Research Working Paper 4594. World Bank, Washington, DC.

IWGIA (International Work Group for Indigenous Affairs). 2008. *The Indigenous World 2008*. Edison, NJ: Transaction Publishers.

Iyigun, M., and D. Rodrik. 2004. "On the Efficacy of Reforms: Policy Tinkering, Institutional Change and Entrepreneurship." Discussion Paper 4399. Centre for Economic Policy Research, London.

Jackson, M., and A. Rosencranz. 2003. "The Delhi Pollution Case: Can the Supreme Court Manage the Environment?" *Environment Policy and Law* 33 (2): 88–91.

Jacoby H., M. Rabassa, and E. Skoufias. Forthcoming. "On the Distributional Implications of Climate Change: The Case of India." Policy Research Working Paper. World Bank, Washington, DC.

Jensen, R. 2000. "Agricultural Volatility and Investments in Children." *American Economic Review* 90 (2): 399–404.

Jevrejeva, S., A. Grinsted, J. C. Moore, and S. Holgate. 2006. "Nonlinear Trends and Multiyear Cycles in Sea Level Records." *Journal of Geophysical Research* 111: 1–11.

Jha, S., and I. Pereira. 2011. "Existing Measures of Sustainability: A Review." Background Paper for the 2011 *Human Development Report*. UNDP–HDRO, New York.

Jin, Y., H. Wang, and D. Wheeler. 2010. "Environmental Performance Rating and Disclosure. An Empirical Investigation of China's Green Watch Program." Policy Research Working Paper 5420. World Bank, Washington, DC. http://www-wds.worldbank.org/servlet/WDSContentServer/WDSP/IB/2010/09/16/000158349_20100916105353/Rendered/PDF/WPS5420.pdf. Accessed 15 June 2011.

Kammen, D. M., K. Kapadia, and M. Fripp. 2004. "Putting Renewables to Work: How Many Jobs Can the Clean Energy Industry Generate?" Renewable and Appropriate Energy Lab Report. University of California–Berkeley, Berkeley, CA.

Kan, H., S. J. London, G Chen, Y. Zhang, G. Song, N. Zhao, L. Jiang, and B. Chen. 2008. "Season, Sex, Age, and Education as Modifiers of the Effects of Outdoor Air Pollution on Daily Mortality in Shanghai, China: The Public Health and Air Pollution in Asia Study." *Environmental Health Perspectives* 116 (9): 1183–88.

Kelman, I., and J. J. West. 2009. "Climate Change and Small Island Developing States: A Critical Review." *Ecological and Environmental Anthropology* 5 (1): 1–16.

Kenya National Coordinating Agency for Population and Development. 2008. "An Output-Based Approach to Reproductive Health: Vouchers for Health in Kenya." Policy Brief 2. Nairobi.

Khan, A., and M. Khan. 2010. "Population Programs in Bangladesh: Problems, Prospects And Policy Issues." Gillespie Foundation, Pasadena, CA. http://gillespiefoundation.org/uploads/Population_Problems_in_Bangladesh_Problem__Prospects_and_Policy_Issues.pdf. Accessed 4 April 2011.

Khandker, S. R., D. F. Barnes, and H. A. Samad. 2009. "Welfare Impacts of Rural Electrification: A Case Study from Bangladesh." Policy Research Working Paper 4859, World Bank, Washington, DC. http://ssrn.com/abstract=1368068. Accessed 6 May 2011.

Khandker, S. R., D. F. Barnes, H. A. Samad, and N. H. Minh. 2009. "Welfare Impacts of Rural Electrification: Evidence from Vietnam." Policy Research Working Paper 5057. World Bank, Washington, DC.

Khilyuk, L. F., and G. V. Chilingar. 2006. "On Global Forces of Nature Driving the Earth's Climate. Are Humans Involved?" *Environmental Geology* 50: 899–910.

Kim, J., J. Corfee-Morlot, and P. T. Serclaes. 2009. "Linking Mitigation Actions in Developing Countries with Mitigation Support: A Conceptual Framework." Organisation for Economic Co-operation and Development, Environment Directorate, and International Energy Agency, Paris. www.oecd.org/dataoecd/27/24/42474721.pdf. Accessed 5 May 2011.

Kimenyi, M. S. 2011. "The Arab Democracy Paradox." The Brookings Institution, 4 March 04 2011. www.brookings.edu/opinions/2011/0304_arab_democracy_kimenyi.aspx. Accessed 15 May 2011.

King, M., A. Smith and M. Gracey. 2009. "Indigenous Health Part 2: The Underlying Causes of the Health Gap." *The Lancet* 374 (9683): 76–85.

Kjellstrom, T. M. Lodh, T. McMichael, G. Ranmuthugala, R. Shrestha, and S. Kingsland. 2006. "Air and Water Pollution: Burden and Strategies for Control." In *Disease Control Priorities in Developing Countries*, ed. D. T. Jamison, J. G. Breman, A. R. Measham, G. Alleyne, M. Claeson, D. B. Evans, P. Jha, A. Mills, and P. Musgrove. Washington, DC and New York: World Bank and Oxford University Press.

Klein, A.-M., C. Müller, P. Hoehn, and C. Kremen. 2009. "Understanding the Role of Species Richness for Crop Pollination Services." In *Biodiversity, Ecosystem Functioning, and Human Wellbeing*, ed. N. Shahid, D. E. Bunker, A. Hector, M. Loreau, and C. Perrings. Oxford, UK: Oxford University Press.

Klopfenstein, L., L. Petrasky, V. Winton, and J. Brown. 2011. "Addressing Water Quality Issues in Rural Cameroon and Household Biosand Filters." *International Journal for Service Learning in Engineering* 6 (1): 64–80.

Klugman, J., F. Rodriguez, and H. J. Choi. 2011. "The HDI 2010: New Controversies, Old Critiques." Human Development Research Paper 1. UNDP–HDRO, New York.

Knutson, T. R., J. L. McBride, J. Chan, K. Emanuel, G. Holland, C. Landsea, I. Held, J. P. Kossin, A. K. Srivastava, and M. Sugi. 2010. "Tropical Cyclones and Climate Change." *Nature Geoscience* 3: 157–63.

Kockler, H. 2005. *Coping Strategies of Households Exposed to Unequal Environmental Quality in Germany*. Paper for the 4th Global Conference Environmental Justice and Global Citizenship: Environment, Sustainability and Technologies, 5–7 July, Oxford, UK. www.inter-disciplinary.net/ptb/ejgc/ejgc4/paper_koeckler1.pdf. Accessed 25 May 2011.

Kojima, M., and R. Bacon. 2006. "Coping with Higher Oil Prices." World Bank, Energy Sector Management Assistance Program, Washington, DC.

Koolwal, G., and D. van de Walle. 2010. "Access to Water, Women's Work and Child Outcomes." Policy Research Working Paper 5302. World Bank, Washington, DC.

Kramarae, C., and D. Spender, eds. 2000. *Routledge International Encyclopedia of Women: Global Women's Issues and Knowledge. Education: Health to Hypertension Vol. 2*. New York: Routledge.

Kriström, B., and S. Wibe. 1997. "Environmental Policy in Sweden." In *Comparative Environmental Policy and Politics*, ed. U. Desai. New York: State University of New York Press.

Kruize, H., and A. A. Bouwman. 2004. "Environmental (In)equity in the Netherlands: A Case Study on the Distribution of Environmental Quality in the Rijnmond Region." RIVM Report 550012003. Dutch National Institute for Public Health and the Environment, Bilthoven, The Netherlands. www.rivm.nl/bibliotheek/rapporten/550012003.pdf. Accessed 5 June 2011.

Kumar, S. K., and D. Hotchkiss. 1989. "Consequences of Deforestation for Women's Time Allocation, Agricultural Production and Nutrition in Hill Areas of Nepal." Research Report 69. International Food Policy Research Institute, Washington, DC.

Lama, J. R., C. R. Seas, R. León-Barúa, E. Gotuzzo, and R. B. Sack. 2004. "Environmental Temperature, Cholera, and Acute Diarrohea in Adults in Lima, Peru." *Journal of Health Population and Nutrition* 22 (4): 399–403.

Laurian, L. 2008. "Environmental Justice in France." *Journal of Environmental Planning Management* 51: 55–79.

Leading Group on Innovative Financing for Development. 2010. *Globalizing Solidarity: The Case for Financial Levies*. Report of the Committee of Experts to the Taskforce on International Financial Transactions and Development. Paris: Permanent Leading Group Secretariat, French Ministry of Foreign and International Affairs.

Lohror, J. 2010. "A Physicist Solves the City." *New York Times Magazine*, 19 December. www.nytimes.com/2010/12/19/magazine/19Urban_West-t.html. Accessed 15 June 2011.

Leisher, C., M. Sanjayan, J. Blockhus, A. Kontoleon, S. N. Larsen. 2010. *Does Conserving Biodiversity Work To Reduce Poverty? A State of Knowledge Review*. Cambridge, UK: The Nature Conservancy, University of Cambridge, International Institution for Environment and Development, and Poverty and Conservation Learning Group.

Leonhardt, D. 2011. "The Big Thirst: The Future of Water." Economix (blog), *New York Times*, 3 May. http://economix.blogs.nytimes.com/2011/05/03/the-big-thirst-the-future-of-water/. Accessed 5 May 2011.

Li, Q., and R. Reuveny. 2006. "Democracy and Environmental Degradation." *International Studies Quarterly* 50: 935–56.

Lieuw-Kie-Song, M. R. 2009. "Green Jobs for the Poor: A Public Employment Approach." Poverty Reduction Discussion Paper 2009/02. United Nations Development Programme, New York.

Lin, J. 2010. "New Structural Economics: A Framework for Rethinking Development." Policy Research Working Paper 5197. World Bank, Washington, DC.

Lindsay S. W., and Martens W. J. M. 1998. "Malaria in the African highlands: Past, Present and Future." *Bulletin of the World Health Organization* 76: 33–45.

Liu, J., and P. Raven. 2010. "China's Environmental Challenges and Implications for the World." *Environmental Science and Technology* 40: 823–51.

Llavador, H., J. Roemer, and J. Silvestre. 2011. "Sustainability in the Presence of Global Warming: Theory and Empirics." Human Development Research Paper 5. UNDP–HDRO, New York.

Lloyd-Smith, M., and L. Bell. 2003. "Toxic Disputes and the Rise of Environmental Justice in Australia." *International Journal of Occupational and Environmental Health* 9: 14–23. http://ntn.org.au/wp-content/uploads/2010/02/envjusticeinaust.pdf. Accessed 15 July 2011.

Lobell, D. B., M. B. Burke, C. Tebaldi, M. D. Mastrandrea, W. P. Falcon, and R. L. Naylor. 2008. "Prioritizing Climate Change Adaptation Needs for Food Security in 2030." *Science* 319: 607–10.

Lobell, D. B., W. Schlenker, and J. Costa-Roberts. 2011. "Climate Trends and Global Crop Production since 1980." *Science* 333 (6402): 616–20.

Lopez-Calva, L., and N. Lustig, eds. 2010. *Declining Inequality in Latin America: A Decade of Progress?* Brookings Institution Press and the United Nations Development Programme: Washington, DC, and New York.

Lopez Carr, D., and L. Grandia. 2011. "Implications of Urban vs. Rural Fertility Rates: The Case of Guatemala." The New Security Beat (blog), The Woodrow Wilson Center Environmental Change and Security Program, 22 March. www.newsecuritybeat.org/2011/03/watch-david-lopez-carr-and-liza-grandia.html. Accessed 18 May 2011.

Loughran, D., and L. Pritchett. 1997. "Environmental Scarcity, Resource Collection, and the Demand for Children in Nepal." Working Paper. World Bank, Washington, DC.

Lundqvist, L. 1972. "Sweden's Environmental Policy." *Ambio* 1 (3): 90–101. www.jstor.org/stable/4311956. Accessed 13 May 2011.

Lwin Oo, Y. 2010. "Global Hand-Washing Day Inspires Children of Myanmar to Regular Hand-Washing." UNICEF Myanmar. www.unicef.org/myanmar/water_sanitation_14579.html. Accessed 23 May 2011.

Mansour, M., J. B. Mansour, and A. H. El Swesy. 2010. "Scaling up Proven Public Health Interventions through a Locally Owned and Sustained Leadership Development Programme in Rural Upper Egypt." *Human Resources for Health* 8 (1). www.human-resources-health.com/content/8/1/1. Accessed 15 July 2011.

Manus, P. 2006. "Indigenous People, Environmental Rights and Evolving Common Law Perspectives in Canada, Australia and the United States." *Boston College Environmental Affairs Law Review* 33 (1). http://lawdigitalcommons.bc.edu/ealr/vol33/iss1/2. Accessed 19 April 2011.

Marchiori , L., J.-F. Maystadt, and I. Schumacher. 2011. "The Impact of Climate Variations on Migration in Sub-Saharan Africa." Presentation at the Conference on Adaptation to Climate Change, 18–19 May, Washington, DC. www.gwu.edu/~iiep/adaptation/docs/Maystadt,%20the%20Impact%20of%20Climate%20Variations%20on%20Migration%20in%20sub-Saharan%20Africa.pdf. Accessed 15 July 2011.

Marín, A., S. Gelchich, G. Araya, G. Olea, M. Espíndola, and J. C. Castilla. 2010. "The 2010 Tsunami in Chile: Devastation and Survival of Coastal Mall-Scale Fishing Communities." *Marine Policy* 34 (6): 1381–84.

Martin, P. L. 2011. "Pay to Preserve: The Global Politics of Ecuador's Yasuní-ITT Proposal." *Revue internationale de politique de développement* 2 http://poldev.revues.org/770. Accessed 25 July 2011.

May, J. R. 2006. "Constituting Fundamental Environmental Rights Worldwide." *Pace Environmental Law Review* 23 (1). http://digitalcommons.pace.edu/cgi/viewcontent.cgi?article=1075&context=pelr. Accessed 5 June 2011.

Mayer, A. L., P. E. Kauppi, P. K. Angelstam, Y. Shang, and P. M. Tikka. 2005. "Importing Timber, Exporting Ecological Impact." *Science* 308 (5720): 359–60.

Mayer, A. L., P. E. Kauppi, P. M. Tikka, and P. K. Angelstam. 2006. "Conservation Implications of Exporting Domestic Wood Harvest to Neighboring Countries." *Environmental Science and Policy* 9 (3): 228–36.

Mayer-Foulkes, D. 2011. "A Cross-Country Causal Panorama of Human Development and Sustainability." Background Paper for the 2011 *Human Development Report*. UNDP–HDRO, New York.

Mayers, J. 2007. "Trees, Poverty and Targets: Forests and the Millennium Development Goals," Briefing. International Institute for Environment and Development, London.

McGillivray, M. 2011. "Global Inequality in Health: Disparities in Human Longevity." In *Health Inequality and Development*, ed. M. McGillivray, I. Dutta, and D. Lawson. New York and Helsinki: Palgrave McMillan in association with the United Nations University World Institute for Development Economics Research.

McGranahan, G., P. Jacobi, J. Songsor, C. Surjadi, and M. Kjellen. 2001. *The Citizens at Risk, from Urban Sanitation to Sustainable Cities*. London: Earthscan.

McKinsey and Company. 2009. "Pathways to a Low-Carbon Economy: Version 2 of the Global Greenhouse Gas Abatement Cost Curve." https://solutions.mckinsey.com/ClimateDesk/default.aspx. Accessed 15 July 2011.

McSweeney, K.. 2004. "Forest Product Sale as Natural Insurance." *Society and Natural Resources, 17* (1): 39–56.

Measure DHS. 2008. "Description of the Demographic and Health Surveys: Individual Recode: Data File." Version 1.0. Calverton, MD. www.measuredhs.com/pubs/pdf/DHSG4/Recode4DHS.pdf. Accessed 10 June 2011.

Mehta, L., and S. Movik, eds. 2011. *Shit Matters: The Potential of Community-Led Total Sanitation*. Warwickshire, UK: Practical Action Publishing.

Meier, P., V. Tuntivate, D. F. Barnes, S. V. Bogach, and D. Farchy. 2010. "Peru: National Survey of Rural Household Energy Use." Special Report 007/10. World Bank, Energy Sector Management Assistance Program, World Bank, Washington, DC. www.esmap.org/esmap/sites/esmap.org/files/ESMAP_PeruNationalSurvey_Web_0.pdf. Accessed 5 May 2011.

Meinshausen, M., N. Meinshausen, W. Hare, S. C. B. Raper, J. Frieler, R. Knutti, D. J. Frame, and M. R. Allen. 2009. "Greenhouse-Gas Emission Targets for Limiting Global Warming to 2°C." *Nature* 458 (30): 1158–63.

Meyfroidt, P., T. K. Rudel, and E. F. Lambin. 2010. "Forest Transitions, Trade, and the Global Displacement of Land Use." *Proceedings of the National Academy of Sciences of the United States of America* 107 (49): 20917–22.

Miguel, E., S. Satyanath, and E. Sergenti. 2004 . "Economic Shocks and Civil Convict: An Instrumental Variables Approach." *Journal of Political Economy* 112 (4): 725–53.

Milanovic, B. 2009. "Global Inequality and the Global Inequality Extraction Ratio." Policy Research Working Paper 5044. World Bank, Washington, DC.

———. 2011."Global Income Inequality." Household Survey Data for 1998–2002. World Bank, Washington, DC. http://econ.worldbank.org/WBSITE/EXTERNAL/EXTDEC/EXTRESEARCH/0,,contentMDK:22261771~pagePK:64214825~piPK:64214943~theSitePK:469382,00.html. Accessed 23 May 2011.

Milinksi, M., R. D. Sommerfeld, H.-J. Krambeck, F. A. Reed, and J. Marotzke. 2008. "The Collective-Risk Social Dilemma and the Prevention of Simulated Dangerous Climate Change." *Proceedings of the National Academy of Sciences of the United States of America* 105 (7): 2291–94.

Millennium Ecosystem Assessment. 2005. *Ecosystems and Human Well-Being: Desertification Synthesis*. Washington, DC: World Resources Institute. www.maweb.org/documents/document.355.aspx.pdf. Accessed 15 May 2011.

Millman, A., D. Tang, and F. P. Perera. 2008. "Air Pollution Threatens the Health of Children in China." *Pediatrics* 122 (3): 620–28.

Mills, S., E. Bos, E. Suzuki. 2010. "Unmet Need for Contraception." Washington, DC: World Bank.

Milly, P. C. D., K. A. Dunne, and A. V. Vecchia. 2005. "Global Pattern of Trends in Stream Flow and Water Availability in a Changing Climate." *Nature* 438 (17): 347–50.

Milton, A. H., S. M. Shahidullah, W. Smith, K. S. Hossain, Z. Hasan, and K. T. Ahmed. 2010. "Association between Chronic Arsenic Exposure and Nutritional Status among the Women of Child Bearing Age: A Case-Control Study in Bangladesh." *International Journal for Environmental Research and Public Health* 7 (7): 2811–21.

Mimura, N., L. Nurse, R. McLean, J. Agard, L. Briguglio, P. Lefale, R. Payet, and G. Sem. 2007. "Small

Islands." In *Climate Change 2007: Impacts, Adaptation and Vulnerability. Contribution of Working Group II to the Fourth Assessment Report of the Intergovernmental Panel on Climate Change*, ed. M. L. Parry, O. F. Canziani, J. P. Palutikof, P. J. van der Linden, and C. E. Hanson. Cambridge, UK: Cambridge University Press. www.ipcc.ch/pdf/assessment-report/ar4/wg2/ar4-wg2-chapter16.pdf. Accessed 19 May 2011.

Mitchell, G., and D. Dorling. 2003. "An Environmental Justice Analysis of British Air Quality." *Environment and Planning A* 35 (5): 909–29.

Mitra, A. 2011. "Environmental Resource Consumption Pattern in Rural Arunachal Pradesh." *Forest Policy and Economics* 13 (3): 166–70.

Mitra, A., and D. K. Mishra. 2011. "Environmental Resource Consumption Pattern in Rural Arunachal Pradesh." *Forest Policy and Economics* 13 (3): 166–170.

Molnar, A., S. J. Scherr, and A. Khare. 2004. *Who Conserves the World's Forests? Community Driven Strategies to Protect Forests and Respect Rights*. Washington, DC: Forest Trends and Ecoagriculture Partners.

Mulongoy, K. J., and S. B. Gidda. 2008. *The Value of Nature: Ecological, Economic, Cultural and Social Benefits of Protected Areas*. Montreal, Canada: Secretariat of the Convention on Biological Diversity.

Myers, N., and A. H. Knoll. 2001. "The Biotic Crisis and the Future of Evolution." *Proceedings of the National Academy of Sciences of the United States of America* 98 (10): 5389–92.

Nagendra, H. 2011. "Heterogeneity and Collective Action for Forest Management." Human Development Research Paper 2. UNDP–HDRO, New York.

Namibia Ministry of Environment and Tourism, Directorate of Parks and Wildlife Management. 2010. *Climate Change Vulnerability and Adaptation Assessment for Namibia's Biodiversity and Protected Area System*. Windhoek.

Nankhuni, F., and J. L. Findeis. 2004. "Natural Resource Collection Work and Children's Schooling in Malawi." *Agricultural Economics* 31 (2–3): 123–34.

Ndiritu, S. W., and W. Nyangena. 2010. "Environmental Goods Collection and Children's Schooling: Evidence from Kenya." *Regional Environmental Change*. www.springerlink.com/content/470430708568p4qj/. Accessed 22 May 2011.

Nellemann, C., M. MacDevette, T. Manders, B. Eickhout, D. Svihus, a. G. Prins, B. P. Kaltenborn, eds. 2009. *The Environmental Food Crisis: The Environment's Role in Averting Future Food Crises*. A UNEP Rapid Response Assessment. United Nations Environment Programme, GRID-Arendal, Norway.

Nelson, G. C., M. W. Rosegrant, J. Koo, R. Robertson, T. Sulser, T. Zhu, C. Ringler, S. Msangi, A. Palazzo, M. Batka, M. Magalhaes, R. Valmonte-Santos, M. Ewing, and D. Lee. 2009. *Climate Change: Impact on Agriculture and Costs of Adaptation*. Food Policy Report. International Food Policy Research Institute, Washington, DC.

Nelson, G. C., M. W. Rosegrant, A. Palazzo, I. Gray, C. Ingersoll, R. Robertson, S. Tokgoz, T. Zhu, T.

B. Sulser, C. Ringler, S. Msangi, and L. You. 2010. *Food Security, Farming, and Climate Change to 2050: Scenarios, Results, amd Policy Options*. Washington, DC: International Food Policy Research Institute.

Nelson, S. 2011. "Environmental Services Program Spurs Water Innovation for the Urban Poor." *Global Waters*, March. www.usaid.gov/our_work/cross-cutting_programs/water/globalwaters/mar2011/3_mar11.html. Accessed 3 May 2011.

Nepal Water for Health. 2004. "Easy Access to Sanitation Materials in Rural Nepal: An Evaluation of a SaniMart Pilot Project." Water for Health, Panchawati, Nepal.

Neubert, S. 2009. "Wastewater Reuse: How "Integrated" and Sustainable is the Strategy?" *Water Policy* 11: 37–53.

Neumayer, E. 2002. "Do Democracies Exhibit Stronger International Environmental Commitment? A Cross-Country Analysis." *Journal of Peace Research* 39 (2): 139–64.

———. 2003. "Beyond Income: Convergence in Living Standards, Big Time." *Structural Change and Economic Dynamics* 14 (3): 275–96.

———. 2004. "Sustainability and Well-Being Indicators." Research Paper 2004/23. United Nations University World Institute for Development Economics Research, Helsinki.

———. 2010a. *Weak versus Strong Sustainability: Exploring the Limits of Two Opposing Paradigms*. Cheltenham, UK: Edward Elgar Publishing

———. 2010b. "Human Development and Sustainability." Human Development Research Paper 210/05. UNDP–HDRO, New York. http://hdr.undp.org/en/reports/global/hdr2010/papers/HDRP_2010_05.pdf. Accessed 10 June 2011.

———. 2011. "Sustainability and Inequality in Human Development." Human Development Research Paper 4. UNDP–HDRO, New York.

Neumayer, E., and F. Barthel. 2011. "Normalizing Economic Loss from Natural Disasters: A Global Analysis." *Global Environmental Change* 21: 13–24.

Neumayer, E., and T. Plumper. 2007. "The Gendered Nature of Natural Disasters: The Impact of Catastrophic Events on the Gender Gap in Life Expectancy, 1981–2002." *Annals of the Association of American Geographers* 97 (3): 551–66.

Newell, P. 2008. "Civil Society, Corporate Accountability and the Politics of Climate Change." *Global Environmental Politics* 8 (3): 122–153.

Newell, P., J. Phillips, and D. Mulvaney. 2011. "Pursuing Clean Energy Equitably." Human Development Research Paper 3. UNDP–HDRO, New York.

New York Times. 2011. "The Court and Global Warming." 18 April. www.nytimes.com/2011/04/19/opinion/19tue1.html . Accessed 15 July 2011.

Nishikiori, N., T. Abe, D. G. Costa, S. D. Dharmaratne, O. Kunii, and K. Moji. 2006. "Who Died as a Result of the Tsunami? Risk Factors of Mortality among Internally Displaced Persons in Sri Lanka: A Retrospective Cohort Analysis." *BMC Public Health*: 6–73.

Nordhaus, W. 2004. *Retrospective on the 1970s Productivity Slowdown*. Working Paper 10950. Cambridge, MA: National Bureau of Economic Research.

Norgaard, K., and R. York. 2005. "Gender Equality and State Environmentalism." *Gender and Society* 19 (4): 506–22.

Norton Rose Group. 2011. "Asia Pacific Climate Change Series: China." Issue 2. Sydney, Australia. www.nortonrose.com/files/asia-pacific-climate-change-policy-series-china-52306.pdf. Accessed 1 July 2011.

Noy, I. 2009. "The Macroeconomic Consequences of Disasters." *Journal of Development Economics* 88: 221–31.

Nugent, C., and J. M. Shandra. 2009. "State Environmental Protection Efforts, Women's Status, and World Polity: A Cross-National Analysis." *Organization Environment* 22 (2): 208–29.

Nussbaum, M. 1998. *Plato's Republic: The Good Society and the Deformation of Desire*. Washington, DC: Library of Congress.

———. 2006. *Frontiers of Justice: Disability, Nationality, Species Membership*. Cambridge, MA: Harvard University Press.

O'Donnell, O., E. van Doorslaer, A. Wagstaff, and M. Lindelow. 2008. *Analyzing Health Equity Using Household Survey Data*. WBI Learning Resources Series. Washington, DC: World Bank.

O'Neill, B. C., M. Dalton, R. Fuchs, L. Jiang, S. Pachauri, and K. Zigova. 2010. "Global Demographic Trends and Future Carbon Emissions." *Proceedings of the National Academy of Science of the United States of America* 107 (41): 17521–26.

OECD (Organisation for Economic Co-operation and Development. 2010a. *Tackling Inequalities in Brazil, China, India and South Africa: The Role of Labour Markets and Social Policies*. Paris: Organisation for Economic Co-operation and Development. http://dx.doi.org/10.1787/9789264088368-en. Accessed 10 April 2011.

———. 2010b. *Cities and Climate change*. Paris.

———. 2010c. "Green Growth Strategy Interim Report: Implementing Our Commitment For A Sustainable Future." Meeting of the OECD Council at Ministerial Level, 27–28 May, Paris.

———. 2010d. *Innovative Financing Mechanisms for the Water Sector*. Paris.

———. 2011a. *Tackling Inequality*. Issues Paper. Paris. www.oecd.org/dataoecd/32/20/47723414.pdf. Accessed 10 May 2011.

———. 2011b. "Development Aid Reaches an Historic High in 2010." OECD, Development Co-operation Directorate, Paris. www.oecd.org/document/35/0,3746,en_2649_34447_47515235_1_1_1_1,00.html. Accessed 15 July 2011.

Okello, V. 2005. "The Upesi Rural Stoves Project." *Boiling Point* 51: 2-5.

Ostrom, E. 1992. *Governing the Commons: The Evolution of Institutions for Collective Action*. Natural Resources 32. Cambridge, UK: Cambridge University Press.

Oxfam International. 2005. "The Tsunami's Impact on Women." Briefing Note. Oxfam International, Oxford, UK. www.oxfam.org/sites/www.oxfam.org/files/women. pdf. Accessed 15 July 2011.

———. 2007. "Blind Spot: The Continued Failure of the World Bank and the IMF to Fully Assess the Impact of Their Advice." Joint NGO Briefing Note. Oxfam International, Oxford, UK.

Parry, M. L., O. F. Canziani, J. P. Palutikof, J. van der Linden, and C. E. Hanson, eds. 2007. *Climate Change 2007: Impacts, Adaptation and Vulnerability.* Contribution of Working Group II to the Fourth Assessment Report of the Intergovernmental Panel on Climate Change. Cambridge, UK: Cambridge University Press.

Parry, M. L., J. Lowe, and C. Hanson. 2009. "Overshoot, Adapt and Recover." *Nature* 458: 1102–03.

Pastor, M. 2007. "Environmental Justice: Reflections from the United States." In *Reclaiming Nature: Environmental Justice and Ecological Restoration*, ed. J. K. Boyce, S. Narain, and E. A. Stanton. London and New York: Anthem Press.

Pattanayak, S. K., and E. Sills. 2001. "Do Tropical Forests Provide Natural Insurance? The Microeconomics of Non-Timber Forest Products Collection in the Brazilian Amazon." *Land Economics* 77 (4): 595–612.

Pedersen, O. W. 2008. "European Environmental Human Rights and Environmental Rights: A Long Time Coming?" *Georgetown International Environmental Law Review* 21 (1).

Pellow, D. 2004. "The Politics of Illegal Dumping: An Environmental Justice Framework." *Qualitative Sociology* 27 (4).

Pepper, D. 2007. "India's Rivers are Drowning in Pollution." *CNN Money*, 11 June. http://money.cnn.com/magazines/fortune/fortune_archive/2007/06/11/100083453/index.htm. Accessed 15 May 2011.

Perez, E., C. Amelink, B. Briceno, J. Cardosi, J. Devine, A. Grossman, A. Kamasan, C. Kullman, C. A. Kumar, I. Moise, K. Mwambuli, A. Orsola-Vidal, and D. Wartono. 2011. *Global Scaling Up Rural Sanitation Project: Progress Report.* Washington, DC: Water and Sanitation Program.

Perrings, C., and D. W. Pearce. 1994. "Threshold Effects and Incentives for the Conservation of Biodiversity." *Environment and Resource Economics* 4 (1). 13–28.

Peru Ministry of Housing, Construction and Sanitation. 2006. *2006–2015 National Sanitation Plan.* Lima.

The PEW Charitables Trusts. 2010. "Who's Winning the Clean Energy Race? Growth, Competition and Opportunity in the World's Largest Economies." Washington, DC. www.pewtrusts.org/uploadedFiles/wwwpewtrustsorg/Reports/Global_warming/G-20%20Report.pdf. Accessed 15 July 2011.

Potts, M., and L. Marsh. 2010. *The Population Factor: How Does it Relate to Climate Change? Climate Adaptation*, February.

Pradhan, M., D. Sahn, and S. Younger. 2003. "Decomposing World Health Inequality." *Journal of Health Economics* 22 (2): 271–93.

Price, G. N. 2008. "Hurricane Katrina: Was There a Political Economy of Death." *Review of the Black Political Economy* 35 (4): 163–80.

Prüss-Üstün A., R. Bos, F. Gore, and J. Bartram. 2008. *Safer Water, Better Health: Costs, Benefits and Sustainability of Interventions to Protect and Promote Health.* Geneva: World Health Organization.

Prüss-Üstün, A., and C. Corvalán. 2006. *Preventing Disease through Healthy Environments. Towards an Estimate of the Environmental Burden of Disease.* Geneva: World Health Organization.

Puddephatt, A. 2009. "Exploring the Role of Civil Society in the Formulation and Adoption of Access to Information Laws: The Cases of Bulgaria, India, Mexico, South Africa and the United Kingdom." Access to Information Working Paper Series. World Bank, Washington, DC. http://siteresources.worldbank.org/EXTGOVACC/Resources/atICivSocietyFinalWeb.pdf. Accessed 10 May 2011.

Raleigh, C., and H. Urdal. 2008. "Climate Change, Demography, Environmental Degradation, and Armed Conflict." New Directions in Demographic Security Series. Woodrow Wilson International Center for Scholars, Environmental Change and Security Program, Washington, DC.

Raupach, M. R., G. Marland, P. Ciais, C. Le Quéré, J. G. Canadell, G. Klepper, and C. B. Field. 2007. "Global and Regional Drivers of Accelerating CO2 Emissions." *Proceedings of the National Academy of Sciences of the United States of America* 104 (24): 10288–93.

Rawls, J. 1971. *A Theory of Justice.* Cambridge, MA: Harvard University Press.

Renewable Energy Policy Network for the 21st Century. 2010. *Renewables 2010 Global Status Report.* Paris.

———. 2011. *Renewables 2011 Global Status Report.* Paris.

Riojas-Rodríguez, H., J. A. Escamailla-Cejudo, J. A. González-Hermosillo, M. M. Téllez-Rojo, M. Vallejo, C. Santos-Burgoa, and L. Rojas-Bracho. 2006. "Personal PM2.5 and CO Exposures and Heart Rate Variability in Subjects with Known Schemic heart Disease in Mexico City." *Journal of Exposure Science and Environmental Epidemiology* 16: 131–37.

Robinson, B. H. 2009. "E-Waste: An Assessment of Global Production and Environmental Impact." *Science of Total Environment* 408: 183–91.

Rockström, J., W. Steffen, K. Noone, Å. Persson, F. S. Chapin, III, E. Lambin, T. M. Lenton, M. Scheffer, C. Folke, H. Schellnhuber, B. Nykvist, C. A. De Wit, T. Hughes, S. van der Leeuw, H. Rodhe, S. Sörlin, P. K. Snyder, R. Costanza, U. Svedin, M. Falkenmark, L. Karlberg, R. W. Corell, V. J. Fabry, J. Hansen, B. Walker, D. Liverman, K. Richardson, P. Crutzen, and J. Foley. 2009. "Planetary Boundaries: Exploring the Safe Operating Space for Humanity." *Ecology and Society* 14(2).

Rodriguez-Oreggia, E., A. de la Fuente, R. de la Torre, H. Moreno, and C. Rodriguez. 2010. *The Impact of Natural Disasters on Human Development and Poverty at the Municipal Level in Mexico.* Working Paper 43. Harvard University, Center for International Development, Cambridge, MA.

Rodrik, D. 2005. "Feasible Globalizations." In *Globalization: What's New?*, ed. M. Weinstein. New York: Columbia University Press.

———. 2006. "Goodbye Washington Consensus, Hello Washington Confusion? A Review of the World Bank's Economic Growth in the 1990s: Learning from a Decade of Reform." *Journal of Economic Literature* 64: 973–87.

Rodrik, D., A. Subramanian, and F. Trebbi. 2004. "Institutions Rule: The Primacy of Institutions over Geography and Integration in Economic Development." *Journal of Economic Growth* 9 (2): 131–65.

Roper, L., E. Utz, and J. Harvey. 2006. "The Tsunami learning project, Lessons for Grantmakers in Natural Disaster Response." Grantmakers without Borders, San Francisco, CA.

Roscher, C., J. Schumacher, O. Foitzik, and E. D. Schulze. 2007. "Resistance to Rust Fungi in Lolium Perenne Depends on Within Species Variation and Performance of the Host Species in Grasslands of Different Plant Diversity." *Community Ecology* 153 (1): 173–83.

Rose, E. 1999. "Consumption Smoothing and Excess Female Mortality in Rural India." *Review of Economics and Statistics* 8 (1): 41–49.

Roseinweig, F. 2008. "Synthesis of Four Country Enabling Environment Assessments for Scaling Up Sanitation Programs." Water and Sanitation Program, Washington, DC.

Ross, A. 2009. "Modern Interpretations of Sustainable Development." *Journal of Law and Society* 36 (1): 32–54.

Roudi, F. 2009. "A Perspective of Fertility Behavior of Iranian Women." Research paper presented at the International Union for the Scientific Study of Population's International Population Conference, 27 September–2 October, Marrakech.

Sala-i-Martin, X. 2006. "The World Distribution of Income: Falling Poverty and… Convergence, Period." *Quarterly Journal of Economics* CXXI (2): 351–97.

Sanchez, T. 2010. *The Hidden Energy Crisis: How Policies Are Failing the World's Poor.* Rugby, UK: Practical Action.

Sarfo-Mensah, P., and W. Oduro. 2007. "Traditional Natural Resources Management Practices and Biodiversity Conservation in Ghana: A Review of Local Concepts and Issues on Change and Sustainability." Working Paper 90.2007. Fondazione Eni Enrico Mattei, Milan. http://papers.ssrn.com/sol3/papers.cfm?abstract_id=1017238. Accessed 15 July 2011.

Sarkar, S., J. E. Greenleaf, A. Gupta, D. Ghosh, L. M. Blaney, P. Bandyopadhyay, R. K. Biswas, A. K. Dutta, and A. K. SenGupta. 2010. "Evolution of Community-Based Arsenic Removal Systems in Remote Villages in West Bengal, India: Assessment of Decade-long Operation." *Water Research* 44 (2010): 5813–22.

Schmidt, R. 2008. *The Currency Transaction Tax, Rate and Revenue Estimates.* Tokyo: United Nations University Press, War on Want and the North-South Institute.

Schmidt, R., and A. Bhushan. 2011. "The Currency Transactions Tax: Feasibility, Revenue Estimates, and Potential Use of Revenues." Human Development Research Paper 9. UNDP–HDRO, New York.

Scholtes, F. 2011. "Environmental Sustainability in a Perspective of the Human Development and Capability Approach." Background Paper for the 2011 *Human Development Report*. UNDP–HDRO, New York.

Schreckenberg, K., and C. Luttrell. 2009. "Participatory Forest Management: A Route to Poverty Reduction?" *International Forestry Review* 11: 221–38.

Schreiber, M. A. Forthcoming. "The Evolution of Legal Instruments and the Sustainability of the Peruvian Anchovy Fishery." *Marine Policy*.

Seballos, T. T., M. Tarazona, and J. Gallegos. 2011. *Children and Disasters: Understanding Impact and Enabling Agency*. Brighton, UK: Children in a Changing Climate. www.childreninachangingclimate.org/database/CCC/Publications/IMPACTS%20and%20AGENCY_FINAL.pdf. Accessed 15 June 2011.

Secretariat of the Convention on Biological Diversity. 2010. *Global Biodiversity Outlook 3*. Montreal, Canada. www.cbd.int/doc/publications/gbo/gbo3-final-en.pdf. Accessed 20 June 2011.

Secretariat of the Pacific Community. 2011. "Climate Change May Halve Pacific Islands' Coastal Fish Catches." 4 March. www.spc.int/en/component/content/article/216-about-spc-news/683-climate-change-may-halve-paci. Accessed 15 May 2011.

Sen, A. 1979. "Equality of What?" Stanford University. The Tanner Lecture on Human Values, 22 May, Palo Alto, CA. http://culturability.fondazioneunipolis.org/wp-content/blogs.dir/1/files_mf/1270288635equalityofwhat.pdf. Accessed 15 June 2011.

———. 2003. "Continuing the Conversation: Amartya Sen Talks with Bina Agarwal, Jane Humphries, and Ingrid Robeyns." *Feminist Economist* 9 (2–3): 319–32.

———. 2006. "Human Rights and the Limits of the Law." *Cardozo Law Review* 27 (6): 2913–27.

———. 2009. *The Idea of Justice*. Cambridge, MA: Harvard University Press.

———. 2010. "The Place of Capability in a Theory of Justice." In *Measuring Justice: Primary Goods and Capabilities*, ed. H. Brighouse and I. Robeyns. Cambridge, MA: Cambridge University Press.

Senbet, D. 2010. "Determinants of Child Labor Versus Schooling in Rural Ethiopia." *European Journal of Social Sciences* 17 (3). www.eurojournals.com/ejss_17_3_10.pdf. Accessed 15 July 2011.

Shafik, N. 2011. "The Future of Development Finance." Working Paper 250. Center for Global Development, Washington, DC. www.cgdev.org/content/publications/detail/1425068. Accessed 15 July 2011.

Shandra, J. M., C. L. Shandra, and B. London. 2008. "Women, Non-Governmental Organizations, and Deforestation: A Cross-National Study." *Population and Environment* 30(1–2): 48–72.

Shelton, D. L. 2010. "Developing Substantive Environmental Rights." *Journal of Human Rights and the Environment* 1 (1): 89–120.

Simms, A., J. M. Maldonado, and H. Reid. 2006. *Up in Smoke? Latin America and the Caribbean: The Threat from Climate Change to the Environment and Human Development*. The Third Report from the Working Group on Climate Change and Development. London: New Economics Foundation.

Skoufias, E., B. Essama-Nssah, and R. Katayama. 2010. "Too Little Too Late: Welfare Impacts of Rainfall Shocks in Rural Indonesia." World Bank, Washington, DC.

Skoufias, E., M. Rabassa, and S. Olivieri. 2011. "The Poverty Impacts of Climate Change: A Review of the Evidence." Policy Research Working Paper 5622. World Bank, Washington, DC.

Smith, K. R., S. Mehta, and M. Maeusezahl-Feuz. 2004. "Indoor Air Pollution from Household Use of Solid Fuels." In *Comparative Quantification of Health Risks: Global and Regional Burden of Disease Attributable to Selected Major Risk Factors*, eds. M. Ezzati, A. D. Lopez, A. Rodgers, and C. J. L. Murray. Geneva: World Health Organization.

Sobrevila, C. 2008. *The Role of Indigenous Peoples in Biodiversity Conservation: The Natural but Often Forgotten Partners*. Washington, DC: World Bank. http://siteresources.worldbank.org/INTBIODIVERSITY/Resources/RoleofIndigenousPeoplesinBiodiversityConservation.pdf. Accessed 15 June 2011.

Solow, R. M. 1973. "Is the End of the World at Hand?" *Challenge* 16 (1): 39–50.

———. 1974. "The Economics of Resources or the Resources of Economics." Papers and Proceedings of the Eighty-Sixth Annual Meeting of the American Economic Association. *The American Economic Review* 64 (2): 1–14

———. 1993. "An Almost Practical Step toward Sustainability." *Resources Policy* 19 (3): 162–72.

Sonak, S., M. Sonak, and A. Giriyan. 2008. "Shipping Hazardous Waste: Implications for Economically Developing Countries." *International Environmental Agreements* 8: 143–59.

South Africa Department of Environmental Affairs and UNEP (United Nations Environment Programme). 2011. *Working for the Environment*. Pretoria: South Africa Department of Environmental Affairs. www.grida.no/files/publications/savg_ebook.pdf. Accessed 20 June 2011.

Speck, S. 2010. "Options for Promoting Environmental Fiscal Reform in EC Development Cooperation: South Africa Country Case Study." UNEP-UNDP Poverty-Environment Initiative, Nairobi. www.unpei.org/PDF/budgetingfinancing/southafrica-case-study-fiscalreforms.pdf. Accessed 20 July 2011.

Speelmon E. C., W. Checkley, R. H. Gilman, J. Patz, M. Calderon, and S. Manga. 2000. "Cholera Incidence and El Niño–Related Higher Ambient Temperature." *Journal of American Medical Association* 283 (23): 3072–74.

Speth, J. G. 2008. *The Bridge at the Edge of the World: Capitalism, the Environment, and Crossing from Crisis to Sustainability*. New Haven, CT: Yale University Press.

Stern, N. 2007. *The Economics of Climate Change. The Stern Review*. New York: Cambridge University Press.

Stern, N., and C. Taylor. 2007. "Climate Change: Risk, Ethics and the Stern Review." *Science* 317: 203–04.

———. 2010. "What Do the Appendices to the Copenhagen Accord Tell Us about Global Greenhouse Gas Emissions and the Prospects for Avoiding a Rise in Global Average Temperature of More Than 2°C?" Policy Paper. Center for Climate Change Economics and Policy, Grantham Research Institute on Climate Change and the Environment and United Nations Environment Programme, London and New York.

Stiglitz, J. E. 2011. "Gambling with the Planet." *Project Syndicate*, 6 April 2011. www.project-syndicate.org/commentary/stiglitz137/English. Accessed 16 May 2011.

Stiglitz, J. E., A. Sen, and J.-P. Fitoussi. 2009. *Report of the Commission on the Measurement of Economic Performance and Social Progress*. Paris.

Stockholm International Peace Research Institute (SIPRI). 2010. *Yearbook 2010*. Stockholm.

Sze, J., and J. K. London. 2008. "Environmental Justice at the Crossroads." *Sociology Compass* 2/4: 1331–54

Tachamo, R. D., O. Moog, D. N. Shah, and S. Sharma. 2009. "The Cause and Implications of Urban River Pollution: Mitigative Measures and Benthic Macroinvertebrates as River Monitoring Tool." In *Water and Urban Development Paradigms towards an Integration of Engineering, Design and Management Approaches*, ed. J. Feyen, K. Shannon, and M. Neville. London: Taylor and Francis Group.

Takasaki, Y., B. L. Barham, and O. T. Coomes. 2004. "Risk Coping Strategies in Tropical Forests: Floods, Illnesses and Resource Extraction." *Environment and Development Economics* 9 (2): 203–24.

Thomas, R., E. Rignot, G. Casassa, P. Kanagaratnam, C. Acuña, T. Akins, H. Brecher, E. Frederick, P. Gogineni, W. Krabill, S. Manizde, H. Ramamoorthy, A. Rivera, R. Russell, J. Sonntag, R. Swift, J. Yungel, and J. Zwally. 2004. "Accelerated Sea Level Rise from West Antarctica." *Science* 306 (5694): 255–58.

Thomas, V., and M. Ahmad. 2009. "A Historical Perspective on the Mirab System: A Case Study of the Jangharoq Canal, Baghlan." Case Study Series. Afghanistan Research and Evaluation Unit. www.areu.org.af/Uploads/EditionPdfs/908E-The%20Mirab%20System-CS-web.pdf. Accessed 1 August 2011.

Thornton, P. K., P. G. Jones, G. Alagarswamy, and J. Andresen. 2009. "Spatial Variation of Crop Yield Response to Climate Change in East Africa." *Global Environmental Change* 19: 54–65.

Timsina, N. P. 2003. "Promoting Social Justice and Conserving Mountain Forest Environments: A Case Study of Nepal's Community Forestry Programme." *Geographical Journal* 169 (3): 236–42.

Tole, L. 2010. "Reforms from the Ground Up: A Review of Community-Based Forest Management in Tropical Developing Countries." *Environmental Management* 45 (6): 1312–31.

Torras, M. 2006. "The Impact of Power Equality, Income, and the Environment on Human Health: Some Inter-Country Comparisons." *International Review of Applied Economics* 20 (1): 1–20.

———. 2011. "A Survey of the Effects of Inequality on the Environment and Sustainability." Background Paper for the 2011 *Human Development Report*. UNDP–HDRO, New York.

Torras, M., and J. K. Boyce 1998. "Income, Inequality, and Pollution: A Reassessment of the Environmental Kuznets Curve." *Ecological Economics* 25: 147–60.

Transparency International. 2011. *The Global Corruption Report: Climate Change*. London and Washington, DC: Earthscan.

Tucker, J. 2010. "Are Mexico's Conditional Cash Transfers missing the target?" Policy Matters 7 (2): 4-9.

Ulimwengu, J. M., and R. Ramadan. 2009. "How Does Food Price Increase Affect Ugandan Households? An Augmented Market Approach." Discussion Paper 00884. International Food Policy Research Institute, Washington, DC.

UN (United Nations). 1992. "1992 Rio Declaration on Environment and Development." Conference on Environment and Development, 3–14 June, Rio de Janeiro.

———. 1997. "Programme for the Further Implementation of Agenda 21." Agenda Item 8, A/RES/S-19/2. United Nations General Assembly, New York.

———. 2002. "United Nations Declaration on Sustainable Development." Adopted at the World Summit on Sustainable Development. 2–4 September, Johannesburg.

———. 2008. *Innovation for Sustainable Development: Local Case Studies from Africa*. New York.

———. 2010. *The Millennium Development Goals Report 2010*. New York: United Nations.

———. 2011. "International Year of Sustainable Energy for All." Sixty-fifth Session, Agenda item 20 and 151, A/65/151. UN General Assembly, New York. http://daccess-dds-ny.un.org/doc/UNDOC/GEN/N10/521/60/PDF/N1052160.pdf?OpenElement. Accessed 14 July 2011.

UN Habitat (United Nations Human Settlements Programme). 2003. *Water and Sanitation in the World's Cities: Local Action for Global Goals*. London and New York: Earthscan.

UN Millennium Project. 2005. *Investing in Development: A Practical Plan to Achieve the Millennium Development Goals. Overview*. New York.

UN Water. 2006. "Gender, Water and Sanitation: A Policy Brief." UN Water, Inter-Agency Task Force on Gender and Water, New York.

———.2010a. *Global Annual Assessment of Sanitation and Drinking-Water: Targeting Resources for Better Results*. Geneva: World Health Organization.

———. 2010b. *Progress on Sanitation and Drinking-Water*. Geneva: World Health Organization and United Nations Children's Fund. www.unwater.org/downloads/JMP_report_2010.pdf. Accessed 15 July 2011.

UNDESA (United Nations Department for Economic and Social Affairs). 2006. *Trends in Sustainable Development*. New York: United Nations. www.un.org/esa/sustdev/publications/trends2008/fullreport.pdf. Accessed 15 June 2011.

———. 2008. *World Population Prospects: 2008 Revision*, New York: United Nations.

———. 2009. *World Economic and Social Survey 2009: Promoting Development, Saving the Planet*. New York: United Nations.

———. 2010a. *Promoting Development, Saving the Planet*. New York: United Nations.

———. 2010b. *The World's Women 2010: Trends and Statistics*. New York: United Nations.

———. 2011a. *World Economic and Social Survey 2011: The Great Green Technological Transformation*. New York: United Nations.

———. 2011b. *World Population Prospects: The 2010 Revision*. CD-ROM Edition. New York: United Nations.

UNDP (United Nations Development Programme). 2002. *Arab Human Development Report 2002: Creating Opportunities for Future Generations*. New York: United Nations Development Programme.

———. 2008. "Mid-Term Review of the Global Environment Facility: Resource Allocation Framework." Technical Paper 3. United Nations Development Programme, Global Environment Facility, New York.

———. 2009. *Arab Human Development Report 2009: Challenges to Human Security in Arab Countries*. New York: United Nations Development Programme.

———. 2010. "Fostering Social Accountability: From Principle to Practice." Guidance Note. Oslo Governance Centre, Democratic Governance Group, Bureau for Development Policy, Oslo.

———. 2011a. "Western Balkans: Assessment of Capacities for Low-Carbon and Climate Resilient Development— Presentation Transcript." www.slideshare.net/undpeuropeandcis/undp-survey-results-assessment -of-capacities-for-lowcarbon-and-climate-resilient -development. Accessed 28 July 2011.

———. 2011b. *Energy for People-Centered Sustainable Development*. New York: United Nations Development Programme.

———. 2011c. *Sharing Innovative Experiences: Successful Social Protection Floor Experiences*. Vol. 18. New York.

———. n.d. "Community Water Initiative." www.undp.org/water/community-water-initiative.shtml. Accessed 15 May 2011.

UNDP (United Nations Development Programme) Bhutan. 2008. *Bhutan's Progress: Midway to the Millennium Development Goals*. Thiampu: United Nations Development Programme.

UNDP (United Nations Development Programme) Costa Rica Country Office, Observatorio del Desarrollo, and Universidad de Costa Rica. 2011. "Sustainability and Equity: Challenges for Human Development." Human Development Report 2011 Case Study. San José.

UNDP (United Nations Development Programme) and GEF (Global Environment Facility). 2010. "Annual Performance Report: Project Implementation Report. PIMS 3121: Strengthening the Protected Area Network." Unpublished internal document, New York.

UNDP (United Nations Development Programme)– Human Development Report Office. 1990–2010.

Human Development Reports 1990–2010. New York: Oxford University Press through 2005; and Palgrave Macmillan since 2006.

UNDP (United Nations Development Programme)– UNEP (United Nations Environment Programme) Poverty-Environment Initiative. 2008. "Environment, Climate Change and the MDGs: Reshaping the Development Agenda." A Poverty Environment Partnership Event in Support of the UN High Level Event on MDGs." Nairobi.

UNDP (United Nations Development Programme), UNEP (United Nations Environment Programme), World Bank and WRI (World Resources Institute). 2005. *World Resources 2005: The Wealth of the Poor: Managing Ecosystems to Fight Poverty*. Washington, DC: World Resources Institute.

UNDP (United Nations Development Programme) Water Governance Programme. 2010. "Djibouti." *Country Sector Assessments* Volume 2. United Nations Development Programme, Governance, Advocacy and Leadership for Water, Sanitation and Hygiene, New York.

UNDP (United Nations Development Programme) and WHO (World Health Organization). 2009. *The Energy Access Situation in Developing Countries: A Review Focusing on the Least Developed Countries and Sub-Saharan Africa*. New York: United Nations Development Programme.

———. 2011. *Sharing Innovative Experiences: Successful Social Protection Floor Experiences (vol. 18)*. United Nations Development Programme, Special Unit for the South-South Cooperation, New York.

UNECE (United Nations Economic Commission for Europe). 2011. "Summary of the Report on Measuring Sustainable Development Proposed Indicators, and Results of Electronic Consultation." ESA/STAT/AC.238, UNCEEA/6/14. Sixth Meeting of the UN Committee of Experts on Environmental-Economic Accounting, 15–17 June, New York.

UNEP (United Nations Environment Programme). 2007. "Interlinkages: Governance for Sustainability." In *Global Environment Outlook (GEO 4)*. Nairobi: United Nations Environment Programme.

———. 2009. *From Conflict to Peacebuilding: The Role of Natural Resources and the Environment*. Nairobi: United Nations Environment Programme.

———. 2010. *Green Economy: Developing Countries Success Stories*. Nairobi: United Nations Environment Programme.

———. 2011. *Towards a Green Economy; Pathways to Sustainable Development and Poverty Eradication*. Nairobi: United Nations Environment Programme.

UNEP (United Nations Environment Programme) and GRID Europe. 2009. "E-Waste, the Hidden Side of IT Equipment's Manufacturing and Use." United Nations Environment Programme, Geneva. www.grid.unep.ch/product/publication/download/ew_ewaste.en.pdf. Accessed 18 June 2011.

UNEP (United Nations Environment Programme) and UNU (United Nations University). 2009. "Recycling from E-Waste to Resources." United Nations Environment Programme, Division of Technology, Industry and

Economics, and the StEP Initiative (Solving the E-waste Problem Initiative), Paris and Bonn. www.uneptie.org/shared/publications/pdf/DTIx1192xPA-Recycling%20from%20ewaste%20to%20Resources.pdf. Accessed 30 May 2011.

UNFPA (United Nations Population Fund). 2009. *State of the World Population 2009: Financing a Changing World, Women, Population and Climate.* New York.

———. 2010. *Recent Success Stories in Reproductive Health.* New York.

UNHCR (United Nations High Commissioner for Refugees). 2002. "A Critical Time for the Environment." *Refugees* 12 (127). Geneva.

UNICEF (United Nations Children's Fund). 2010. "Water, Sanitation and Hygiene." New York. www.unicef.org/wash/. Accessed 1 May 2011.

UNICEF (United Nations Children's Fund) Madagascar Water Sanitation and Hygiene. 2007. "UNICEF WASH in Schools Madagascar: An Assessment Report." www.scribd.com/doc/48617354/UNICEF-WASH-in-Schools-Madagascar-2007. Accessed 5 May 2011.

United Church of Christ. 1987. *Toxic Wastes and Race in the United States.* New York: Commission for Racial Justice.

United Nations Statistics Division. 2010. "UNSD Environmental Indicators." www.unstats.un.org/unsd/ENVIRONMENT/qindicators.htm. Accessed 15 July 2011.

United States Environmental Protection Agency. 2011. "Inventory of U.S. Greenhouse Gas Emissions and Sinks: 1990–2009: Executive Summary." Washington, DC.

United States National Academy of Sciences. 1992. *Policy Implications of Greenhouse Warming: Mitigation, Adaptation, and the Science Base.* Washington, DC: National Academy Press.

USAID (United States Agency for International Development). 2008. "Environmental Health at USAID. What's New?" Arlington, VA. www.ehproject.org/phe/phe_projects.html. Accessed 15 May 2011.

USEIA (United States Energy Information Administration). 2008. "World Nominal Oil Price Chronology 1970–2007." Washington, DC. www.eia.doe.gov/cabs/AOMC/Overview.html. Accessed 28 June 2011.

Vankoningsveld, M., J. P. M. Mulder, M. J. F. Stive, L. VanDerValk, and A. W. VanDerWeck. 2008. "Living with Sea-Level Rise and Climate Change: A Case Study of the Netherlands." *Journal of Coastal Research* 24 (2): 367 79.

Vedeld, P., A. Angelsen, E. Sjaastad, and G. Kobugabe-Berg. 2004. "Counting on the Environment: Forest Incomes and the Rural Poor." Environment Department Paper 98. World Bank, Washington, DC.

Vennemo, H., K. Aunan, H. Lindhjem, and H. M. Seip. 2009. "Environmental Pollution in China: Status and Trends." *Review of Environmental Economics and Policy* 3 (2): 209–30.

Veron, S. R., J. M. Paruelo, and M. Oesterheld. 2006. "Assessing Desertification." *Journal of Arid Environments* 66: 751–63.

Vidal, J. 2011. "Bolivia Enshrines Natural World's Rights with Equal Status for Mother Earth." 10 April. www.guardian.co.uk/environment/2011/apr/10/bolivia-enshrines-natural-worlds-rights. Accessed 16 June 2011.

Vié, J.-C., C. Hilton-Taylor, and S. N. Stuart, eds. 2009. *Wildlife in a Changing World—An Analysis of the 2008 IUCN Red List of Threatened Species.* Gland, Switzerland: International Union for Conservation of Nature.

Viel, J.-F., M. Hägi, E. Upegui, and L. Laurian. 2010. "Environmental Justice in a French Industrial Region: Are Polluting Industrial Facilities Equally Distributed?" *Health and Place* 17 (1): 257–62.

Vincent, K. 2011. "Sustaining Equitable Progress: Gender Equality in the Context of Climate Change." Background Paper for the 2011 *Human Development Report.* UNDP–HDRO, New York.

Vizard, P., S. Fukuda-Parr, and D. Elson. 2011. "Introduction: The Capability Approach and Human Rights." *Journal of Human Development and Capabilities* 12 (1): 1–22.

Volker, M., and H. Waible. 2010. "Do Rural Households Extract More Forest Products in Times of Crisis? Evidence from the Mountainous Uplands of Vietnam." *Forest Policy and Economics* 12 (6): 407–14.

Walker, A. 2010. "In Rural India, IKEA Solar-Powered Lamps Light a Path for Girl Students." IKEA Social Initiative projects. www.unicef.org/infobycountry/india_53698.html. Accessed 28 May 2011.

Walton, M. 2010. "Capitalism, the State and the Underlying Drivers of Human Development." Human Development Research Paper 9. United Nations Development Programme, Human Development Report Office, New York.

Wang, H., J. Bi, D. Wheeler, J. Wang, D. Cao, G. Lu, and Y. Wang. 2002. "Environmental Performance Rating and Disclosure: China's Green-Watch Program." Policy Research Working Paper 2889. World Bank, Washington, DC.

Wang, L., S. Bandyopadhyay, M. Cosgrove-Davies, and H. Samad. 2011. "Quantifying Carbon and Distributional Benefits of Solar Home System Programs in Bangladesh." Policy Research Working Paper 5545. World Bank, Washington, DC.

Watts, J. 2006. "Doctors Blame Air Pollution for China's Asthma Increases." *The Lancet* 368 (9537): 719–20.

———. 2011. "A Report Card for China's Environment." Environmental Blog, The Guardian, 3 June. www.guardian.co.uk/environment/blog/2011/jun/03/report-card-for-china-environment. Accessed 16 June 2011.

WCED (United Nations World Commission on Environment and Development). 1987. *Our Common Future.* Oxford, UK: Oxford University Press.

Weikard, H.-P. 1999. *Wahlfreiheit für zukünftige Generationen. Neue Grundlagen für eine Ressourcenökonomik.* Marburg, Germany: Metropolis Press.

Weitzman, M. L. 2009a. "Some Basic Economics of Extreme Climate Change." In *Changing Climate, Changing Economy,* ed. Jean-Philippe Touffut. Northampton, MA : Edward Elgar.

———. 2009b. "On Modelling and Interpreting the Economics of Catastrophic Climate Change." *Review of Economics and Statistics* 91 (1): 1–19. www.economics.harvard.edu/faculty/weitzman/files/RESstatModeling.pdf. Accessed 23 May 2011.

Wheeler, D. 2009. "Country Profile of Environmental Burden of Disease: China, based on 2004 WHO Statistics." Geneva.

———. 2011. "Quantifying Vulnerability to Climate Change: Implications for Adaptation Assistance." Working Paper 240. Center for Global Development, Washington, DC. www.cgdev.org/content/publications/detail/1424759. Accessed 29 May 2011.

Widmer, R., H. Oswald-Krapf, D. Sinha-Khetriwal, M. Schnellmann, and H. Böni. 2005. "Global Perspectives on E-Waste." *Environmental Impact Assessment Review* 25 (5): 436–58

Wilkinson, M., N. Moilwa, and B. Taylor. 2004. "The Design and Development of a Sanitation Hand Washing Dispenser: A South African Case Study." 30th Water, Engineering and Development Centre International Conference, 25–29 October, Vientiane, Lao PDR.

Willenbockel, D. 2011. "Environmental Tax Reform in Vietnam: An Ex Ante General Equilibrium Assessment." Paper presented at EcoMod conference, 29 June–1 July, University of the Azores, Ponta Delgada, Portugal.

Wire, T. 2009. "Fewer Emitters, Lower Emissions, Less Cost Reducing Future Carbon Emissions by Investing in Family Planning a Cost/Benefit Analysis." M.Sc. dissertation. London, UK: London School of Economics and Political Science. www.optimumpopulation.org/reducingemissions.pdf. Accessed 3 July 2011.

Wodon, Q., and Y. Ying. 2010. "Domestic Work Time in Sierra Leone." Working Paper 27736. Munich Personal RePEc Archive, Munich. http://mpra.ub.uni-muenchen.de/27736/1/MPRA_paper_27736.pdf. Accessed 19 April 2011.

Wong, C.-M., C. Q. Ou, K. P. Chan, Y.K. Chau, T.Q. Thach, L. Yang, R. Yat-Nork Chung, G. N. Thomas, J. S. M. Peiris, T.W. Wong, A. J. Hedley, and T.-H. Lam. 2008. "The Effects of Air Pollution on Mortality in Socially Deprived Urban Areas in Hong Kong, China." *Environmental Health Perspectives* 116 (9): 1189–94.

Wong, C.-M., T. Q. Thach, P. Y. K. Chau, E. K. Chan, R. Y. Chung, C. Q. Ou, L. Yang, J. S. Peiris, G. N. Thomas, T. H. Lam, T. W. Wong, A. J. Hedley, and HEI Health Review Committee. 2010. "Interaction between Air Pollution and Respiratory Viruses: Time-Series Study of Daily Mortality and Hospital Admissions in Hong Kong." In *Public Health and Air Pollution in Asia: Coordinated Studies of Short-Term Exposure to Air Pollution and Daily Mortality in Four Cities, Part 4.* Research Report 154. Boston, MA: Health Effects Institute.

Wood, S., K. Sebastian, and S. J. Scherr. 2000. *Pilot Analysis of Global Ecosystems: Agro Ecosystems.* Washington, DC: International Food Policy Research Institute and World Resources Institute.

Wooldridge, J. M. 2003. *Introductory Econometrics: A Modern Approach.* Berkeley, CA: South Western College Publications.

World Bank. 2007. *Making the Most of Scarcity: Accountability for Better Water Management Results in the Middle East and North Africa.* World Bank: Washington, DC.

———. 2008a. *Environmental Health and Child Survival.* Washington, DC: World Bank.

———. 2008b. "Project Performance Assessment Report Lao People's Democratic Republic Southern Provinces Rural Electrification Project." Credit 3047-LA. World Bank, Independent Evaluation Group, Sector Thematic and Global Evaluation Division, Washington, DC.

———. 2008c. "Economic Impacts of Sanitation in Southeast Asia: A Four-Country Study Conducted in Cambodia, Indonesia, the Philippines and Vietnam under the Economics of Sanitation Initiative (ESI)." World Bank, Jakarta.

———. 2008d. *Forests Sourcebook: Practical Guidance for Sustaining Forests in Development Cooperation.* Washington, DC: World Bank.

———. 2009. "Poverty and Social Impact Analysis of Groundwater Over-exploitation in Mexico." World Bank, Latin America and Caribbean Region, Washington, DC.

———. 2010a. "Maji ni Maisha: Innovative Finance for Community Water Schemes in Kenya." 3 May. Washington, DC. http://go.worldbank.org/HX72K0KP00. Accessed 20 May 2011.

———. 2010b. "Monitoring Climate Finance and ODA." Issues Brief 1. World Bank, Sustainable Development Vice Presidency, Environment Department, Washington, DC.

———. 2010c. "Enabling Reforms: A Stakeholder-Based Analysis of the Political Economy of Tanzania's Charcoal Sector and the Poverty and Social Impacts of Proposed Reforms." World Bank, Sustainable Development Vice Presidency, Environment Department, Washington, DC.

———. 2011a. "Applying Innovative Approaches to Improve Rural Sanitation at Large Scale." http://water.worldbank.org/water/news/applying-innovative-approaches-improve-rural-sanitation-large-scale. Accessed 20 June 2011.

———. 2011b. *World Development Indicators.* Washington, DC: World Bank.

World Resources Institute. 2005. *World Resources 2005: The Wealth of the Poor, Managing Ecosystems to Fight Poverty.* Washington, DC: World Resources Institute.

World Water Assessment Programme. 2006. *The United Nations World Water Development Report 2: Water a Shared Responsibility.* Paris: United Nations Educational, Scientific and Cultural Organization.

———. 2009. *The United Nations World Water Development Report 3: Water in a Changing World.* Paris: United Nations Educational, Scientific and Cultural Organization.

Würtenberger, L., T. Koellner, and C. R. Binder. 2005. "Virtual Land Use and Agricultural Trade: Estimating Environmental and Socio-Economic Impacts." *Ecological Economics* 57 (4): 679–97.

Yemiru, T., A. Roos, B. M. Campbell, and F. Bohlin. 2010. "Forest Incomes and Poverty Alleviation under Participatory Forest Management in the Bale Highlands, Southern Ethiopia." *International Forestry Review* 12 (1): 66–77.

Yonghuan, M., S. Fan, L. Zhou, Z. Dong, K. Zhang, and J. Feng. 2007. "The Temporal Change of Driving Factors during the Course of Land Desertification in Arid Region of North China: The Case of Minqin County." *Environmental Geology* 51: 999–1008.

Zacune, J. 2011. "World Bank: Catalyzing Catastrophic Climate Change: The World Bank's Role in Dirty Energy Investment and Carbon Markets." Issue 122. Friends of the Earth International, Amsterdam,.

Zambrano, E. 2011a. "An Axiomatization of the Human Development Index." Human Development Research Paper 10. UNDP–HDRO, New York.

———. 2011b. "Functionings, Capabilities and the 2010 Human Development Index." Human Development Research Paper 11. UNDP–HDRO, New York.

Zhan, J., D. L. Mauzerall, T. Zhu, S. Liang, M. Ezzati, and J.V. Remais. 2010. "Environmental Health in China: Progress towards Clean Air and Safe Water." *The Lancet* 375 (9720): 1110–19.

**Statistical
Annex**

Human development
statistical annex

Readers guide

The 10 statistical tables provide an overview of key aspects of human development at the country and regional levels as well as for key country groupings. The tables include composite indices estimated by the Human Development Report Office (HDRO), using the methods detailed in *Technical notes 1–4*. Data in the tables are those available to the HDRO as of 15 May 2011, unless otherwise noted.

The tables include data for as many of the 192 UN member states as possible as well as Hong Kong Special Administrative Region of China and the Occupied Palestinian Territory. Data availability determines Human Development Index (HDI) country coverage. Where reliable data are unavailable or there is significant uncertainty about the validity of the data, countries are excluded from calculations in order to ensure the statistical credibility of the *HDR*.

Countries and areas are ranked by their 2011 HDI value. The *Key to countries* on the inside back cover of the Report lists countries alphabetically with their HDI ranks.

All the indicators are available online in several formats at http://hdr.undp.org/en/statistics, which includes interactive tools, maps of all the human development indices and selected animations, descriptive materials such as country factsheets, and guidance on how to calculate the indices. These materials are also available in French and Spanish.

Sources and definitions

The HDRO is primarily a user, not a producer, of statistics. It relies on international data agencies with the mandate, resources and expertise to collect and compile national data on specific indicators. Where data are not available from international data suppliers, data from other credible sources are used.

Definitions of indicators and sources for original data components are given at the end of each table, with full references in the *Statistical references*. For more detailed technical information about the indicators, the websites of the respective source agencies should be consulted; links to these sources are at http://hdr.undp.org/en/statistics.

Comparisons over time and across editions of the Report

Because international data agencies continually improve their data series, the data—including the HDI values and ranks—presented in this Report are not comparable to those published in earlier editions. For the HDI, trends using consistent data—calculated at five-year intervals for 1980–2011—are presented in table 2.

Discrepancies between national and international estimates

When compiling data series, international agencies apply international standards and harmonization procedures to make national data comparable across countries. When data for a country are missing, an international agency may produce an estimate if other relevant information is available. In some cases international data series may not incorporate the most recent national data. All these factors can lead to discrepancies between national and international estimates.

When HDRO becomes aware of discrepancies, these are brought to the attention of national and international data authorities. The HDRO continues to advocate for improving international data and actively supports efforts to enhance data quality.

Country groupings and aggregates

In addition to country-level data, several population-weighted aggregates are presented. In general, an aggregate is shown for a country grouping only when the relevant data are available for at least half the countries and represent at least two-thirds of the available population in that classification. Aggregates for each classification represent only the countries for which data are available, unless otherwise noted. Occasionally aggregates are those from the original source rather than weighted averages; these values are indicated with a superscript "T".

Human development classification

HDI classifications are relative—based on quartiles of HDI distribution across countries and denoted very high, high, medium and low HDI. Because there are 187 countries, the four groups do not have the same number of countries: the very high, high and medium HDI groups have 47 countries each, and the low HDI group has 46 countries.

Country groupings

Countries are grouped based on UNDP regional classification. Other groupings are based on UN classifications such as Least Developed Countries and Small Island Developing States. The composition of each region is presented in *Regions*.

Country notes

Data for China do not include Hong Kong Special Administrative Region of China, Macao Special Administrative Region of China or Taiwan Province of China, unless otherwise noted. Data for Sudan include South Sudan unless otherwise noted but are often based on information collected from the northern part of the country only.

Symbols

A dash between two years, as in 2005–2011, indicates that the data are the most recent year available in the period specified, unless otherwise noted. Growth rates are usually average annual rates of growth between the first and last years of the period shown.

A slash between years such as 2005/2011 indicates average for the years shown, unless otherwise noted.

The following symbols are used in the tables:

..	Not available
0 or 0.0	Nil or negligible
—	Not applicable
<	Less than

Statistical tables

Composite measures

Dimensions of human development

Key to HDI countries and ranks, 2011

Country	Rank	Country	Rank	Country	Rank
Afghanistan	172	Georgia	75	Occupied Palestinian Territory	114
Albania	70	Germany	9	Oman	89
Algeria	96	Ghana	135	Pakistan	145
Andorra	32	Greece	29	Palau	49
Angola	148	Grenada	67	Panama	58
Antigua and Barbuda	60	Guatemala	131	Papua New Guinea	153
Argentina	45	Guinea	178	Paraguay	107
Armenia	86	Guinea-Bissau	176	Peru	80
Australia	2	Guyana	117	Philippines	112
Austria	19	Haiti	158	Poland	39
Azerbaijan	91	Honduras	121	Portugal	41
Bahamas	53	Hong Kong, China (SAR)	13	Qatar	37
Bahrain	42	Hungary	38	Romania	50
Bangladesh	146	Iceland	14	Russian Federation	66
Barbados	47	India	134	Rwanda	166
Belarus	65	Indonesia	124	Saint Kitts and Nevis	72
Belgium	18	Iran, Islamic Republic of	88	Saint Lucia	82
Belize	93	Iraq	132	Saint Vincent and the Grenadines	85
Benin	167	Ireland	7	Samoa	99
Bhutan	141	Israel	17	São Tomé and Príncipe	144
Bolivia, Plurinational State of	108	Italy	24	Saudi Arabia	56
Bosnia and Herzegovina	74	Jamaica	79	Senegal	155
Botswana	118	Japan	12	Serbia	59
Brazil	84	Jordan	95	Seychelles	52
Brunei Darussalam	33	Kazakhstan	68	Sierra Leone	180
Bulgaria	55	Kenya	143	Singapore	26
Burkina Faso	181	Kiribati	122	Slovakia	35
Burundi	185	Korea, Republic of	15	Slovenia	21
Cambodia	139	Kuwait	63	Solomon Islands	142
Cameroon	150	Kyrgyzstan	126	South Africa	123
Canada	6	Lao People's Democratic Republic	138	Spain	23
Cape Verde	133	Latvia	43	Sri Lanka	97
Central African Republic	179	Lebanon	71	Sudan	169
Chad	183	Lesotho	160	Suriname	104
Chile	44	Liberia	182	Swaziland	140
China	101	Libya	64	Sweden	10
Colombia	87	Liechtenstein	8	Switzerland	11
Comoros	163	Lithuania	40	Syrian Arab Republic	119
Congo	137	Luxembourg	25	Tajikistan	127
Congo, Democratic Republic of the	187	Madagascar	151	Tanzania, United Republic of	152
Costa Rica	69	Malawi	171	Thailand	103
Côte d'Ivoire	170	Malaysia	61	Timor-Leste	147
Croatia	46	Maldives	109	Togo	162
Cuba	51	Mali	175	Tonga	90
Cyprus	31	Malta	36	Trinidad and Tobago	62
Czech Republic	27	Mauritania	159	Tunisia	94
Denmark	16	Mauritius	77	Turkey	92
Djibouti	165	Mexico	57	Turkmenistan	102
Dominica	81	Micronesia, Federated States of	116	Uganda	161
Dominican Republic	98	Moldova, Republic of	111	Ukraine	76
Ecuador	83	Mongolia	110	United Arab Emirates	30
Egypt	113	Montenegro	54	United Kingdom	28
El Salvador	105	Morocco	130	United States	4
Equatorial Guinea	136	Mozambique	184	Uruguay	48
Eritrea	177	Myanmar	149	Uzbekistan	115
Estonia	34	Namibia	120	Vanuatu	125
Ethiopia	174	Nepal	157	Venezuela, Bolivarian Republic of	73
Fiji	100	Netherlands	3	Viet Nam	128
Finland	22	New Zealand	5	Yemen	154
Former Yugoslav Republic of Macedonia	78	Nicaragua	129	Zambia	164
France	20	Niger	186	Zimbabwe	173
Gabon	106	Nigeria	156		
Gambia	168	Norway	1		

TABLE 1

Human Development Index and its components

HDI rank	Human Development Index (HDI) Value 2011	Life expectancy at birth (years) 2011	Mean years of schooling (years) 2011[a]	Expected years of schooling (years) 2011[a]	Gross national income (GNI) per capita (constant 2005 PPP $) 2011	GNI per capita rank minus HDI rank 2011	Nonincome HDI Value 2011
VERY HIGH HUMAN DEVELOPMENT							
1 Norway	0.943	81.1	12.6	17.3	47,557	6	0.975
2 Australia	0.929	81.9	12.0	18.0	34,431	16	0.979
3 Netherlands	0.910	80.7	11.6[b]	16.8	36,402	9	0.944
4 United States	0.910	78.5	12.4	16.0	43,017	6	0.931
5 New Zealand	0.908	80.7	12.5	18.0	23,737	30	0.978
6 Canada	0.908	81.0	12.1[b]	16.0	35,166	10	0.944
7 Ireland	0.908	80.6	11.6	18.0	29,322	19	0.959
8 Liechtenstein	0.905	79.6	10.3[c]	14.7	83,717[d]	−6	0.877
9 Germany	0.905	80.4	12.2[b]	15.9	34,854	8	0.940
10 Sweden	0.904	81.4	11.7[b]	15.7	35,837	4	0.936
11 Switzerland	0.903	82.3	11.0[b]	15.6	39,924	0	0.926
12 Japan	0.901	83.4	11.6[b]	15.1	32,295	11	0.940
13 Hong Kong, China (SAR)	0.898	82.8	10.0	15.7	44,805	−4	0.910
14 Iceland	0.898	81.8	10.4	18.0	29,354	11	0.943
15 Korea, Republic of	0.897	80.6	11.6[b]	16.9	28,230	12	0.945
16 Denmark	0.895	78.8	11.4[b]	16.9	34,347	3	0.926
17 Israel	0.888	81.6	11.9	15.5	25,849	14	0.939
18 Belgium	0.886	80.0	10.9[b]	16.1	33,357	2	0.914
19 Austria	0.885	80.9	10.8[b]	15.3	35,719	−4	0.908
20 France	0.884	81.5	10.6[b]	16.1	30,462	4	0.919
21 Slovenia	0.884	79.3	11.6[b]	16.9	24,914	11	0.935
22 Finland	0.882	80.0	10.3	16.8	32,438	0	0.911
23 Spain	0.878	81.4	10.4[b]	16.6	26,508	6	0.920
24 Italy	0.874	81.9	10.1[b]	16.3	26,484	6	0.914
25 Luxembourg	0.867	80.0	10.1	13.3	50,557	−20	0.854
26 Singapore	0.866	81.1	8.8[b]	14.4[e]	52,569	−22	0.851
27 Czech Republic	0.865	77.7	12.3	15.6	21,405	14	0.917
28 United Kingdom	0.863	80.2	9.3	16.1	33,296	−7	0.879
29 Greece	0.861	79.9	10.1[b]	16.5	23,747	5	0.902
30 United Arab Emirates	0.846	76.5	9.3	13.3	59,993	−27	0.813
31 Cyprus	0.840	79.6	9.8	14.7	24,841	2	0.866
32 Andorra	0.838	80.9	10.4[f]	11.5	36,095[g]	−19	0.836
33 Brunei Darussalam	0.838	78.0	8.6	14.1	45,753	−25	0.819
34 Estonia	0.835	74.8	12.0	15.7	16,799	13	0.890
35 Slovakia	0.834	75.4	11.6	14.9	19,998	8	0.875
36 Malta	0.832	79.6	9.9	14.4	21,460	4	0.866
37 Qatar	0.831	78.4	7.3	12.0	107,721	−36	0.757
38 Hungary	0.816	74.4	11.1[b]	15.3	16,581	11	0.862
39 Poland	0.813	76.1	10.0[b]	15.3	17,451	7	0.853
40 Lithuania	0.810	72.2	10.9	16.1	16,234	10	0.853
41 Portugal	0.809	79.5	7.7	15.9	20,573	1	0.833
42 Bahrain	0.806	75.1	9.4	13.4	28,169	−14	0.806
43 Latvia	0.805	73.3	11.5[h]	15.0	14,293	12	0.857
44 Chile	0.805	79.1	9.7	14.7	13,329	14	0.862
45 Argentina	0.797	75.9	9.3	15.8	14,527	9	0.843
46 Croatia	0.796	76.6	9.8[b]	13.9	15,729	5	0.834
47 Barbados	0.793	76.8	9.3	13.4[h]	17,966	−3	0.818
HIGH HUMAN DEVELOPMENT							
48 Uruguay	0.783	77.0	8.5[b]	15.5	13,242	12	0.828
49 Palau	0.782	71.8	12.1[i]	14.7	9,744[j,k]	29	0.853
50 Romania	0.781	74.0	10.4	14.9	11,046	20	0.841
51 Cuba	0.776	79.1	9.9	17.5	5,416[l]	52	0.904
52 Seychelles	0.773	73.6	9.4[m]	13.3	16,729	−4	0.794
53 Bahamas	0.771	75.6	8.5[m]	12.0	23,029[n]	−15	0.768
54 Montenegro	0.771	74.6	10.6	13.7[h]	10,361[o]	20	0.831
55 Bulgaria	0.771	73.4	10.6[b]	13.7	11,412	14	0.822
56 Saudi Arabia	0.770	73.9	7.8	13.7	23,274	−19	0.765
57 Mexico	0.770	77.0	8.5	13.9	13,245	2	0.808

Human Development Index and its components

TABLE 1

HDI rank	Human Development Index (HDI) Value	Life expectancy at birth (years)	Mean years of schooling (years)	Expected years of schooling (years)	Gross national income (GNI) per capita (constant 2005 PPP $)	GNI per capita rank minus HDI rank	Nonincome HDI Value
	2011	2011	2011[a]	2011[a]	2011	2011	2011
58 Panama	0.768	76.1	9.4	13.2	12,335	7	0.811
59 Serbia	0.766	74.5	10.2[b]	13.7	10,236	16	0.824
60 Antigua and Barbuda	0.764	72.6	8.9[h]	14.0	15,521	−8	0.786
61 Malaysia	0.761	74.2	9.5	12.6	13,685	−5	0.790
62 Trinidad and Tobago	0.760	70.1	9.2	12.3	23,439[p]	−26	0.750
63 Kuwait	0.760	74.6	6.1	12.3	47,926	−57	0.705
64 Libya	0.760	74.8	7.3	16.6	12,637[q]	0	0.795
65 Belarus	0.756	70.3	9.3[r]	14.6	13,439	−8	0.785
66 Russian Federation	0.755	68.8	9.8	14.1	14,561	−13	0.777
67 Grenada	0.748	76.0	8.6	16.0	6,982	30	0.829
68 Kazakhstan	0.745	67.0	10.4	15.1	10,585	4	0.786
69 Costa Rica	0.744	79.3	8.3	11.7	10,497	4	0.785
70 Albania	0.739	76.9	10.4	11.3	7,803	18	0.804
71 Lebanon	0.739	72.6	7.9[m]	13.8	13,076	−10	0.760
72 Saint Kitts and Nevis	0.735	73.1	8.4	12.9	11,897	−4	0.762
73 Venezuela, Bolivarian Republic of	0.735	74.4	7.6[b]	14.2	10,656	−2	0.771
74 Bosnia and Herzegovina	0.733	75.7	8.7[r]	13.6	7,664	16	0.797
75 Georgia	0.733	73.7	12.1[r]	13.1	4,780	36	0.843
76 Ukraine	0.729	68.5	11.3	14.7	6,175	24	0.810
77 Mauritius	0.728	73.4	7.2	13.6	12,918	−14	0.745
78 Former Yugoslav Republic of Macedonia	0.728	74.8	8.2[r]	13.3	8,804	2	0.776
79 Jamaica	0.727	73.1	9.6	13.8	6,487	19	0.802
80 Peru	0.725	74.0	8.7	12.9	8,389	2	0.775
81 Dominica	0.724	77.5	7.7[m]	13.2	7,889	6	0.779
82 Saint Lucia	0.723	74.6	8.3	13.1	8,273	2	0.773
83 Ecuador	0.720	75.6	7.6	14.0	7,589	9	0.776
84 Brazil	0.718	73.5	7.2	13.8	10,162	−7	0.748
85 Saint Vincent and the Grenadines	0.717	72.3	8.6	13.2	8,013	1	0.766
86 Armenia	0.716	74.2	10.8	12.0	5,188	22	0.806
87 Colombia	0.710	73.7	7.3	13.6	8,315	−4	0.752
88 Iran, Islamic Republic of	0.707	73.0	7.3	12.7	10,164	−12	0.731
89 Oman	0.705	73.0	5.5[m]	11.8	22,841	−50	0.671
90 Tonga	0.704	72.3	10.3[b]	13.7	4,186	26	0.808
91 Azerbaijan	0.700	70.7	8.6[m]	11.8	8,666	−10	0.733
92 Turkey	0.699	74.0	6.5	11.8	12,246	−25	0.704
93 Belize	0.699	76.1	8.0[b]	12.4	5,812	9	0.766
94 Tunisia	0.698	74.5	6.5	14.5	7,281	2	0.745
MEDIUM HUMAN DEVELOPMENT							
95 Jordan	0.698	73.4	8.6	13.1	5,300	9	0.773
96 Algeria	0.698	73.1	7.0	13.6	7,658	−5	0.739
97 Sri Lanka	0.691	74.9	8.2	12.7	4,943	12	0.768
98 Dominican Republic	0.689	73.4	7.2[b]	11.9	8,087	−13	0.720
99 Samoa	0.688	72.4	10.3[m]	12.3	3,931[s]	22	0.788
100 Fiji	0.688	69.2	10.7[b]	13.0	4,145	18	0.781
101 China	0.687	73.5	7.5	11.6	7,476	−7	0.725
102 Turkmenistan	0.686	65.0	9.9[i]	12.5[h]	7,306	−7	0.724
103 Thailand	0.682	74.1	6.6	12.3	7,694	−14	0.714
104 Suriname	0.680	70.6	7.2[r]	12.6	7,538	−11	0.712
105 El Salvador	0.674	72.2	7.5	12.1	5,925	−4	0.724
106 Gabon	0.674	62.7	7.5	13.1	12,249	−40	0.667
107 Paraguay	0.665	72.5	7.7	12.1	4,727	5	0.729
108 Bolivia, Plurinational State of	0.663	66.6	9.2	13.7	4,054	11	0.742
109 Maldives	0.661	76.8	5.8[b]	12.4	5,276	−3	0.714
110 Mongolia	0.653	68.5	8.3	14.1	3,391	17	0.743
111 Moldova, Republic of	0.649	69.3	9.7	11.9	3,058	21	0.746
112 Philippines	0.644	68.7	8.9[b]	11.9	3,478	11	0.725
113 Egypt	0.644	73.2	6.4	11.0	5,269	−6	0.686
114 Occupied Palestinian Territory	0.641	72.8	8.0[m]	12.7	2,656[k,t]	23	0.750
115 Uzbekistan	0.641	68.3	10.0[r]	11.4	2,967	19	0.736
116 Micronesia, Federated States of	0.636	69.0	8.8[i]	12.1[u]	2,935[v]	19	0.729
117 Guyana	0.633	69.9	8.0	11.9	3,192	11	0.715
118 Botswana	0.633	53.2	8.9	12.2	13,049	−56	0.602

HDI rank		Human Development Index (HDI) Value	Life expectancy at birth (years)	Mean years of schooling (years)	Expected years of schooling (years)	Gross national income (GNI) per capita (constant 2005 PPP $)	GNI per capita rank minus HDI rank	Nonincome HDI Value
		2011	2011	2011[a]	2011[a]	2011	2011	2011
119	Syrian Arab Republic	0.632	75.9	5.7[b]	11.3	4,243	−5	0.686
120	Namibia	0.625	62.5	7.4	11.6	6,206	−21	0.643
121	Honduras	0.625	73.1	6.5	11.4	3,443	4	0.694
122	Kiribati	0.624	68.1	7.8	12.1	3,140	8	0.701
123	South Africa	0.619	52.8	8.5[b]	13.1	9,469	−44	0.604
124	Indonesia	0.617	69.4	5.8	13.2	3,716	−2	0.674
125	Vanuatu	0.617	71.0	6.7	10.4	3,950	−5	0.668
126	Kyrgyzstan	0.615	67.7	9.3	12.5	2,036	19	0.734
127	Tajikistan	0.607	67.5	9.8	11.4	1,937	20	0.726
128	Viet Nam	0.593	75.2	5.5	10.4	2,805	8	0.662
129	Nicaragua	0.589	74.0	5.8	10.8	2,430	10	0.669
130	Morocco	0.582	72.2	4.4	10.3	4,196	−15	0.606
131	Guatemala	0.574	71.2	4.1	10.6	4,167	−14	0.595
132	Iraq	0.573	69.0	5.6	9.8	3,177	−3	0.616
133	Cape Verde	0.568	74.2	3.5[i]	11.6	3,402	−7	0.603
134	India	0.547	65.4	4.4	10.3	3,468	−10	0.568
135	Ghana	0.541	64.2	7.1	10.5	1,584	20	0.633
136	Equatorial Guinea	0.537	51.1	5.4[r]	7.7	17,608	−91	0.458
137	Congo	0.533	57.4	5.9	10.5	3,066	−6	0.555
138	Lao People's Democratic Republic	0.524	67.5	4.6	9.2	2,242	4	0.569
139	Cambodia	0.523	63.1	5.8	9.8	1,848	11	0.584
140	Swaziland	0.522	48.7	7.1	10.6	4,484	−27	0.512
141	Bhutan	0.522	67.2	2.3[r]	11.0	5,293	−36	0.500
LOW HUMAN DEVELOPMENT								
142	Solomon Islands	0.510	67.9	4.5[i]	9.1	1,782	10	0.567
143	Kenya	0.509	57.1	7.0	11.0	1,492	15	0.584
144	São Tomé and Príncipe	0.509	64.7	4.2[i]	10.8	1,792	7	0.564
145	Pakistan	0.504	65.4	4.9	6.9	2,550	−7	0.526
146	Bangladesh	0.500	68.9	4.8	8.1	1,529	11	0.566
147	Timor-Leste	0.495	62.5	2.8[i]	11.2	3,005	−14	0.499
148	Angola	0.486	51.1	4.4[r]	9.1	4,874	−38	0.455
149	Myanmar	0.483	65.2	4.0	9.2	1,535	7	0.536
150	Cameroon	0.482	51.6	5.9	10.3	2,031	−4	0.509
151	Madagascar	0.480	66.7	5.2[i]	10.7	824	26	0.605
152	Tanzania, United Republic of	0.466	58.2	5.1	9.1	1,328	10	0.523
153	Papua New Guinea	0.466	62.8	4.3	5.8	2,271	−12	0.475
154	Yemen	0.462	65.5	2.5	8.6	2,213	−11	0.471
155	Senegal	0.459	59.3	4.5	7.5	1,708	−2	0.488
156	Nigeria	0.459	51.9	5.0[r]	8.9	2,069	−12	0.471
157	Nepal	0.458	68.8	3.2	8.8	1,160	8	0.524
158	Haiti	0.454	62.1	4.9	7.6[u]	1,123	12	0.520
159	Mauritania	0.453	58.6	3.7	8.1	1,859	−10	0.472
160	Lesotho	0.450	48.2	5.9[b]	9.9	1,664	−6	0.475
161	Uganda	0.446	54.1	4.7	10.8	1,124	7	0.506
162	Togo	0.435	57.1	5.3	9.6	798	16	0.526
163	Comoros	0.433	61.1	2.8[i]	10.7	1,079	9	0.488
164	Zambia	0.430	49.0	6.5	7.9	1,254	0	0.469
165	Djibouti	0.430	57.9	3.8[r]	5.1	2,335	−25	0.420
166	Rwanda	0.429	55.4	3.3	11.1	1,133	1	0.477
167	Benin	0.427	56.1	3.3	9.2	1,364	−6	0.456
168	Gambia	0.420	58.5	2.8	9.0	1,282	−5	0.450
169	Sudan	0.408	61.5	3.1	4.4	1,894	−21	0.402
170	Côte d'Ivoire	0.400	55.4	3.3	6.3	1,387[p]	−10	0.412
171	Malawi	0.400	54.2	4.2	8.9	753	8	0.470
172	Afghanistan	0.398	48.7	3.3	9.1	1,416	−13	0.407
173	Zimbabwe	0.376	51.4	7.2	9.9	376[n]	11	0.529
174	Ethiopia	0.363	59.3	1.5[i]	8.5	971	0	0.383
175	Mali	0.359	51.4	2.0[b]	8.3	1,123	−6	0.366
176	Guinea-Bissau	0.353	48.1	2.3[r]	9.1	994	−3	0.366
177	Eritrea	0.349	61.6	3.4	4.8	536	6	0.421
178	Guinea	0.344	54.1	1.6[w]	8.6	863	−2	0.364
179	Central African Republic	0.343	48.4	3.5	6.6	707	2	0.379

Human Development Index and its components

TABLE
1

HDI rank		Human Development Index (HDI) Value 2011	Life expectancy at birth (years) 2011	Mean years of schooling (years) 2011[a]	Expected years of schooling (years) 2011[a]	Gross national income (GNI) per capita (constant 2005 PPP $) 2011	GNI per capita rank minus HDI rank 2011	Nonincome HDI Value 2011
180	Sierra Leone	0.336	47.8	2.9	7.2	737	0	0.365
181	Burkina Faso	0.331	55.4	1.3[r]	6.3	1,141	−15	0.323
182	Liberia	0.329	56.8	3.9	11.0	265	5	0.504
183	Chad	0.328	49.6	1.5[i]	7.2	1,105	−12	0.320
184	Mozambique	0.322	50.2	1.2	9.2	898	−9	0.325
185	Burundi	0.316	50.4	2.7	10.5	368	0	0.412
186	Niger	0.295	54.7	1.4	4.9	641	−4	0.311
187	Congo, Democratic Republic of the	0.286	48.4	3.5	8.2	280	−1	0.399
OTHER COUNTRIES OR TERRITORIES								
	Korea, Democratic People's Rep. of	..	68.8	..	..	..	..	..
	Marshall Islands	..	72.0	9.8[i]	10.8	..	..	0.752
	Monaco	..	82.2	..	17.5	..	..	..
	Nauru	..	79.9	..	9.3	..	..	..
	San Marino	..	81.8	..	..	..	..	..
	Somalia	..	51.2	..	2.4	..	..	..
	Tuvalu	..	67.2	..	10.8	..	..	..
Human Development Index groups								
	Very high human development	0.889	80.0	11.3	15.9	33,352	—	0.918
	High human development	0.741	73.1	8.5	13.6	11,579	—	0.769
	Medium human development	0.630	69.7	6.3	11.2	5,276	—	0.658
	Low human development	0.456	58.7	4.2	8.3	1,585	—	0.478
Regions								
	Arab States	0.641	70.5	5.9	10.2	8,554	—	0.643
	East Asia and the Pacific	0.671	72.4	7.2	11.7	6,466	—	0.709
	Europe and Central Asia	0.751	71.3	9.7	13.4	12,004	—	0.785
	Latin America and the Caribbean	0.731	74.4	7.8	13.6	10,119	—	0.767
	South Asia	0.548	65.9	4.6	9.8	3,435	—	0.569
	Sub-Saharan Africa	0.463	54.4	4.5	9.2	1,966	—	0.467
Least developed countries		0.439	59.1	3.7	8.3	1,327	—	0.467
Small island developing states		0.640	69.6	7.3	10.8	5,200	—	0.675
World		0.682	69.8	7.4	11.3	10,082	—	0.683

NOTES

a. Data refer to 2011 or the most recent year available.
b. Updated by HDRO based on UNESCO (2011) data.
c. Assumes the same adult mean years of schooling as Switzerland before the most recent update.
d. Estimated using the purchasing power parity (PPP) and projected growth rate of Switzerland.
e. Calculated by the Singapore Ministry of Education.
f. Assumes the same adult mean years of schooling as Spain before the most recent update.
g. Estimated using the PPP and projected growth rate of Spain.
h. Based on cross-country regression.
i. Based on data on years of schooling of adults from household surveys from World Bank (2010).
j. Based on UNESCAP (2011) and UNDESA (2011) projected growth rates.
k. Based on unpublished estimates from the World Bank.
l. PPP estimate based on cross-country regression; projected growth rate based on ECLAC (2011) and UNDESA (2011) projected growth rates.
m. Based on UNESCO (2011) estimates of education attainment distribution.
n. Based on PPP data from IMF (2011).
o. Based on EBRD (2011) and UNDESA (2011) projected growth rates.
p. Based on World Bank (2011b).
q. Based on OECD and others (2011) and UNDESA (2011) projected growth rates.
r. Based on data from UNICEF (2000–2010).
s. Based on ADB (2011) projected growth rate.
t. Based on UNESCWA (2011) and UNDESA (2011) projected growth rates.
u. Refers to primary and secondary education only. United Nations Educational, Scientific and Cultural Organization Institute for Statistics estimate.
v. Based on ADB (2011) and UNDESA (2011) projected growth rates.
w. Based on data from ICF Macro (2011).

DEFINITIONS

Human Development Index (HDI): A composite index measuring average achievement in three basic dimensions of human development—a long and healthy life, knowledge and a decent standard of living. See *Technical note 1* for details on how the HDI is calculated.
Life expectancy at birth: Number of years a newborn infant could expect to live if prevailing patterns of age-specific mortality rates at the time of birth stay the same throughout the infant's life.
Mean years of schooling: Average number of years of education received by people ages 25 and older, converted from education attainment levels using official durations of each level.
Expected years of schooling: Number of years of schooling that a child of school entrance age can expect to receive if prevailing patterns of age-specific enrolment rates persist throughout the child's life.
Gross national income (GNI) per capita: Aggregate income of an economy generated by its production and its ownership of factors of production, less the incomes paid for the use of factors of production owned by the rest of the world, converted to international dollars using purchasing power parity (PPP) rates, divided by midyear population.
GNI per capita rank minus HDI rank: Difference in rankings by GNI per capita and by the HDI. A negative value means that the country is better ranked by GNI than by the HDI.
Nonincome HDI: Value of the HDI computed from the life expectancy and education indicators only.

MAIN DATA SOURCES

Column 1: HDRO calculations based on data from UNDESA (2011), Barro and Lee (2010b), UNESCO Institute for Statistics (2011), World Bank (2011a), UNSD (2011) and IMF (2011).
Column 2: UNDESA (2011).
Column 3: HDRO updates of Barro and Lee (2010b) estimates based on UNESCO Institute for Statistics data on education attainment (2011) and Barro and Lee (2010a) methodology.
Column 4: UNESCO Institute for Statistics (2011).
Column 5: HDRO calculations based on data from World Bank (2011a), IMF (2011) and UNSD (2011).
Column 6: Calculated based on data in columns 1 and 5.
Column 7: Calculated based on data in columns 2, 3 and 4.

TABLE 2

Human Development Index trends, 1980–2011

HDI rank	Human Development Index (HDI) Value							HDI rank Change[a]		Average annual HDI growth (%)		
	1980	1990	2000	2005	2009	2010	2011	2006–2011	2010–2011	1980–2011	1990–2011	2000–2011
VERY HIGH HUMAN DEVELOPMENT												
1 Norway	0.796	0.844	0.913	0.938	0.941	0.941	0.943	0	0	0.55	0.53	0.29
2 Australia	0.850	0.873	0.906	0.918	0.926	0.927	0.929	0	0	0.29	0.30	0.23
3 Netherlands	0.792	0.835	0.882	0.890	0.905	0.909	0.910	5	0	0.45	0.41	0.29
4 United States	0.837	0.870	0.897	0.902	0.906	0.908	0.910	−1	0	0.27	0.21	0.13
5 New Zealand	0.800	0.828	0.878	0.899	0.906	0.908	0.908	0	0	0.41	0.44	0.31
6 Canada	0.817	0.857	0.879	0.892	0.903	0.907	0.908	3	0	0.34	0.28	0.30
7 Ireland	0.735	0.782	0.869	0.898	0.905	0.907	0.908	−3	0	0.68	0.71	0.40
8 Liechtenstein	..	..	..	..	..	0.904	0.905	..	0	..	..	..
9 Germany	0.730	0.795	0.864	0.895	0.900	0.903	0.905	−2	0	0.69	0.62	0.43
10 Sweden	0.785	0.816	0.894	0.896	0.898	0.901	0.904	−2	0	0.45	0.49	0.09
11 Switzerland	0.810	0.833	0.873	0.890	0.899	0.901	0.903	1	0	0.35	0.38	0.30
12 Japan	0.778	0.827	0.868	0.886	0.895	0.899	0.901	1	0	0.47	0.41	0.33
13 Hong Kong, China (SAR)	0.708	0.786	0.824	0.850	0.888	0.894	0.898	14	1	0.77	0.64	0.78
14 Iceland	0.762	0.807	0.863	0.893	0.897	0.896	0.898	−3	−1	0.53	0.51	0.36
15 Korea, Republic of	0.634	0.742	0.830	0.866	0.889	0.894	0.897	3	0	1.13	0.91	0.72
16 Denmark	0.783	0.809	0.861	0.885	0.891	0.893	0.895	−2	0	0.43	0.48	0.35
17 Israel	0.763	0.802	0.856	0.874	0.884	0.886	0.888	−1	0	0.49	0.49	0.34
18 Belgium	0.757	0.811	0.876	0.873	0.883	0.885	0.886	−1	0	0.51	0.42	0.10
19 Austria	0.740	0.790	0.839	0.860	0.879	0.883	0.885	1	0	0.58	0.55	0.48
20 France	0.722	0.777	0.846	0.869	0.880	0.883	0.884	−1	0	0.66	0.62	0.40
21 Slovenia	..	..	0.805	0.848	0.876	0.882	0.884	4	0	..	..	0.85
22 Finland	0.759	0.794	0.837	0.875	0.877	0.880	0.882	−7	0	0.49	0.51	0.48
23 Spain	0.691	0.749	0.839	0.857	0.874	0.876	0.878	0	0	0.77	0.76	0.42
24 Italy	0.717	0.764	0.825	0.861	0.870	0.873	0.874	−3	0	0.64	0.64	0.52
25 Luxembourg	0.728	0.788	0.854	0.865	0.863	0.865	0.867	−3	0	0.56	0.45	0.13
26 Singapore	..	..	0.801	0.835	0.856	0.864	0.866	3	0	..	..	0.71
27 Czech Republic	..	..	0.816	0.854	0.863	0.863	0.865	−1	0	..	..	0.53
28 United Kingdom	0.744	0.778	0.833	0.855	0.860	0.862	0.863	0	0	0.48	0.50	0.33
29 Greece	0.720	0.766	0.802	0.856	0.863	0.862	0.861	−5	0	0.58	0.56	0.64
30 United Arab Emirates	0.629	0.690	0.753	0.807	0.841	0.845	0.846	3	0	0.96	0.97	1.06
31 Cyprus	..	0.747	0.800	0.809	0.837	0.839	0.840	5	0	..	0.56	0.44
32 Andorra	..	..	..	..	..	0.838	0.838	..	0	..	..	..
33 Brunei Darussalam	0.750	0.784	0.818	0.830	0.835	0.837	0.838	−2	0	0.36	0.32	0.22
34 Estonia	..	0.717	0.776	0.821	0.828	0.832	0.835	−2	0	..	0.73	0.66
35 Slovakia	..	0.747	0.779	0.810	0.829	0.832	0.834	0	0	..	0.53	0.62
36 Malta	0.703	0.753	0.799	0.825	0.827	0.830	0.832	−3	0	0.54	0.48	0.37
37 Qatar	0.703	0.743	0.784	0.818	0.818	0.825	0.831	−1	0	0.54	0.54	0.53
38 Hungary	0.700	0.706	0.775	0.803	0.811	0.814	0.816	0	0	0.50	0.70	0.48
39 Poland	..	..	0.770	0.791	0.807	0.811	0.813	2	0	..	..	0.50
40 Lithuania	..	..	0.749	0.793	0.802	0.805	0.810	0	1	..	..	0.70
41 Portugal	0.639	0.708	0.778	0.789	0.805	0.808	0.809	2	−1	0.76	0.64	0.35
42 Bahrain	0.651	0.721	0.773	0.795	0.805	0.805	0.806	−3	0	0.69	0.54	0.38
43 Latvia	..	0.693	0.732	0.784	0.798	0.802	0.805	−1	0	..	0.72	0.87
44 Chile	0.630	0.698	0.740	0.770	0.790	0.802	0.805	3	0	0.78	0.68	0.65
45 Argentina	0.669	0.697	0.749	0.765	0.788	0.794	0.797	3	1	0.57	0.64	0.57
46 Croatia	..	..	0.748	0.780	0.793	0.794	0.796	0	−1	..	..	0.57
47 Barbados	..	..	..	0.787	0.790	0.791	0.793	−2	0	..	..	..
HIGH HUMAN DEVELOPMENT												
48 Uruguay	0.658	0.686	0.736	0.748	0.773	0.780	0.783	5	0	0.56	0.63·	0.56
49 Palau	..	..	0.774	0.788	0.777	0.779	0.782	−5	0	..	..	0.09
50 Romania	..	0.700	0.704	0.748	0.778	0.779	0.781	2	0	..	0.52	0.95
51 Cuba	..	0.677	0.681	0.725	0.770	0.773	0.776	10	0	..	0.65	1.19
52 Seychelles	..	..	0.764	0.766	0.767	0.771	0.773	−3	0	..	..	0.11
53 Bahamas	..	..	0.752	0.766	0.769	0.770	0.771	−3	0	..	..	0.23
54 Montenegro	..	..	..	0.757	0.768	0.769	0.771	−3	1	..	..	..
55 Bulgaria	..	0.698	0.715	0.749	0.766	0.768	0.771	0	1	..	0.48	0.68
56 Saudi Arabia	0.651	0.693	0.726	0.746	0.763	0.767	0.770	0	2	0.55	0.50	0.55
57 Mexico	0.593	0.649	0.718	0.741	0.762	0.767	0.770	2	0	0.85	0.82	0.64

Human Development Index trends, 1980–2011

TABLE 2

HDI rank	Human Development Index (HDI) Value							HDI rank Change[a]		Average annual HDI growth (%)		
	1980	1990	2000	2005	2009	2010	2011	2006–2011	2010–2011	1980–2011	1990–2011	2000–2011
58 Panama	0.628	0.660	0.718	0.740	0.760	0.765	0.768	2	1	0.65	0.73	0.62
59 Serbia	..	..	0.719	0.744	0.761	0.764	0.766	−2	1	..	..	0.58
60 Antigua and Barbuda	..	..	..	..	..	0.763	0.764	..	1	..	..	..
61 Malaysia	0.559	0.631	0.705	0.738	0.752	0.758	0.761	2	3	1.00	0.90	0.69
62 Trinidad and Tobago	0.673	0.676	0.701	0.728	0.755	0.758	0.760	2	1	0.40	0.56	0.74
63 Kuwait	0.688	0.712	0.754	0.752	0.757	0.758	0.760	−8	−1	0.32	0.31	0.07
64 Libya	..	..	..	0.741	0.763	0.770	0.760	−5	−10	..	..	..
65 Belarus	..	..	..	0.723	0.746	0.751	0.756	1	0	..	..	..
66 Russian Federation	..	..	0.691	0.725	0.747	0.751	0.755	−1	0	..	..	0.81
67 Grenada	..	..	..	..	..	0.746	0.748	..	0	..	..	..
68 Kazakhstan	..	..	0.657	0.714	0.733	0.740	0.745	2	1	..	..	1.15
69 Costa Rica	0.614	0.656	0.703	0.723	0.738	0.742	0.744	−1	−1	0.62	0.60	0.51
70 Albania	..	0.656	0.691	0.721	0.734	0.737	0.739	−1	1	..	0.57	0.61
71 Lebanon	..	..	..	0.711	0.733	0.737	0.739	3	−1	..	..	..
72 Saint Kitts and Nevis	..	..	..	..	..	0.735	0.735	..	0	..	..	..
73 Venezuela, Bolivarian Republic of	0.623	0.629	0.656	0.692	0.732	0.734	0.735	7	0	0.54	0.74	1.04
74 Bosnia and Herzegovina	..	..	..	0.717	0.730	0.731	0.733	−2	0	..	..	..
75 Georgia	..	..	..	0.707	0.724	0.729	0.733	1	0	..	..	..
76 Ukraine	..	0.707	0.669	0.712	0.720	0.725	0.729	−3	3	..	0.15	0.78
77 Mauritius	0.546	0.618	0.672	0.703	0.722	0.726	0.728	1	0	0.93	0.78	0.73
78 Former Yugoslav Republic of Macedonia	..	..	..	0.704	0.725	0.726	0.728	1	−2	..	..	..
79 Jamaica	0.607	0.637	0.680	0.702	0.724	0.726	0.727	−2	−1	0.59	0.64	0.62
80 Peru	0.574	0.612	0.674	0.691	0.714	0.721	0.725	4	1	0.75	0.81	0.67
81 Dominica	..	..	0.699	0.709	0.722	0.723	0.724	−7	−1	..	..	0.33
82 Saint Lucia	..	..	..	..	..	0.720	0.723	..	0	..	..	..
83 Ecuador	0.591	0.636	0.668	0.695	0.716	0.718	0.720	0	0	0.64	0.59	0.69
84 Brazil	0.549	0.600	0.665	0.692	0.708	0.715	0.718	3	1	0.87	0.86	0.69
85 Saint Vincent and the Grenadines	..	..	..	..	..	0.715	0.717	..	−1	..	..	..
86 Armenia	..	..	0.643	0.689	0.712	0.714	0.716	−3	0	..	..	0.99
87 Colombia	0.550	0.594	0.652	0.675	0.702	0.707	0.710	4	1	0.83	0.85	0.77
88 Iran, Islamic Republic of	0.437	0.534	0.636	0.671	0.703	0.707	0.707	2	−1	1.57	1.35	0.97
89 Oman	..	..	..	0.694	0.703	0.704	0.705	−2	0	..	..	..
90 Tonga	..	0.649	0.681	0.696	0.701	0.703	0.704	−5	0	..	0.39	0.30
91 Azerbaijan	..	..	..	..	..	0.699	0.700	..	0	..	..	..
92 Turkey	0.463	0.558	0.634	0.671	0.690	0.696	0.699	2	3	1.34	1.08	0.90
93 Belize	0.619	0.651	0.668	0.689	0.696	0.698	0.699	−3	−1	0.39	0.34	0.42
94 Tunisia	0.450	0.542	0.630	0.667	0.692	0.698	0.698	3	−1	1.43	1.21	0.94
MEDIUM HUMAN DEVELOPMENT												
95 Jordan	0.541	0.591	0.646	0.673	0.694	0.697	0.698	1	−1	0.83	0.80	0.70
96 Algeria	0.454	0.551	0.624	0.667	0.691	0.696	0.698	2	0	1.40	1.13	1.03
97 Sri Lanka	0.539	0.583	0.633	0.662	0.680	0.686	0.691	2	1	0.80	0.81	0.80
98 Dominican Republic	0.532	0.577	0.640	0.658	0.680	0.686	0.689	2	2	0.83	0.84	0.67
99 Samoa	..	..	0.657	0.676	0.685	0.686	0.688	−6	0	..	..	0.43
100 Fiji	0.566	0.624	0.668	0.678	0.685	0.687	0.688	−5	−3	0.63	0.47	0.27
101 China	0.404	0.490	0.588	0.633	0.674	0.682	0.687	6	0	1.73	1.62	1.43
102 Turkmenistan	..	..	..	0.654	0.677	0.681	0.686	1	0	..	..	..
103 Thailand	0.486	0.566	0.626	0.656	0.673	0.680	0.682	−1	0	1.10	0.89	0.78
104 Suriname	..	..	..	0.659	0.674	0.677	0.680	−3	0	..	..	..
105 El Salvador	0.466	0.524	0.619	0.652	0.669	0.672	0.674	−1	0	1.20	1.21	0.79
106 Gabon	0.522	0.605	0.621	0.648	0.664	0.670	0.674	0	0	0.83	0.52	0.75
107 Paraguay	0.544	0.572	0.612	0.635	0.651	0.662	0.665	1	0	0.65	0.71	0.76
108 Bolivia, Plurinational State of	0.507	0.560	0.612	0.649	0.656	0.660	0.663	−3	0	0.87	0.81	0.73
109 Maldives	..	..	0.576	0.619	0.650	0.658	0.661	2	0	..	..	1.27
110 Mongolia	..	0.540	0.555	0.611	0.642	0.647	0.653	4	0	..	0.91	1.49
111 Moldova, Republic of	..	..	0.586	0.631	0.638	0.644	0.649	−2	0	..	..	0.92
112 Philippines	0.550	0.571	0.602	0.622	0.636	0.641	0.644	1	1	0.51	0.58	0.62
113 Egypt	0.406	0.497	0.585	0.611	0.638	0.644	0.644	2	−1	1.50	1.24	0.88
114 Occupied Palestinian Territory	..	..	..	..	..	0.640	0.641	..	0	..	..	..
115 Uzbekistan	..	..	..	0.611	0.631	0.636	0.641	2	0	..	..	..
116 Micronesia, Federated States of	..	..	..	0.633	0.635	0.635	0.636	−5	0	..	..	..
117 Guyana	0.501	0.489	0.579	0.606	0.624	0.629	0.633	1	2	0.76	1.23	0.81
118 Botswana	0.446	0.594	0.585	0.601	0.626	0.631	0.633	1	−1	1.14	0.30	0.71
119 Syrian Arab Republic	0.497	0.548	0.583	0.621	0.630	0.631	0.632	−6	−1	0.78	0.68	0.73
120 Namibia	..	0.564	0.577	0.593	0.617	0.622	0.625	2	1	..	0.49	0.72

HDI rank		Human Development Index (HDI) Value							HDI rank Change[a]		Average annual HDI growth (%)		
		1980	1990	2000	2005	2009	2010	2011	2006–2011	2010–2011	1980–2011	1990–2011	2000–2011
121	Honduras	0.451	0.513	0.569	0.597	0.619	0.623	0.625	−1	−1	1.06	0.94	0.86
122	Kiribati	..	..	..	..	..	0.621	0.624	..	0	..	..	..
123	South Africa	0.564	0.615	0.616	0.599	0.610	0.615	0.619	−1	1	0.30	0.03	0.05
124	Indonesia	0.423	0.481	0.543	0.572	0.607	0.613	0.617	2	1	1.23	1.19	1.17
125	Vanuatu	..	..	..	..	..	0.615	0.617	..	−2	..	..	..
126	Kyrgyzstan	..	..	0.577	0.595	0.611	0.611	0.615	−1	0	..	..	0.59
127	Tajikistan	..	..	0.527	0.575	0.600	0.604	0.607	−1	0	..	..	1.30
128	Viet Nam	..	0.435	0.528	0.561	0.584	0.590	0.593	1	0	..	1.50	1.06
129	Nicaragua	0.457	0.473	0.533	0.566	0.582	0.587	0.589	−1	0	0.83	1.05	0.92
130	Morocco	0.364	0.435	0.507	0.552	0.575	0.579	0.582	0	0	1.52	1.39	1.26
131	Guatemala	0.428	0.462	0.525	0.550	0.569	0.573	0.574	2	0	0.95	1.04	0.81
132	Iraq	..	..	..	0.552	0.565	0.567	0.573	−1	0	..	..	..
133	Cape Verde	..	..	0.523	0.543	0.564	0.566	0.568	−1	0	..	..	0.75
134	India	0.344	0.410	0.461	0.504	0.535	0.542	0.547	1	0	1.51	1.38	1.56
135	Ghana	0.385	0.418	0.451	0.484	0.527	0.533	0.541	5	1	1.10	1.23	1.66
136	Equatorial Guinea	..	..	0.488	0.516	0.534	0.534	0.537	−2	−1	..	..	0.88
137	Congo	0.465	0.502	0.478	0.506	0.523	0.528	0.533	0	0	0.44	0.28	0.99
138	Lao People's Democratic Republic	..	0.376	0.448	0.484	0.514	0.520	0.524	3	1	..	1.59	1.44
139	Cambodia	..	..	0.438	0.491	0.513	0.518	0.523	−1	2	..	..	1.62
140	Swaziland	..	0.526	0.492	0.493	0.515	0.520	0.522	−1	−2	..	−0.03	0.54
141	Bhutan	..	..	..	..	..	0.518	0.522	..	−1	..	..	..
LOW HUMAN DEVELOPMENT													
142	Solomon Islands	..	..	0.479	0.502	0.504	0.507	0.510	−5	0	..	..	0.58
143	Kenya	0.420	0.456	0.443	0.467	0.499	0.505	0.509	2	1	0.62	0.52	1.27
144	São Tomé and Príncipe	..	..	..	0.483	0.503	0.506	0.509	−1	−1	..	..	..
145	Pakistan	0.359	0.399	0.436	0.480	0.499	0.503	0.504	−1	0	1.10	1.12	1.33
146	Bangladesh	0.303	0.352	0.422	0.462	0.491	0.496	0.500	1	0	1.63	1.69	1.55
147	Timor-Leste	..	..	0.404	0.448	0.487	0.491	0.495	1	0	..	..	1.86
148	Angola	..	..	0.384	0.445	0.481	0.482	0.486	1	0	..	..	2.18
149	Myanmar	0.279	0.298	0.380	0.436	0.474	0.479	0.483	2	1	1.78	2.32	2.21
150	Cameroon	0.370	0.427	0.427	0.449	0.475	0.479	0.482	0	1	0.85	0.58	1.11
151	Madagascar	..	..	0.427	0.465	0.483	0.481	0.480	−5	−2	..	..	1.07
152	Tanzania, United Republic of	..	0.352	0.364	0.420	0.454	0.461	0.466	7	1	..	1.35	2.27
153	Papua New Guinea	0.313	0.368	0.423	0.435	0.457	0.462	0.466	1	−1	1.29	1.12	0.87
154	Yemen	..	..	0.374	0.422	0.452	0.460	0.462	4	0	..	..	1.93
155	Senegal	0.317	0.365	0.399	0.432	0.453	0.457	0.459	−2	0	1.20	1.10	1.28
156	Nigeria	..	..	..	0.429	0.449	0.454	0.459	−4	1	..	..	..
157	Nepal	0.242	0.340	0.398	0.424	0.449	0.455	0.458	0	−1	2.08	1.43	1.30
158	Haiti	0.332	0.397	0.421	0.429	0.449	0.449	0.454	−2	1	1.02	0.64	0.68
159	Mauritania	0.332	0.353	0.410	0.432	0.447	0.451	0.453	−4	−1	1.01	1.20	0.92
160	Lesotho	0.418	0.470	0.427	0.417	0.440	0.446	0.450	1	0	0.24	−0.22	0.47
161	Uganda	..	0.299	0.372	0.401	0.438	0.442	0.446	3	0	..	1.93	1.65
162	Togo	0.347	0.368	0.408	0.419	0.429	0.433	0.435	0	0	0.73	0.80	0.58
163	Comoros	..	..	..	0.428	0.430	0.431	0.433	−3	0	..	..	..
164	Zambia	0.401	0.394	0.371	0.394	0.419	0.425	0.430	2	1	0.23	0.42	1.37
165	Djibouti	..	..	..	0.402	0.425	0.427	0.430	0	−1	..	..	..
166	Rwanda	0.275	0.232	0.313	0.376	0.419	0.425	0.429	2	0	1.44	2.97	2.92
167	Benin	0.252	0.316	0.378	0.409	0.422	0.425	0.427	−4	0	1.71	1.44	1.10
168	Gambia	0.272	0.317	0.360	0.384	0.413	0.418	0.420	−1	0	1.41	1.35	1.41
169	Sudan	0.264	0.298	0.357	0.383	0.403	0.406	0.408	0	0	1.41	1.52	1.23
170	Côte d'Ivoire	0.347	0.361	0.374	0.383	0.397	0.401	0.400	0	0	0.45	0.50	0.61
171	Malawi	0.270	0.291	0.343	0.351	0.387	0.395	0.400	0	0	1.27	1.52	1.41
172	Afghanistan	0.198	0.246	0.230	0.340	0.387	0.394	0.398	0	0	2.28	2.32	5.10
173	Zimbabwe	0.366	0.425	0.372	0.347	0.349	0.364	0.376	0	0	0.09	−0.58	0.11
174	Ethiopia	..	..	0.274	0.313	0.353	0.358	0.363	2	0	..	..	2.57
175	Mali	0.174	0.204	0.275	0.319	0.352	0.356	0.359	2	0	2.37	2.74	2.47
176	Guinea-Bissau	..	..	..	0.340	0.348	0.351	0.353	−2	0	..	..	..
177	Eritrea	..	..	..	..	..	0.345	0.349	..	0	..	..	..
178	Guinea	..	..	..	0.326	0.341	0.342	0.344	−2	0	..	..	..
179	Central African Republic	0.283	0.310	0.306	0.311	0.334	0.339	0.343	0	0	0.62	0.48	1.05
180	Sierra Leone	0.248	0.241	0.252	0.306	0.329	0.334	0.336	0	0	0.99	1.61	2.65
181	Burkina Faso	..	..	..	0.302	0.326	0.329	0.331	1	0	..	..	..
182	Liberia	0.335	..	0.306	0.300	0.320	0.325	0.329	1	1	−0.06	..	0.64
183	Chad	..	..	0.286	0.312	0.323	0.326	0.328	−2	−1	..	..	1.26

TABLE 2

TABLE 2

HDI rank	Human Development Index (HDI) Value							HDI rank Change[a]		Average annual HDI growth (%)		
	1980	1990	2000	2005	2009	2010	2011	2006–2011	2010–2011	1980–2011	1990–2011	2000–2011
184 Mozambique	..	0.200	0.245	0.285	0.312	0.317	0.322	0	0	..	2.28	2.49
185 Burundi	0.200	0.250	0.245	0.267	0.308	0.313	0.316	0	0	1.49	1.12	2.33
186 Niger	0.177	0.193	0.229	0.265	0.285	0.293	0.295	0	0	1.67	2.05	2.33
187 Congo, Democratic Republic of the	0.282	0.289	0.224	0.260	0.277	0.282	0.286	0	0	0.05	−0.04	2.25
Human Development Index groups												
Very high human development	0.766	0.810	0.858	0.876	0.885	0.888	0.889	—	—	0.48	0.44	0.33
High human development	0.614[b]	0.648[b]	0.687	0.716	0.734	0.739	0.741	—	—	0.61	0.64	0.70
Medium human development	0.420[b]	0.480	0.548	0.587	0.618	0.625	0.630	—	—	1.31	1.30	1.28
Low human development	0.316	0.347	0.383	0.422	0.448	0.453	0.456	—	—	1.19	1.31	1.59
Regions												
Arab States	0.444	0.516	0.578	0.609	0.634	0.639	0.641	—	—	1.19	1.04	0.94
East Asia and the Pacific	0.428[b]	0.498[b]	0.581	0.622	0.658	0.666	0.671	—	—	1.46	1.43	1.31
Europe and Central Asia	0.644[b]	0.680[b]	0.695	0.728	0.744	0.748	0.751	—	—	0.50	0.47	0.71
Latin America and the Caribbean	0.582	0.624	0.680	0.703	0.722	0.728	0.731	—	—	0.73	0.76	0.66
South Asia	0.356	0.418	0.468	0.510	0.538	0.545	0.548	—	—	1.40	1.31	1.45
Sub-Saharan Africa	0.365	0.383	0.401	0.431	0.456	0.460	0.463	—	—	0.77	0.90	1.31
Least developed countries	0.288[b]	0.320[b]	0.363	0.401	0.431	0.435	0.439	—	—	1.37	1.51	1.73
Small island developing states	0.529[b]	0.565[b]	0.596[b]	0.616	0.635	0.638	0.640	—	—	0.62	0.59	0.65
World	0.558[b]	0.594	0.634	0.660	0.676	0.679	0.682	—	—	0.65	0.66	0.66

NOTES

a. A positive value indicates improvement in rank.
b. Based on less than half the countries in the group or region.

DEFINITION

Human Development Index (HDI): A composite index measuring average achievement in three basic dimensions of human development—a long and healthy life, knowledge and a decent standard of living. See *Technical note 1* for details on how the HDI is calculated.

MAIN DATA SOURCES

Columns 1–7: HDRO calculations based on data from UNDESA (2011), Barro and Lee (2010b), UNESCO Institute for Statistics (2011), World Bank (2011a), UNSD (2011) and IMF (2011).
Columns 8–12: Calculated based on Human Development Index values in the relevant year.

TABLE 3

Inequality-adjusted Human Development Index

HDI rank	Human Development Index (HDI) Value	Inequality-adjusted HDI			Inequality-adjusted life expectancy index		Inequality-adjusted education index		Inequality-adjusted income index		Quintile income ratio	Income Gini coefficient
		Value	Overall loss (%)	Change in rank[a]	Value	Loss (%)	Value	Loss (%)	Value	Loss (%)		
	2011	2011	2011	2011	2011	2011	2011	2011	2011	2011	2000–2011[b]	2000–2011[b]
VERY HIGH HUMAN DEVELOPMENT												
1 Norway	0.943	0.890	5.6	0	0.928	3.7	0.964	2.2	0.789	10.6	3.9	25.8
2 Australia	0.929	0.856	7.9	0	0.931	4.7	0.964	1.7	0.698	16.6	7.0	..
3 Netherlands	0.910	0.846	7.0	−1	0.917	4.3	0.895	3.9	0.739	12.5	5.1	..
4 United States	0.910	0.771	15.3	−19	0.863	6.6	0.905	3.7	0.587	32.4	8.5	40.8
5 New Zealand	0.908	..	..	..	0.907	5.2	..	..	..	..	6.8	..
6 Canada	0.908	0.829	8.7	−7	0.914	5.0	0.897	3.2	0.696	17.1	5.5	32.6
7 Ireland	0.908	0.843	7.2	0	0.915	4.3	0.933	3.2	0.701	13.8	5.7	34.3
8 Liechtenstein	0.905	..	..	..	..	..	..	..	..	..	..	..
9 Germany	0.905	0.842	6.9	0	0.915	4.0	0.911	1.8	0.717	14.5	4.3	28.3
10 Sweden	0.904	0.851	5.9	5	0.937	3.3	0.869	3.9	0.756	10.3	4.0	25.0
11 Switzerland	0.903	0.840	7.0	0	0.943	4.1	0.854	2.0	0.735	14.3	5.4	33.7
12 Japan	0.901	..	..	..	0.965	3.5	..	..	..	..	3.4	..
13 Hong Kong, China (SAR)	0.898	..	..	..	0.961	2.9	..	..	..	..	9.6	43.4
14 Iceland	0.898	0.845	5.9	5	0.945	3.0	0.888	2.6	0.718	11.8	..	..
15 Korea, Republic of	0.897	0.749	16.5	−17	0.916	4.3	0.696	25.5	0.659	18.4	4.7	..
16 Denmark	0.895	0.842	6.0	4	0.887	4.4	0.895	3.1	0.751	10.2	4.3	..
17 Israel	0.888	0.779	12.3	−8	0.934	3.9	0.835	7.9	0.607	23.7	7.9	39.2
18 Belgium	0.886	0.819	7.6	−1	0.905	4.4	0.825	6.5	0.735	11.7	4.9	33.0
19 Austria	0.885	0.820	7.4	1	0.920	4.2	0.838	2.4	0.715	15.1	4.4	29.1
20 France	0.884	0.804	9.1	0	0.930	4.2	0.791	9.1	0.705	13.9	5.6	..
21 Slovenia	0.884	0.837	5.3	7	0.898	4.1	0.904	3.1	0.723	8.5	4.8	31.2
22 Finland	0.882	0.833	5.6	7	0.909	3.9	0.858	2.1	0.740	10.6	3.8	26.9
23 Spain	0.878	0.799	8.9	2	0.929	4.1	0.826	5.5	0.666	16.7	6.0	34.7
24 Italy	0.874	0.779	10.9	−2	0.938	3.9	0.758	11.4	0.665	16.8	6.5	36.0
25 Luxembourg	0.867	0.799	7.8	3	0.913	3.5	0.724	6.2	0.771	13.5	..	..
26 Singapore	0.866	..	..	..	0.936	2.9	..	..	..	..	9.8	..
27 Czech Republic	0.865	0.821	5.0	9	0.874	3.9	0.912	1.3	0.695	9.6	3.5	..
28 United Kingdom	0.863	0.791	8.4	4	0.903	4.8	0.797	2.2	0.688	17.3	7.2	..
29 Greece	0.861	0.756	12.2	−2	0.900	4.8	0.738	14.3	0.649	17.1	6.2	34.3
30 United Arab Emirates	0.846	..	..	..	0.836	6.3	..	..	..	..	..	..
31 Cyprus	0.840	0.755	10.1	−2	0.901	4.1	0.678	15.0	0.704	10.9	..	..
32 Andorra	0.838	..	..	..	..	..	..	..	..	..	..	..
33 Brunei Darussalam	0.838	..	..	..	0.862	5.8	..	..	..	..	..	..
34 Estonia	0.835	0.769	7.9	2	0.813	6.0	0.891	2.7	0.627	14.5	6.3	36.0
35 Slovakia	0.834	0.787	5.7	7	0.825	5.7	0.861	1.6	0.686	9.6	4.0	..
36 Malta	0.832	..	..	..	0.892	5.1	..	..	..	..	..	..
37 Qatar	0.831	..	..	..	0.854	7.2	..	..	..	..	13.3	41.1
38 Hungary	0.816	0.759	7.0	3	0.809	5.7	0.831	4.0	0.650	11.2	4.8	31.2
39 Poland	0.813	0.734	9.7	0	0.834	5.8	0.768	6.6	0.619	16.3	5.6	34.2
40 Lithuania	0.810	0.730	9.8	0	0.765	7.2	0.847	4.1	0.601	17.5	6.7	37.6
41 Portugal	0.809	0.726	10.2	0	0.893	4.9	0.697	5.6	0.616	19.3	7.9	..
42 Bahrain	0.806	..	..	..	0.815	6.2	..	..	..	..	..	..
43 Latvia	0.805	0.717	10.9	−1	0.782	7.1	0.840	3.8	0.561	21.0	6.3	35.7
44 Chile	0.805	0.652	19.0	−11	0.871	6.6	0.688	13.7	0.462	34.1	3.6	52.1
45 Argentina	0.797	0.641	19.5	−13	0.796	9.7	0.708	12.1	0.468	34.4	12.3	45.8
46 Croatia	0.796	0.675	15.1	−3	0.844	5.5	0.697	10.4	0.523	27.8	5.2	33.7
47 Barbados	0.793	..	..	..	0.814	9.2	..	..	..	..	..	..
HIGH HUMAN DEVELOPMENT												
48 Uruguay	0.783	0.654	16.4	−7	0.815	9.3	0.681	10.8	0.505	27.8	8.7	42.4
49 Palau	0.782	..	..	..	..	..	..	..	..	..	..	..
50 Romania	0.781	0.683	12.6	1	0.770	9.6	0.789	5.0	0.524	22.2	4.9	31.2
51 Cuba	0.776	..	..	..	0.883	5.4	..	..	..	..	..	..
52 Seychelles	0.773	..	..	..	..	..	..	..	..	..	2.7	19.0
53 Bahamas	0.771	0.658	14.7	−3	0.782	10.9	0.618	7.9	0.588	24.5	..	..
54 Montenegro	0.771	0.718	6.9	7	0.803	6.8	0.782	2.5	0.589	11.3	4.6	30.0
55 Bulgaria	0.771	0.683	11.4	3	0.776	7.8	0.754	5.9	0.543	19.9	10.2	45.3
56 Saudi Arabia	0.770	..	..	..	0.753	11.5	..	..	..	..	..	..
57 Mexico	0.770	0.589	23.5	−15	0.801	10.9	0.567	21.9	0.451	35.6	14.4	51.7

Inequality-adjusted Human Development Index

TABLE 3

HDI rank	Human Development Index (HDI) Value	Inequality-adjusted HDI Value	Overall loss (%)	Change in rank[a]	Inequality-adjusted life expectancy index Value	Loss (%)	Inequality-adjusted education index Value	Loss (%)	Inequality-adjusted income index Value	Loss (%)	Quintile income ratio	Income Gini coefficient
	2011	2011	2011	2011	2011	2011	2011	2011	2011	2011	2000–2011[b]	2000–2011[b]
58 Panama	0.768	0.579	24.6	−15	0.776	12.4	0.611	17.8	0.410	40.5	15.8	52.3
59 Serbia	0.766	0.694	9.5	9	0.788	8.3	0.712	9.9	0.595	10.3	4.1	28.2
60 Antigua and Barbuda	0.764	..	..	..	..	..	..	..	..	..	..	..
61 Malaysia	0.761	..	..	..	0.798	6.7	..	..	..	0.0	11.4	46.2
62 Trinidad and Tobago	0.760	0.644	15.3	−2	0.659	16.6	0.665	6.6	0.610	21.9	8.3	..
63 Kuwait	0.760	..	..	..	0.803	6.7	..	..	..	..	..	..
64 Libya	0.760	..	..	..	0.781	9.7	..	..	..	..	..	..
65 Belarus	0.756	0.693	8.3	10	0.736	7.4	0.735	5.4	0.617	12.1	4.0	27.2
66 Russian Federation	0.755	0.670	11.3	7	0.687	10.8	0.696	11.2	0.628	11.9	8.2	42.3
67 Grenada	0.748	..	..	..	0.798	9.6	..	..	..	..	..	..
68 Kazakhstan	0.745	0.656	11.9	5	0.621	16.2	0.790	5.3	0.576	13.8	4.6	30.9
69 Costa Rica	0.744	0.591	20.5	−7	0.863	7.8	0.543	17.7	0.442	33.7	13.2	50.3
70 Albania	0.739	0.637	13.9	0	0.797	11.2	0.635	11.9	0.510	18.3	5.3	34.5
71 Lebanon	0.739	0.570	22.8	−9	0.718	13.5	0.528	24.1	0.489	30.0	..	..
72 Saint Kitts and Nevis	0.735	..	..	..	..	..	..	..	..	..	..	..
73 Venezuela, Bolivarian Republic of	0.735	0.540	26.6	−16	0.753	12.2	0.567	18.1	0.368	44.9	10.0	43.5
74 Bosnia and Herzegovina	0.733	0.649	11.6	7	0.794	9.6	0.685	5.2	0.502	19.3	6.4	36.2
75 Georgia	0.733	0.630	14.1	2	0.720	15.1	0.812	3.3	0.428	22.7	8.9	41.3
76 Ukraine	0.729	0.662	9.2	14	0.684	10.5	0.806	6.1	0.526	10.9	3.9	27.5
77 Mauritius	0.728	0.631	13.3	5	0.760	9.8	0.570	13.5	0.581	16.6	..	..
78 Former Yugoslav Republic of Macedonia	0.728	0.609	16.4	2	0.784	9.4	0.574	17.5	0.502	21.8	9.3	44.2
79 Jamaica	0.727	0.610	16.2	4	0.710	15.3	0.704	8.3	0.454	24.1	9.8	45.5
80 Peru	0.725	0.557	23.2	−5	0.726	14.8	0.535	24.0	0.444	30.0	13.5	48.0
81 Dominica	0.724	..	..	..	..	..	..	..	..	..	..	..
82 Saint Lucia	0.723	..	..	..	0.773	10.4	..	..	..	..	..	42.6
83 Ecuador	0.720	0.535	25.8	−10	0.753	14.1	0.535	22.1	0.379	38.8	12.8	49.0
84 Brazil	0.718	0.519	27.7	−13	0.723	14.4	0.492	25.7	0.392	40.7	17.6	53.9
85 Saint Vincent and the Grenadines	0.717	..	..	..	0.710	14.0	..	..	..	..	..	..
86 Armenia	0.716	0.639	10.8	13	0.728	14.9	0.710	6.5	0.504	10.8	4.5	30.9
87 Colombia	0.710	0.479	32.5	−24	0.731	13.7	0.515	22.8	0.292	53.9	24.8	58.5
88 Iran, Islamic Republic of	0.707	..	..	..	0.701	16.1	..	..	..	..	7.0	38.3
89 Oman	0.705	..	..	..	0.776	7.2	..	..	..	..	..	..
90 Tonga	0.704	..	..	..	0.712	13.8	..	..	..	..	..	..
91 Azerbaijan	0.700	0.620	11.4	11	0.636	20.6	0.615	8.3	0.610	4.5	5.3	33.7
92 Turkey	0.699	0.542	22.5	−2	0.742	12.8	0.423	27.4	0.506	26.5	8.0	39.7
93 Belize	0.699	..	..	..	0.776	12.2	..	..	..	..	17.2	..
94 Tunisia	0.698	0.523	25.2	−7	0.751	12.6	0.396	38.7	0.480	21.8	8.0	40.8
MEDIUM HUMAN DEVELOPMENT												
95 Jordan	0.698	0.565	19.0	5	0.732	13.1	0.551	22.4	0.449	21.1	6.3	37.7
96 Algeria	0.698	..	..	..	0.716	14.5	..	..	..	..	6.1	..
97 Sri Lanka	0.691	0.579	16.2	9	0.785	9.4	0.558	17.9	0.442	20.8	6.9	40.3
98 Dominican Republic	0.689	0.510	25.9	−9	0.707	16.0	0.451	26.8	0.417	33.8	12.2	48.4
99 Samoa	0.688	..	..	..	0.717	13.4	..	..	..	..	..	..
100 Fiji	0.688	..	..	..	0.676	13.0	..	..	..	..	..	..
101 China	0.687	0.534	22.3	−1	0.730	13.5	0.478	23.2	0.436	29.5	8.4	41.5
102 Turkmenistan	0.686	..	..	..	0.520	26.7	..	..	..	..	7.9	..
103 Thailand	0.682	0.537	21.3	2	0.768	10.1	0.490	18.0	0.411	34.0	15.0	53.6
104 Suriname	0.680	0.518	23.8	−3	0.678	15.0	0.508	20.1	0.403	34.9	..	52.8
105 El Salvador	0.674	0.495	26.6	−11	0.698	15.2	0.431	32.4	0.403	31.1	12.1	46.9
106 Gabon	0.674	0.543	19.5	8	0.486	27.8	0.612	7.3	0.536	22.1	7.9	41.5
107 Paraguay	0.665	0.505	24.0	−4	0.680	17.8	0.515	19.8	0.368	33.4	14.9	52.0
108 Bolivia, Plurinational State of	0.663	0.437	34.1	−12	0.550	25.1	0.542	27.6	0.280	47.2	21.8	57.3
109 Maldives	0.661	0.495	25.2	−6	0.832	7.3	0.334	41.2	0.436	23.2	6.8	37.4
110 Mongolia	0.653	0.563	13.8	15	0.622	18.8	0.680	5.8	0.422	16.4	6.2	36.5
111 Moldova, Republic of	0.649	0.569	12.2	18	0.691	11.2	0.673	6.1	0.397	18.9	6.7	38.0
112 Philippines	0.644	0.516	19.9	4	0.652	15.2	0.592	13.5	0.356	30.0	9.0	44.0
113 Egypt	0.644	0.489	24.1	−5	0.723	13.9	0.331	40.9	0.487	14.2	4.6	32.1
114 Occupied Palestinian Territory	0.641	..	..	..	0.725	13.1	..	..	..	..	..	..
115 Uzbekistan	0.641	0.544	15.1	17	0.577	24.3	0.701	1.4	0.399	17.9	6.2	36.7
116 Micronesia, Federated States of	0.636	0.390	38.6	−12	0.624	19.2	0.534	22.4	0.179	63.1	..	..
117 Guyana	0.633	0.492	22.3	−1	0.616	21.7	0.574	11.7	0.337	32.1	..	43.2
118 Botswana	0.633	..	..	..	0.396	24.3	..	..	..	..	21.0	..

HDI rank	Human Development Index (HDI) Value	Inequality-adjusted HDI Value	Overall loss (%)	Change in rank[a]	Inequality-adjusted life expectancy index Value	Loss (%)	Inequality-adjusted education index Value	Loss (%)	Inequality-adjusted income index Value	Loss (%)	Quintile income ratio	Income Gini coefficient
	2011	2011	2011	2011	2011	2011	2011	2011	2011	2011	2000–2011[b]	2000–2011[b]
119 Syrian Arab Republic	0.632	0.503	20.4	4	0.793	10.0	0.366	31.5	0.439	18.3	5.7	35.8
120 Namibia	0.625	0.353	43.5	−14	0.528	21.1	0.445	27.8	0.187	68.3	52.2	..
121 Honduras	0.625	0.427	31.7	−3	0.693	17.4	0.392	31.8	0.287	43.4	30.4	57.7
122 Kiribati	0.624	..	..	..	..	..	..	..	..	..	..	..
123 South Africa	0.619	..	..	..	0.370	28.4	0.558	20.8	..	..	20.2	57.8
124 Indonesia	0.617	0.504	18.3	8	0.648	16.8	0.465	20.4	0.426	17.7	5.9	36.8
125 Vanuatu	0.617	..	..	..	0.679	15.6	..	..	..	..	..	..
126 Kyrgyzstan	0.615	0.526	14.4	17	0.604	19.8	0.637	11.1	0.379	12.2	4.9	33.4
127 Tajikistan	0.607	0.500	17.6	8	0.546	27.2	0.638	9.4	0.360	15.3	4.2	29.4
128 Viet Nam	0.593	0.510	14.0	14	0.754	13.4	0.417	17.1	0.423	11.4	6.2	37.6
129 Nicaragua	0.589	0.427	27.5	3	0.734	13.9	0.350	33.3	0.303	33.6	15.0	52.3
130 Morocco	0.582	0.409	29.7	2	0.685	16.7	0.242	45.8	0.412	23.0	7.4	40.9
131 Guatemala	0.574	0.393	31.6	1	0.657	18.6	0.280	36.1	0.329	38.5	17.0	53.7
132 Iraq	0.573	..	..	..	0.617	20.3	..	..	..	..	..	..
133 Cape Verde	0.568	..	..	..	0.746	12.7	0.295	30.7	..	..	..	50.4
134 India	0.547	0.392	28.3	1	0.522	27.1	0.267	40.6	0.433	14.7	5.6	36.8
135 Ghana	0.541	0.367	32.2	−1	0.506	27.5	0.339	40.9	0.288	27.2	9.3	42.8
136 Equatorial Guinea	0.537	..	..	..	0.268	45.4	0.303	29.2	..	..	..	..
137 Congo	0.533	0.367	31.1	−1	0.371	37.0	0.390	25.4	0.342	30.3	10.6	47.3
138 Lao People's Democratic Republic	0.524	0.405	22.8	6	0.586	21.7	0.300	30.5	0.376	15.5	5.9	36.7
139 Cambodia	0.523	0.380	27.2	3	0.484	28.8	0.346	31.1	0.328	21.4	7.8	44.4
140 Swaziland	0.522	0.338	35.4	−4	0.295	35.0	0.406	29.8	0.322	40.9	12.4	50.7
141 Bhutan	0.522	..	..	..	0.565	24.1	0.185	44.8	..	..	..	46.7
LOW HUMAN DEVELOPMENT												
142 Solomon Islands	0.510	..	..	..	0.599	20.7	..	..	..	..	..	..
143 Kenya	0.509	0.338	33.6	−2	0.386	34.1	0.403	30.7	0.248	36.0	11.3	47.7
144 São Tomé and Príncipe	0.509	0.348	31.5	1	0.502	28.8	0.365	19.1	0.231	44.2	10.8	50.8
145 Pakistan	0.504	0.346	31.4	1	0.485	32.3	0.207	46.4	0.413	11.0	4.7	32.7
146 Bangladesh	0.500	0.363	27.4	5	0.593	23.2	0.252	39.4	0.321	17.7	4.3	31.0
147 Timor-Leste	0.495	0.332	32.9	−1	0.468	30.2	0.195	47.4	0.401	17.8	4.6	31.9
148 Angola	0.486	..	..	..	0.264	46.1	..	..	0.278	50.0	31.0	58.6
149 Myanmar	0.483	..	..	..	0.533	25.3	..	..	..	..	..	..
150 Cameroon	0.482	0.321	33.4	−2	0.284	43.0	0.336	35.3	0.345	19.9	9.1	44.6
151 Madagascar	0.480	0.332	30.7	2	0.548	25.6	0.347	30.1	0.193	36.1	8.6	47.2
152 Tanzania, United Republic of	0.466	0.332	28.8	1	0.407	32.4	0.305	32.8	0.294	20.6	6.6	37.6
153 Papua New Guinea	0.466	..	..	..	0.505	25.2	..	..	..	..	12.5	..
154 Yemen	0.462	0.312	32.3	0	0.537	25.1	0.155	49.8	0.365	17.6	6.3	37.7
155 Senegal	0.459	0.304	33.8	0	0.430	30.7	0.211	45.1	0.309	23.9	7.4	39.2
156 Nigeria	0.459	0.278	39.3	−6	0.283	43.8	0.247	44.2	0.309	28.8	9.5	42.9
157 Nepal	0.458	0.301	34.3	0	0.620	19.5	0.201	43.6	0.220	37.4	8.9	47.3
158 Haiti	0.454	0.271	40.2	−9	0.459	30.9	0.241	40.7	0.180	47.9	25.2	59.5
159 Mauritania	0.453	0.298	34.2	1	0.389	36.2	0.208	43.2	0.329	21.5	7.4	39.0
160 Lesotho	0.450	0.288	35.9	−1	0.292	34.3	0.384	24.3	0.213	47.0	18.8	52.5
161 Uganda	0.446	0.296	33.6	2	0.328	39.1	0.322	32.2	0.246	29.1	8.7	44.3
162 Togo	0.435	0.289	33.5	2	0.367	37.2	0.277	41.5	0.238	20.0	8.7	34.4
163 Comoros	0.433	..	..	..	0.437	32.6	0.193	47.4	..	..	..	64.3
164 Zambia	0.430	0.303	29.5	7	0.266	41.9	0.366	23.8	0.287	20.8	15.3	50.7
165 Djibouti	0.430	0.275	35.0	0	0.377	36.0	0.166	47.0	0.366	21.3	..	39.9
166 Rwanda	0.429	0.276	35.7	2	0.328	41.3	0.282	30.7	0.228	34.5	13.9	53.1
167 Benin	0.427	0.274	35.8	1	0.340	40.3	0.212	42.0	0.286	23.6	6.7	38.6
168 Gambia	0.420	..	..	..	0.402	33.9	..	..	..	..	11.0	47.3
169 Sudan	0.408	..	..	..	0.438	33.0	..	..	..	..	..	..
170 Côte d'Ivoire	0.400	0.246	38.6	−3	0.347	37.8	0.173	43.2	0.247	34.4	11.0	46.1
171 Malawi	0.400	0.272	32.0	2	0.324	39.9	0.267	34.7	0.232	19.7	6.6	39.0
172 Afghanistan	0.398	..	..	..	0.222	50.9	0.223	39.3	..	..	..	..
173 Zimbabwe	0.376	0.268	28.7	1	0.343	30.6	0.452	20.1	0.124	34.5	12.1	..
174 Ethiopia	0.363	0.247	31.9	1	0.400	35.4	0.146	38.2	0.258	20.8	4.2	29.8
175 Mali	0.359	..	..	..	0.266	46.3	0.170	36.9	..	..	7.1	39.0
176 Guinea-Bissau	0.353	0.207	41.4	−4	0.221	50.1	0.181	40.3	0.222	32.5	6.0	35.5
177 Eritrea	0.349	..	..	..	0.481	26.6	..	..	..	..	..	..
178 Guinea	0.344	0.211	38.8	−2	0.308	42.7	0.143	42.0	0.213	31.1	7.2	39.4
179 Central African Republic	0.343	0.204	40.6	−3	0.242	46.0	0.174	45.9	0.201	28.1	9.5	43.6

TABLE 3

Inequality-adjusted Human Development Index

TABLE
3

HDI rank	Human Development Index (HDI) Value	Inequality-adjusted HDI			Inequality-adjusted life expectancy index		Inequality-adjusted education index		Inequality-adjusted income index		Quintile income ratio	Income Gini coefficient
		Value	Overall loss (%)	Change in rank[a]	Value	Loss (%)	Value	Loss (%)	Value	Loss (%)		
	2011	2011	2011	2011	2011	2011	2011	2011	2011	2011	2000–2011[b]	2000–2011[b]
180 Sierra Leone	0.336	0.196	41.6	−3	0.240	45.3	0.160	47.4	0.197	31.0	8.1	42.5
181 Burkina Faso	0.331	0.215	35.1	3	0.326	41.7	0.117	37.3	0.260	25.3	6.7	39.6
182 Liberia	0.329	0.213	35.3	3	0.362	37.6	0.235	46.4	0.113	19.0	7.0	52.6
183 Chad	0.328	0.196	40.1	−1	0.224	52.0	0.124	43.4	0.272	21.0	7.4	39.8
184 Mozambique	0.322	0.229	28.9	7	0.282	40.8	0.181	18.2	0.233	25.8	9.9	45.6
185 Burundi	0.316	..	..	..	0.261	45.6	..	..	..	..	4.8	33.3
186 Niger	0.295	0.195	34.2	0	0.314	42.6	0.107	39.5	0.218	17.9	5.2	34.0
187 Congo, Democratic Republic of the	0.286	0.172	39.9	0	0.224	50.0	0.245	31.2	0.093	36.8	9.2	44.4
OTHER COUNTRIES OR TERRITORIES												
Korea, Democratic People's Rep. of	..	..	..	..	0.640	16.9	..	..	..	..	..	..
Marshall Islands	..	..	..	..	..	..	..	..	..	..	..	..
Monaco	..	..	..	..	..	..	..	..	..	..	..	..
Nauru	..	..	..	..	..	..	..	..	..	..	..	..
San Marino	..	..	..	..	..	..	..	..	..	..	..	..
Somalia	..	..	..	..	0.260	47.1	..	..	..	..	..	..
Tuvalu	..	..	..	..	..	..	..	..	..	..	..	..
Human Development Index groups												
Very high human development	0.889	0.787	11.5	—	0.897	5.2	0.838	6.2	0.648	22.2	—	—
High human development	0.741	0.590[c]	20.5[c]	—	0.734	12.4	0.580[c]	18.9[c]	0.482	28.2[c]	—	—
Medium human development	0.630	0.480	23.7	—	0.633	19.2	0.396	29.4	0.441	22.3	—	—
Low human development	0.456	0.304	33.3	—	0.393	35.6	0.238	39.2	0.300	24.2	—	—
Regions												
Arab States	0.641	0.472[c]	26.4[c]	—	0.654	18.0	0.307[c]	40.8[c]	0.524[c]	17.8[c]	—	—
East Asia and the Pacific	0.671	0.528[c]	21.3[c]	—	0.709	14.3	0.477[c]	21.9[c]	0.435[c]	26.8[c]	—	—
Europe and Central Asia	0.751	0.655	12.7	—	0.715	11.7	0.681	10.7	0.578	15.7	—	—
Latin America and the Caribbean	0.731	0.540	26.1	—	0.743	13.4	0.528	23.2	0.401	39.3	—	—
South Asia	0.548	0.393	28.4	—	0.529	26.9	0.266	40.9	0.430	15.1	—	—
Sub-Saharan Africa	0.463	0.303	34.5	—	0.331	39.0	0.276	35.6	0.306	28.4	—	—
Least developed countries	0.439	0.296	32.4	—	0.403	34.7	0.233	36.8	0.277	25.3	—	—
Small island developing states	0.640	0.458[c]	28.4[c]	—	0.633	19.1	0.417[c]	29.6[c]	0.364[c]	35.6[c]	—	—
World	0.682	0.525	23.0	—	0.637	19.0	0.450	26.2	0.506	23.4	—	—

NOTES
a. Change in rank is based on countries for which the Inequality-adjusted Human Development Index is calculated.
b. Data refer to the most recent year available during the period specified.
c. Based on less than half the countries in the group or region.

DEFINITIONS
Human Development Index (HDI): A composite index measuring average achievement in three basic dimensions of human development—a long and healthy life, knowledge and a decent standard of living. See *Technical note 1* for details on how the HDI is calculated.
Inequality-adjusted HDI (IHDI): HDI value adjusted for inequalities in the three basic dimensions of human development. See *Technical note 2* for details on how the IHDI is calculated.
Overall loss: The loss in potential human development due to inequality, calculated as the percentage difference between the HDI and the IHDI.
Inequality-adjusted life expectancy index: The HDI life expectancy index adjusted for inequality in distribution of expected length of life based on data from life tables listed in *Main data sources*.
Inequality-adjusted education index: The HDI education index adjusted for inequality in distribution of years of schooling based on data from household surveys listed in *Main data sources*.
Inequality-adjusted income index: The HDI income index adjusted for inequality in income distribution based on data from household surveys listed in *Main data sources*.
Quintile income ratio: Ratio of the average income of the richest 20 percent of the population to the average income of the poorest 20 percent of the population.

Income Gini coefficient: Measure of the deviation of the distribution of income (or consumption) among individuals or households within a country from a perfectly equal distribution. A value of 0 represents absolute equality, a value of 100 absolute inequality.

MAIN DATA SOURCES
Column 1: HDRO calculations based on data from UNDESA (2011), Barro and Lee (2010b), UNESCO Institute for Statistics (2011), World Bank (2011a) and IMF (2011).
Column 2: Calculated as the geometric mean of the values in columns 5, 7 and 9 using the methodology in *Technical note 2*.
Column 3: Calculated based on data in columns 1 and 2.
Column 4: Calculated based on HDI rank and data in column 2.
Columns 5, 7 and 9: HDRO calculations based on data from United Nations Department of Economic and Social Affairs life tables, the Luxembourg Income Study, Eurostat's European Union Survey of Income and Living Conditions, the World Bank's International Income Distribution Database, the United Nations Children's Fund's Multiple Indicator Cluster Surveys, ICF Macro Demographic and Health Surveys, the World Health Organization's World Health Survey and the United Nations University's World Institute for Development Economics Research's World Income Inequality Database using the methodology in *Technical note 2*. The list of surveys and years of surveys used for each index are available at http://hdr.undp.org.
Column 6: Calculated based on data in column 5 and the unadjusted life expectancy index.
Column 8: Calculated based on data in column 7 and the unadjusted education index.
Column 10: Calculated based on data in column 9 and the unadjusted income index.
Columns 11 and 12: World Bank (2011a).

TABLE 4

Gender Inequality Index and related indicators

HDI rank	Gender Inequality Index		Maternal mortality ratio	Adolescent fertility rate	Seats in national parliament (% female)	Population with at least secondary education (% ages 25 and older)		Labour force participation rate (%)		REPRODUCTIVE HEALTH			Total fertility rate
										Contraceptive prevalence rate, any method (% of married women ages 15–49)	At least one antenatal visit (%)	Births attended by skilled health personnel (%)	
	Rank	Value				Female	Male	Female	Male				
	2011	2011	2008	2011[a]	2011	2010	2010	2009	2009	2005–2009[b]	2005–2009[b]	2005–2009[b]	2011[a]
VERY HIGH HUMAN DEVELOPMENT													
1 Norway	6	0.075	7	9.0	39.6	99.3	99.1	63.0	71.0	88.0	..	..	2.0
2 Australia	18	0.136	8	16.5	28.3	95.1	97.2	58.4	72.2	71.0	100.0	100.0	2.0
3 Netherlands	2	0.052	9	5.1	37.8	86.3	89.2	59.5	72.9	69.0	..	100.0	1.8
4 United States	47	0.299	24	41.2	16.8[c]	95.3	94.5	58.4	71.9	73.0	..	99.0	2.1
5 New Zealand	32	0.195	14	30.9	33.6	71.6	73.5	61.8	75.7	75.0	95.0	100.0	2.1
6 Canada	20	0.140	12	14.0	24.9	92.3	92.7	62.7	73.0	74.0	..	98.0	1.7
7 Ireland	33	0.203	3	17.5	11.1	82.3	81.5	54.4	73.0	89.0	..	100.0	2.1
8 Liechtenstein	..	..	..	..	24.0	..	..	..	..	..	..	..	..
9 Germany	7	0.085	7	7.9	31.7	91.3	92.8	53.1	66.8	75.0	..	..	1.5
10 Sweden	1	0.049	5	6.0	45.0	87.9	87.1	60.6	69.2	..	..	..	1.9
11 Switzerland	4	0.067	10	4.6	27.6	63.6	73.8	60.6	73.7	82.0	..	..	1.5
12 Japan	14	0.123	6	5.0	13.6	80.0	82.3	47.9	71.8	54.0	..	100.0	1.4
13 Hong Kong, China (SAR)	..	..	..	3.2	..	67.3	71.0	52.2	68.9	84.0	..	..	1.1
14 Iceland	9	0.099	5	14.6	42.9	66.3	57.7	71.7	83.1	..	..	..	2.1
15 Korea, Republic of	11	0.111	18	2.3	14.7	79.4	91.7	50.1	72.0	80.0	..	100.0	1.4
16 Denmark	3	0.060	5	6.0	38.0	59.0	65.6	60.3	70.6	..	..	..	1.9
17 Israel	22	0.145	7	14.0	19.2	78.9	77.2	51.9	62.5	..	..	..	2.9
18 Belgium	12	0.114	5	14.2	38.5	75.7	79.8	46.7	60.8	75.0	..	..	1.8
19 Austria	16	0.131	5	12.8	28.3	67.3	85.9	53.2	68.1	51.0	100.0	100.0	1.4
20 France	10	0.106	8	7.2	20.0	79.6	84.6	50.5	62.2	71.0	99.0	99.0	2.0
21 Slovenia	28	0.175	18	5.0	10.8	60.6[d,e]	81.9[d,e]	52.8	65.4	74.0	98.0	100.0	1.5
22 Finland	5	0.075	8	9.3	42.5	70.1	70.1	57.0	64.9	..	100.0	100.0	1.9
23 Spain	13	0.117	6	12.7	34.7	70.9	75.7	49.1	68.5	66.0	..	..	1.5
24 Italy	15	0.124	5	6.7	20.3	67.8	78.9	38.4	60.6	60.0	..	..	1.5
25 Luxembourg	26	0.169	17	10.1	20.0	66.4	73.9	48.0	63.3	..	..	100.0	1.7
26 Singapore	8	0.086	9	4.8	23.4	57.3	64.7	53.7	75.6	62.0	..	100.0	1.4
27 Czech Republic	17	0.136	8	11.1	21.0	85.5	87.6	48.8	67.6	72.0	99.0	100.0	1.5
28 United Kingdom	34	0.209	12	29.6	21.0	68.8	67.8	55.3	69.5	84.0	..	99.0	1.9
29 Greece	24	0.162	2	11.6	17.3	64.4	72.0	42.9	65.0	61.0	..	..	1.5
30 United Arab Emirates	38	0.234	10	26.7	22.5	76.9	77.3	41.9	92.1	28.0	97.0	99.0	1.7
31 Cyprus	21	0.141	10	6.6	12.5	61.8	73.2	54.3	70.8	..	..	..	1.5
32 Andorra	..	..	..	8.4	53.6	49.3[d,e]	49.5[d,e]	..	..	..	..	..	..
33 Brunei Darussalam	..	..	21	25.1	..	66.6	61.2	59.7	74.8	..	100.0	99.0	2.0
34 Estonia	30	0.194	12	22.7	19.8	94.4	94.6	54.8	69.0	70.0	..	100.0	1.7
35 Slovakia	31	0.194	6	20.2	16.0	80.8	87.1	51.2	68.5	80.0	..	100.0	1.4
36 Malta	42	0.272	8	17.3	8.7	64.4	73.5	31.6	67.5	86.0	..	98.0	1.3
37 Qatar	111	0.549	8	16.2	0.0[f]	62.1	54.7	49.9	93.0	43.0	..	99.0	2.2
38 Hungary	39	0.237	13	16.5	9.1	93.2	96.7	42.5	58.8	77.0	..	100.0	1.4
39 Poland	25	0.164	6	14.8	17.9	79.7	83.9	46.2	61.9	49.0	..	100.0	1.4
40 Lithuania	29	0.192	13	19.7	19.1	91.9	95.7	50.2	62.1	47.0	..	100.0	1.5
41 Portugal	19	0.140	7	16.8	27.4	40.4	41.9	56.2	69.4	67.0	..	100.0	1.3
42 Bahrain	44	0.288	19	14.9	15.0	74.4	80.4	32.4	85.0	62.0	97.0	98.0	2.4
43 Latvia	36	0.216	20	18.0	20.0	94.8	96.2	54.3	70.2	48.0	..	100.0	1.5
44 Chile	68	0.374	26	58.3	13.9	67.3	69.8	41.8	73.4	58.0	95.0	100.0	1.8
45 Argentina	67	0.372	70	56.9	37.8	57.0	54.9	52.4	78.4	78.0	99.0	95.0	2.2
46 Croatia	27	0.170	14	13.5	23.5	57.4	72.3	46.3	60.3	..	..	100.0	1.5
47 Barbados	65	0.364	64	42.6	19.6	89.5	87.6	65.8	78.0	55.0	100.0	100.0	1.6
HIGH HUMAN DEVELOPMENT													
48 Uruguay	62	0.352	27	61.1	14.6	56.6	51.7	53.8	75.5	78.0	96.0	100.0	2.0
49 Palau	..	..	..	13.8	6.9	..	..	..	..	21.0	100.0	100.0	..
50 Romania	55	0.333	27	32.0	9.8	83.8	90.5	45.4	60.0	70.0	94.0	99.0	1.4
51 Cuba	58	0.337	53	45.2	43.2	73.9	80.4	40.9	66.9	78.0	100.0	100.0	1.5
52 Seychelles	..	..	..	51.3	23.5	41.2[d,e]	45.4[d,e]	..	..	..	..	..	..
53 Bahamas	54	0.332	49	31.8	17.9	48.5[d,e]	54.5[d,e]	68.3	78.7	45.0	98.0	99.0	1.9
54 Montenegro	..	..	15	18.2	11.1	79.7[d,e]	69.5[d,e]	..	..	39.0	97.0	99.0[g]	1.6
55 Bulgaria	40	0.245	13	42.8	20.8	69.1	70.6	48.2	61.2	63.0	..	100.0	1.6

Gender Inequality Index and related indicators

TABLE
4

		Gender Inequality Index		Maternal mortality ratio	Adolescent fertility rate	Seats in national parliament (% female)	Population with at least secondary education (% ages 25 and older)		Labour force participation rate (%)		REPRODUCTIVE HEALTH			Total fertility rate
											Contraceptive prevalence rate, any method (% of married women ages 15–49)	At least one antenatal visit (%)	Births attended by skilled health personnel (%)	
HDI rank		Rank	Value				Female	Male	Female	Male				
		2011	2011	2008	2011a	2011	2010	2010	2009	2009	2005–2009b	2005–2009b	2005–2009b	2011a
56	Saudi Arabia	135	0.646	24	11.6	0.0 f	50.3	57.9	21.2	79.8	24.0	90.0	91.0	2.6
57	Mexico	79	0.448	85	70.6	25.5	55.8	61.9	43.2	80.6	73.0	94.0	93.0	2.2
58	Panama	95	0.492	71	82.6	8.5	63.5	60.7	48.4	80.7	..	72.0	92.0	2.4
59	Serbia	..	..	8	22.1	21.6	61.7	70.7	..	..	41.0	98.0	99.0 g	1.6
60	Antigua and Barbuda	..	..	..	55.5	19.4	..	..	..	..	53.0	100.0	100.0	..
61	Malaysia	43	0.286	31	14.2	14.0	66.0	72.8	44.4	79.2	55.0	79.0	99.0	2.6
62	Trinidad and Tobago	53	0.331	55	34.7	27.4	67.6	66.6	55.1	78.1	43.0	96.0	98.0	1.6
63	Kuwait	37	0.229	9	13.8	7.7	52.2	43.9	45.4	82.5	52.0	95.0	98.0	2.3
64	Libya	51	0.314	64	3.2	7.7	55.6	44.0	24.7	78.9	45.0	81.0	94.0 g	2.4
65	Belarus	..	..	15	22.1	32.1	..	..	54.8	66.5	73.0	99.0	100.0 g	1.5
66	Russian Federation	59	0.338	39	30.0	11.5	90.6	95.6	57.5	69.2	80.0	..	100.0	1.5
67	Grenada	..	..	..	42.4	21.4	..	..	..	..	54.0	100.0	99.0	2.2
68	Kazakhstan	56	0.334	45	30.0	13.6	92.2	95.0	65.7	76.3	51.0	100.0	100.0 g	2.5
69	Costa Rica	64	0.361	44	65.6	38.6	54.4	52.8	45.1	79.9	80.0	90.0	99.0	1.8
70	Albania	41	0.271	31	17.9	16.4	83.2	89.2	49.3	70.4	69.0	97.0	99.0	1.5
71	Lebanon	76	0.440	26	16.2	3.1	32.4	33.3	22.3	71.5	58.0	96.0	98.0	1.8
72	Saint Kitts and Nevis	..	..	..	42.6	6.7	..	..	..	..	54.0	100.0	100.0	..
73	Venezuela, Bolivarian Republic of	78	0.447	68	89.9	17.0	33.4	29.6	51.7	80.3	77.0	94.0	95.0	2.4
74	Bosnia and Herzegovina	..	..	9	16.4	15.8	..	..	54.9	68.3	36.0	99.0	100.0 g	1.1
75	Georgia	73	0.418	48	44.7	6.5	63.8 d,e	58.9 d,e	55.1	73.8	47.0	96.0	98.0	1.5
76	Ukraine	57	0.335	26	30.8	8.0	91.5	96.1	52.0	65.4	67.0	99.0	99.0	1.5
77	Mauritius	63	0.353	36	35.4	18.8	45.2	52.9	40.8	74.8	76.0	..	98.0	1.6
78	Former Yugoslav Republic of Macedonia	23	0.151	9	22.0	32.5	55.6 d	40.2 d	42.9	65.2	14.0	94.0	100.0 g	1.4
79	Jamaica	81	0.450	89	77.3	16.0	74.0	71.1	56.1	74.0	69.0	91.0	97.0 g	2.3
80	Peru	72	0.415	98	54.7	27.5 h	57.6	76.1	58.2	76.0	73.0	94.0	83.0 g	2.4
81	Dominica	..	..	..	20.0	12.5	11.2 d,e	10.3 d,e	..	..	50.0	100.0	100.0	..
82	Saint Lucia	..	..	..	61.7	20.7	..	..	51.0	75.8	47.0	99.0	100.0	1.9
83	Ecuador	85	0.469	140	82.8	32.3	44.2	45.8	47.1	77.7	73.0	84.0	98.0 g	2.4
84	Brazil	80	0.449	58	75.6	9.6	48.8	46.3	60.1	81.9	81.0	97.0	97.0	1.8
85	Saint Vincent and the Grenadines	..	..	..	58.9	14.3	..	..	56.0	78.8	48.0	100.0	99.0	2.0
86	Armenia	60	0.343	29	35.7	9.2	94.1	94.8	59.6	74.6	53.0	93.0	100.0	1.7
87	Colombia	91	0.482	85	74.3	13.8	48.0	47.6	40.7	77.6	78.0	94.0	96.0 g	2.3
88	Iran, Islamic Republic of	92	0.485	30	29.5	2.8	39.0	57.2	31.9	73.0	79.0	98.0	97.0	1.6
89	Oman	49	0.309	20	9.2	9.0	26.7	28.1	25.4	76.9	32.0	100.0	99.0	2.2
90	Tonga	..	..	..	22.3	3.6 i	84.0	87.8	54.6	74.7	23.0	..	95.0	3.8
91	Azerbaijan	50	0.314	38	33.8	16.0	65.4 d,e	61.9 d,e	59.5	66.8	51.0	77.0	88.0 g	2.2
92	Turkey	77	0.443	23	39.2	9.1	27.1	46.7	24.0	69.6	73.0	92.0	91.0	2.0
93	Belize	97	0.493	94	78.7	11.1	35.2	32.8	47.4	80.6	34.0	94.0	95.0 g	2.7
94	Tunisia	45	0.293	60	5.7	23.3	33.5	48.0	25.6	70.6	60.0	96.0	95.0	1.9
MEDIUM HUMAN DEVELOPMENT														
95	Jordan	83	0.456	59	26.5	12.2	57.1	74.2	23.3	73.9	59.0	99.0	99.0	2.9
96	Algeria	71	0.412	120	7.3	7.0	36.3	49.3	37.2	79.6	61.0	89.0	95.0	2.1
97	Sri Lanka	74	0.419	39	23.6	5.3	56.0	57.6	34.2	75.1	68.0	99.0	99.0	2.2
98	Dominican Republic	90	0.480	100	108.7	19.1	49.7	41.8	50.5	79.8	73.0	99.0	98.0	2.5
99	Samoa	..	..	..	28.3	4.1	64.2 d,e	60.0 d,e	37.9	75.4	25.0	..	100.0	3.8
100	Fiji	..	..	26	45.2	..	86.6	88.6	38.7	78.4	35.0	..	99.0	2.6
101	China	35	0.209	38	8.4	21.3	54.8	70.4	67.4	79.7	85.0	91.0	99.0	1.6
102	Turkmenistan	..	..	77	19.5	16.8	..	..	62.4	74.0	48.0	99.0	100.0	2.3
103	Thailand	69	0.382	48	43.3	14.0	25.6	33.7	65.5	80.7	77.0	98.0	97.0	1.5
104	Suriname	..	..	100	39.5	9.8	..	..	38.5	66.0	46.0	90.0	90.0 g	2.3
105	El Salvador	93	0.487	110	82.7	19.0	40.5	47.5	45.9	76.7	73.0	94.0	96.0	2.2
106	Gabon	103	0.509	260	89.9	16.1	53.8	34.7	70.0	81.1	33.0	94.0	86.0	3.2
107	Paraguay	87	0.476	95	72.3	13.6	45.4	50.4	57.0	86.6	79.0	96.0	82.0	2.9
108	Bolivia, Plurinational State of	88	0.476	180	78.2	30.1	55.1	67.9	62.1	82.0	61.0	86.0	71.0	3.2
109	Maldives	52	0.320	37	12.2	6.5	31.3	37.3	57.1	77.0	39.0	81.0	84.0	1.7
110	Mongolia	70	0.410	65	20.8	3.9	83.0	81.8	67.8	78.2	55.0	100.0	99.0	2.5
111	Moldova, Republic of	46	0.298	32	33.8	18.8	85.8	92.3	46.5	53.1	68.0	98.0	100.0 g	1.5
112	Philippines	75	0.427	94	54.1	21.5	65.9	63.7	49.2	78.5	51.0	91.0	62.0	3.1
113	Egypt	..	..	82	46.6	.. j	43.4	59.3	22.4	75.3	60.0	74.0	79.0	2.6
114	Occupied Palestinian Territory	..	..	..	53.5	..	36.5 d,e	29.0 d,e	16.5	68.4	50.0	99.0	99.0	4.3

HDI rank		Gender Inequality Index Rank 2011	Gender Inequality Index Value 2011	Maternal mortality ratio 2008	Adolescent fertility rate 2011[a]	Seats in national parliament (% female) 2011	Population with at least secondary education (% ages 25 and older) Female 2010	Population with at least secondary education Male 2010	Labour force participation rate (%) Female 2009	Labour force participation rate Male 2009	REPRODUCTIVE HEALTH Contraceptive prevalence rate, any method (% of married women ages 15–49) 2005–2009[b]	At least one antenatal visit (%) 2005–2009[b]	Births attended by skilled health personnel (%) 2005–2009[b]	Total fertility rate 2011[a]
115	Uzbekistan	..	..	30	13.8	19.2	..	..	58.4	71.0	65.0	99.0	100.0[g]	2.3
116	Micronesia, Federated States of				25.4	0.0					45.0	..	88.0	3.3
117	Guyana	106	0.511	270	68.3	30.0	42.6	43.7	44.7	81.2	43.0	92.0	92.0[g]	2.2
118	Botswana	102	0.507	190	52.1	7.9	73.6	77.5	72.3	80.9	53.0	94.0	95.0[g]	2.6
119	Syrian Arab Republic	86	0.474	46	42.8	12.4	24.7	24.1	21.1	79.5	58.0	84.0	93.0[g]	2.8
120	Namibia	84	0.466	180	74.4	25.0	49.6	46.1	51.8	62.6	55.0	95.0	81.0	3.1
121	Honduras	105	0.511	110	93.1	18.0	31.9	38.3	40.1	80.2	65.0	92.0	67.0[g]	3.0
122	Kiribati	..	..	..	22.2	4.3	..	..	..	..	22.0	88.0	63.0	..
123	South Africa	94	0.490	410	59.2	42.7	66.3	68.0	47.0	63.4	60.0	92.0	91.0	2.4
124	Indonesia	100	0.505	240	45.1	18.0	24.2	31.1	52.0	86.0	57.0	93.0	75.0[g]	2.1
125	Vanuatu	..	..	..	54.0	3.8	..	..	79.3	88.3	38.0	84.0	74.0	3.8
126	Kyrgyzstan	66	0.370	81	34.1	23.3	81.0	81.2	54.8	79.1	48.0	97.0	98.0[g]	2.6
127	Tajikistan	61	0.347	64	28.4	17.5	93.2	85.8	57.0	77.7	37.0	89.0	88.0[g]	3.2
128	Viet Nam	48	0.305	56	26.8	25.8	24.7	28.0	68.0	76.0	80.0	91.0	88.0[g]	1.8
129	Nicaragua	101	0.506	100	112.7	20.7	30.8	44.7	47.1	78.4	72.0	90.0	74.0	2.5
130	Morocco	104	0.510	110	15.1	6.7	20.1	36.3	26.2	80.1	63.0	68.0	63.0	2.2
131	Guatemala	109	0.542	110	107.2	12.0	15.6	21.0	48.1	87.9	54.0	93.0	51.0	3.8
132	Iraq	117	0.579	75	98.0	25.2	22.0	42.7	13.8	68.9	50.0	84.0	80.0	4.5
133	Cape Verde	..	..	94	81.6	20.8	..	..	53.5	81.3	61.0	98.0	78.0[g]	2.3
134	India	129	0.617	230	86.3	10.7	26.6	50.4	32.8	81.1	54.0	75.0	53.0[g]	2.5
135	Ghana	122	0.598	350	71.1	8.3	33.9	83.1	73.8	75.2	24.0	90.0	57.0	4.0
136	Equatorial Guinea	..	..	280	122.9	10.0	..	..	39.7	92.0	..	86.0	65.0[g]	5.0
137	Congo	132	0.628	580	118.7	9.2	43.8	48.7	62.9	82.6	44.0	86.0	83.0	4.4
138	Lao People's Democratic Republic	107	0.513	580	39.0	25.0	22.9	36.8	77.7	78.9	38.0	35.0	20.0[g]	2.5
139	Cambodia	99	0.500	290	41.8	19.0	11.6	20.6	73.6	85.6	40.0	69.0	44.0	2.4
140	Swaziland	110	0.546	420	83.9	21.9	49.9	46.1	53.1	74.9	51.0	85.0	69.0[g]	3.2
141	Bhutan	98	0.495	200	50.2	13.9	16.2[d,e]	19.4[d,e]	53.4	70.6	35.0	88.0	71.0	2.3
LOW HUMAN DEVELOPMENT														
142	Solomon Islands	..	..	100	70.3	0.0	..	..	24.2	50.0	27.0	74.0	70.0	4.0
143	Kenya	130	0.627	530	100.2	9.8	20.1	38.6	76.4	88.1	46.0	92.0	44.0	4.6
144	São Tomé and Príncipe	..	..	..	66.1	18.2	..	..	44.5	76.0	38.0	98.0	82.0	3.5
145	Pakistan	115	0.573	260	31.6	21.0	23.5	46.8	21.7	84.9	30.0	61.0	39.0[g]	3.2
146	Bangladesh	112	0.550	340	78.9	18.6	30.8	39.3	58.7	82.5	53.0	51.0	24.0[g]	2.2
147	Timor-Leste	..	..	370	65.8	29.2	..	..	58.9	82.8	22.0	61.0	18.0	5.9
148	Angola	..	..	610	171.1	38.6	..	..	74.5	88.4	6.0	80.0	47.0[g]	5.1
149	Myanmar	96	0.492	240	16.3	4.0	18.0	17.6	63.1	85.1	41.0	80.0	64.0	1.9
150	Cameroon	134	0.639	600	127.8	13.9	21.1	34.9	53.5	80.7	29.0	82.0	63.0	4.3
151	Madagascar	..	..	440	134.3	12.1	..	..	84.2	88.7	40.0	86.0	44.0[g]	4.5
152	Tanzania, United Republic of	119	0.590	790	130.4	36.0	5.6	9.2	86.3	90.6	26.0	76.0	43.0[g]	5.5
153	Papua New Guinea	140	0.674	250	66.9	0.9	12.4	24.4	71.6	74.2	32.0	79.0	53.0	3.8
154	Yemen	146	0.769	210	78.8	0.7	7.6	24.4	19.9	73.5	28.0	47.0	36.0	4.9
155	Senegal	114	0.566	410	105.9	29.6	10.9	19.4	64.8	88.6	12.0	87.0	52.0[g]	4.6
156	Nigeria	..	..	840	118.3	7.3	..	..	39.2	73.4	15.0	58.0	39.0[g]	5.4
157	Nepal	113	0.558	380	103.4	33.2	17.9	39.9	63.3	80.3	48.0	44.0	19.0	2.6
158	Haiti	123	0.599	300	46.4	4.2	22.5	36.3	57.5	82.9	32.0	85.0	26.0[g]	3.2
159	Mauritania	126	0.605	550	79.2	19.2	8.0	20.8	59.0	81.0	9.0	75.0	61.0[g]	4.4
160	Lesotho	108	0.532	530	73.5	22.9	24.3	20.3	70.8	77.7	47.0	92.0	62.0[g]	3.1
161	Uganda	116	0.577	430	149.9	37.2	9.1	20.8	78.3	90.6	24.0	94.0	42.0	5.9
162	Togo	124	0.602	350	65.3	11.1	15.3	45.1	63.6	85.7	17.0	84.0	62.0[g]	3.9
163	Comoros	..	..	340	58.0	3.0	..	..	73.7	85.4	26.0	75.0	62.0[g]	4.7
164	Zambia	131	0.627	470	146.8	14.0	25.7	44.2	59.5	79.2	41.0	94.0	47.0[g]	6.3
165	Djibouti	..	..	300	22.9	13.8	..	..	61.5	78.7	23.0	92.0	93.0[g]	3.6
166	Rwanda	82	0.453	540	38.7	50.9	7.4	8.0	86.7	85.1	36.0	96.0	52.0[g]	5.3
167	Benin	133	0.634	410	111.7	8.4	11.3	25.9	67.4	77.9	17.0	84.0	74.0[g]	5.1
168	Gambia	127	0.610	400	76.6	7.5	16.9	31.4	70.6	85.2	18.0	98.0	57.0[g]	4.7
169	Sudan	128	0.611	750	61.9	24.2	12.8	18.2	30.8	73.9	8.0	64.0	49.0[g]	4.2
170	Côte d'Ivoire	136	0.655	470	129.4	8.9	13.6	25.2	50.8	82.1	13.0	85.0	57.0	4.2
171	Malawi	120	0.594	510	119.2	20.8	10.4	20.4	75.0	78.8	41.0	92.0	54.0	6.0
172	Afghanistan	141	0.707	1,400	118.7	27.6	5.8	34.0	33.1	84.5	10.0	16.0	14.0	6.0
173	Zimbabwe	118	0.583	790	64.6	17.9	48.8	62.0	60.0	74.3	65.0	93.0	60.0	3.1

TABLE 4

TABLE
4

Gender Inequality Index and related indicators

HDI rank	Gender Inequality Index Rank	Gender Inequality Index Value	Maternal mortality ratio	Adolescent fertility rate	Seats in national parliament (% female)	Population with at least secondary education (% ages 25 and older) Female	Population with at least secondary education (% ages 25 and older) Male	Labour force participation rate (%) Female	Labour force participation rate (%) Male	REPRODUCTIVE HEALTH Contraceptive prevalence rate, any method (% of married women ages 15–49)	REPRODUCTIVE HEALTH At least one antenatal visit (%)	REPRODUCTIVE HEALTH Births attended by skilled health personnel (%)	Total fertility rate
	2011	2011	2008	2011[a]	2011	2010	2010	2009	2009	2005–2009[b]	2005–2009[b]	2005–2009[b]	2011[a]
174 Ethiopia	..	..	470	72.4	25.5	..	..	80.7	90.3	15.0	28.0	6.0	3.9
175 Mali	143	0.712	830	186.3	10.2	3.2	8.4	37.6	67.0	8.0	70.0	49.0[g]	6.1
176 Guinea-Bissau	..	..	1,000	111.1	10.0	..	..	59.6	83.8	10.0	78.0	39.0[g]	4.9
177 Eritrea	..	..	280	66.6	22.0	..	..	62.5	83.4	8.0	70.0	28.0[g]	4.2
178 Guinea	..	..	680	157.4	..[k]	..	..	79.2	89.2	9.0	88.0	46.0[g]	5.0
179 Central African Republic	138	0.669	850	106.6	9.6[h]	10.3	26.2	71.6	86.7	19.0	69.0	44.0[g]	4.4
180 Sierra Leone	137	0.662	970	143.7	13.2	9.5	20.4	65.4	67.5	8.0	87.0	42.0[g]	4.7
181 Burkina Faso	121	0.596	560	124.8	15.3	34.7[d,e]	35.1[d,e]	78.2	90.8	17.0	85.0	54.0	5.8
182 Liberia	139	0.671	990	142.6	13.8	15.7	39.2	66.6	75.8	11.0	79.0	46.0	5.0
183 Chad	145	0.735	1,200	164.5	14.3	0.9[d,e]	9.9[d,e]	62.7	78.2	3.0	39.0	14.0	5.7
184 Mozambique	125	0.602	550	149.2	39.2	1.5	6.0	84.8	86.9	16.0	92.0	55.0[g]	4.7
185 Burundi	89	0.478	970	18.6	36.1	5.2	9.2	91.0	87.5	9.0	92.0	34.0	4.1
186 Niger	144	0.724	820	207.1	13.1	2.5	7.6	38.9	87.5	11.0	46.0	33.0	6.9
187 Congo, Democratic Republic of the	142	0.710	670	201.4	9.4	10.7	36.2	56.5	85.6	21.0	85.0	74.0[g]	5.5
OTHER COUNTRIES OR TERRITORIES													
Korea, Democratic People's Rep. of	..	..	250	0.7	15.6	..	..	55.1	77.5	69.0	97.0	97.0	2.0
Marshall Islands	..	..	..	53.5	3.0	..	..	..	..	45.0	81.0	86.0	..
Monaco	..	..	..	1.6	26.1	..	..	..	..	..	..	..	..
Nauru	..	..	..	31.2	0.0	..	..	..	..	36.0	95.0	97.0	..
San Marino	..	..	..	2.5	16.7	..	..	..	..	..	..	..	..
Somalia	..	..	1,200	70.1	6.8	..	..	56.5	84.7	15.0	26.0	33.0[g]	6.3
Tuvalu	..	..	..	23.3	0.0	..	..	..	..	31.0	97.0	98.0	..
Human Development Index groups													
Very high human development	..	0.224	16	23.8	21.5	82.0	84.6	52.8	69.8	69.5	98.6	99.2	1.8
High human development	..	0.409	51	51.6	13.5	61.0	64.6	47.8	75.0	72.4	94.4	96.1	1.9
Medium human development	..	0.475	135	50.1	17.3	41.2	57.7	51.1	80.0	67.7	85.1	78.1	2.1
Low human development	..	0.606	532	98.2	18.2	18.7	32.4	54.6	82.7	27.8	64.9	39.6	4.2
Regions													
Arab States	..	0.563	192	44.4	12.0	32.9	46.2	26.0	77.1	46.1	76.4	76.1	3.1
East Asia and the Pacific	..	..	79	19.8	20.2	48.1	61.3	64.2	80.3	76.9	90.7	91.9	1.8
Europe and Central Asia	..	0.311	29	28.0	13.4	78.0	83.3	49.7	67.8	67.7	95.3	97.9	1.7
Latin America and the Caribbean	..	0.445	80	73.7	18.7	50.5	52.2	51.7	79.9	74.8	94.8	92.0	2.2
South Asia	..	0.601	252	77.4	12.5	27.3	49.2	34.6	81.2	52.1	71.3	50.5	2.6
Sub-Saharan Africa	..	0.610	619	119.7	19.8	22.2	34.9	62.9	81.2	24.3	73.6	47.7	4.8
Least developed countries	..	0.594	537	106.1	20.3	16.8	27.4	64.4	84.0	28.7	63.7	38.2	4.1
Small island developing states	..	..	..	66.4	20.6	50.3	54.9	52.6	75.8	53.3	90.8	74.3	2.7
World	..	0.492	176	58.1	17.7	50.8	61.7	51.5	78.0	61.6	82.7	76.4	2.4

NOTES

a. Annual average for 2010–2015.
b. Data refer to the most recent year available during the period specified.
c. The denominator of the calculation refers to voting members of the House of Representatives only.
d. UNESCO Institute for Statistics (2011).
e. Refers to an earlier year than that specified.
f. For purposes of calculating the Gender Inequality Index, a value of 0.1 percent was used.
g. Includes deliveries by cadres of health workers other than doctors, nurses and midwives.
h. Data are for 2010.
i. No women were elected in 2010; however, one woman was appointed to the cabinet.
j. The People's Assembly and the Shoura Assembly were dissolved by the Egypt Supreme Council of Armed Forces on 13 February 2011.
k. The parliament was dissolved following the December 2008 coup.

DEFINITIONS

Gender Inequality Index: A composite measure reflecting inequality in achievements between women and men in three dimensions: reproductive health, empowerment and the labour market. See *Technical note 3* for details on how the Gender Inequality Index is calculated.
Maternal mortality ratio: Ratio of the number of maternal deaths to the number of live births in a given year, expressed per 100,000 live births.
Adolescent fertility rate: Number of births to women ages 15–19 per 1,000 women ages 15–19.
Seats in national parliament: Proportion of seats held by women in a lower or single house or an upper house or senate, expressed as percentage of total seats.
Population with at least secondary education: Percentage of the population ages 25 and older that have reached secondary education.

Labour force participation rate: Proportion of a country's working-age population that engages in the labour market, either by working or actively looking for work, expressed as a percentage of the working-age population.
Contraceptive prevalence rate, any method: Percentage of women of reproductive age (ages 15–49) who are using, or whose partners are using, any modern or traditional form of contraception.
At least one antenatal visit: Percentage of women who used antenatal care provided by skilled health personnel for reasons related to pregnancy at least once during pregnancy, as a percentage of live births.
Births attended by skilled health personnel: Percentage of deliveries attended by personnel (including doctors, nurses and midwives) trained to give the necessary care, supervision and advice to women during pregnancy, labour and postpartum; to conduct deliveries on their own; and to care for newborns.
Total fertility rate: Number of children that would be born to each woman if she were to live to the end of her child-bearing years and bear children at each age in accordance with prevailing age-specific fertility rates.

MAIN DATA SOURCES

Columns 1 and 2: HDRO calculations based on UNICEF (2011), UNDESA (2011), IPU (2011), Barro and Lee (2010b), UNESCO (2011) and ILO (2011).
Column 3: WHO, UNICEF, UNFPA and World Bank (2010).
Columns 4 and 13: UNDESA (2011).
Column 5: IPU (2011).
Columns 6 and 7: HDRO updates of Barro and Lee (2010b) estimates based on UNESCO Institute for Statistics data on education attainment (2011) and Barro and Lee (2010a) methodology.
Columns 8 and 9: ILO (2011).
Columns 10–12: UNICEF (2011).

TABLE 5

Multidimensional Poverty Index

		Multidimensional Poverty Index		Population in multidimensional poverty[a]			Population vulnerable to poverty	Population in severe poverty	Share of multidimensional poor with deprivations in environmental services			Population below income poverty line	
				Headcount		Intensity of deprivation			Clean water	Improved sanitation	Modern fuels	PPP $1.25 a day	National poverty line
HDI rank		Year[b]	Value[a]	(%)	(thousands)	(%)	(%)	(%)	(%)	(%)	(%)	(%)	(%)
												2000–2009[c]	2000–2009[c]
VERY HIGH HUMAN DEVELOPMENT													
21	Slovenia	2003 (W)	0.000[d]	0.0[d]	0[d]	0.0[d]	0.4[d]	0.0[d]	0.0	0.0	0.0	0.0	..
27	Czech Republic	2003 (W)	0.010	3.1	316	33.4	0.0	0.0	0.0	0.0	0.0	..	..
30	United Arab Emirates	2003 (W)	0.002	0.6	20	35.3	2.0	0.0	0.1	0.1	0.0	..	..
34	Estonia	2003 (W)	0.026	7.2	97	36.5	1.3	0.2	0.3	0.6	2.4	0.0	..
35	Slovakia	2003 (W)	0.000[d]	0.0[d]	0[d]	0.0[d]	0.0[d]	0.0[d]	0.0	0.0	0.0	0.0	..
38	Hungary	2003 (W)	0.016	4.6	466	34.3	0.0	0.0	0.0	0.0	0.0	0.0	..
39	Poland	..	..	..	..	..	..	..	..	..	..	0.0	16.6
40	Lithuania	..	..	..	..	..	..	..	..	..	..	0.0	..
43	Latvia	2003 (W)	0.006[e]	1.6[e]	37[e]	37.9[e]	0.0[e]	0.0[e]	0.0	0.8	0.1	0.0	5.9
44	Chile	..	..	..	..	..	..	..	..	..	..	0.8	15.1
45	Argentina	2005 (N)	0.011[f]	3.0[f]	1,160[f]	37.7[f]	5.7[f]	0.2[f]	0.2[f]	2.2[f]	2.2[f]	0.9	..
46	Croatia	2003 (W)	0.016	4.4	196	36.3	0.1	0.3	0.1	0.3	1.2	0.0	11.1
HIGH HUMAN DEVELOPMENT													
48	Uruguay	2003 (W)	0.006	1.7	56	34.7	0.1	0.0	0.0	0.0	0.3	0.0	20.5
50	Romania	..	..	..	..	..	..	..	..	..	..	0.5	13.8
52	Seychelles	..	..	..	..	..	..	..	..	..	..	0.3	..
54	Montenegro	2005 (M)	0.006	1.5	9	41.6	1.9	0.3	0.2	0.4	0.9	0.0	4.9
55	Bulgaria	..	..	..	..	..	..	..	..	..	..	1.0	12.8
57	Mexico	2006 (N)	0.015	4.0	4,313	38.9	5.8	0.5	0.6	2.1	2.8	3.4	47.4
58	Panama	..	..	..	..	..	..	..	..	..	..	9.5	32.7
59	Serbia	2005 (M)	0.003	0.8	79	40.0	3.6	0.1	0.1	0.2	0.7	0.1	6.6
61	Malaysia	..	..	..	..	..	..	..	..	..	..	0.0	3.8
62	Trinidad and Tobago	2006 (M)	0.020	5.6	74	35.1	0.4	0.3	0.3	0.5	0.0	..	..
65	Belarus	2005 (M)	0.000	0.0	0	35.1	0.8	0.0	0.0	0.0	0.0	0.0	5.4
66	Russian Federation	2003 (W)	0.005[e]	1.3[e]	1,883[e]	38.9[e]	0.8[e]	0.2[e]	0.1	0.4	0.1	0.0	11.1
68	Kazakhstan	2006 (M)	0.002	0.6	92	36.9	5.0	0.0	0.3	0.1	0.5	0.2	15.4
69	Costa Rica	..	..	..	..	..	..	..	..	..	..	0.7	21.7
70	Albania	2009 (D)	0.005	1.4	45	37.7	7.4	0.1	0.3	0.4	1.1	0.6	12.4
73	Venezuela, Bolivarian Republic of	..	..	..	..	..	..	..	..	..	..	3.5	29.0
74	Bosnia and Herzegovina	2006 (M)	0.003	0.8	30	37.2	7.0	0.1	0.1	0.1	0.5	0.0	14.0
75	Georgia	2005 (M)	0.003	0.8	36	35.2	5.3	0.0	0.4	0.3	0.8	14.7	23.6
76	Ukraine	2007 (D)	0.008	2.2	1,018	35.5	1.0	0.2	0.1	0.1	0.3	0.1	7.9
78	Former Yugoslav Republic of Macedonia	2005 (M)	0.008	1.9	39	40.9	6.7	0.3	0.4	0.8	1.5	0.3	19.0
79	Jamaica	..	..	..	..	..	..	..	..	..	..	0.2	9.9
80	Peru	2004 (D)	0.086	19.9	5,421	43.2	16.9	6.0	14.1	19.4	19.2	5.9	34.8
83	Ecuador	2003 (W)	0.009	2.2	286	41.6	2.1	0.6	0.7	0.6	0.3	5.1	36.0
84	Brazil	2006 (N)	0.011	2.7	5,075	39.3	7.0	0.2	1.0	1.1	..	3.8	21.4
86	Armenia	2005 (D)	0.004	1.1	34	36.2	3.9	0.0	0.2	0.4	0.3	1.3	26.5
87	Colombia	2010 (D)	0.022	5.4	2,500	40.9	6.4	1.1	2.4	2.6	3.6	16.0	45.5
88	Iran, Islamic Republic of	..	..	..	..	..	..	..	..	..	..	1.5	..
91	Azerbaijan	2006 (D)	0.021	5.3	461	30.4	12.5	0.6	3.1	2.4	1.6	1.0	15.0
92	Turkey	2003 (D)	0.028	6.6	4,378	42.0	7.3	1.3	2.0	3.2	..	2.7	18.1
93	Belize	2006 (M)	0.024	5.6	16	42.6	7.6	1.1	1.9	2.5	4.1	..	33.5
94	Tunisia	2003 (W)	0.010[e]	2.8[e]	272[e]	37.1[e]	4.9[e]	0.2[e]	1.2	1.4	0.5	2.6	3.8
MEDIUM HUMAN DEVELOPMENT													
95	Jordan	2009 (D)	0.008	2.4	145	34.4	1.3	0.1	0.2	0.0	0.0	0.4	13.3
97	Sri Lanka	2003 (W)	0.021[e]	5.3[e]	1,027[e]	38.7[e]	14.4[e]	0.6[e]	3.0	2.6	5.3	7.0	15.2
98	Dominican Republic	2007 (D)	0.018	4.6	438	39.4	8.6	0.7	1.5	2.7	2.9	4.3	50.5
100	Fiji	..	..	..	..	..	..	..	..	..	..	..	31.0
101	China	2003 (W)	0.056	12.5	161,675	44.9	6.3	4.5	3.0	7.7	9.1	15.9	2.8
103	Thailand	2005 (M)	0.006	1.6	1,067	38.5	9.9	0.2	0.5	0.5	1.2	10.8	8.1
104	Suriname	2006 (M)	0.039	8.2	41	47.2	6.7	3.3	5.2	6.5	5.3	..	..
105	El Salvador	..	..	..	..	..	..	..	..	..	..	5.1	37.8
106	Gabon	2000 (D)	0.161[d]	35.4[d]	437[d]	45.5[d]	22.4[d]	13.2[d]	19.4	32.6	26.9	4.8	32.7
107	Paraguay	2003 (W)	0.064	13.3	755	48.5	15.0	6.1	8.8	11.2	12.4	5.1	35.1
108	Bolivia, Plurinational State of	2008 (D)	0.089	20.5	1,972	43.7	18.7	5.8	8.2	19.8	17.7	14.0	60.1
109	Maldives	2009 (D)	0.018	5.2	16	35.6	4.8	0.3	0.2	0.4	0.9	1.5	..

Multidimensional Poverty Index

HDI rank	Multidimensional Poverty Index		Population in multidimensional poverty[a]			Population vulnerable to poverty	Population in severe poverty	Share of multidimensional poor with deprivations in environmental services			Population below income poverty line	
	Year[b]	Value[a]	Headcount		Intensity of deprivation			Clean water	Improved sanitation	Modern fuels	PPP $1.25 a day	National poverty line
			(%)	(thousands)	(%)	(%)	(%)	(%)	(%)	(%)	(%)	(%)
											2000–2009[c]	2000–2009[c]
110 Mongolia	2005 (M)	0.065	15.8	402	41.0	20.6	3.2	11.6	13.7	15.7	22.4	35.2
111 Moldova, Republic of	2005 (D)	0.007	1.9	72	36.7	6.4	0.1	0.5	1.0	1.5	1.9	29.0
112 Philippines	2008 (D)	0.064	13.4	12,083	47.4	9.1	5.7	2.9	6.1	11.0	22.6	26.5
113 Egypt	2008 (D)	0.024	6.0	4,699	40.7	7.2	1.0	0.3	1.0	..	2.0	22.0
114 Occupied Palestinian Territory	2007 (N)	0.005	0.4	52	37.3	8.8	0.1	0.6	0.2	0.1	..	21.9
115 Uzbekistan	2006 (M)	0.008	2.3	603	36.2	8.1	0.1	0.6	0.1	0.9	46.3	..
117 Guyana	2005 (D)	0.053	13.4	100	39.5	6.7	2.1	1.6	4.6	2.5	..	..
118 Botswana	..	..										30.6
119 Syrian Arab Republic	2006 (M)	0.021[d]	5.5[d]	1,041[d]	37.5[d]	7.1[d]	0.5[d]	1.7	1.0	0.1	1.7	..
120 Namibia	2007 (D)	0.187	39.6	855	47.2	23.6	14.7	14.7	36.4	37.5	..	38.0
121 Honduras	2006 (D)	0.159	32.5	2,281	48.9	22.0	11.3	11.9	23.0	29.6	23.3	60.0
123 South Africa	2008 (N)	0.057	13.4	6,609	42.3	22.2	2.4	4.6	9.6	8.0	17.4	23.0
124 Indonesia	2007 (D)	0.095	20.8	48,352	45.9	12.2	7.6	10.2	13.2	15.5	18.7	13.3
125 Vanuatu	2007 (M)	0.129	30.1	67	42.7	33.5	6.5	7.9	20.1	29.5	..	..
126 Kyrgyzstan	2006 (M)	0.019	4.9	249	38.8	9.2	0.9	1.6	1.0	2.8	1.9	43.1
127 Tajikistan	2005 (M)	0.068	17.1	1,104	40.0	23.0	3.1	10.5	3.4	10.1	21.5	47.2
128 Viet Nam	2002 (D)	0.084	17.7	14,249	47.2	18.5	6.0	15.3	10.0	..	13.1	14.5
129 Nicaragua	2006 (D)	0.128	28.0	1,538	45.7	17.4	11.2	20.4	27.7	27.4	15.8	46.2
130 Morocco	2007 (N)	0.048[e]	10.6[e]	3,287[e]	45.3[e]	12.3[e]	3.3[e]	4.4	6.5	4.9	2.5	9.0
131 Guatemala	2003 (W)	0.127[e]	25.9[e]	3,134[e]	49.1[e]	9.8[e]	14.5[e]	3.7	6.6	23.0	16.9	51.0
132 Iraq	2006 (M)	0.059	14.2	3,996	41.3	14.3	3.1	6.4	5.1	2.7	4.0	22.9
133 Cape Verde	..	..	..	..	..	..	..	..	..	..	21.0	26.6
134 India	2005 (D)	0.283	53.7	612,203	52.7	16.4	28.6	11.9	48.2	51.1	41.6	27.5
135 Ghana	2008 (D)	0.144	31.2	7,258	46.2	21.6	11.4	12.2	29.9	31.0	30.0	28.5
137 Congo	2009 (D)	0.208	40.6	1,600	51.2	17.7	22.9	17.2	38.9	35.9	54.1	50.1
138 Lao People's Democratic Republic	2006 (M)	0.267	47.2	2,757	56.5	14.1	28.1	27.8	38.6	47.1	33.9	27.6
139 Cambodia	2005 (D)	0.251	52.0	6,946	48.4	21.3	22.0	28.6	48.3	51.6	28.3	30.1
140 Swaziland	2007 (D)	0.184	41.4	469	44.5	24.4	13.0	24.0	37.8	37.8	62.9	69.2
141 Bhutan	2010 (M)	0.119	27.2	197	43.9	17.2	8.5	2.6	16.9	22.1	26.2	23.2
LOW HUMAN DEVELOPMENT												
143 Kenya	2009 (D)	0.229	47.8	18,863	48.0	27.4	19.8	30.8	42.6	47.6	19.7	45.9
144 São Tomé and Príncipe	2009 (D)	0.154	34.5	56	44.7	24.3	10.7	9.4	29.6	31.3	28.6	53.8
145 Pakistan	2007 (D)	0.264[e]	49.4[e]	81,236[e]	53.4[e]	11.0[e]	27.4[e]	6.9	32.1	40.5	22.6	22.3
146 Bangladesh	2007 (D)	0.292	57.8	83,207	50.4	21.2	26.2	2.5	48.2	56.7	49.6	40.0
147 Timor-Leste	2009 (D)	0.360	68.1	749	52.9	18.2	38.7	35.7	47.6	67.6	37.4	49.9
148 Angola	2001 (M)	0.452	77.4	11,137	58.4	10.7	54.8	51.3	68.5	71.0	54.3	..
149 Myanmar	2000 (M)	0.154[e]	31.8[e]	14,297[e]	48.3[e]	13.4[e]	9.4[e]	25.2	19.1	..	..	..
150 Cameroon	2004 (D)	0.287	53.3	9,149	53.9	19.3	30.4	32.5	48.5	52.5	9.6	39.9
151 Madagascar	2009 (D)	0.357	66.9	13,463	53.3	17.9	35.4	49.4	66.5	66.9	67.8	68.7
152 Tanzania, United Republic of	2008 (D)	0.367	65.2	27,569	56.3	23.0	43.7	47.3	64.1	65.0	67.9	33.4
154 Yemen	2006 (M)	0.283	52.5	11,176	53.9	13.0	31.9	31.9	25.7	28.4	17.5	34.8
155 Senegal	2005 (D)	0.384	66.9	7,273	57.4	11.6	44.4	31.7	51.4	53.2	33.5	50.8
156 Nigeria	2008 (D)	0.310	54.1	81,510	57.3	17.8	33.9	35.7	39.6	52.8	64.4	54.7
157 Nepal	2006 (D)	0.350	64.7	18,008	54.0	15.6	37.1	14.4	56.3	63.4	55.1	30.9
158 Haiti	2006 (D)	0.299	56.4	5,346	53.0	18.8	32.3	35.6	52.2	56.2	54.9	77.0
159 Mauritania	2007 (M)	0.352[e]	61.7[e]	1,982[e]	57.1[e]	15.1[e]	40.7[e]	45.4	54.5	53.4	21.2	46.3
160 Lesotho	2009 (D)	0.156	35.3	759	44.1	26.7	11.1	18.4	31.2	32.8	43.4	56.6
161 Uganda	2006 (D)	0.367	72.3	21,235	50.7	19.4	39.7	60.3	69.1	72.3	28.7	24.5
162 Togo	2006 (M)	0.284	54.3	3,003	52.4	21.6	28.7	33.4	52.9	54.2	38.7	61.7
163 Comoros	2000 (M)	0.408[d]	73.9[d]	416[d]	55.2[d]	16.0[d]	43.8[d]	45.0	72.8	72.3	46.1	44.8
164 Zambia	2007 (D)	0.328	64.2	7,740	51.2	17.2	34.8	49.8	57.4	63.0	64.3	59.3
165 Djibouti	2006 (M)	0.139	29.3	241	47.3	16.1	12.5	6.7	16.3	8.8	18.8	..
166 Rwanda	2005 (D)	0.426	80.2	7,380	53.2	14.9	50.6	63.5	65.7	80.2	76.8	58.5
167 Benin	2006 (D)	0.412	71.8	5,652	57.4	13.2	47.2	33.2	69.5	71.3	47.3	39.0
168 Gambia	2006 (M)	0.324	60.4	935	53.6	17.6	35.5	20.8	32.1	60.3	34.3	58.0
170 Côte d'Ivoire	2005 (D)	0.353	61.5	11,083	57.4	15.3	39.3	25.0	51.9	..	23.8	42.7
171 Malawi	2004 (D)	0.381	72.1	8,993	52.8	20.0	40.4	44.0	71.6	72.0	73.9	52.4
172 Afghanistan	..	..	..	..	..	..	..	..	..	..	..	36.0
173 Zimbabwe	2006 (D)	0.180	39.7	4,974	45.3	24.0	14.8	24.2	31.6	39.0	..	72.0
174 Ethiopia	2005 (D)	0.562	88.6	65,798	63.5	6.1	72.3	53.8	83.7	88.3	39.0	38.9

HDI rank	Multidimensional Poverty Index		Population in multidimensional poverty[a]		Intensity of deprivation (%)	Population vulnerable to poverty (%)	Population in severe poverty (%)	Share of multidimensional poor with deprivations in environmental services			Population below income poverty line	
			Headcount					Clean water (%)	Improved sanitation (%)	Modern fuels (%)	PPP $1.25 a day (%)	National poverty line (%)
	Year[b]	Value[a]	(%)	(thousands)							2000–2009[c]	2000–2009[c]
175 Mali	2006 (D)	0.558	86.6	11,771	64.4	7.6	68.4	43.7	79.5	86.5	51.4	47.4
176 Guinea-Bissau	..	..	..	..	..	..	..	..	..	..	48.8	64.7
178 Guinea	2005 (D)	0.506	82.5	7,459	61.3	9.3	62.3	37.7	75.6	82.5	43.3	53.0
179 Central African Republic	2000 (M)	0.512	86.4	3,198	59.3	11.8	55.4	53.6	53.3	86.1	62.8	62.0
180 Sierra Leone	2008 (D)	0.439	77.0	4,321	57.0	13.1	53.2	50.3	71.1	76.9	53.4	66.4
181 Burkina Faso	2006 (M)	0.536	82.6	12,078	64.9	8.6	65.8	43.0	69.6	82.4	56.5	46.4
182 Liberia	2007 (D)	0.485	83.9	2,917	57.7	9.7	57.5	33.5	78.9	83.9	83.7	63.8
183 Chad	2003 (W)	0.344	62.9	5,758	54.7	28.2	44.1	42.9	58.4	61.3	61.9	55.0
184 Mozambique	2009 (D)	0.512	79.3	18,127	64.6	9.5	60.7	44.1	63.2	78.7	60.0	54.7
185 Burundi	2005 (M)	0.530	84.5	6,127	62.7	12.2	61.9	51.6	63.1	84.3	81.3	66.9
186 Niger	2006 (D)	0.642	92.4	12,437	69.4	4.0	81.8	64.1	89.3	92.3	43.1	59.5
187 Congo, Democratic Republic of the	2007 (D)	0.393	73.2	44,485	53.7	16.1	46.5	55.5	62.0	72.8	59.2	71.3
OTHER COUNTRIES OR TERRITORIES												
Somalia	2006 (M)	0.514	81.2	6,941	63.3	9.5	65.6	70.0	69.1	81.0	..	..

TABLE 5

NOTES

a. Not all indicators were available for all countries; caution should thus be used in cross-country comparisons. Where data are missing, indicator weights are adjusted to total 100 percent. For details on countries missing data, see Alkire and others (2011).
b. *D* indicates data are from Demographic and Health Surveys, *M* indicates data are from Multiple Indicator Cluster Surveys, *W* indicates data are from World Health Surveys and *N* indicates data are from national surveys.
c. Data refer to the most recent year available during the period specified.
d. Upper bound estimate.
e. Lower bound estimate.
f. Refers to only part of the country.

DEFINITIONS

Multidimensional Poverty Index: Percentage of the population that is multidimensionally poor adjusted by the intensity of the deprivations. See *Technical note 4* for details on how the Multidimensional Poverty Index is calculated.
Multidimensional poverty headcount: Percentage of the population with a weighted deprivation score of at least 33 percent.
Intensity of deprivation of multidimensional poverty: Average percentage of deprivation experienced by people in multidimensional poverty.
Population vulnerable to poverty: Percentage of the population at risk of suffering multiple deprivations—that is, those with a deprivation score of 20–33 percent.
Population in severe poverty: Percentage of the population in severe multidimensional poverty—that is, those with a deprivation score of 50 percent or more.
Share of multidimensional poor with deprivations in clean water: Percentage of the multidimensionally poor population without access to clean water that is less than a 30 minute walk from home. Clean water is defined using the Millennium Development Goal definition and includes piped water into dwelling, plot or yard; public tap/standpipe; borehole/tube well; protected dug well; protected spring; rainwater collection; and bottled water (if a secondary available source is also improved). It does not include unprotected well, unprotected spring, water provided by carts with small tanks/drums, tanker truck-provided water and bottled water (if secondary source is not an improved source); or surface water taken directly from rivers, ponds, streams, lakes, dams or irrigation channels.
Share of multidimensional poor with deprivations in improved sanitation: Percentage of the multidimensionally poor population without access to an improved sanitation facility. Improved sanitation facilities are defined using the Millennium Development Goal definition and include flush or pour-flush to piped sewer system or septic tank, ventilated improved pit latrine, pit latrine with slab and composting toilet. Facilities are not considered improved when they are shared with other households or open to the public.
Share of multidimensional poor with deprivations in modern fuels: Percentage of the multidimensionally poor population without access to modern fuels. Households are considered deprived of modern fuels if they cook with wood, charcoal or dung.
Population below PPP $1.25 a day: Percentage of the population living below the international poverty line $1.25 (in purchasing power parity terms) a day.
Population below national poverty line: Percentage of the population living below the national poverty line, which is the poverty line deemed appropriate for a country by its authorities. National estimates are based on population-weighted subgroup estimates from household surveys.

MAIN DATA SOURCES

Columns 1 and 2: Calculated from various household surveys, including ICF Macro Demographic and Health Surveys, United Nations Children's Fund Multiple Indicator Cluster Surveys and World Health Organization World Health Surveys conducted between 2000 and 2010.
Columns 3–10: Calculated based on data on household deprivations in education, health and living standards from various household surveys as listed in column 1.
Columns 11 and 12: World Bank (2011a).

TABLE 6

Environmental sustainability

		COMPOSITE MEASURES OF SUSTAINABILITY			PRIMARY ENERGY SUPPLY[a]		CARBON DIOXIDE EMISSIONS		POLLUTION		NATURAL RESOURCE DEPLETION AND BIODIVERSITY				
							Per capita		Greenhouse gas emissions per capita	Urban pollution		Fresh water withdrawals	Forest area	Change in forest area	Endangered species
HDI rank		Adjusted net savings (% of GNI)	Ecological footprint (hectares per capita)	Environmental performance index (0–100)	Fossil fuels (% of total)	Renewables (% of total)	(tonnes)	(average annual % growth)	(tonnes of carbon dioxide equivalent)	(micrograms per cubic metre)	Natural resource depletion (% of GNI)	(% of total renewable water resources)	(% of land area)	(%)	(% of all species)
		2005–2009[b]	2007	2010	2007	2007	2008	1970/2008	2005	2008	2009	2003–2010[b]	2008	1990–2008	2010
VERY HIGH HUMAN DEVELOPMENT															
1	Norway	12.8	5.6	81.1	58.6	45.3	10.5	1.0	5.8	16	10.6	0.8	32.4	8.6	7
2	Australia	1.7	6.8	65.7	94.6	5.4	19.0	1.3	9.6	14	5.1	..	19.7	−2.2	22
3	Netherlands	11.6	6.2	66.4	92.5	4.4	10.5	−0.1	2.4	31	0.8	11.7	10.8	5.8	5
4	United States	−0.8	8.0	63.5	85.0	5.4	17.3	−0.6	3.7	19	0.7	15.6	33.2	2.3	21
5	New Zealand	8.0	4.9	73.4	66.7	33.1	7.8	1.2	10.0	12	0.9	..	31.5	7.3	25
6	Canada	5.8	7.0	66.4	74.9	17.0	16.4	0.1	4.7	15	2.3	..	34.1	0.0	7
7	Ireland	−1.1	6.3	67.1	90.2	3.8	9.8	1.1	5.8	13	0.1	..	10.5	55.1	7
8	Liechtenstein	..	..	..	..	..	..	..	..	17	..	..	43.1	6.2	1
9	Germany	11.4	5.1	73.2	80.1	8.9	9.6	..	1.9	16	0.1	21.0	31.8	3.1	9
10	Sweden	16.0	5.9	86.0	33.1	32.4	5.3	−2.0	2.1	11	0.2	1.5	68.7	3.4	5
11	Switzerland	21.6	5.0	89.1	52.7	20.6	5.3	−0.5	1.2	22	..	..	30.8	6.9	6
12	Japan	12.1	4.7	72.5	83.0	3.4	9.5	0.7	1.0	27	0.0	..	68.5	0.0	15
13	Hong Kong, China (SAR)	..	..	..	94.9	0.4	5.5	2.6	0.5	..	..	..	..	..	9
14	Iceland	4.1	..	93.5	17.1	82.9	7.1	0.1	3.3	14	..	0.1	0.3[c]	223.0	9
15	Korea, Republic of	20.0	4.9	57.0	81.2	1.5	10.6	5.0	1.2	31	0.0	..	64.3	−2.1	10
16	Denmark	10.7	8.3	69.2	80.4	18.9	8.4	−1.1	2.9	16	1.5	10.8	12.7	21.3	6
17	Israel	12.2	4.8	62.4	96.6	4.9	5.4	−0.1	1.1	28	0.2	101.9	7.1	17.0	12
18	Belgium	13.2	8.0	58.1	73.8	4.2	9.9	−0.5	1.8	21	0.0	34.0	22.3	..	5
19	Austria	15.0	5.3	78.1	71.6	27.1	8.1	0.5	1.9	29	0.1	..	47.0	2.7	11
20	France	7.0	5.0	78.2	51.0	7.6	6.1	−0.9	2.3	13	0.0	15.0	29.0	9.1	14
21	Slovenia	13.6	5.3	65.0	69.4	11.2	8.5	..	2.6	29	0.2	3.0	62.0	..	13
22	Finland	8.1	6.2	74.7	48.0	26.1	10.7	0.5	3.4	15	0.1	1.5	72.9	1.2	4
23	Spain	9.7	5.4	70.6	81.7	7.9	7.4	2.0	1.7	28	0.0	29.0	35.7	29.0	16
24	Italy	6.1	5.0	73.1	89.9	8.2	7.5	0.8	1.4	23	0.1	..	30.6	18.5	14
25	Luxembourg	7.6	9.4	67.8	88.0	3.0	21.9	−1.6	3.5	13	..	..	33.5	..	2
26	Singapore	33.0	5.3	69.6	100.0	0.0	7.0	−0.6	1.4	31	..	..	3.3	0.0	17
27	Czech Republic	11.3	5.7	71.6	81.2	5.4	11.3	..	2.1	18	0.3	14.8	34.3	..	5
28	United Kingdom	2.2	4.9	74.2	90.2	2.8	8.5	−0.8	1.8	13	1.2	8.8	11.8	9.8	10
29	Greece	−7.9	5.4	60.9	92.8	5.6	8.8	3.1	1.4	32	0.2	12.7	29.8	16.5	16
30	United Arab Emirates	..	10.7	40.7	100.0	0.0	34.6	−1.8	6.2	89	..	2,032.0	3.8	28.7	9
31	Cyprus	0.4	..	56.3	96.0	4.0	9.9	3.4	1.3	34	..	19.3	18.7	7.4	8
32	Andorra	..	..	..	..	..	6.4	..	..	17	..	..	34.0	0.0	3
33	Brunei Darussalam	−1.8	..	60.8	100.0	0.0	27.0	−2.2	17.9	51	..	..	72.8	−7.1	9
34	Estonia	14.4	7.9	63.8	88.3	12.0	13.6	..	2.3	13	0.7	14.0	52.6	..	3
35	Slovakia	19.8	4.1	74.5	70.0	5.7	7.0	..	1.4	13	0.3	1.4	40.2	..	5
36	Malta	..	..	76.3	99.9	0.1	6.3	3.0	0.9	..	..	..	0.9	0.0	7
37	Qatar	..	10.5	48.9	100.0	0.0	53.5	−0.6	18.0	35	..	455.2	0.0	0.0	8
38	Hungary	4.5	3.0	69.1	77.8	6.3	5.5	−0.6	1.6	16	0.2	5.4	22.4	11.6	8
39	Poland	9.7	4.3	63.1	93.8	6.3	8.3	−0.3	2.7	35	1.0	19.4	30.5	4.5	5
40	Lithuania	6.0	4.7	68.3	60.8	9.3	4.5	..	2.5	17	0.2	9.6	34.2	..	4
41	Portugal	−1.8	4.5	73.0	78.3	18.3	5.3	3.1	1.8	21	0.1	..	37.7	3.6	19
42	Bahrain	10.6	..	42.0	100.3	0.0	29.0	2.4	4.3	49	..	219.8	0.6	145.0	8
43	Latvia	20.4	5.6	72.5	64.3	30.8	3.4	..	2.3	13	0.3	..	53.6	..	4
44	Chile	3.2	3.2	73.3	77.6	22.1	4.4	1.4	1.6	62	10.0	..	21.7	5.8	10
45	Argentina	10.6	2.6	61.0	89.8	7.1	4.8	0.9	3.9	68	4.9	..	10.9	−14.1	9
46	Croatia	12.3	3.7	68.7	85.1	8.7	5.3	..	1.5	27	0.8	0.6	34.2	..	13
47	Barbados	..	..	..	..	..	5.3	2.9	..	38	..	..	19.4	0.0	8
HIGH HUMAN DEVELOPMENT															
48	Uruguay	6.1	5.1	59.1	64.9	33.2	2.5	0.5	8.1	160	0.4	..	9.5	79.8	12
49	Palau	..	..	..	..	..	10.4	..	..	..	..	..	87.6	..	13
50	Romania	18.8	2.7	67.0	79.4	14.1	4.4	−0.8	1.7	12	1.3	3.2	28.3	2.0	9
51	Cuba	..	1.9	78.1	89.9	10.1	2.8	0.7	1.4	21	..	..	26.3	36.1	18
52	Seychelles	..	..	..	..	..	8.1	7.4	..	..	..	..	88.5	0.0	18
53	Bahamas	..	..	..	..	..	6.4	−2.3	..	..	..	..	51.4	0.0	10
54	Montenegro	..	..	..	..	..	3.1	..	..	..	..	..	40.4	..	11
55	Bulgaria	6.1	4.1	62.5	76.2	5.3	6.7	−0.2	2.0	51	1.1	28.7	35.1	14.7	9

HDI rank	Adjusted net savings (% of GNI)[b] 2005–2009[b]	Ecological footprint (hectares per capita) 2007	Environmental performance index (0–100) 2010	Fossil fuels (% of total) 2007	Renewables (% of total) 2007	Per capita (tonnes) 2008	Per capita (average annual % growth) 1970/2008	Greenhouse gas emissions per capita (tonnes of carbon dioxide equivalent) 2005	Urban pollution (micrograms per cubic metre) 2008	Natural resource depletion (% of GNI) 2009	Fresh water withdrawals (% of total renewable water resources)[b] 2003–2010[b]	Forest area (% of land area) 2008	Change in forest area (%) 1990–2008	Endangered species (% of all species) 2010
56 Saudi Arabia	–3.9	5.1	55.3	100.0	0.0	17.2	2.1	2.5	104	28.9	943.3	0.5[c]	0.0	9
57 Mexico	9.1	3.0	67.3	88.8	9.9	4.4	1.8	1.7	33	5.4	17.5	33.5	–7.4	17
58 Panama	28.4	2.9	71.4	75.7	24.1	2.0	0.9	1.4	34	..	..	44.0	–13.6	6
59 Serbia	..	2.4	..	89.5	10.5	5.1	..	2.3	..	0.4	..	29.6	..	7
60 Antigua and Barbuda	..	..	69.8	..	..	5.2	–0.7	..	13	..	..	22.3	–4.9	8
61 Malaysia	15.4	4.9	65.0	95.1	5.0	7.7	4.7	2.4	20	7.9	..	62.8	–7.8	18
62 Trinidad and Tobago	–32.4	3.1	54.2	99.9	0.1	37.3	3.7	7.8	105	28.2	..	44.4	–5.3	6
63 Kuwait	15.7	6.3	51.1	100.0	0.0	26.3	–0.6	6.3	95	..	..	0.3[c]	70.6	9
64 Libya	..	3.1	50.1	99.1	0.9	9.3	–1.5	2.7	76	30.5	..	0.1[c]	0.0	9
65 Belarus	16.9	3.8	65.4	92.1	5.5	6.5	..	2.4	7	0.9	..	42.2	..	4
66 Russian Federation	–0.8	4.4	61.2	90.9	3.0	12.1	..	4.9	16	14.5	..	49.4	..	9
67 Grenada	..	..	..	..	..	2.4	4.4	..	21	..	..	50.0	0.0	10
68 Kazakhstan	–1.2	4.5	57.3	98.8	1.1	15.3	..	4.3	15	22.0	..	1.2	..	8
69 Costa Rica	15.2	2.7	86.4	45.6	54.5	1.8	2.5	0.9	32	0.2	..	50.1	–0.2	7
70 Albania	8.2	1.9	71.4	63.7	26.2	1.3	–0.7	1.1	46	1.3	..	28.4	–1.3	15
71 Lebanon	2.7	2.9	57.9	95.4	3.7	4.1	2.5	0.4	36	..	28.1	13.4	4.4	10
72 Saint Kitts and Nevis	..	..	..	..	..	4.9	..	..	17	..	..	42.3	0.0	8
73 Venezuela, Bolivarian Republic of	2.9	2.9	62.9	87.6	12.5	6.0	–0.4	3.0	9	9.8	..	53.1	–9.9	8
74 Bosnia and Herzegovina	..	2.7	55.9	92.8	9.6	8.3	..	1.2	19	1.6	0.9	42.7	..	10
75 Georgia	–7.1	1.8	63.6	66.6	33.7	1.2	..	1.4	49	0.1	2.6	39.5	..	9
76 Ukraine	5.6	2.9	58.2	81.8	1.4	7.0	..	2.1	18	3.8	..	16.7	..	8
77 Mauritius	8.0	4.3	80.6	..	..	3.1	4.4	..	18	0.0	26.4	17.2	–9.9	18
78 Former Yugoslav Republic of Macedonia	11.6	5.7	60.6	84.2	8.2	5.8	..	1.0	20	0.1	16.1	39.2	..	14
79 Jamaica	6.9	1.9	58.0	88.5	11.5	4.5	1.4	0.7	37	0.7	..	31.2	–1.9	15
80 Peru	8.6	1.5	69.3	76.1	23.9	1.4	0.1	0.9	51	5.9	..	53.4	–2.7	8
81 Dominica	..	..	..	..	..	1.9	4.4	..	22	0.0	..	60.3	–9.6	9
82 Saint Lucia	..	..	..	..	..	2.3	3.4	..	34	0.0	..	77.0	7.3	9
83 Ecuador	4.4	1.9	69.3	83.9	15.7	2.0	2.7	1.7	20	9.9	..	41.3	–25.7	12
84 Brazil	4.6	2.9	63.4	52.6	44.5	2.1	2.0	4.0	21	3.1	0.7	61.9	–8.9	10[d]
85 Saint Vincent and the Grenadines	–8.8	..	..	..	..	1.9	4.7	..	24	..	..	68.1	4.9	8
86 Armenia	9.6	1.8	60.4	73.5	5.2	1.8	..	1.3	69	0.5	36.4	9.5	..	7
87 Colombia	5.4	1.9	76.8	72.7	27.7	1.5	0.3	1.8	20	6.2	..	54.7	–2.9	11
88 Iran, Islamic Republic of	..	2.7	60.0	99.4	0.7	7.3	2.2	2.1	55	17.9	67.7	6.8	0.0	9
89 Oman	–7.9	5.0	45.9	100.0	0.0	16.4	11.0	7.1	94	..	86.6	0.0[c]	0.0	9
90 Tonga	..	..	..	..	..	1.7	5.0	..	..	0.0	..	12.5	0.0	10
91 Azerbaijan	5.4	1.9	59.1	98.9	1.5	5.4	..	4.7	33	32.7	35.2	11.3	..	8
92 Turkey	2.9	2.7	60.4	90.6	9.5	3.9	3.2	1.4	37	0.2	18.8	14.4	14.6	15
93 Belize	9.2	..	69.9	..	..	1.4	0.9	..	13	..	..	61.9	–11.0	6
94 Tunisia	14.6	1.9	60.6	86.3	13.7	2.5	3.2	1.0	26	4.6	..	6.3	51.4	11
MEDIUM HUMAN DEVELOPMENT														
95 Jordan	3.0	2.1	56.1	98.0	1.7	3.5	3.3	0.5	33	1.1	99.4	1.1	0.0	10
96 Algeria	..	1.6	67.4	99.8	0.2	3.2	2.9	1.8	69	16.9	..	0.6	–9.4	13
97 Sri Lanka	16.4	1.2	63.7	43.4	56.6	0.6	1.9	0.6	74	0.5	24.5	30.1	–19.6	19
98 Dominican Republic	0.4	1.5	68.4	79.2	20.8	2.2	3.1	0.9	16	0.5	..	40.8	43.3	17
99 Samoa	..	..	..	..	..	0.9	3.9	..	..	0.3	..	60.4	31.5	12
100 Fiji	3.4	..	65.9	..	..	1.5	1.1	..	19	..	..	55.1	5.7	15
101 China	39.7	2.2	49.0	86.9	12.3	5.2	4.6	1.5	66	3.1	19.5	21.6	28.1	12
102 Turkmenistan	..	3.9	38.4	100.7	0.0	9.5	..	6.7	65	30.4	..	8.8	..	8
103 Thailand	20.5	2.4	62.2	80.6	19.3	4.3	6.3	1.6	55	3.2	13.1	37.1	–3.1	14
104 Suriname	..	..	68.2	..	..	4.7	0.2	..	24	..	..	94.6	–0.1	3
105 El Salvador	3.7	2.0	69.1	38.4	61.6	1.0	2.5	0.8	28	0.5	..	14.3	–21.5	12
106 Gabon	1.8	1.4	56.4	43.8	56.2	1.7	–2.1	6.4	7	29.2	..	85.4	0.0	6
107 Paraguay	5.2	3.2	63.5	28.2	163.1	0.7	2.1	4.1	67	..	..	45.2	–15.2	4
108 Bolivia, Plurinational State of	6.2	2.6	44.3	82.1	17.9	1.3	2.1	4.9	74	11.2	..	53.4	–7.9	4
109 Maldives	31.4	..	65.9	..	..	3.0	..	..	29	..	15.7	3.0	0.0	10
110 Mongolia	24.9	..	42.8	96.2	3.3	4.1	1.6	3.7	111	11.1	..	7.1	–11.8	7
111 Moldova, Republic of	16.2	1.4	58.8	89.1	2.8	1.3	..	1.1	36	0.2	..	11.5	..	6
112 Philippines	28.0	1.3	65.7	56.9	43.1	0.9	0.8	0.8	19	1.0	17.0	25.3	15.0	19
113 Egypt	3.1	1.7	62.0	96.1	4.0	2.6	3.9	0.9	97	7.3	..	0.1[c]	56.4	10
114 Occupied Palestinian Territory	..	..	..	..	..	0.5	..	..	..	..	49.9	1.5	1.0	..
115 Uzbekistan	..	1.7	42.3	98.1	1.9	4.6	..	1.9	40	17.8	..	7.7	..	7
116 Micronesia, Federated States of	..	..	..	..	..	0.6	..	..	..	..	..	91.5	..	15

TABLE 6

Environmental sustainability

		COMPOSITE MEASURES OF SUSTAINABILITY			PRIMARY ENERGY SUPPLY[a]		CARBON DIOXIDE EMISSIONS		POLLUTION		NATURAL RESOURCE DEPLETION AND BIODIVERSITY				
							Per capita		Green-house gas emissions per capita (tonnes of carbon dioxide equivalent)	Urban pollution (micrograms per cubic metre)	Natural resource depletion (% of GNI)	Fresh water withdrawals (% of total renewable water resources)	Forest area (% of land area)	Change in forest area (%)	Endangered species (% of all species)
HDI rank		Adjusted net savings (% of GNI)	Ecological footprint (hectares per capita)	Environmental performance index (0–100)	Fossil fuels (% of total)	Renewables (% of total)	(tonnes)	(average annual % growth)							
		2005–2009[b]	2007	2010	2007	2007	2008	1970/2008	2005	2008	2009	2003–2010[b]	2008	1990–2008	2010
117	Guyana	−0.4	..	59.2	..	..	2.0	−0.3	..	22	3.4	..	77.2	0.0	3
118	Botswana	9.6	2.7	41.3	67.2	22.3	2.5	..	4.1	69	2.8	..	20.4	−15.5	2
119	Syrian Arab Republic	−14.1	1.5	64.6	98.7	1.3	3.4	3.1	0.9	69	10.2	99.8	2.6	28.8	13
120	Namibia	21.9	2.2	59.3	71.6	18.1	1.9	..	4.4	48	0.3	..	9.0	−15.1	5
121	Honduras	9.5	1.9	49.9	54.1	45.9	1.2	2.2	1.2	42	0.4	..	48.5	−33.2	7
122	Kiribati	..	..	..	..	..	0.3	−0.8	..	..	..	..	15.0	0.0	14
123	South Africa	0.4	2.3	50.8	87.2	10.5	8.8	0.7	1.9	22	5.4	..	7.6	0.0	15
124	Indonesia	11.0	1.2	44.6	65.6	34.4	1.8	4.8	1.5	72	6.5	..	52.9	−19.2	16
125	Vanuatu	12.4	..	..	..	..	0.4	−0.4	..	15	..	..	36.1	0.0	14
126	Kyrgyzstan	9.4	1.2	59.7	69.2	32.4	1.1	..	1.0	26	0.5	..	4.8	..	6
127	Tajikistan	6.2	1.0	51.3	42.3	54.7	0.5	..	0.9	43	0.2	..	2.9	..	6
128	Viet Nam	16.6	1.4	59.0	54.0	45.6	1.5	2.1	1.3	53	7.2	9.3	43.6	44.3	12
129	Nicaragua	3.4	1.6	57.1	38.5	61.5	0.8	0.7	1.7	23	0.8	..	27.0	−27.9	4
130	Morocco	25.0	1.2	65.6	93.6	3.9	1.5	3.1	0.5	27	1.4	..	11.5	1.2	16
131	Guatemala	4.0	1.8	54.0	42.9	57.2	0.9	1.9	1.1	60	1.2	..	35.2	−20.6	8
132	Iraq	..	1.3	41.0	99.4	0.2	3.4	1.0	0.7	138	45.7	..	1.9	2.6	9
133	Cape Verde	..	..	..	..	..	0.6	4.1	..	..	..	..	21.0	46.1	13
134	India	24.1	0.9	48.3	71.1	28.1	1.5	3.8	0.7	59	4.2	40.1	22.9	6.6	13
135	Ghana	−4.7	1.8	51.3	27.8	72.5	0.4	0.5	0.6	24	6.9	..	22.7	−30.6	5
136	Equatorial Guinea	..	..	41.9	..	..	7.3	11.3	..	7	66.0	..	58.8	−11.3	6
137	Congo	−44.7	1.0	54.0	43.5	53.7	0.6	0.7	2.7	68	50.6	..	65.7	−1.3	4
138	Lao People's Democratic Republic	17.8	1.3	59.6	..	..	0.3	0.5	..	39	..	..	68.9	−8.1	9
139	Cambodia	13.0	1.0	41.7	29.7	69.7	0.3	1.8	1.9	41	0.2	0.5	58.6	−20.0	13
140	Swaziland	−0.9	1.5	54.4	..	..	1.0	0.4	..	35	0.1	..	32.2	17.4	2
141	Bhutan	..	..	68.0	..	..	1.1	12.5	..	22	5.3	0.4	84.1	6.3	7
LOW HUMAN DEVELOPMENT															
142	Solomon Islands	−3.7	..	51.1	..	..	0.4	1.0	..	26	10.9	..	79.5	−4.3	17
143	Kenya	13.1	1.1	51.4	16.2	83.8	0.3	−0.2	0.9	30	1.2	8.9	6.1	−5.9	8
144	São Tomé and Príncipe	..	..	57.3	..	..	0.8	3.8	..	29	1.0	..	28.1	0.0	..
145	Pakistan	10.7	0.8	48.0	61.8	37.7	0.9	2.2	1.1	109	3.1	81.5	2.3	−29.8	9
146	Bangladesh	27.1	0.6	44.0	68.4	31.6	0.3	..	0.7	134	2.6	3.0	11.1	−3.1	9
147	Timor-Leste	..	0.4	..	..	..	0.2	..	..	..	..	..	51.4	−20.9	5
148	Angola	−29.2	1.0	36.3	33.5	66.5	1.4	2.2	5.1	55	29.1	..	47.1	−3.7	4
149	Myanmar	..	1.8	51.3	31.0	69.0	0.3	1.0	2.2	46	..	..	49.6	−17.4	8
150	Cameroon	6.8	1.0	44.6	23.9	76.1	0.3	3.1	1.6	47	4.8	..	43.1	−16.3	11
151	Madagascar	3.9	1.8	49.2	..	..	0.1	−0.8	..	33	0.2	..	21.8	−7.5	23
152	Tanzania, United Republic of	13.5	1.2	47.9	10.6	89.4	0.1	0.3	1.4	22	2.5	..	38.6	−17.5	12
153	Papua New Guinea	..	2.1	44.3	..	..	0.3	0.5	..	18	19.9	..	64.1	−8.0	12
154	Yemen	..	0.9	48.3	99.0	1.0	1.0	..	0.5	67	13.2	..	1.0	0.0	10
155	Senegal	7.8	1.1	42.3	57.3	42.4	0.4	0.7	1.0	81	0.3	..	44.4	−8.5	6
156	Nigeria	..	1.4	40.2	18.3	81.7	0.6	1.3	1.1	46	15.0	..	10.8	−42.8	7
157	Nepal	29.1	3.6	68.2	10.9	89.1	0.1	4.7	1.0	32	4.2	..	25.4	−24.5	6
158	Haiti	..	0.7	39.5	28.3	71.7	0.3	3.1	0.6	35	..	..	3.7	−11.6	19
159	Mauritania	..	2.6	33.7	..	..	0.6	1.4	..	68	18.8	..	0.2[c]	−39.3	7
160	Lesotho	24.4	1.1	49.8	..	..	..	..	..	46	1.4	..	1.4	9.0	3
161	Uganda	8.6	1.5	49.8	..	..	0.1	−0.9	..	12	4.7	..	16.1	−33.4	7
162	Togo	..	1.0	36.4	14.3	83.4	0.2	1.4	0.8	29	3.6	..	6.0	−52.3	4
163	Comoros	..	..	..	..	..	0.2	..	..	34	1.0	..	2.0	−68.3	13
164	Zambia	1.4	0.9	47.0	7.5	92.3	0.1	−4.7	3.8	..	11.5	..	67.0	−5.7	3
165	Djibouti	..	..	60.5	..	..	0.6	−0.8	..	49	0.3	..	0.2[c]	0.0	9
166	Rwanda	8.8	1.0	44.6	..	..	0.1	4.2	..	26	2.4	..	16.8	30.5	6
167	Benin	4.1	1.2	39.6	37.1	61.0	0.5	4.1	0.9	45	1.2	..	42.1	−19.1	4
168	Gambia	12.9	3.4	50.3	..	..	0.3	2.2	..	62	1.0	..	47.6	7.8	4
169	Sudan	−7.1	1.7	47.1	31.2	68.8	0.3	0.1	3.0	159	11.1	..	29.5	−8.3	5
170	Côte d'Ivoire	7.3	1.0	54.3	25.0	75.5	0.3	−0.9	1.0	32	3.1	..	32.7	1.8	7
171	Malawi	..	0.7	51.4	..	..	0.1	−0.8	..	35	0.9	..	35.1	−15.2	9
172	Afghanistan	..	0.6	..	..	..	0.0	−3.5	..	37	..	..	2.1	0.0	5
173	Zimbabwe	..	1.2	47.8	26.1	69.1	0.7	−2.0	1.3	..	3.5	..	42.1	−26.6	3
174	Ethiopia	8.3	1.1	43.1	6.7	93.3	0.1	0.7	1.1	59	4.5	..	12.6	..	7
175	Mali	13.5	1.9	39.4	..	..	0.0	0.2	..	112	..	..	10.4	−10.1	2
176	Guinea-Bissau	..	1.0	44.7	..	..	0.2	1.2	..	47	..	..	72.6	−7.9	5
177	Eritrea	..	0.9	54.6	19.9	80.1	0.1	..	0.8	71	0.8	9.2	15.3	..	8

HDI rank	Adjusted net savings (% of GNI) 2005–2009[b]	Ecological footprint (hectares per capita) 2007	Environmental performance index (0–100) 2010	Fossil fuels (% of total) 2007	Renewables (% of total) 2007	Per capita (tonnes) 2008	(average annual % growth) 1970/2008	Greenhouse gas emissions per capita (tonnes of carbon dioxide equivalent) 2005	Urban pollution (micrograms per cubic metre) 2008	Natural resource depletion (% of GNI) 2009	Fresh water withdrawals (% of total renewable water resources) 2003–2010[b]	Forest area (% of land area) 2008	Change in forest area (%) 1990–2008	Endangered species (% of all species) 2010
178 Guinea	−4.2	1.7	44.4	..	..	0.1	−0.9	..	53	6.6	..	26.9	−8.9	8
179 Central African Republic	..	1.3	33.3	..	..	0.1	−1.2	..	34	0.0	..	36.4	−2.3	1
180 Sierra Leone	1.2	1.1	32.1	..	..	0.3	−0.6	..	38	2.1	..	38.6	−11.3	7
181 Burkina Faso	2.3	1.3	47.3	..	..	0.1	3.9	..	64	1.6	..	21.1	−15.7	3
182 Liberia	−18.3	1.3	..	..	..	0.1	−5.0	..	31	11.0	..	45.6	−11.0	8
183 Chad	..	1.7	40.8	..	..	0.0	0.2	..	81	25.2	..	9.3	−10.9	3
184 Mozambique	2.0	0.8	51.2	7.3	95.9	0.1	−2.7	1.1	26	3.8	..	50.2	−9.1	7
185 Burundi	−6.8	0.9	43.9	..	..	0.0	1.9	..	31	10.6	..	6.8	−39.2	5
186 Niger	16.2	2.3	37.6	..	..	0.1	1.0	..	96	1.2	..	1.0	−36.8	3
187 Congo, Democratic Republic of the	..	0.8	51.6	4.0	96.2	0.0	−3.3	1.9	40	10.7	..	68.3	−3.5	6
OTHER COUNTRIES OR TERRITORIES														
Korea, Democratic People's Rep. of	..	1.3	41.8	88.9	11.1	3.3	−1.2	1.0	59	..	..	49.2	−27.8	9
Marshall Islands	..	..	..	..	..	1.6	..	..	..	..	..	70.2	..	12
Monaco	..	..	..	..	..	..	..	..	..	..	..	..	..	8
Nauru	..	..	..	..	..	14.2	..	..	..	..	..	0.0	0.0	14
San Marino	..	..	..	..	..	..	..	..	8	..	..	0.0	0.0	0
Somalia	..	1.4	..	..	..	0.1	0.5	..	31	..	22.4	11.0	−16.7	7
Tuvalu	..	..	..	..	..	..	..	..	..	..	..	33.3	0.0	15
Human Development Index groups														
Very high human development	6.6	5.9	68.2	81.9	7.2	11.3	0.3	2.7	24	0.8	..	5.8	1.2	14
High human development	5.0	3.1	63.5	81.2	15.9	5.9	1.8	2.9	30	8.7	..	10.2	−3.4	11
Medium human development	27.2	1.6	50.3	77.3	22.2	3.2	3.9	1.2	61	4.4	..	2.9	8.3	13
Low human development	..	1.2	46.3	..	..	0.4	0.6	..	69	8.7	..	1.6	−13.9	8
Regions														
Arab States	..	2.1	56.4	88.9	10.9	4.6	2.3	1.5	89	..	..	1.1	1.8	10
East Asia and the Pacific	..	..	..	..	..	4.2	4.2	..	..	..	..	8.5	12.6	13
Europe and Central Asia	4.7	3.5	60.4	87.7	6.7	7.8	..	2.9	25	6.8	..	24.3	..	9
Latin America and the Caribbean	6.2	2.6	65.2	69.2	30.4	2.9	1.5	2.7	33	..	..	12.2	−7.5	11
South Asia	22.9	1.0	49.0	69.8	29.7	1.5	3.4	0.8	70	6.2	30.1	5.5	−1.3	12
Sub-Saharan Africa	4.7	1.3	45.7	..	..	0.9	0.2	..	43	9.8	..	1.6	−13.8	7
Least developed countries	..	1.2	46.7	..	..	0.2	0.1	..	68	10.0	..	2.0	−12.2	8
Small island developing states	..	..	..	..	..	2.6	1.9	..	..	..	..	14.2	1.1	15
World	18.3	2.4	54.4	72.3	25.1	4.4	2.5	1.7	52	2.4	..	1.7	−1.2	12

NOTES

a. The sum of the shares of fossil fuels and renewable energy resources may be greater than 100 percent because some countries generate more electricity than they consume and export the excess.
b. Data refer to the most recent year available during the period specified.
c. Less than 1 percent.
d. For certain amphibian species endemic to Brazil, there was not time for the Global Amphibian Assessment (GAA) Coordinating Team and the experts on the species in Brazil to reach agreement on the Red List Categories. The data for amphibians included in the data displayed here are those that were agreed at the GAA Brazil workshop in April 2003. However, a subsequent GAA check found that many of the assessments were inconsistent with the approach adopted elsewhere in the world, and a "consistent Red List Category" was also assigned to these species. Therefore, data displayed here may not match data in the Global Species Assessment.

DEFINITIONS

Adjusted net savings: Rate of savings in an economy that takes into account investments in human capital, depletion of natural resources and damage caused by pollution (including particulate emissions), expressed as a percentage of gross national income (GNI). A negative value implies an unsustainable path.
Ecological footprint: Amount of biologically productive land and sea area that a country requires to produce the resources it consumes and to absorb the waste it generates.
Environmental performance index: Index comprising 25 performance indicators across 10 policy categories covering both environmental public health and ecosystem vitality.
Primary energy supply, fossil fuels: Percentage of total energy supply that comes from natural resources formed from biomass in the geological past (such as coal, oil and natural gas).
Primary energy supply, renewables: Percentage of total energy supply that comes from constantly replenished natural processes, including solar, wind, biomass, geothermal, hydropower and ocean resources and some waste. Nuclear energy is not included.
Carbon dioxide emissions, per capita: Human-originated carbon dioxide emissions stemming from the burning of fossil fuels, gas flaring and the production of cement, divided by midyear population.
Greenhouse gas emissions per capita: Emissions from methane, nitrous oxide and other greenhouse gases, including hydrofluorocarbons, perfluorocarbons and sulfur hexafluoride, divided by midyear population. Carbon dioxide emissions are not included.

Urban pollution: Particulate matter concentrations in terms of fine suspended particulates of human-made or natural origin less than 10 microns (PM10) in diameter that are capable of penetrating deep into the respiratory tract. Data are urban population–weighted PM10 levels in residential areas of cities with more than 100,000 residents. The estimates represent the average annual exposure level of an urban resident to outdoor particulate matter.
Natural resource depletion: Monetary expression of energy, mineral and forest depletion, expressed as a percentage of total gross national income (GNI).
Fresh water withdrawals: Total fresh water withdrawn in a given year, expressed as a percentage of total renewable water resources.
Forest area: Percentage of total land area spanning more than 0.5 hectares with trees higher than 5 metres and a canopy cover of more than 10 percent, or trees able to reach these thresholds, unless under agricultural or urban land use.
Change in forest area: Percentage change in area under forest cover.
Endangered species: Percentage of animal species (including mammals, birds, reptiles, amphibians, fish and invertebrates) classified as either critically endangered, endangered or vulnerable by the International Union for the Conservation of Nature.

MAIN DATA SOURCES

Columns 1 and 9: World Bank (2011a).
Column 2: Global Footprint Network (2010).
Column 3: Emerson and others (2010).
Columns 4 and 5: HDRO calculations based on data on total primary energy supply from IEA (2011).
Columns 6 and 7: HDRO calculations based on data from Boden, Marland and Andres (2009).
Column 8: HDRO calculations based on data from World Bank (2011a) and UNDESA (2011).
Column 10: HDRO calculations based on World Bank (2011a).
Column 11: FAO (2011a).
Columns 12 and 13: HDRO calculations based on data on forest and total land area from FAO (2011a).
Column 14: IUCN (2010).

TABLE 6

TABLE 7

Human development effects of environmental threats

			IMPACT OF NATURAL DISASTERS		Deaths due to					
	Population under age 5 suffering from		Number of deaths (average annual per million people)	Population affected (average annual per million people)	Water pollution (per million people)	Indoor air pollution (per million people)	Outdoor air pollution (per million people)	Malaria (per million people)	Dengue (per million people)	Population living on degraded land (%)
HDI rank	Stunting (%)	Wasting (%)								
	2000–2009ᵃ	2000–2009ᵃ	2001/2010	2001/2010	2004	2004	2004	2009	2001–2010ᵃ	2010
VERY HIGH HUMAN DEVELOPMENT										
1 Norway	..	..	0	33	..	..	65	..	..	0.2 ᵇ
2 Australia	..	..	3	1,378	..	..	35	..	0	9.0
3 Netherlands	..	..	12	0ᵇ	..	..	203	..	..	5.4
4 United States	3.9	1.3	1	6,689	..	..	138	..	..	1.1
5 New Zealand	..	..	0	175	..	..	0ᵇ	..	..	5.3
6 Canada	..	..	0	54	..	..	85	..	..	2.7
7 Ireland	..	..	0ᵇ	11	..	..	0ᵇ	..	..	0.5ᵇ
8 Liechtenstein	..	..		..	..	..	..	..	..	..
9 Germany	1.3	1.1	12	404	..	..	124	..	..	8.1
10 Sweden	..	..	0	0	..	..	56	..	..	0.3ᵇ
11 Switzerland	..	..	14	77	..	..	109	..	..	0.5ᵇ
12 Japan	..	..	1	709	..	..	196	..	..	0.3ᵇ
13 Hong Kong, China (SAR)	..	..	0	271	..	..	..	..	..	..
14 Iceland	..	..	..	..	..	..	0ᵇ	..	..	..
15 Korea, Republic of	..	..	1	1,158	..	..	152	0.0	..	2.9
16 Denmark	..	..	0	0	..	..	111	..	..	8.5
17 Israel	..	..	1	270	..	..	216	..	..	12.9
18 Belgium	..	..	20	31	..	..	203	..	..	10.5
19 Austria	..	..	4	735	..	..	147	..	..	2.7
20 France	..	..	34	891	..	..	81	..	..	3.9
21 Slovenia	..	..	15	52	..	..	150	..	..	8.4
22 Finland	..	..	0	7	..	..	19	..	..	0.0ᵇ
23 Spain	..	..	33	14	..	..	136	..	..	1.4
24 Italy	..	..	33	29	..	..	137	..	..	2.2
25 Luxembourg	..	..	34	0	..	..	..	..	..	..
26 Singapore	4.4	3.3	..	..	..	..	264	..	5	..
27 Czech Republic	2.6	2.1	5	2,098	..	..	167	..	..	4.2
28 United Kingdom	..	..	1	617	..	..	189	..	..	2.7
29 Greece	..	..	1	112	..	..	224	..	..	1.1
30 United Arab Emirates	..	..	..	..	..	..	55	..	..	1.9
31 Cyprus	..	..	0	4	..	..	197	..	..	11.4
32 Andorra	..	..	..	..	..	..	..	..	..	..
33 Brunei Darussalam	..	..	..	..	..	..	..	..	..	..
34 Estonia	..	..	0	7	..	0ᵇ	74	..	..	5.0
35 Slovakia	..	..	2	212	..	..	74	..	..	9.1
36 Malta	..	..	..	..	..	..	..	..	..	..
37 Qatar	..	..	..	..	..	..	0ᵇ	..	..	0.1ᵇ
38 Hungary	..	..	7	467	..	..	208	..	..	17.1
39 Poland	..	..	3	318	..	..	162	..	..	13.2
40 Lithuania	..	..	1	0	..	..	204	..	..	4.8
41 Portugal	..	..	26	1,418	..	..	190	..	..	2.3
42 Bahrain	..	..	..	..	..	..	0ᵇ	..	..	..
43 Latvia	..	..	3	0	..	..	0ᵇ	..	..	1.8
44 Chile	2.0	0.5	1	3,051	12	..	149	..	0	1.1
45 Argentina	8.2	2.3	0	1,790	8	..	342	0.0	0	1.7
46 Croatia	..	..	18	59	..	0ᵇ	225	..	..	17.5
47 Barbados	..	..	0	1,968	..	..	..	..	0	..
HIGH HUMAN DEVELOPMENT										
48 Uruguay	13.9	6.0	1	4,548	..	0ᵇ	422	..	0	5.7
49 Palau	..	..	..	..	..	..	..	..	49	..
50 Romania	12.8	3.5	3	764	..	18	439	..	..	13.5
51 Cuba	4.6	3.9	0	87,392	18	53	160	..	0	17.0
52 Seychelles	..	..	0	7,860	..	..	..	..	..	..
53 Bahamas	..	..	4	5,979	..	..	..	0.0	0	..

HDI rank	Population under age 5 suffering from Stunting (%) 2000–2009[a]	Wasting (%) 2000–2009[a]	IMPACT OF NATURAL DISASTERS Number of deaths (average annual per million people) 2001/2010	Population affected (average annual per million people) 2001/2010	Deaths due to Water pollution (per million people) 2004	Indoor air pollution (per million people) 2004	Outdoor air pollution (per million people) 2004	Malaria (per million people) 2009	Dengue (per million people) 2001–2010[a]	Population living on degraded land (%) 2010
54 Montenegro	7.9	2.2	0	1,249	..	..	..	..	..	8.0
55 Bulgaria	8.8	1.6	1	179	..	0[b]	437	..	..	7.8
56 Saudi Arabia	9.3	5.3	1	86	..	..	108	0.0	..	4.3
57 Mexico	15.5	3.4	1	7,097	43	41	88	0.0	0	3.8
58 Panama	19.1	3.9	2	3,612	63	63	63	0.0	0	4.1
59 Serbia	8.1	1.8	0	213	..	..	..	..	..	18.5
60 Antigua and Barbuda	..	..	0	34,720	0	..	..	..	0	..
61 Malaysia	..	..	0	1,573	35	0[b]	23	0.0	4	1.2
62 Trinidad and Tobago	5.3	4.4	0	131	..	0[b]	0[b]	..	9	..
63 Kuwait	..	..	..	..	..	..	137	..	..	0.6
64 Libya	21.0	5.6	..	..	..	0[b]	318	..	..	8.5
65 Belarus	4.5	1.3	0	19	..	10	..	..	..	4.7
66 Russian Federation	..	..	40	1,332	5	4	231	0.0[c]	..	3.1
67 Grenada	..	..	38	59,003	..	..	..	..	0	..
68 Kazakhstan	17.5	4.9	1	442	193	7	159	..	..	23.5
69 Costa Rica	..	..	2	7,367	24	47	47	0.2	0	1.3
70 Albania	27.0	6.6	0	19,215	32	0[b]	64	..	..	5.7
71 Lebanon	16.5	4.2	0[b]	414	50	..	100	..	..	1.2
72 Saint Kitts and Nevis	..	..	..	..	..	..	..	..	0	..
73 Venezuela, Bolivarian Republic of	15.6	3.7	1	704	61	8	..	0.0	0	1.9
74 Bosnia and Herzegovina	11.8	1.6	0	10,673	..	0[b]	79	..	..	6.1
75 Georgia	14.7	2.3	0[b]	94	89	44	288	0.0	..	1.9
76 Ukraine	22.9	4.1	2	1,421	2	6	305	..	..	6.2
77 Mauritius	..	..	0	81	..	..	80	..	..	..
78 Former Yugoslav Republic of Macedonia	11.5	1.8	2	53,874	..	0[b]	148	..	..	7.1
79 Jamaica	3.7	2.2	3	15,757	75	188	75	0.0	0	3.3
80 Peru	29.8	5.4	6	20,752	92	37	117	0.1	0	0.7
81 Dominica	..	..	7	11,372	..	..	..	..	0	..
82 Saint Lucia	..	..	6	1,721	..	..	..	..	0	..
83 Ecuador	29.0	6.2	1	3,769	83	0[b]	38	0.0	0	1.6
84 Brazil	7.1	2.2	1	3,440	137	58	74	0.4	0	7.9
85 Saint Vincent and the Grenadines	..	..	4	918	..	..	0[b]	..	0	..
86 Armenia	18.2	4.2	0	0	33	131	882	0.0	..	9.6
87 Colombia	16.2	5.1	4	14,482	50	57	61	0.3	0	2.0
88 Iran, Islamic Republic of	..	..	1	2,156	..	4	132	0.0	..	25.1
89 Oman	..	..	5	722	..	..	126	0.7	..	5.8
90 Tonga	..	..	0	15,857	..	..	..	..	..	..
91 Azerbaijan	26.8	8.4	0	1,159	212	130	177	0.0	..	3.8
92 Turkey	15.6	3.5	0	224	97	51	299	0.0[c]	..	5.5
93 Belize	22.2	4.9	13	28,239	..	..	..	0.0	0	1.1
94 Tunisia	9.0	3.3	0	320	82	10	82	..	..	36.7
MEDIUM HUMAN DEVELOPMENT										
95 Jordan	12.0	3.6	0	0	77	..	134	..	..	22.0
96 Algeria	15.9	3.7	4	564	247	12	65	0.0	..	28.8
97 Sri Lanka	17.3	21.1	2	22,052	41	210	51	0.0	2	21.1
98 Dominican Republic	10.1	3.4	9	3,480	142	33	88	1.4	1	7.0
99 Samoa	..	..	5	0	..	0[b]	..	..	..	..
100 Fiji	..	..	8	10,511	0[b]	0[b]	..	..	0	..
101 China	21.8	6.8	1	93,151	42	422	230	0.0[c]	0	8.6
102 Turkmenistan	..	..	..	..	532	..	170	0.0	..	11.1
103 Thailand	15.7	7.0	2	58,220	121	159	61	1.0	1	17.0
104 Suriname	..	..	1	6,013	0[b]	..	..	0.0	0	..
105 El Salvador	24.6	6.1	7	9,436	116	50	50	0.0	0	6.3
106 Gabon	26.3	8.8	0	149	298	74	..	133.3	..	..
107 Paraguay	..	..	0	7,307	86	52	86	..	1	1.3
108 Bolivia, Plurinational State of	27.1	4.3	5	18,429	378	145	111	0.0	0	2.0
109 Maldives	31.9	25.7	0	522	0[b]	0[b]	0[b]	..	0	..
110 Mongolia	27.5	5.3	4	59,135	199	119	..	..	..	31.5
111 Moldova, Republic of	11.3	3.2	1	6,532	0[b]	78	261	..	..	21.8
112 Philippines	33.8	20.7	10	48,370	182	86	54	0.3	5	2.2

TABLE 7

Human development effects of environmental threats

TABLE 7

	Population under age 5 suffering from		IMPACT OF NATURAL DISASTERS		Deaths due to					Population living on degraded land (%)
	Stunting (%)	Wasting (%)	Number of deaths (average annual per million people)	Population affected (average annual per million people)	Water pollution (per million people)	Indoor air pollution (per million people)	Outdoor air pollution (per million people)	Malaria (per million people)	Dengue (per million people)	
HDI rank	2000–2009ª	2000–2009ª	2001/2010	2001/2010	2004	2004	2004	2009	2001–2010ª	2010
113 Egypt	30.7	6.8	0	5	137	8	213	0.0ᶜ	..	25.3
114 Occupied Palestinian Territory	..	..	0	12	..	..	..	..	..	..
115 Uzbekistan	19.6	4.4	0	5	335	241	148	0.0	..	27.0
116 Micronesia, Federated States of	..	..	43	7,771	0ᵇ	..	..	..	..	..
117 Guyana	18.2	10.8	5	54,311	269	0ᵇ	..	0.0	0	..
118 Botswana	29.1	10.7	0	499	486	270	0ᵇ	3.0	..	22.0
119 Syrian Arab Republic	28.6	10.0	1	6,371	89	39	100	0.0	..	33.3
120 Namibia	29.6	17.5	7	40,481	98	49	0ᵇ	20.5	..	28.5
121 Honduras	29.9	8.6	4	13,628	178	119	89	0.1	1	15.0
122 Kiribati	..	..	0	85	..	..	..	..	..	..
123 South Africa	..	..	1	30,398	260	68	23	0.9	..	17.5
124 Indonesia	40.1	19.6	2	1,364	141	202	144	3.8	5	3.1
125 Vanuatu	..	..	2	24,519	0ᵇ	0ᵇ	..	8.6	..	9.7
126 Kyrgyzstan	18.1	2.7	2	37,899	259	418	80	0.0	..	9.7
127 Tajikistan	33.1	14.9	3	47,642	751	516	47	0.0	..	10.5
128 Viet Nam	30.5	20.2	3	19,794	72	289	81	0.3	1	8.0
129 Nicaragua	18.8	4.3	7	11,487	168	131	19	0.0	2	13.9
130 Morocco	23.1	9.9	1	419	140	17	30	0.0ᶜ	..	39.1
131 Guatemala	54.3	17.7	14	26,888	314	113	40	0.0	0	9.1
132 Iraq	27.5	7.1	0	226	879	23	387	0.0	..	4.5
133 Cape Verde	..	..	1	6,048	214	0ᵇ	0ᵇ	4.1	..	..
134 India	47.9	43.5	2	41,245	405	435	107	0.9	0	9.6
135 Ghana	28.6	14.3	1	2,925	961	308	33	141.8	..	1.4
136 Equatorial Guinea	35.0	10.6	..	..	1,187	..	..	33.8	..	..
137 Congo	31.2	11.8	0	2,102	435	290	145	29.4	..	0.1ᵇ
138 Lao People's Democratic Republic	47.6	31.6	1	15,096	406	459	0ᵇ	0.8	1	4.1
139 Cambodia	39.5	28.8	1	34,829	826	500	23	20.0	1	39.3
140 Swaziland	29.5	6.1	0	117,337	456	274	0ᵇ	11.1	..	..
141 Bhutan	37.5	12.0	2	0	467	311	..	5.6	0	0.1ᵇ
LOW HUMAN DEVELOPMENT										
142 Solomon Islands	32.8	11.5	4	4,672	219	219	..	101.1	..	..
143 Kenya	35.8	16.5	2	27,446	683	412	17	0.0	..	31.0
144 São Tomé and Príncipe	29.3	13.1	..	..	665	0ᵇ	..	141.5	..	..
145 Pakistan	41.5	31.3	3	18,218	380	360	192	0.0	..	4.5
146 Bangladesh	43.2	41.3	6	47,203	469	356	68	0.3	0	11.3
147 Timor-Leste	55.7	40.6	0	1,177	308	..	..	48.2	35	..
148 Angola	50.8	27.5	2	4,989	3,014	2,099	169	567.5	..	3.3
149 Myanmar	40.6	29.6	290	6,551	432	393	96	20.4	3	19.2
150 Cameroon	36.4	16.6	0	204	1,066	664	128	257.8	..	15.3
151 Madagascar	52.8	36.8	5	17,121	1,175	732	35	8.6	..	0.0ᵇ
152 Tanzania, United Republic of	44.4	16.7	0	13,270	865	500	32	18.8	..	25.0
153 Papua New Guinea	43.9	18.1	4	3,987	471	269	..	90.1	0	..
154 Yemen	57.7	43.1	2	135	734	335	55	1.6	..	32.4
155 Senegal	20.1	14.5	0	7,377	1,219	595	170	47.4	..	16.2
156 Nigeria	41.0	26.7	0	1,295	1,304	699	136	48.7	..	11.5
157 Nepal	49.3	38.8	7	9,738	520	326	30	0.3	0	2.3
158 Haiti	29.7	18.9	66	12,565	619	402	65	0.0	..	15.2
159 Mauritania	24.2	16.7	1	41,693	776	405	67	26.9	..	23.8
160 Lesotho	45.2	16.6	0	45,203	195	98	0ᵇ	..	..	63.6
161 Uganda	38.7	16.4	2	9,460	988	716	4	194.5	..	23.5
162 Togo	26.9	20.5	1	4,972	908	605	38	263.6	..	5.1
163 Comoros	46.9	25.0	0	381	479	160	0ᵇ	..	..	..
164 Zambia	45.8	14.9	1	32,196	1,135	777	98	303.5	..	4.6
165 Djibouti	32.6	29.6	6	82,450	630	0ᵇ	252	0.0	..	7.5
166 Rwanda	51.7	18.0	1	9,919	1,854	1,387	33	78.5	..	10.1
167 Benin	44.7	20.2	1	12,662	1,271	770	54	159.9	..	1.6
168 Gambia	27.6	15.8	1	4,106	753	411	137	142.7	..	17.9
169 Sudan	37.9	31.7	1	13,909	477	371	141	32.9	..	39.9
170 Côte d'Ivoire	40.1	16.7	0	96	1,246	705	51	938.3	..	1.3
171 Malawi	53.2	15.5	4	64,924	1,459	1,042	48	451.9	..	19.4

		Population under age 5 suffering from		IMPACT OF NATURAL DISASTERS		Deaths due to					Population living on degraded land (%)
		Stunting (%)	Wasting (%)	Number of deaths (average annual per million people)	Population affected (average annual per million people)	Water pollution (per million people)	Indoor air pollution (per million people)	Outdoor air pollution (per million people)	Malaria (per million people)	Dengue (per million people)	
HDI rank		2000–2009[a]	2000–2009[a]	2001/2010	2001/2010	2004	2004	2004	2009	2001–2010[a]	2010
172	Afghanistan	59.3	32.9	11	9,799	2,499	2,023	15	1.0	..	11.0
173	Zimbabwe	35.8	14.0	0	78,319	532	302	48	1.1	..	29.4
174	Ethiopia	50.7	34.6	2	35,049	1,546	998[b]	34	13.8	..	72.3
175	Mali	38.5	27.9	0	11,678	1,769	1,198	78	156.3	..	59.5
176	Guinea-Bissau	28.1	17.2	0	12,575	2,088	1,268	149	248.6	..	1.0
177	Eritrea	43.7	34.5	0	32,492	741	440	46	4.5	..	58.8
178	Guinea	40.0	20.8	0	3,355	1,080	641	67	60.0	..	0.8
179	Central African Republic	44.6	21.8	0	1,696	1,088	759	0[b]	154.5	..	..
180	Sierra Leone	37.4	21.3	3	361	3,271	2,181	141	302.1	..	..
181	Burkina Faso	44.5	37.4	1	2,723	1,733	1,197	87	499.4	..	73.2
182	Liberia	39.4	20.4	0	924	2,134	1,261	32	444.7	..	..
183	Chad	44.8	33.9	2	33,141	1,509	1,013	84	20.2	..	45.4
184	Mozambique	47.0	21.2	1	25,059	840	548	44	163.9	..	1.9
185	Burundi	63.1	38.9	2	29,916	2,088	1,449	43	87.4	..	18.5
186	Niger	54.8	39.9	0	96,596	3,212	2,192	80	144.2	..	25.0
187	Congo, Democratic Republic of the	45.8	28.2	0	325	1,924	1,356	72	329.7	..	0.1[b]
OTHER COUNTRIES OR TERRITORIES											
	Korea, Democratic People's Rep. of	43.1	20.6	5	7,513	191	..	242	0.0	..	2.9
	Marshall Islands	..	..	0	1,110	..	..	..	..	0	..
	Monaco	..	..	..	..	..	..	..	..	..	..
	Nauru	..	..	..	..	..	..	..	..	..	..
	San Marino	..	..	..	..	..	..	..	..	..	..
	Somalia	42.1	32.8	2	69,471	2,068	1,383	36	4.9	..	26.3
	Tuvalu	10.0	1.6	..	..	..	..	..	..	..	..
Human Development Index groups											
	Very high human development	..	..	8	2,331	..	..	150	..	..	3.2
	High human development	..	..	7	4,890	..	..	159	..	..	7.4
	Medium human development	35.7	24.7	2	54,444	212	357	156	1.8	..	10.0
	Low human development	43.8	28.3	14	19,221	1,035	696[b]	91	92.5	..	18.8
Regions											
	Arab States	29.8	15.2	1	4,529	..	..	146	..	..	24.9
	East Asia and the Pacific	..	..	9	69,648	84	..	..	..	..	..
	Europe and Central Asia	..	..	13	2,357	..	..	240	..	..	8.6
	Latin America and the Caribbean	15.8	4.4	3	8,741	104	..	103	0.2	0	5.3
	South Asia	46.8	41.2	2	36,336	443	424	109	0.7	0	9.9
	Sub-Saharan Africa	42.9	24.5	1	16,966	1,286	798	70	143.7	..	22.1
Least developed countries		45.5	29.6	20	23,357	1,151	794	63	99.0	..	23.3
Small island developing states		..	..	16	25,300	..	..	..	..	..	..
World		..	..	6	32,575	..	..	145	..	..	10.1

TABLE **7**

NOTES
a. Data refer to the most recent year available during the period specified.
b. Less than 1.
c. Less than 0.05.

DEFINITIONS
Population under age 5 suffering from stunting: Percentage of children under age 5 falling two standard deviations or more below the median height-for-age of the reference population.
Population under age 5 suffering from wasting: Percentage of children under age 5 falling two standard deviations or more below the median weight-for-height of the reference population.
Number of deaths due to natural disasters: People confirmed as dead, or missing and presumed dead, as a result of natural disasters, which include drought, extreme temperature, flood, mass movement, wet storm and wildfire.
Population affected by natural disasters: People requiring immediate assistance during a period of emergency as a result of a natural disaster (as defined above), including displaced, evacuated, homeless and injured people.
Deaths due to water pollution: Deaths due to diarrhoea attributable to poor water, sanitation or hygiene.
Deaths due to indoor air pollution: Deaths due to acute respiratory infections (children under age 5), chronic obstructive pulmonary disease (adults over age 30) and lung cancer (adults over age 30) attributable to indoor smoke from solid fuels.

Deaths due to outdoor air pollution: Deaths due to respiratory infections and diseases, lung cancer and selected cardiovascular diseases attributable to outdoor air pollution.
Deaths due to malaria: Deaths due to malaria.
Deaths due to dengue: Deaths due to dengue fever, dengue haemorrhagic fever and dengue shock syndrome.
Population living on degraded land: Percentage of the population living on severely and very severely degraded land. Land degradation estimates consider biomass, soil health, water quantity and biodiversity, and range in severity.

MAIN DATA SOURCES
Columns 1 and 2: WHO (2010b).
Columns 3 and 4: WHO Collaborating Centre for Research on the Epidemiology of Disasters (2011) and UNDESA (2011).
Columns 5–7: HDRO calculations based on WHO (2009) and UNDESA (2011).
Column 8: WHO (2010c).
Column 9: HDRO calculations based on WHO (2011) and UNDESA (2011).
Column 10: FAO (2011b).

TABLE 8

Perceptions about well-being and the environment

HDI rank	WELL-BEING		ENVIRONMENT					
	Overall life satisfaction (0, least satisfied; 10, most satisfied)	Humans cause global warming (% yes)	Global warming threat (% serious[a])	Active in environmental group (% yes)	Satisfaction with government to reduce emissions (% satisfied)	Satisfaction with actions to preserve the environment (% satisfied)	Satisfaction with air quality (% satisfied)	Satisfaction with water quality (% satisfied)
	2006–2010[b]	2006–2010[b]	2006–2010[b]	2006–2010[b]	2006–2010[b]	2006–2010[b]	2006–2010[b]	2006–2010[b]
VERY HIGH HUMAN DEVELOPMENT								
1 Norway	7.6	46.8	43.7	11.6	..	51.5	89.3	95.3
2 Australia	7.5	45.1	70.5	19.5	..	63.8	93.1	93.4
3 Netherlands	7.5	43.6	52.6	15.5	..	66.1	81.5	94.2
4 United States	7.2	35.9	54.7	17.6	43.9	57.8	87.8	89.5
5 New Zealand	7.2	41.1	59.0	24.6	..	74.8	93.0	89.0
6 Canada	7.7	55.8	73.9	19.3	34.0	61.7	84.5	91.3
7 Ireland	7.3	47.6	58.7	..	..	58.9	94.8	90.6
8 Liechtenstein	..					..	..	
9 Germany	6.7	59.7	60.4	12.8	49.1	61.8	86.3	95.0
10 Sweden	7.5	50.1	48.6	11.4	47.6	62.9	89.3	96.7
11 Switzerland	7.5	..	..	..	54.4	63.9	83.7	96.1
12 Japan	6.1	83.7	77.3	14.1	33.0	46.8	78.2	87.8
13 Hong Kong, China (SAR)	5.6	80.0	68.6	..	21.6	41.4	27.8	78.4
14 Iceland	6.9	37.9	34.4	12.5	..	56.0	85.2	96.9
15 Korea, Republic of	6.1	85.3	82.8	9.4	29.3	36.4	72.0	81.6
16 Denmark	7.8	45.3	32.8	18.1	33.5	64.3	91.6	97.4
17 Israel	7.4	40.9	67.4	14.3	..	37.7	58.4	55.7
18 Belgium	6.9	42.6	63.1	21.4	..	56.0	74.0	84.7
19 Austria	7.3	52.7	60.4	..	41.3	63.9	88.0	97.1
20 France	6.8	58.6	65.5	10.0	..	57.5	76.6	83.9
21 Slovenia	6.1	65.1	69.2	..	..	55.9	80.2	90.0
22 Finland	7.4	55.1	41.7	..	..	57.3	89.7	95.0
23 Spain	6.2	63.2	70.9	10.4	..	46.0	82.0	83.6
24 Italy	6.4	57.0	87.0	14.6	..	29.7	69.8	80.6
25 Luxembourg	7.1	53.7	62.1	15.5	..	76.8	85.7	92.3
26 Singapore	6.5	57.2	72.7	19.8	69.8	80.5	91.1	92.9
27 Czech Republic	6.2	45.2	35.5	13.0	26.6	56.6	69.0	89.2
28 United Kingdom	7.0	38.5	58.8	17.2	..	66.8	88.8	94.8
29 Greece	5.8	81.3	95.5	6.0	16.0	19.8	68.7	64.7
30 United Arab Emirates	7.1	29.2	71.0	..	..	89.7	81.5	84.4
31 Cyprus	6.4	79.4	89.4	..	..	45.7	63.0	67.4
32 Andorra	..	..	..	..	..	..	..	..
33 Brunei Darussalam	..	..	..	..	..	..	..	..
34 Estonia	5.1	44.3	36.0	6.8	16.8	45.2	75.0	66.8
35 Slovakia	6.1	56.9	54.7	..	..	42.8	70.4	86.0
36 Malta	5.8	66.8	85.8	13.0	..	53.8	44.4	64.0
37 Qatar	6.8	39.3	67.4	..	..	87.1	80.6	79.6
38 Hungary	4.7	51.0	74.5	6.1	..	32.7	83.5	86.2
39 Poland	5.8	43.2	55.1	6.2	17.5	43.6	80.3	79.6
40 Lithuania	5.1	51.4	49.7	4.3	11.0	29.9	70.2	69.7
41 Portugal	4.9	61.5	90.7	10.0	28.5	37.2	85.7	90.0
42 Bahrain	5.9	35.4	74.3	..	..	65.3	85.6	85.0
43 Latvia	4.7	49.2	39.6	3.9	21.2	38.9	75.1	65.3
44 Chile	6.6	68.5	93.1	7.6	26.8	42.1	69.5	84.5
45 Argentina	6.4	80.4	97.4	4.2	7.0	33.9	75.0	73.8
46 Croatia	5.6	61.5	..	..	..	38.1	75.0	81.2
47 Barbados	..	..	..	..	..	..	..	..
HIGH HUMAN DEVELOPMENT								
48 Uruguay	6.1	72.9	85.6	4.1	32.7	70.5	85.6	92.9
49 Palau	..	..	..	..	..			
50 Romania	4.9	44.9	74.3	3.5	17.4	14.3	71.4	69.5
51 Cuba	5.4	..	..	..	..	54.5	52.8	59.3
52 Seychelles	..		..		..	..		
53 Bahamas	..				..	..	..	..
54 Montenegro	5.5	59.9	..	..	..	50.1	66.2	78.2
55 Bulgaria	4.2	49.3	66.0	..	10.9	19.4	69.3	60.8

HDI rank	WELL-BEING			ENVIRONMENT				
	Overall life satisfaction (0, least satisfied; 10, most satisfied)	Humans cause global warming (% yes)	Global warming threat (% serious[a])	Active in environmental group (% yes)	Satisfaction with government to reduce emissions (% satisfied)	Satisfaction with actions to preserve the environment (% satisfied)	Satisfaction with air quality (% satisfied)	Satisfaction with water quality (% satisfied)
	2006–2010[b]	2006–2010[b]	2006–2010[b]	2006–2010[b]	2006–2010[b]	2006–2010[b]	2006–2010[b]	2006–2010[b]
56 Saudi Arabia	6.3	34.6	78.6	10.6	..	53.3	55.5	60.4
57 Mexico	6.8	70.9	94.5	6.1	22.7	46.8	78.0	67.7
58 Panama	7.3	66.6	97.0	9.2	16.5	44.1	85.2	75.9
59 Serbia	4.5	64.1	..	..	..	28.1	61.9	60.2
60 Antigua and Barbuda	..	..	..	..	..	..	..	..
61 Malaysia	5.6	65.5	71.1	27.3	17.1	64.2	82.3	82.9
62 Trinidad and Tobago	6.7	75.8	98.2	6.2	..	26.3	75.8	74.0
63 Kuwait	6.8	33.3	58.8	..	..	69.2	55.7	67.8
64 Libya	4.9	22.8	64.3	..	..	65.0	69.9
65 Belarus	5.5	48.7	48.6	5.0	20.0	50.6	65.1	62.6
66 Russian Federation	5.4	48.0	48.9	5.7	9.4	18.3	57.6	52.8
67 Grenada	..	..	..	..	..	..	..	..
68 Kazakhstan	5.5	43.8	57.2	8.7	14.3	37.4	61.6	55.7
69 Costa Rica	7.3	80.5	92.2	13.0	33.2	59.6	86.3	88.7
70 Albania	5.3	30.7	..	..	..	27.4	54.5	50.2
71 Lebanon	5.0	68.2	79.7	..	..	23.7	50.5	47.3
72 Saint Kitts and Nevis	..	..	..	..	..	..	..	..
73 Venezuela, Bolivarian Republic of	7.5	61.4	97.9	5.8	27.2	59.8	77.1	67.9
74 Bosnia and Herzegovina	4.7	66.4	..	..	..	22.1	71.2	71.7
75 Georgia	4.1	40.8	78.2	3.6	15.2	38.0	67.4	66.4
76 Ukraine	5.1	60.9	68.2	5.1	3.2	8.8	55.4	51.0
77 Mauritius	..	..	..	..	..	..	..	..
78 Former Yugoslav Republic of Macedonia	4.2	54.8	..	..	..	39.8	73.0	69.7
79 Jamaica	6.2	..	..	..	..	32.9	85.8	88.8
80 Peru	5.6	66.5	96.0	10.7	15.5	35.5	64.7	67.8
81 Dominica	..	..	..	..	..	..	..	..
82 Saint Lucia	..	..	..	..	..	..	..	..
83 Ecuador	5.8	58.6	97.7	9.1	33.0	39.1	60.7	62.4
84 Brazil	6.8	81.3	94.9	7.2	29.6	48.2	68.2	83.1
85 Saint Vincent and the Grenadines	..	..	..	..	..	..	..	..
86 Armenia	4.4	31.6	80.0	9.8	12.4	27.8	58.9	61.3
87 Colombia	6.4	73.1	96.1	12.5	30.6	53.5	73.7	80.2
88 Iran, Islamic Republic of	5.1	61.7	77.6	9.2	..	55.2	66.6	58.4
89 Oman	..	..	..	..	..	..	..	..
90 Tonga	..	..	..	..	..	..	..	..
91 Azerbaijan	4.2	37.3	85.2	13.0	21.1	28.1	65.4	51.0
92 Turkey	5.5	55.1	86.0	12.4	12.9	41.9	72.3	64.1
93 Belize	6.5	59.0	85.7	20.3	..	30.3	70.7	63.3
94 Tunisia	5.1	33.0	58.6	..	..	66.7	66.7	50.3
MEDIUM HUMAN DEVELOPMENT								
95 Jordan	5.6	60.2	68.7	2.9	..	59.4	71.1	59.0
96 Algeria	5.3	39.4	59.6	..	..	42.4	57.1	60.7
97 Sri Lanka	4.0	56.5	76.3	10.0	40.1	61.7	91.7	88.0
98 Dominican Republic	4.7	54.6	92.0	15.8	14.7	53.1	69.2	69.7
99 Samoa	..	..	..	..	..	..	..	..
100 Fiji	..	..	..	..	..	..	..	..
101 China	4.7	47.5	31.7	11.6	33.4	73.0	75.1	73.3
102 Turkmenistan	6.6	29.4	..	..	..	..	80.8	71.2
103 Thailand	6.2	74.9	66.7	43.8	28.7	75.5	83.0	82.8
104 Suriname	..	..	..	..	..	..	..	..
105 El Salvador	6.7	72.0	92.8	12.9	23.3	39.7	74.0	70.4
106 Gabon	..	..	..	..	..	..	..	..
107 Paraguay	5.8	72.4	95.2	8.6	13.5	45.5	87.7	83.9
108 Bolivia, Plurinational State of	5.8	72.5	95.6	11.6	20.1	45.5	72.8	74.4
109 Maldives	..	..	..	..	..	..	..	..
110 Mongolia	4.6	58.6	65.5	11.4	..	16.7	55.4	59.7
111 Moldova, Republic of	5.6	48.6	83.2	11.3	4.5	15.5	62.8	60.1
112 Philippines	4.9	76.2	92.9	30.4	26.8	86.2	82.4	83.4
113 Egypt	4.7	45.1	66.7	4.1	..	25.7	83.2	76.1
114 Occupied Palestinian Territory	4.7	47.4	58.0	11.8	..	28.4	62.3	58.4
115 Uzbekistan	5.1	16.9	67.0	6.2	44.5	71.4	86.5	82.1
116 Micronesia, Federated States of	..	..	..	..	..	..	..	..

TABLE 8

Perceptions about well-being and the environment

		WELL-BEING		ENVIRONMENT				
HDI rank	Overall life satisfaction (0, least satisfied; 10, most satisfied)	Humans cause global warming (% yes)	Global warming threat (% serious[a])	Active in environmental group (% yes)	Satisfaction with government to reduce emissions (% satisfied)	Satisfaction with actions to preserve the environment (% satisfied)	Satisfaction with air quality (% satisfied)	Satisfaction with water quality (% satisfied)
	2006–2010[b]	2006–2010[b]	2006–2010[b]	2006–2010[b]	2006–2010[b]	2006–2010[b]	2006–2010[b]	2006–2010[b]
117 Guyana	6.0	36.2	83.3	27.8	..	34.1	78.7	53.8
118 Botswana	3.6	25.6	79.9	26.1	..	76.1	70.1	72.4
119 Syrian Arab Republic	4.5	53.2	50.0	..	..	50.4	55.7	49.8
120 Namibia	4.9	48.6	75.4	17.6	..	57.9	76.4	81.6
121 Honduras	5.9	54.1	88.9	25.3	12.2	39.3	74.4	69.7
122 Kiribati	..	..	..	..	..	..	..	..
123 South Africa	4.7	37.2	70.4	26.8	34.5	55.7	85.7	53.4
124 Indonesia	5.5	75.5	88.1	18.9	28.7	48.2	82.1	86.9
125 Vanuatu	..	..	..	..	..	..	..	..
126 Kyrgyzstan	5.0	46.4	68.9	15.5	5.7	27.7	87.3	82.9
127 Tajikistan	4.4	16.7	66.7	24.9	31.4	42.8	84.0	65.0
128 Viet Nam	5.3	71.3	68.8	16.8	14.9	67.6	62.9	62.3
129 Nicaragua	5.7	70.6	94.8	14.7	21.5	56.2	82.4	68.5
130 Morocco	4.7	67.4	89.0	3.2	..	32.6	57.9	63.9
131 Guatemala	6.3	74.9	94.6	16.9	14.7	39.1	82.4	66.8
132 Iraq	5.1	40.1	62.3	..	..	15.8	61.5	44.4
133 Cape Verde	..	..	..	..	..	..	..	..
134 India	5.0	49.4	83.4	11.6	41.6	45.4	79.1	62.7
135 Ghana	4.6	58.6	69.0	27.8	33.9	59.9	89.1	72.0
136 Equatorial Guinea	..	..	..	..	..	..	..	..
137 Congo	3.8	58.3	75.4	12.9	..	27.8	65.5	33.5
138 Lao People's Democratic Republic	5.0	71.6	63.3	47.9	..	72.5	88.6	82.7
139 Cambodia	4.1	41.4	89.6	8.6	42.8	85.5	83.1	73.0
140 Swaziland	..	..	..	..	..	..	..	..
141 Bhutan	..	..	..	..	..	..	..	..
LOW HUMAN DEVELOPMENT								
142 Solomon Islands	..	..	..	..	..	..	..	..
143 Kenya	4.3	62.8	82.9	23.7	17.9	63.2	86.0	51.8
144 São Tomé and Príncipe	..	..	..	..	..	..	..	..
145 Pakistan	5.8	32.4	71.6	10.1	24.9	21.1	77.6	55.0
146 Bangladesh	4.9	66.7	92.1	11.9	45.2	47.3	83.1	69.5
147 Timor-Leste	..	..	..	..	..	..	..	..
148 Angola	4.2	70.0	89.2	32.0	..	69.9	59.9	47.4
149 Myanmar	5.3	..	..	..	..	..	88.4	..
150 Cameroon	4.6	57.2	68.2	14.6	15.7	44.2	82.9	51.4
151 Madagascar	4.6	66.8	94.0	6.4	..	43.8	81.0	52.6
152 Tanzania, United Republic of	3.2	52.9	83.5	47.1	30.6	51.3	61.7	34.7
153 Papua New Guinea	..	..	..	..	..	..	..	..
154 Yemen	4.4	65.7	65.8	..	..	30.1	80.0	56.4
155 Senegal	4.4	41.0	72.0	17.3	15.3	30.8	77.9	67.3
156 Nigeria	4.8	37.5	67.5	39.6	10.9	32.2	73.9	46.8
157 Nepal	4.3	59.7	88.6	24.9	19.3	42.4	87.9	81.8
158 Haiti	3.8	12.6	79.6	32.6	..	24.9	38.8	26.0
159 Mauritania	4.8	51.2	74.2	15.9	..	32.1	64.2	57.4
160 Lesotho	..	..	..	..	..	..	..	..
161 Uganda	4.2	52.8	73.1	25.6	33.7	47.9	81.4	59.6
162 Togo	2.8	43.1	77.3	16.7	..	23.4	52.4	33.8
163 Comoros	3.8	34.4	82.1	..	..	36.6	76.7	55.8
164 Zambia	5.3	63.0	66.5	31.4	22.1	45.0	82.4	53.9
165 Djibouti	5.0	51.9	82.4	55.4	..	54.0	69.0	63.5
166 Rwanda	4.0	48.1	74.4	31.2	76.8	90.3	78.5	54.5
167 Benin	3.7	45.7	71.3	12.0	..	34.6	78.1	55.6
168 Gambia	..	..	..	..	..	..	..	..
169 Sudan	4.4	58.5	80.1	19.0	..	38.9	80.3	62.4
170 Côte d'Ivoire	4.2	79.8	..	..	5.8	32.1	74.8	52.1
171 Malawi	5.1	46.9	..	..	60.8	82.3	91.1	61.8
172 Afghanistan	4.8	31.2	75.6	12.2	14.2	45.5	67.1	60.7
173 Zimbabwe	4.7	36.5	53.5	..	10.2	50.1	73.1	62.3
174 Ethiopia	4.4	..	..	..	..	36.6	72.0	29.2
175 Mali	3.8	64.6	93.9	21.4	26.2	44.7	79.5	57.0
176 Guinea-Bissau	..	..	..	..	..	..	..	..
177 Eritrea	..	..	..	..	..	..	..	..

TABLE 8

HDI rank	WELL-BEING		ENVIRONMENT					
	Overall life satisfaction (0, least satisfied; 10, most satisfied)	Humans cause global warming (% yes)	Global warming threat (% serious[a])	Active in environmental group (% yes)	Satisfaction with government to reduce emissions (% satisfied)	Satisfaction with actions to preserve the environment (% satisfied)	Satisfaction with air quality (% satisfied)	Satisfaction with water quality (% satisfied)
	2006–2010[b]	2006–2010[b]	2006–2010[b]	2006–2010[b]	2006–2010[b]	2006–2010[b]	2006–2010[b]	2006–2010[b]
178 Guinea	4.3	39.8	78.4	30.8	..	22.7	54.9	38.3
179 Central African Republic	3.6	67.2	77.3	..	..	63.5	87.0	41.2
180 Sierra Leone	4.1	52.1	74.0	50.8	..	29.8	72.7	36.6
181 Burkina Faso	4.0	52.5	96.3	14.3	..	48.5	73.8	39.4
182 Liberia	4.2	32.1	71.8	43.2	..	34.4	79.4	50.7
183 Chad	3.7	55.0	96.0	29.9	12.9	56.8	57.1	34.9
184 Mozambique	4.7	53.0	87.8	8.4	..	53.6	79.1	71.4
185 Burundi	3.8	45.8	91.6	16.1	28.1	55.7	84.9	52.1
186 Niger	4.1	..	..	14.4	25.9	58.3	90.9	63.0
187 Congo, Democratic Republic of the	4.0	47.7	..	..	16.3	31.0	70.5	22.1
Human Development Index groups								
Very high human development	6.7	54.4	66.3	..	..	52.4	81.7	87.2
High human development	5.9	62.3	..	..	..	40.9	67.5	67.0
Medium human development	4.9	52.1	62.2	..	..	58.2	77.2	69.8
Low human development	4.7	49.6	78.4	..	..	39.9	76.7	51.8
Regions								
Arab States	5.0	48.2	69.1	..	..	37.3	69.7	62.8
East Asia and the Pacific	..	..	..	..	..	..	..	..
Europe and Central Asia	5.3	47.6	62.8	..	..	30.8	67.1	63.2
Latin America and the Caribbean	6.5	72.8	94.8	8.8	..	46.3	71.8	74.6
South Asia	5.0	49.7	82.6	11.6	39.2	43.6	78.8	62.9
Sub-Saharan Africa	4.4	49.5	..	..	..	44.5	75.7	46.6
Least developed countries	4.4	..	..	..	..	45.5	76.8	52.6
Small island developing states	..	..	..	..	..	..	..	..
World	5.3	53.5	67.9	..	..	51.6	76.5	69.2

TABLE
8

NOTES

The typical World Poll survey includes at least 1,000 surveys of randomly selected individuals. In some countries oversamples are collected in major cities or areas of special interest. Additionally, in some large countries, such as China and the Russian Federation, sample sizes of at least 2,000 are collected. Although rare, in some instances the sample size is between 500 and 1,000. Quality control procedures are used to validate that correct samples are selected and that the correct person is randomly selected in each household. Gallup's methodology ensures that the reported data are representative of 95 percent of the world's adult population (ages 15 and older). For further information, see https://worldview.gallup.com/content/methodology.aspx.

a. Very serious and somewhat serious.

b. Data refer to the most recent year available during the period specified.

SURVEY QUESTIONS

Overall life satisfaction: Please imagine a ladder, with steps numbered from zero at the bottom to ten at the top. Suppose we say that the top of the ladder represents the best possible life for you, and the bottom of the ladder represents the worst possible life for you. On which step of the ladder would you say you personally feel you stand at this time, assuming that the higher the step the better you feel about your life, and the lower the step the worse you feel about it? Which step comes closest to the way you feel?

Humans cause global warming: Temperature rise is a part of global warming or climate change. Do you think rising temperatures are a result of human activities? (Asked of those who said they know something or a great deal about global warming and climate change.)

Global warming threat: How serious of a threat is global warming to you and your family? (Asked of those who said they know something or a great deal about global warming and climate change.)

Active in environmental group: Which of these, if any, have you done in the past year? Been active in a group or organization that works to protect the environment?

Satisfaction with government to reduce emissions: Do you think the government of this country is doing enough to reduce emissions of gases released by motor vehicles and factories, or not?

Satisfaction with actions to preserve the environment: In this country, are you satisfied or dissatisfied with the efforts to preserve the environment?

Satisfaction with air quality: In the city or area where you live, are you satisfied or dissatisfied with the quality of air?

Satisfaction with water quality: In the city or area where you live, are you satisfied or dissatisfied with the quality of water?

MAIN DATA SOURCE

Columns 1–8: Gallup (2011).

TABLE 9

Education and health

		EDUCATION					HEALTH							
		Adult literacy rate (% ages 15 and older)	Gross enrolment ratio			Primary education resources		One-year-olds lacking immunization against		Mortality			HIV prevalence Youth (% ages 15–24)		Health-adjusted life expectancy[a] (years)
			Primary (%)	Secondary (%)	Tertiary (%)	Pupil–teacher ratio (pupils per teacher)	School teachers trained to teach (%)	DTP (%)	Measles (%)	Under five (per 1,000 live births)	Adult (per 1,000 people)				
HDI rank											Female	Male	Female	Male	
		2005–2010[b]	2001–2010[b]	2001–2010[b]	2001–2010[b]	2005–2010[b]	2005–2010[b]	2009	2009	2009	2009	2009	2009	2009	2007
VERY HIGH HUMAN DEVELOPMENT															
1	Norway	..	98.7	110.4	73.5	..	..	8	8	3	50	83	<0.1	<0.1	73
2	Australia	..	106.4	132.7	82.3	..	..	8	6	5	45	79	0.1	0.1	74
3	Netherlands	..	106.9	120.8	61.6	..	..	3	4	4	56	75	<0.1	0.1	73
4	United States	..	98.2	93.6	85.9	13.9	..	5	8	8	78	134	0.2	0.3	70
5	New Zealand	..	101.2	126.3	83.5	14.6	..	8	11	6	57	86	<0.1	<0.1	73
6	Canada	..	98.4	102.2	62.3	..	..	20	7	6	53	87	0.1	0.1	73
7	Ireland	..	104.6	118.1	60.6	15.8	..	7	11	4	57	97	0.1	0.1	73
8	Liechtenstein	..	108.9	105.0	34.7	6.5		..	..	2	..	..	..	..	..
9	Germany	..	103.6	101.7	..	13.0	..	7	4	4	53	99	<0.1	0.1	73
10	Sweden	..	96.2	102.6	71.5	9.3	..	2	3	3	47	74	<0.1	<0.1	74
11	Switzerland	..	103.4	96.0	51.2	..	..	5	10	4	43	74	0.1	0.2	75
12	Japan	..	102.3	101.0	58.6	18.1	..	2	6	3	42	86	<0.1	<0.1	76
13	Hong Kong, China (SAR)	..	104.0	82.1	56.6	15.9	95.1	..	..	..	..	..	..	..	..
14	Iceland	..	98.3	108.3	74.3	..	..	4	8	3	43	65	0.1	0.1	74
15	Korea, Republic of	..	104.3	97.2	100.0	22.4	..	6	7	5	46	109	<0.1	<0.1	71
16	Denmark	..	98.6	118.4	77.0	..	..	11	16	4	65	107	0.1	0.1	72
17	Israel	..	111.1	89.1	62.5	13.1	..	7	4	4	45	78	<0.1	0.1	73
18	Belgium	..	103.4	107.5	66.3	11.1	..	1	6	5	59	105	<0.1	<0.1	72
19	Austria	..	98.7	100.4	59.3	11.4	..	17	17	4	50	102	0.2	0.3	72
20	France	..	108.7	113.0	55.3	18.7	..	1	10	4	54	117	0.1	0.2	73
21	Slovenia	99.7	98.4	96.8	87.6	17.2	..	4	5	3	54	131	<0.1	<0.1	71
22	Finland	..	97.4	109.0	90.9	13.6	..	1	2	3	56	124	<0.1	0.1	72
23	Spain	97.7	107.2	120.8	73.4	12.6	..	4	2	4	43	94	0.1	0.2	74
24	Italy	98.9	103.3	100.5	67.2	10.3	..	4	9	4	41	77	<0.1	<0.1	74
25	Luxembourg	..	100.4	96.0	10.0	11.9	..	1	4	3	57	95	0.1	0.1	73
26	Singapore	94.7	..	..	..	17.4	94.3	3	5	3	42	76	<0.1	<0.1	73
27	Czech Republic	..	103.5	95.1	60.9	18.5	..	1	2	4	63	138	<0.1	<0.1	70
28	United Kingdom	..	106.4	99.0	59.0	18.3	..	7	14	6	58	95	0.1	0.2	72
29	Greece	97.2	101.2	101.8	90.8	10.3	..	1	1	3	44	106	0.1	0.1	72
30	United Arab Emirates	90.0	105.4	95.2	30.4	15.6	100.0	8	8	7	66	84	..	..	68
31	Cyprus	97.9	105.4	98.4	52.0	14.2	..	1	13	4	41	81	..	..	70
32	Andorra	..	89.0	80.8	10.3	10.3	100.0	1	2	4	44	94	..	..	74
33	Brunei Darussalam	95.3	106.5	98.2	17.1	11.9	84.1	1	1	7	82	105	..	..	66
34	Estonia	99.8	100.2	99.3	63.7	12.2	..	5	5	6	77	234	0.2	0.3	66
35	Slovakia	..	102.1	92.0	55.8	15.7	..	1	1	7	74	184	<0.1	<0.1	67
36	Malta	92.4	98.6	100.3	32.2	10.5	..	27	18	7	44	76	<0.1	<0.1	72
37	Qatar	94.7	105.9	85.2	10.2	11.2	48.9	1	1	11	48	69	<0.1	<0.1	67
38	Hungary	99.4	99.7	98.8	62.5	10.5	..	1	1	6	99	229	<0.1	<0.1	66
39	Poland	99.5	97.1	98.9	71.4	9.6	..	1	2	7	76	197	<0.1	<0.1	67
40	Lithuania	99.7	97.2	99.2	79.5	12.8	..	2	4	6	95	274	<0.1	<0.1	63
41	Portugal	94.9	112.3	106.8	61.2	11.2	..	4	5	4	54	123	0.2	0.3	71
42	Bahrain	91.4	106.6	96.4	51.2	..	..	2	1	12	87	127	..	..	66
43	Latvia	99.8	98.7	92.7	67.3	10.4	..	5	4	8	105	284	0.1	0.2	64
44	Chile	98.6	106.4	90.4	54.8	24.6	..	3	4	9	59	116	0.1	0.2	70
45	Argentina	97.7	116.7	85.9	69.4	16.3	..	6	1	14	88	160	0.2	0.3	67
46	Croatia	98.8	95.3	95.2	48.9	14.8	..	4	2	5	60	153	<0.1	<0.1	68
47	Barbados	..	..	..	..	14.1	58.1	7	6	11	80	136	1.1	0.9	67
HIGH HUMAN DEVELOPMENT															
48	Uruguay	98.3	113.6	87.9	64.9	15.0	..	5	6	13	84	156	0.2	0.3	67
49	Palau	..	101.4	95.7	37.9	12.5	..	51	25	15	110	229	..	..	64
50	Romania	97.7	99.3	93.5	67.1	15.8	..	3	3	12	90	219	<0.1	0.1	65
51	Cuba	99.8	103.6	89.6	117.8	9.4	100.0	4	4	6	78	120	0.1	0.1	69
52	Seychelles	91.8	106.2	105.0	..	13.8	99.4	1	3	12	108	227	..	..	63
53	Bahamas	..	103.4	93.3	..	15.8	91.1	4	2	12	126	202	3.1	1.4	65

HDI rank	Adult literacy rate (% ages 15 and older)	Gross enrolment ratio			Primary education resources		One-year-olds lacking immunization against		Mortality			HIV prevalence Youth (% ages 15–24)		Health-adjusted life expectancy[a]
		Primary (%)	Secondary (%)	Tertiary (%)	Pupil–teacher ratio (pupils per teacher)	School teachers trained to teach (%)	DTP (%)	Measles (%)	Under five (per 1,000 live births)	Adult (per 1,000 people) Female	Adult Male	Female	Male	(years)
	2005–2010[b]	2001–2010[b]	2001–2010[b]	2001–2010[b]	2005–2010[b]	2005–2010[b]	2009	2009	2009	2009	2009	2009	2009	2007
54 Montenegro	..	106.1	102.1	..	..	..	8	14	9	85	161	..	..	65
55 Bulgaria	98.3	101.5	87.6	53.6	17.3	..	6	4	10	86	205	<0.1	<0.1	66
56 Saudi Arabia	86.1	98.9	96.8	32.8	11.4	91.5	2	2	21	102	186	..	..	62
57 Mexico	93.4	116.6	90.2	27.9	28.1	95.6	11	5	17	88	157	0.1	0.2	67
58 Panama	93.6	109.0	72.7	45.1	23.6	91.5	16	15	23	82	145	0.3	0.4	67
59 Serbia	97.8	97.7	91.5	49.8	16.2	94.2	5	5	7	90	184	0.1	..	65
60 Antigua and Barbuda	99.0	99.8	110.5	14.7	16.2	57.1	1	1	12	158	197	..	..	66
61 Malaysia	92.5	94.6	68.7	36.5	14.6	..	5	5	6	95	175	<0.1	0.1	64
62 Trinidad and Tobago	98.7	104.2	88.8	11.6	17.6	88.0	10	6	35	120	225	0.7	1	62
63 Kuwait	93.9	94.8	89.9	18.9	8.6	100.0	2	3	10	50	66	..	..	69
64 Libya	88.9	110.3	93.5	55.7	..	..	2	2	19	101	175	..	..	64
65 Belarus	99.7	99.0	90.1	77.0	15.0	99.9	4	1	12	117	324	0.1	<0.1	62
66 Russian Federation	99.6	96.8	84.8	77.2	17.4	..	2	2	12	144	391	0.3	0.2	60
67 Grenada	..	107.2	99.1	53.5	17.1	68.8	1	1	15	143	248	..	..	61
68 Kazakhstan	99.7	108.8	98.5	39.5	16.2	..	2	1	29	185	432	0.2	0.1	56
69 Costa Rica	96.1	109.9	96.1	25.3	18.4	87.6	14	19	11	69	115	0.1	0.2	69
70 Albania	95.9	118.9	72.4	19.3	20.2	..	2	3	15	88	126	..	..	64
71 Lebanon	89.6	103.2	82.1	52.5	13.9	..	26	47	12	85	166	<0.1	0.1	62
72 Saint Kitts and Nevis	..	95.7	96.3	18.4	14.3	61.6	1	1	15	90	185	..	..	64
73 Venezuela, Bolivarian Republic of	95.2	103.2	82.1	78.2	14.5	86.3	17	17	18	92	196	..	..	66
74 Bosnia and Herzegovina	97.8	108.9	91.2	37.0	..	..	10	7	14	67	145	..	..	67
75 Georgia	99.7	107.8	87.5	25.8	8.9	94.6	12	17	29	97	235	<0.1	<0.1	64
76 Ukraine	99.7	97.5	94.5	81.1	15.6	99.9	10	6	15	148	395	0.3	0.2	60
77 Mauritius	87.9	100.0	87.2	25.9	21.6	100.0	1	1	17	99	219	0.2	0.3	63
78 Former Yugoslav Republic of Macedonia	97.1	88.9	83.2	40.6	16.4	..	4	4	11	79	144	..	..	66
79 Jamaica	86.4	93.3	91.2	24.2	27.7	..	10	12	31	131	224	0.7	1	64
80 Peru	89.6	109.1	89.1	34.5	20.9	..	7	9	21	96	123	0.1	0.2	67
81 Dominica	..	112.3	105.5	3.5	16.1	57.8	1	1	10	103	192	..	..	66
82 Saint Lucia	..	96.7	95.8	16.0	20.0	87.6	5	1	20	90	188	..	..	66
83 Ecuador	84.2	117.5	75.4	42.4	19.2	77.9	25	34	24	96	173	0.2	0.2	64
84 Brazil	90.0	127.5	100.8	34.4	23.0	..	1	1	21	102	205	..	..	64
85 Saint Vincent and the Grenadines	..	106.9	109.1	..	17.0	79.6	1	1	12	110	204	..	..	63
86 Armenia	99.5	98.5	93.1	50.1	19.3	77.5	7	4	22	103	246	<0.1	<0.1	61
87 Colombia	93.2	120.2	94.6	37.0	29.3	100.0	8	5	19	80	166	0.1	0.2	66
88 Iran, Islamic Republic of	85.0	102.8	83.1	36.5	20.3	98.4	1	1	31	90	144	<0.1	<0.1	61
89 Oman	86.6	83.9	91.3	26.4	11.8	100.0	2	3	12	85	157	<0.1	<0.1	65
90 Tonga	99.0	111.8	102.7	6.4	22.3	..	1	1	19	233	135	..	..	63
91 Azerbaijan	99.5	95.1	99.4	19.1	11.1	99.9	27	33	34	134	221	0.1	<0.1	59
92 Turkey	90.8	99.3	82.0	38.4	..	..	4	3	20	73	134	<0.1	<0.1	66
93 Belize	..	121.9	75.6	11.2	22.6	42.5	3	3	18	129	202	1.8	0.7	60
94 Tunisia	77.6	108.2	90.2	34.4	17.0	..	1	2	21	70	129	<0.1	<0.1	66
MEDIUM HUMAN DEVELOPMENT														
95 Jordan	92.2	96.8	88.2	40.7	..	..	2	5	25	111	195	..	..	63
96 Algeria	72.6	107.7	96.5	30.6	23.0	99.3	7	12	32	106	136	<0.1	0.1	62
97 Sri Lanka	90.6	96.9	87.0	..	23.1	..	3	4	15	82	275	<0.1	<0.1	63
98 Dominican Republic	88.2	106.2	76.8	33.3	25.2	83.6	18	21	32	149	172	0.7	0.3	63
99 Samoa	98.8	100.3	76.1	7.4	31.7	..	28	51	25	167	198	..	..	61
100 Fiji	..	94.2	80.9	15.4	26.0	97.8	1	6	18	157	263	0.1	0.1	62
101 China	94.0	112.7	78.2	24.5	17.2	..	3	6	19	87	142	..	..	66
102 Turkmenistan	99.6	..	..	..	..	..	4	1	45	212	380	..	..	55
103 Thailand	93.5	91.1	77.0	45.0	16.0	..	1	2	14	139	270	..	..	62
104 Suriname	94.6	113.8	75.4	12.3	16.0	100.0	13	12	26	124	217	0.4	0.6	61
105 El Salvador	84.1	115.0	63.6	24.6	32.6	93.2	9	5	17	128	281	0.3	0.4	61
106 Gabon	87.7	134.3	53.1	..	..	..	55	45	69	262	321	3.5	1.4	52
107 Paraguay	94.6	99.4	66.8	36.5	26.5	..	8	9	23	98	168	0.1	0.2	64
108 Bolivia, Plurinational State of	90.7	107.2	81.3	38.3	24.2	..	15	14	51	132	203	0.1	0.1	58
109 Maldives	98.4	111.0	83.7	—	12.7	74.1	2	2	13	70	97	<0.1	<0.1	64
110 Mongolia	97.5	110.1	92.2	52.7	30.4	100.0	5	6	29	141	305	<0.1	<0.1	58
111 Moldova, Republic of	98.5	93.6	88.6	38.3	15.7	..	15	10	17	134	309	0.1	0.1	61
112 Philippines	95.4	110.1	82.5	28.7	33.7	..	13	12	33	130	240	<0.1	<0.1	62

TABLE 9

| HDI rank | | Adult literacy rate (% ages 15 and older) | Gross enrolment ratio | | | Primary education resources | | One-year-olds lacking immunization against | | Mortality | | | HIV prevalence Youth (% ages 15–24) | | Health-adjusted life expectancy[a] |
| | | | Primary (%) | Secondary (%) | Tertiary (%) | Pupil–teacher ratio (pupils per teacher) | School teachers trained to teach (%) | DTP (%) | Measles (%) | Under five (per 1,000 live births) | Adult (per 1,000 people) Female | Male | Female | Male | (years) |
		2005–2010[b]	2001–2010[b]	2001–2010[b]	2001–2010[b]	2005–2010[b]	2005–2010[b]	2009	2009	2009	2009	2009	2009	2009	2007
113	Egypt	66.4	101.1	67.2	28.5	27.2	..	3	5	21	130	215	<0.1	<0.1	60
114	Occupied Palestinian Territory	94.6	78.9	87.1	45.7	28.0	100.0	..	..	30	..	..	..	..	..
115	Uzbekistan	99.3	91.8	103.5	9.8	17.1	100.0	2	5	36	139	220	<0.1	<0.1	59
116	Micronesia, Federated States of	..	110.3	90.5	..	16.6	..	9	14	39	161	183	..	..	62
117	Guyana	..	103.0	103.4	11.2	25.6	63.7	2	3	35	224	286	0.8	0.6	53
118	Botswana	84.1	109.4	81.5	7.6	25.2	97.4	4	6	57	324	372	11.8	5.2	49
119	Syrian Arab Republic	84.2	122.2	74.7	..	17.8	..	20	19	16	95	159	..	..	63
120	Namibia	88.5	112.1	64.7	8.9	30.1	95.6	17	24	48	357	540	5.8	2.3	52
121	Honduras	83.6	116.0	64.5	18.7	33.3	36.4	2	1	30	134	237	0.2	0.3	62
122	Kiribati	..	116.5	84.8	..	25.0	85.4	14	18	46	173	325	..	..	58
123	South Africa	88.7	101.2	93.9	..	30.7	87.4	31	38	62	479	521	13.6	4.5	48
124	Indonesia	92.2	120.8	79.5	23.5	16.6	..	18	18	39	143	234	<0.1	0.1	60
125	Vanuatu	82.0	108.1	47.3	4.8	23.8	100.0	32	48	16	159	200	..	..	61
126	Kyrgyzstan	99.2	95.2	84.1	50.8	24.0	65.7	5	1	37	162	327	0.1	0.1	57
127	Tajikistan	99.7	102.2	84.4	19.8	22.7	88.3	7	11	61	160	183	<0.1	<0.1	57
128	Viet Nam	92.8	104.1	66.9	9.7	19.5	99.6	4	3	24	107	173	0.1	0.1	64
129	Nicaragua	78.0	116.9	67.9	18.0	29.2	72.7	2	1	26	122	210	0.1	0.1	64
130	Morocco	56.1	107.4	55.8	12.9	26.6	100.0	1	2	38	87	126	0.1	0.1	62
131	Guatemala	74.5	113.6	56.6	17.7	29.4	..	8	8	40	151	280	0.3	0.5	60
132	Iraq	78.1	102.5	51.5	15.5	17.0	..	35	31	44	145	292	..	..	54
133	Cape Verde	84.8	98.1	81.5	14.9	23.9	86.5	1	4	28	111	272	..	..	61
134	India	62.8	116.9	60.0	13.5	..	..	34	29	66	169	250	0.1	0.1	56
135	Ghana	66.6	105.2	57.2	8.6	33.1	47.6	6	7	69	253	402	1.3	0.5	50
136	Equatorial Guinea	93.3	83.2	26.2	..	27.2	45.3	67	49	145	355	373	5	1.9	46
137	Congo	..	119.5	43.1	6.4	64.4	89.0	9	24	128	320	409	2.6	1.2	48
138	Lao People's Democratic Republic	72.7	111.8	43.9	13.4	30.5	96.9	43	41	59	251	289	0.2	0.1	54
139	Cambodia	77.6	116.5	40.4	7.0	49.1	99.5	6	8	88	190	350	0.1	0.1	53
140	Swaziland	86.9	107.9	53.3	4.4	32.4	94.0	5	5	73	560	674	15.6	6.5	42
141	Bhutan	52.8	109.1	61.7	6.6	27.7	91.5	4	2	79	194	256	<0.1	0.1	55
LOW HUMAN DEVELOPMENT															
142	Solomon Islands	..	107.3	34.8	..	..	..	19	40	36	119	170	..	..	59
143	Kenya	87.0	112.7	59.5	4.1	46.8	96.8	25	26	84	282	358	4.1	1.8	48
144	São Tomé and Príncipe	88.8	130.4	51.0	4.4	26.2	48.1	2	10	78	104	161	..	..	53
145	Pakistan	55.5	85.1	33.1	5.2	39.7	85.2	15	20	87	189	225	<0.1	0.1	55
146	Bangladesh	55.9	95.1	42.3	7.9	45.8	58.4	6	11	52	222	246	<0.1	<0.1	56
147	Timor-Leste	50.6	112.5	51.2	15.2	29.1	..	28	30	56	154	233	..	..	53
148	Angola	70.0	127.7	23.0	2.8	..	..	27	23	161	353	377	1.6	0.6	45
149	Myanmar	92.0	115.8	53.1	10.7	28.4	98.9	10	13	71	188	275	0.3	0.3	50
150	Cameroon	70.7	113.8	41.5	9.0	46.3	61.8	20	26	154	409	420	3.9	1.6	45
151	Madagascar	64.5	160.4	31.5	3.6	47.9	..	22	36	58	198	273	0.1	0.1	52
152	Tanzania, United Republic of	72.9	104.9	27.4	1.4	53.7	100.0	15	9	108	311	456	3.9	1.7	45
153	Papua New Guinea	60.1	54.9	..	..	35.8	..	36	42	68	221	274	0.8	0.3	56
154	Yemen	62.4	85.4	45.7	10.2	..	..	34	42	66	180	237	..	..	54
155	Senegal	49.7	83.7	30.1	8.0	34.7	..	14	21	93	218	266	0.7	0.3	51
156	Nigeria	60.8	89.5	30.5	10.1	46.3	51.2	58	59	138	365	377	2.9	1.2	42
157	Nepal	59.1	114.9	43.5	5.6	31.9	73.7	18	21	48	159	234	0.1	0.2	55
158	Haiti	48.7	..	..	..	..	..	41	41	87	227	278	1.3	0.6	54
159	Mauritania	57.5	104.4	24.5	3.8	39.1	100.0	36	41	117	262	315	0.3	0.4	51
160	Lesotho	89.7	104.4	45.0	3.6	33.8	57.6	17	15	84	573	676	14.2	5.4	40
161	Uganda	73.2	121.6	27.4	4.1	49.3	89.4	36	32	128	348	539	4.8	2.3	42
162	Togo	56.9	115.2	41.3	5.3	41.3	14.6	11	16	98	278	338	2.2	0.9	51
163	Comoros	74.2	119.4	45.8	5.2	30.2	57.4	17	21	104	229	284	<0.1	<0.1	56
164	Zambia	70.9	112.9	..	..	60.5	..	19	15	141	477	580	8.9	4.2	40
165	Djibouti	..	54.5	30.5	3.5	34.1	100.0	11	27	94	271	326	1.9	0.9	48
166	Rwanda	70.7	150.7	26.7	4.8	68.3	93.9	3	8	111	258	304	1.9	1.3	43
167	Benin	41.7	121.9	36.3	5.8	44.9	71.8	17	28	118	246	385	0.7	0.3	50
168	Gambia	46.5	84.7	55.7	4.6	36.6	..	2	4	103	246	296	2.4	0.9	51
169	Sudan	70.2	74.0	38.0	..	38.4	59.7	16	18	108	275	291	1.3	0.5	50
170	Côte d'Ivoire	55.3	73.6	26.3	8.4	42.1	100.0	19	33	119	456	528	1.5	0.7	47
171	Malawi	73.7	119.3	29.5	—	..	..	7	8	110	496	691	6.8	3.1	44

TABLE 9

HDI rank	Adult literacy rate (% ages 15 and older) 2005–2010[b]	Gross enrolment ratio Primary (%) 2001–2010[b]	Gross enrolment ratio Secondary (%) 2001–2010[b]	Gross enrolment ratio Tertiary (%) 2001–2010[b]	Primary education resources Pupil–teacher ratio (pupils per teacher) 2005–2010[b]	Primary education resources School teachers trained to teach (%) 2005–2010[b]	One-year-olds lacking immunization against DTP (%) 2009	One-year-olds lacking immunization against Measles (%) 2009	Mortality Under five (per 1,000 live births) 2009	Mortality Adult (per 1,000 people) Female 2009	Mortality Adult (per 1,000 people) Male 2009	HIV prevalence Youth (% ages 15–24) Female 2009	HIV prevalence Youth (% ages 15–24) Male 2009	Health-adjusted life expectancy[a] (years) 2007
172 Afghanistan	..	103.9	43.8	3.6	42.8		17	24	199	352	440	..	..	36
173 Zimbabwe	91.9	..	..	..	..	..	27	24	90	574	672	6.9	3.3	39
174 Ethiopia	29.8	102.5	34.4	3.6	57.9	84.6	21	25	104	379	445	..	..	50
175 Mali	26.2	97.2	41.6	6.0	50.1	50.0	26	29	191	218	357	0.5	0.2	42
176 Guinea-Bissau	52.2	119.7	35.9	2.9	62.2	..	32	24	193	369	431	2	0.8	42
177 Eritrea	66.6	48.3	31.8	2.0	38.5	92.2	1	5	55	179	249	0.4	0.2	55
178 Guinea	39.5	89.8	37.0	9.2	43.7	73.1	43	49	142	337	474	0.9	0.4	47
179 Central African Republic	55.2	91.3	12.4	2.5	84.3	..	46	38	171	470	461	2.2	1	42
180 Sierra Leone	40.9	85.1	26.5	2.0	..	..	25	29	192	363	414	1.5	0.6	35
181 Burkina Faso	28.7	79.2	21.4	3.4	47.8	86.1	18	25	166	262	443	0.8	0.5	43
182 Liberia	59.1	90.6	..	..	24.3	40.2	36	36	112	337	389	0.7	0.3	48
183 Chad	33.6	89.7	24.1	2.0	60.9	34.6	77	77	209	384	412	2.5	1	40
184 Mozambique	55.1	115.7	25.5	1.5	58.5	75.9	24	23	142	434	557	8.6	3.1	42
185 Burundi	66.6	146.6	21.2	2.7	51.4	91.2	8	9	166	407	424	2.1	1	43
186 Niger	28.7	66.6	13.3	1.4	38.6	96.7	30	27	160	224	229	0.5	0.2	44
187 Congo, Democratic Republic of the	66.8	90.3	36.7	6.0	37.3	93.4	23	24	199	331	442	..	..	45
OTHER COUNTRIES OR TERRITORIES														
Korea, Democratic People's Rep. of	100.0	..	..	..	..	..	7	2	33	126	207	..	..	59
Marshall Islands	..	90.3	78.2	15.9	..	..	7	6	35	386	429	..	..	52
Monaco	..	127.7	153.4	..	..	..	1	1	4	51	112	..	..	73
Nauru	..	93.0	62.9	..	22.4	74.2	1	1	44	303	448	..	..	55
San Marino	..	92.9	95.6	..	6.2	..	8	8	2	48	57	..	..	75
Somalia	..	32.6	7.7	—	35.5	..	69	76	180	350	382	0.6	0.4	45
Tuvalu	..	100.1	79.5	..	..	..	11	10	35	280	255	..	..	58
Human Development Index groups														
Very high human development	..	102.7	99.7	72.9	0.0	..	5	7	6	60	114	..	..	72
High human development	93.2	110.3	90.4	49.3	0.0	..	6	5	19	106	223	..	..	64
Medium human development	81.9	113.3	69.7	20.5	0.0	..	19	18	44	131	204	..	..	61
Low human development	59.8	96.5	35.0	6.2	0.0	..	26	28	117	287	346	..	..	48
Regions														
Arab States	72.9	95.0	66.5	25.8	0.0	..	16	18	49	139	198	..	..	59
East Asia and the Pacific	93.5	112.3	76.9	24.9	0.0	..	7	9	26	103	168	..	..	64
Europe and Central Asia	98.0	98.5	90.7	57.1	0.0	..	4	4	19	118	281	..	..	62
Latin America and the Caribbean	91.0	116.8	90.7	42.7	0.0	91.7	8	7	22	99	181	..	..	65
South Asia	62.8	109.8	55.9	13.1	0.0	77.1	27	25	69	173	245	..	..	56
Sub-Saharan Africa	61.6	100.2	35.3	5.9	0.0	76.0	30	32	129	355	430	..	..	45
Least developed countries	59.2	99.6	35.6	5.7	0.0	..	21	23	120	282	357	..	..	49
Small island developing states	..	95.1	76.9	51.6	0.0	..	24	26	57	155	207	..	..	61
World	80.9	106.9	68.4	27.6	0.0	..	18	18	58	137	211	..	..	61

TABLE
9

NOTES

a. Based on methods described in the statistical annex of WHO (2007). Estimates for 2007 have been revised to take into account the Global Burden of Disease estimates for 2004 and may not be entirely comparable with those for 2002 published in WHO (2004).

b. Data refer to the most recent year available during the period specified.

DEFINITIONS

Adult literacy rate: Percentage of the population ages 15 and older who can, with understanding, both read and write a short simple statement on their everyday life.

Gross enrolment ratio: Total enrolment in a given level of education (primary, secondary or tertiary), regardless of age, expressed as a percentage of the official school-age population for the same level of education.

Pupil–teacher ratio: Average number of pupils (students) per teacher in primary education in a given school year.

School teachers trained to teach: Percentage of primary school teachers who have received the minimum organized teacher training (pre-service or in-service) required for teaching at the primary level of education.

One-year-olds lacking immunization against DTP: Percentage of one-year-olds who have not received three doses of the combined diphtheria, tetanus toxoid and pertussis (DTP) vaccine.

One-year-olds lacking immunization against measles: Percentage of one-year-olds who have not received at least one dose of a measles vaccine.

Under-five mortality: Probability of dying between birth and exactly age 5, expressed per 1,000 live births.

Adult mortality: Probability that a 15-year-old person will die before reaching age 60, expressed per 1,000 adults.

HIV prevalence: Percentage of the population ages 15–24 who are infected with HIV.

Health-adjusted life expectancy at birth: Average number of years that a person can expect to live in "full health" taking into account years lived in less than full health due to disease and injury.

MAIN DATA SOURCES

Columns 1–6: UNESCO Institute for Statistics (2011).
Columns 7, 8, 10, 11 and 14: WHO (2010a).
Columns 9, 12 and 13: UNICEF (2011).

TABLE 10

Population and economy

	POPULATION							ECONOMY					
HDI rank	Total (millions)		Average annual growth (%)		Urban[a] (% of total)	Median age (years)	Dependency ratio (%)	GDP per capita (PPP $)	Foreign direct investment net inflows (% of GDP)	Net official development assistance received (% of GDP)	Remittance inflows (% of GDP)	Public expenditure on education (% of GDP)	Total expenditure on health (% of GDP)
	2011	2030	1990/1995	2010/2015	2011	2010	2011	2009	2009	2009	2009	2006–2009[b]	2009
VERY HIGH HUMAN DEVELOPMENT													
1 Norway	4.9[c]	5.6[c]	0.5[c]	0.7[c]	79.8[c]	38.7	50.7	56,214	3.0	..	0.2	9.7	9.7
2 Australia	22.6[d]	27.8[d]	1.2[d]	1.3[d]	89.3[d]	36.9	48.6	39,539	2.4	..	0.4	8.5	8.5
3 Netherlands	16.7	17.3	0.7	0.3	83.3	40.7	49.8	40,676	4.2	..	0.5	10.8	10.8
4 United States	313.1	361.7	1.0	0.9	82.6	36.9	50.1	45,989	1.0	..	0.0	16.2	16.2
5 New Zealand	4.4	5.2	1.6	1.0	86.2	36.6	50.9	28,993	–1.0	..	0.5	9.7	9.7
6 Canada	34.3	39.8	1.1	0.9	80.7	39.9	44.5	37,808	1.5	..	..	10.9	10.9
7 Ireland	4.5	5.4	0.4	1.1	62.3	34.7	50.0	40,697	11.1	..	0.3	9.7	9.7
8 Liechtenstein	0.0	0.0	1.3	0.8	14.3	..	..	..	..	..	..	..	..
9 Germany	82.2	79.5	0.7	–0.2	74.0	44.3	51.5	36,338	1.2	..	0.3	11.3	11.3
10 Sweden	9.4	10.4	0.6	0.6	84.8	40.7	54.2	37,377	2.8	..	0.2	9.9	9.9
11 Switzerland	7.7	8.1	1.0	0.4	73.7	41.4	47.4	45,224	5.6	..	0.5	11.3	11.3
12 Japan	126.5	120.2	0.4	–0.1	67.0	44.7	57.9	32,418	0.2	..	0.0	8.3	8.3
13 Hong Kong, China (SAR)	7.1	8.5	1.2	1.0	100.0	41.8	32.1	43,229	24.9	..	0.2	..	..
14 Iceland	0.3	0.4	1.0	1.2	93.5	34.8	49.2	36,795	0.5	..	0.2	8.2	8.2
15 Korea, Republic of	48.4	50.3	0.8	0.4	83.3	37.9	38.1	27,100	0.2	..	0.3	6.5	6.5
16 Denmark	5.6	5.9	0.4	0.3	87.1	40.6	53.3	37,720	0.9	..	0.3	11.2	11.2
17 Israel	7.6	9.8	3.4	1.7	91.9	30.1	61.0	27,656	2.0	..	0.6	7.6	7.6
18 Belgium	10.8	11.2	0.3	0.3	97.4	41.2	52.7	36,313	–8.2	..	2.2	11.8	11.8
19 Austria	8.4	8.6	0.7	0.2	67.8	41.8	47.9	38,818	2.3	..	0.9	11.0	11.0
20 France	63.1	68.5	0.4	0.5	85.9	39.9	54.9	33,674	2.3	..	0.6	11.7	11.7
21 Slovenia	2.0	2.1	0.4	0.2	49.5	41.7	44.3	27,133	–1.2	..	0.6	9.1	9.1
22 Finland	5.4	5.6	0.5	0.3	85.4[e]	42.0	52.1	35,265	0.0	..	0.4	9.7	9.7
23 Spain	46.5	50.0	0.3	0.6	77.6	40.1	47.6	32,150	0.4	..	0.7	9.7	9.7
24 Italy	60.8	60.9	0.0	0.2	68.6	43.2	53.1	32,430	1.4	..	0.1	9.5	9.5
25 Luxembourg	0.5	0.6	1.3	1.4	85.4	38.9	46.1	83,820	372.6	..	3.0	7.8	7.8
26 Singapore	5.2	6.0	2.9	1.1	100.0	37.6	35.6	50,633	9.2	..	..	3.9	3.9
27 Czech Republic	10.5	10.8	0.0	0.3	73.6	39.4	41.6	25,581	1.4	..	0.6	7.6	7.6
28 United Kingdom	62.4	69.3	0.3	0.6	79.8	39.8	52.0	35,155	3.4	..	0.3	9.3	9.3
29 Greece	11.4	11.6	1.0	0.2	61.7	41.4	50.1	29,617	0.7	..	0.6	10.6	10.6
30 United Arab Emirates	7.9	10.5	5.2	2.2	84.4	30.1	21.0	57,744	..	..	..	2.8	2.8
31 Cyprus	1.1	1.3	2.2	1.1	70.5	34.2	41.4	30,848	23.6	..	0.6	6.0	6.0
32 Andorra	0.1	0.1	4.1	1.5	87.6	..	..	..	..	..	..	7.5	7.5
33 Brunei Darussalam	0.4	0.5	2.8	1.7	76.1	28.9	41.9	..	..	..	..	3.0	3.0
34 Estonia	1.3	1.3	–1.7	–0.1	69.5	39.7	49.1	19,693	9.2	..	1.7	7.0	7.0
35 Slovakia	5.5	5.5	0.4	0.2	54.9	36.9	37.6	22,882	0.0	..	1.9	8.5	8.5
36 Malta	0.4	0.4	1.0	0.3	94.8	39.5	41.4	24,814	11.2	0.3[f]	0.6	7.5	7.5
37 Qatar	1.9	2.4	1.1	2.9	95.9	31.6	17.7	91,379	..	..	..	2.5	2.5
38 Hungary	10.0	9.6	–0.1	–0.2	68.5	39.8	45.8	20,312	2.2	..	1.7	7.3	7.3
39 Poland	38.3	37.8	0.2	0.0	60.9	38.0	40.0	18,905	3.2	..	1.9	7.1	7.1
40 Lithuania	3.3	3.1	–0.4	–0.4	67.1	39.3	44.9	17,308	0.6	..	3.1	6.6	6.6
41 Portugal	10.7	10.3	0.4	0.0	61.3	41.0	49.6	24,920	1.2	..	1.5	11.3	11.3
42 Bahrain	1.3	1.7	2.5	2.1	88.7	30.1	28.8	..	1.2	0.5[f]	..	4.5	4.5
43 Latvia	2.2	2.1	–1.3	–0.4	67.7	40.2	46.8	16,437	0.4	..	2.3	6.5	6.5
44 Chile	17.3	19.5	1.8	0.9	89.2	32.1	45.4	14,311	7.8	0.1	0.0	8.2	8.2
45 Argentina	40.8	46.8	1.3	0.9	92.6	30.4	54.7	14,538	1.3	0.0	0.2	9.5	9.5
46 Croatia	4.4	4.2	0.7	–0.2	58.0	41.5	47.6	19,986	4.7	0.3	2.3	7.8	7.8
47 Barbados	0.3	0.3	0.3	0.2	45.1	37.5	40.2	..	8.3	–0.1	3.2	6.8	6.8
HIGH HUMAN DEVELOPMENT													
48 Uruguay	3.4	3.6	0.7	0.3	92.6	33.7	56.6	13,189	4.0	0.2	0.3	7.4	7.4
49 Palau	0.0	0.0	2.7	0.8	84.3	..	..	..	..	27.9	..	11.2	11.2
50 Romania	21.4	20.3	–0.5	–0.2	58.0	38.5	43.3	14,278	3.9	..	3.1	5.4	5.4
51 Cuba	11.3	11.0	0.6	0.0	75.2	38.4	42.0	..	..	0.2[f]	..	11.8	11.8
52 Seychelles	0.1	0.1	1.0	0.3	55.9	..	..	19,587	32.5	3.5	1.6	4.0	4.0
53 Bahamas	0.3	0.4	1.8	1.1	84.3	30.9	41.3	..	..	..	..	7.2	7.2
54 Montenegro	0.6	0.6	1.1	0.1	61.5	35.9	46.4	13,086	32.0	1.8	..	9.3	9.3
55 Bulgaria	7.4	6.5	–1.1	–0.7	71.7	41.6	46.3	13,870	9.4	..	3.2	7.4	7.4

		POPULATION						ECONOMY					
		Total (millions)		Average annual growth (%)		Urban[a] (% of total)	Median age (years)	Dependency ratio (%)	GDP per capita (PPP $)	Foreign direct investment net inflows (% of GDP)	Net official development assistance received (% of GDP)	Remittance inflows (% of GDP)	Public expenditure on education (% of GDP)	Total expenditure on health (% of GDP)
HDI rank		2011	2030	1990/1995	2010/2015	2011	2010	2011	2009	2009	2009	2009	2006–2009[b]	2009
56	Saudi Arabia	28.1	38.5	2.7	2.1	82.3	25.9	49.5	23,480	2.8	0.0[f]	0.1	5.0	5.0
57	Mexico	114.8	135.4	1.8	1.1	78.1	26.6	54.1	14,258	1.7	0.0	2.5	6.5	6.5
58	Panama	3.6	4.5	2.1	1.5	75.5	27.3	54.7	13,057	7.2	0.3	0.7	8.3	8.3
59	Serbia	9.9	9.5	1.3	−0.1	56.4	37.6	46.7	11,893	4.5	1.4	12.6	9.9	9.9
60	Antigua and Barbuda	0.1	0.1	2.0	1.0	30.4	..	..	18,778	11.4	0.6	2.2	5.1	5.1
61	Malaysia	28.9	37.3	2.6	1.6	73.0	26.0	53.4	14,012	0.7	0.1	0.6	4.8	4.8
62	Trinidad and Tobago	1.3	1.4	0.7	0.3	14.2	30.8	38.3	25,572	3.3	0.0	0.5	5.7	5.7
63	Kuwait	2.8	4.0	−5.0	2.4	98.4	28.2	41.3	..	..	..	..	3.3	3.3
64	Libya	6.4	7.8	1.9	0.8	78.1	25.9	54.1	16,502	2.7	0.1	0.0	3.9	3.9
65	Belarus	9.6	8.9	0.0	−0.3	75.2	38.3	40.2	13,040	3.8	0.2	0.7	5.8	5.8
66	Russian Federation	142.8	136.4	0.1	−0.1	73.2	37.9	39.1	18,932	3.0	..	0.4	5.4	5.4
67	Grenada	0.1	0.1	0.8	0.4	39.7	25.0	52.6	8,362	14.5	8.3	8.6	7.4	7.4
68	Kazakhstan	16.2	18.9	−0.7	1.0	58.8	29.0	46.4	11,510	11.8	0.3	0.1	4.5	4.5
69	Costa Rica	4.7	5.7	2.4	1.4	64.9	28.4	45.1	11,106	4.6	0.4	1.8	10.5	10.5
70	Albania	3.2	3.3	−0.9	0.3	52.9	30.0	46.9	8,716	8.1	3.0	11.0	6.9	6.9
71	Lebanon	4.3	4.7	3.2	0.7	87.4	29.1	46.3	13,070	13.9	1.8	21.9	8.1	8.1
72	Saint Kitts and Nevis	0.1	0.1	1.1	1.2	32.6	..	..	14,527	24.5	1.1	7.4	6.0	6.0
73	Venezuela, Bolivarian Republic of	29.4	37.0	2.3	1.5	93.6	26.1	53.6	12,323	−1.0	0.0	0.0	6.0	6.0
74	Bosnia and Herzegovina	3.8	3.5	−5.1	−0.2	49.2	39.4	40.8	8,578	1.4	2.4	12.2	10.9	10.9
75	Georgia	4.3	3.8	−1.5	−0.6	52.8	37.3	44.6	4,774	6.1	8.6	6.6	10.1	10.1
76	Ukraine	45.2	40.5	−0.2	−0.5	69.1	39.3	42.5	6,318	4.2	0.6	4.5	7.0	7.0
77	Mauritius	1.3	1.4	1.4	0.5	41.9[g]	32.4	39.8	12,838	3.0	1.8	2.5	5.7	5.7
78	Former Yugoslav Republic of Macedonia	2.1	2.0	0.6	0.1	59.4	35.9	41.4	11,159	2.7	2.2	4.1	6.9	6.9
79	Jamaica	2.8	2.8	0.8	0.4	52.1	27.0	57.4	7,633	4.5	1.3	15.8	5.1	5.1
80	Peru	29.4	35.5	1.9	1.1	77.3	25.6	55.7	8,629	3.7	0.4	1.8	4.6	4.6
81	Dominica	0.1	0.1	0.1	0.0	67.4	..	..	8,883	13.3	10.1	6.1	6.4	6.4
82	Saint Lucia	0.2	0.2	1.3	1.0	28.1	27.4	47.7	9,605	16.5	4.7	2.9	8.1	8.1
83	Ecuador	14.7	17.9	2.1	1.3	67.6	25.5	57.0	8,268	0.6	0.4	4.4	6.1	6.1
84	Brazil	196.7	220.5	1.6	0.8	86.9	29.1	47.3	10,367	1.6	0.0	0.3	9.0	9.0
85	Saint Vincent and the Grenadines	0.1	0.1	0.1	0.0	49.8	27.9	49.1	9,154	18.9	5.5	5.1	5.6	5.6
86	Armenia	3.1	3.1	−1.9	0.3	64.3	32.1	45.2	5,279	8.9	5.9	8.8	4.7	4.7
87	Colombia	46.9	56.9	1.9	1.3	75.4	26.8	51.9	8,959	3.1	0.5	1.8	6.4	6.4
88	Iran, Islamic Republic of	74.8	84.4	1.7	1.0	71.3	27.1	38.9	11,558	0.9	0.0	0.3	5.5	5.5
89	Oman	2.8	3.6	3.6	1.9	73.3	25.3	42.4	..	4.8	0.1[f]	0.1[f]	3.0	3.0
90	Tonga	0.1	0.1	0.2	0.4	23.5	21.3	76.4	4,466	4.7	12.4	27.9	6.2	6.2
91	Azerbaijan	9.3	10.8	1.5	1.2	52.1	29.5	38.0	9,638	1.1	0.6	3.0	5.8	5.8
92	Turkey	73.6	86.7	1.7	1.1	70.1	28.3	47.3	13,668	1.4	0.2	0.2	6.7	6.7
93	Belize	0.3	0.4	2.9	2.0	52.7	21.8	62.3	6,628	7.0	2.0[f]	5.9	4.9	4.9
94	Tunisia	10.6	12.2	1.7	1.0	67.7	28.9	43.4	8,273	4.0	1.3	5.0	6.2	6.2
MEDIUM HUMAN DEVELOPMENT														
95	Jordan	6.3	8.4	5.0	1.9	78.6	20.7	69.0	5,597	9.5	3.0	14.3	9.3	9.3
96	Algeria	36.0	43.5	2.2	1.4	67.1	26.2	45.8	8,172	2.0	0.2	1.5	5.8	5.8
97	Sri Lanka	21.0	23.1	1.0	0.8	14.3	30.7	49.9	4,772	1.0	1.7	8.0	4.0	4.0
98	Dominican Republic	10.1	12.1	1.9	1.2	69.8	25.1	58.8	8,433	4.4	0.3	7.4	5.9	5.9
99	Samoa	0.2	0.2	0.8	0.5	20.1	20.9	73.8	4,405	0.6	16.1	25.1	7.0	7.0
100	Fiji	0.9	1.0	1.3	0.8	52.3	26.4	51.5	4,526	2.0	2.5	5.4	3.4	3.4
101	China	1,347.6[h]	1,393.1[h]	1.2[h]	0.4[h]	47.8[h]	34.5	37.9	6,828	1.6	0.0	1.0	4.6	4.6
102	Turkmenistan	5.1	6.2	2.7	1.2	50.0	24.5	49.0	7,242	6.8	0.2	..	2.3	2.3
103	Thailand	69.5	73.3	0.9	0.5	34.4	34.2	41.3	7,995	1.9	0.0	0.6	4.3	4.3
104	Suriname	0.5	0.6	1.4	0.9	69.8	27.6	53.1	..	..	3.7[f]	0.1	7.6	7.6
105	El Salvador	6.2	7.1	1.4	0.6	64.8	23.2	62.4	6,629	2.0	1.4	16.5	6.4	6.4
106	Gabon	1.5	2.1	3.1	1.9	86.4	21.6	64.9	14,419	0.3	0.8	0.1	3.5	3.5
107	Paraguay	6.6	8.7	2.4	1.7	62.1	23.1	62.1	4,523	1.4	1.1	4.3	7.1	7.1
108	Bolivia, Plurinational State of	10.1	13.4	2.3	1.6	67.0	21.7	67.7	4,419	2.4	4.4	6.2	5.0	5.0
109	Maldives	0.3	0.4	2.5	1.3	41.3	24.6	45.0	5,476	7.6	2.4	0.3	8.0	8.0
110	Mongolia	2.8	3.5	1.0	1.5	62.5	25.4	46.8	3,522	14.8	9.4	4.8	4.7	4.7
111	Moldova, Republic of	3.5	3.1	−0.1	−0.7	47.7	35.2	38.7	2,854	2.4	4.3	22.4	11.9	11.9
112	Philippines	94.9	126.3	2.3	1.7	49.1	22.2	63.2	3,542	1.2	0.2	12.3	3.8	3.8
113	Egypt	82.5	106.5	1.8	1.7	43.5	24.4	57.4	5,673	3.6	0.5	3.8	5.0	5.0
114	Occupied Palestinian Territory	4.2	6.8	4.4	2.8	74.4	18.1	81.0	..	..	25.3[f]	17.6	..	..
115	Uzbekistan	27.8	33.4	2.2	1.1	36.3	24.2	49.8	2,875	2.3	0.6	..	5.2	5.2
116	Micronesia, Federated States of	0.1	0.1	2.1	0.5	22.8	20.8	66.2	3,088	..	42.0	..	13.8	13.8

TABLE
10

HDI rank		Total (millions) 2011	Total (millions) 2030	Average annual growth (%) 1990/1995	Average annual growth (%) 2010/2015	Urban[a] (% of total) 2011	Median age (years) 2010	Dependency ratio (%) 2011	GDP per capita (PPP $) 2009	Foreign direct investment net inflows (% of GDP) 2009	Net official development assistance received (% of GDP) 2009	Remittance inflows (% of GDP) 2009	Public expenditure on education (% of GDP) 2006–2009[b]	Total expenditure on health (% of GDP) 2009
117	Guyana	0.8	0.8	0.1	0.2	28.7	23.8	58.2	3,240	7.1	8.5	12.5	8.1	8.1
118	Botswana	2.0	2.3	2.7	1.1	61.8	22.9	57.2	13,384	2.1	2.5	0.7	10.3	10.3
119	Syrian Arab Republic	20.8	27.9	2.8	1.7	56.2	21.1	67.1	4,730	2.7	0.5	2.6	2.9	2.9
120	Namibia	2.3	3.0	3.1	1.7	38.6	21.2	65.9	6,410	5.3	3.6	0.1	5.9	5.9
121	Honduras	7.8	10.7	2.6	2.0	52.2	21.0	68.3	3,842	3.5	3.3	17.6	6.0	6.0
122	Kiribati	0.1	0.1	1.5	1.5	44.0	..	..	2,432	1.7	15.6	6.4	12.2	12.2
123	South Africa	50.5	54.7	2.4	0.5	62.2	24.9	53.0	10,278	1.9	0.4	0.3	8.5	8.5
124	Indonesia	242.3	279.7	1.6	1.0	44.6	27.8	47.8	4,199	0.9	0.2	1.3	2.4	2.4
125	Vanuatu	0.2	0.4	2.8	2.4	26.0	20.6	70.8	4,438	5.3	16.5	1.0	4.0	4.0
126	Kyrgyzstan	5.4	6.7	0.9	1.1	34.5	23.8	52.3	2,283	4.1	7.1	21.7	6.8	6.8
127	Tajikistan	7.0	9.0	1.7	1.5	26.4	20.4	66.6	1,972	0.3	8.3	35.1	5.3	5.3
128	Viet Nam	88.8	101.5	2.0	1.0	31.0	28.2	41.3	2,953	8.4	4.4	7.4	7.2	7.2
129	Nicaragua	5.9	7.2	2.4	1.4	57.6	22.1	62.7	2,641	7.1	13.1	12.5	9.5	9.5
130	Morocco	32.3	37.5	1.7	1.0	58.8	26.3	49.8	4,494	2.2	1.0	6.9	5.5	5.5
131	Guatemala	14.8	22.7	2.3	2.5	49.9	18.9	83.4	4,720	1.6	1.0	10.8	7.1	7.1
132	Iraq	32.7	55.3	3.1	3.1	66.1	18.3	85.6	3,548	1.6	4.5	0.1[f]	3.9	3.9
133	Cape Verde	0.5	0.6	2.5	0.9	61.8	22.8	58.1	3,644	7.7	13.1	9.4	3.9	3.9
134	India	1,241.5	1,523.5	2.0	1.3	30.3	25.1	54.4	3,296	2.5	0.2	3.6	4.2	4.2
135	Ghana	25.0	36.5	2.8	2.3	52.2	20.5	73.3	1,552	6.4	6.1	0.4	6.9	6.9
136	Equatorial Guinea	0.7	1.1	3.4	2.7	39.9	20.3	72.5	31,779	15.7	0.5	..	3.9	3.9
137	Congo	4.1	6.2	2.7	2.2	62.5	19.6	79.4	4,238	21.7	4.1	0.1	3.0	3.0
138	Lao People's Democratic Republic	6.3	7.8	2.7	1.3	34.3	21.5	60.3	2,255	5.4	7.2	0.6	4.1	4.1
139	Cambodia	14.3	17.4	3.2	1.2	20.4	22.9	54.3	1,915	5.4	7.7	3.4	5.9	5.9
140	Swaziland	1.2	1.5	2.2	1.4	21.3	19.5	70.5	4,998	2.2	2.0	3.1	6.3	6.3
141	Bhutan	0.7	0.9	−1.5	1.5	35.5	24.6	50.7	5,113	2.9	9.6	..	5.5	5.5
LOW HUMAN DEVELOPMENT														
142	Solomon Islands	0.6	0.8	2.8	2.5	18.9	19.9	74.7	2,547	17.9	42.9	0.4	5.4	5.4
143	Kenya	41.6	65.9	3.1	2.7	22.5	18.5	82.1	1,573	0.5	6.1	5.7	4.3	4.3
144	São Tomé and Príncipe	0.2	0.2	1.9	2.0	63.0	19.3	77.4	1,820	3.9	15.8	1.0[f]	7.1	7.1
145	Pakistan	176.7	234.4	2.6	1.8	36.2	21.7	64.7	2,609	1.5	1.7	5.4	2.6	2.6
146	Bangladesh	150.5	181.9	2.2	1.3	28.6	24.2	54.4	1,416	0.8	1.3	11.8	3.4	3.4
147	Timor-Leste	1.2	2.0	2.8	2.9	28.6	16.6	95.3	805	..	9.5	..	12.3	12.3
148	Angola	19.6	30.8	3.2	2.7	59.4	16.6	95.1	5,812	2.9	0.4	0.1[f]	4.6	4.6
149	Myanmar	48.3	54.3	1.4	0.8	34.3	28.2	43.8	..	..	..	..	2.0	2.0
150	Cameroon	20.0	28.8	2.7	2.1	59.2	19.3	78.6	2,205	1.5	2.9	0.7	5.6	5.6
151	Madagascar	21.3	35.3	3.0	2.8	30.6	18.2	84.9	1,004	6.3	5.2	0.1	4.1	4.1
152	Tanzania, United Republic of	46.2	81.9	3.2	3.1	26.9	17.5	92.2	1,362	1.9	13.7	0.1	5.1	5.1
153	Papua New Guinea	7.0	10.2	2.5	2.2	12.6	20.4	71.3	2,281	5.4	5.3	0.2	3.1	3.1
154	Yemen	24.8	41.3	4.7	3.0	32.4	17.4	87.1	2,470	0.5	2.0	4.4	5.6	5.6
155	Senegal	12.8	20.0	2.9	2.6	42.7	17.8	85.0	1,817	1.6	8.0	10.6	5.7	5.7
156	Nigeria	162.5	257.8	2.4	2.5	50.5	18.5	86.1	2,203	3.3	1.0	5.5	5.8	5.8
157	Nepal	30.5	39.9	2.5	1.7	19.2	21.4	65.8	1,155	0.3	6.7	23.8	5.8	5.8
158	Haiti	10.1	12.5	2.0	1.3	53.6	21.5	66.6	1,151	0.6	..	21.2	6.1	6.1
159	Mauritania	3.5	5.2	2.8	2.2	41.7	19.8	73.7	1,929	−1.3	9.4	0.1	2.5	2.5
160	Lesotho	2.2	2.6	1.8	1.0	27.6	20.3	70.3	1,468	4.0	6.4	26.2	8.2	8.2
161	Uganda	34.5	59.8	3.3	3.1	13.5	15.7	103.5	1,217	3.8	11.4	4.7	8.2	8.2
162	Togo	6.2	8.7	2.2	2.0	44.1	19.7	74.6	850	1.8	17.5	10.7	5.9	5.9
163	Comoros	0.8	1.2	2.4	2.5	28.3	18.9	83.0	1,183	1.7	9.5	2.1	3.4	3.4
164	Zambia	13.5	24.5	2.5	3.0	35.9	16.7	98.4	1,430	5.5	11.1	0.3	4.8	4.8
165	Djibouti	0.9	1.3	2.2	1.9	76.3	21.4	63.5	2,319	9.2	14.5	3.1	7.0	7.0
166	Rwanda	10.9	17.6	−4.9	2.9	19.2	18.7	83.6	1,136	2.3	18.0	1.8	9.0	9.0
167	Benin	9.1	14.6	3.4	2.7	42.5	17.9	87.4	1,508	1.4	10.3	3.6	4.2	4.2
168	Gambia	1.8	2.8	3.1	2.7	58.9	17.8	84.8	1,415	5.4	18.5	10.9	6.0	6.0
169	Sudan	44.6	66.9	2.6	2.4	40.8	19.7	76.7	2,210	4.9	4.6	5.5	7.3	7.3
170	Côte d'Ivoire	20.2	29.8	3.2	2.2	51.3	19.2	80.1	1,701	1.6	10.6	0.8	5.1	5.1
171	Malawi	15.4	28.2	1.0	3.2	20.3	16.9	96.0	794	1.3	16.6	0.0	6.2	6.2
172	Afghanistan	32.4	53.3	8.4	3.1	22.9	16.6	93.9	1,321	1.3	45.7[f]	..	7.4	7.4
173	Zimbabwe	12.8	17.6	2.2	2.2	38.8	19.3	73.6	..	1.1	14.1	..	..	..
174	Ethiopia	84.7	118.5	3.3	2.1	16.8	18.7	79.2	934	0.8	13.4	0.9	4.3	4.3
175	Mali	15.8	26.8	2.5	3.0	36.6	16.3	97.6	1,185	1.2	11.0	4.5	5.6	5.6
176	Guinea-Bissau	1.5	2.3	2.0	2.1	30.2	19.0	80.2	1,071	1.7	17.6	5.6	6.1	6.1

TABLE 10

		POPULATION						ECONOMY					
	Total (millions)		Average annual growth (%)		Urban[a] (% of total)	Median age (years)	Dependency ratio (%)	GDP per capita (PPP $)	Foreign direct investment net inflows (% of GDP)	Net official development assistance received (% of GDP)	Remittance inflows (% of GDP)	Public expenditure on education (% of GDP)	Total expenditure on health (% of GDP)
HDI rank	2011	2030	1990/1995	2010/2015	2011	2010	2011	2009	2009	2009	2009	2006–2009[b]	2009
177 Eritrea	5.4	8.4	0.3	2.9	22.1	19.0	78.9	581	0.0	7.8	..	2.2	2.2
178 Guinea	10.2	15.9	5.5	2.5	35.9	18.3	85.6	1,048	1.2	5.8	1.6	5.7	5.7
179 Central African Republic	4.5	6.4	2.5	2.0	39.2	19.4	78.9	757	2.1	11.9	..	4.3	4.3
180 Sierra Leone	6.0	8.5	−0.4	2.1	38.8	18.4	81.4	808	3.8	23.0	2.4	13.1	13.1
181 Burkina Faso	17.0	29.1	2.7	3.0	26.5	17.1	90.6	1,187	2.1	13.5	1.2	6.4	6.4
182 Liberia	4.1	6.5	−0.3	2.6	48.2	18.2	86.2	396	24.9	78.3	6.2	13.2	13.2
183 Chad	11.5	18.4	3.0	2.6	28.2	17.1	93.1	1,300	6.8	9.2	..	7.0	7.0
184 Mozambique	23.9	35.9	3.2	2.2	39.2	17.8	89.5	885	9.0	20.8	1.1	5.7	5.7
185 Burundi	8.6	11.4	1.7	1.9	11.3	20.2	68.2	392	0.0	41.2	2.1	13.1	13.1
186 Niger	16.1	30.8	3.3	3.5	17.2	15.5	104.9	690	13.7	8.9	1.7	6.1	6.1
187 Congo, Democratic Republic of the	67.8	106.0	3.8	2.6	35.9	16.7	95.0	319	9.0	23.9	..	9.5	9.5
OTHER COUNTRIES OR TERRITORIES													
Korea, Democratic People's Rep. of	24.5	26.2	1.6	0.4	60.3	32.9	47.4	..	..	..	..	..	..
Marshall Islands	0.1	0.1	1.5	1.6	72.1	..	..	..	..	32.1	..	16.5	16.5
Monaco	0.0	0.0	1.3	0.0	100.0	..	..	..	..	..	..	3.9	3.9
Nauru	0.0	0.0	1.7	0.6	100.0	..	..	..	..	..	..	..	..
San Marino	0.0	0.0	1.2	0.6	94.1	..	..	..	..	..	..	7.1	7.1
Somalia	9.6	16.4	−0.2	2.6	37.9	17.5	91.2	..	..	..	..	..	..
Tuvalu	0.0	0.0	0.5	0.2	50.9	..	..	..	..	..	..	9.9	9.9
Human Development Index groups													
Very high human development	1,129.5	1,218.5	0.7	0.5	78.3	39.3	49.9	35,768	1.8	..	0.3	11.9	11.2
High human development	972.9	1,082.5	1.1	0.8	75.7	30.5	46.7	12,861	2.5	0.3	1.2	6.5	6.7
Medium human development	3,545.5	4,087.6	1.6	1.0	41.3	28.9	48.1	5,077	2.2	0.5	2.2	4.6	4.5
Low human development	1,259.7	1,857.2	2.8	2.2	33.9	19.8	77.7	1,671	2.7	8.7	5.1	5.0	5.1
Regions													
Arab States	360.7	496.9	2.4	2.0	56.7	23.2	61.9	8,256	3.2	1.9	2.7	5.0	5.3
East Asia and the Pacific	1,978.5	2,135.3	1.3	0.6	46.1	32.3	41.5	6,227	1.9	0.4	1.4	4.4	4.3
Europe and Central Asia	480.5	491.3	0.3	0.2	64.6	34.9	43.3	14,244	3.4	..	1.4	6.4	6.3
Latin America and the Caribbean	591.2	696.0	1.7	1.1	79.8	27.5	53.0	10,739	2.1	0.4	1.5	7.7	7.6
South Asia	1,728.5	2,141.8	2.1	1.4	32.0	24.6	55.7	3,368	2.1	1.4	4.5	4.0	4.1
Sub-Saharan Africa	877.6[T]	1,353.8[T]	2.7[T]	2.4[T]	37.7[T]	18.6[T]	83.5[T]	2,181	3.7	9.9	2.2	6.4	6.2
Least developed countries	851.1[T]	1,256.8[T]	2.7[T]	2.2[T]	29.7[T]	19.7[T]	76.3[T]	1,379	3.2	12.0	5.2	5.4	5.6
Small island developing states	53.2	63.8	1.5	1.1	52.0	26.6	59.0	5,241	3.9	3.7	6.7	5.6	7.0
World	6,974.0[T]	8,321.4[T]	1.5[T]	1.1[T]	50.8[T]	29.2[T]	52.2[T]	10,715	2.3	2.2	0.7	10.2	6.0

TABLE 10

NOTES

a. Because data are based on national definitions of what constitutes a city or metropolitan area, cross-country comparison should be made with caution.
b. Data refer to the most recent year available during the period specified.
c. Includes Svalbard and Jan Mayen Islands.
d. Includes Christmas Island, Cocos (Keeling) Islands and Norfolk Island.
e. Includes Åland Islands.
f. Refers to an earlier year than that specified.
g. Includes Agalega, Rodrigues and Saint Brandon.
h. Includes Taiwan Province of China and excludes Hong Kong Special Administrative Region and Macao Special Administrative Region.

DEFINITIONS

Total population: De facto population in a country, area or region as of 1 July.
Average annual population growth: Average annual exponential growth rate for the period indicated.
Urban population: De facto population living in areas classified as urban according to the criteria used by each area or country as of 1 July.
Median age: Age that divides the population distribution into two equal parts—that is, 50 percent of the population is above that age and 50 percent is below it.
Dependency ratio: Ratio of the sum of the population ages 0–14 and that ages 65 and older to the population ages 15–64.

GDP per capita: Gross domestic product (GDP) expressed in purchasing power parity international dollar terms, divided by midyear population.
Foreign direct investment net inflows: Sum of equity capital, reinvestment of earnings, other long-term capital and short-term capital, expressed as a percentage of gross domestic product (GDP).
Net official development assistance received: Disbursements of loans made on concessional terms (net of repayments of principal) and grants by official agencies to promote economic development and welfare in countries and territories in part I of the Development Assistance Committee list of aid recipients, expressed as a percentage of the recipient country's gross national income (GNI).
Remittance inflows: Earnings and material resources transferred by international migrants or refugees to recipients in their country of origin or countries in which the migrant formerly resided, expressed as a percentage of the receiving country's GDP.
Public expenditure on education: Total public expenditure (current and capital) on education, expressed as a percentage of gross domestic product (GDP).
Total expenditure on health: The sum of public and private health expenditure. It includes the provision of health services (preventive and curative), family planning activities, nutrition activities and emergency aid designated for health but does not include provision of water and sanitation.

MAIN DATA SOURCES
Columns 1–4, 6 and 7: UNDESA (2011).
Column 5: UNDESA (2010).
Columns 8–13: World Bank (2011a).

Technical notes

Calculating the human development indices—graphical presentation

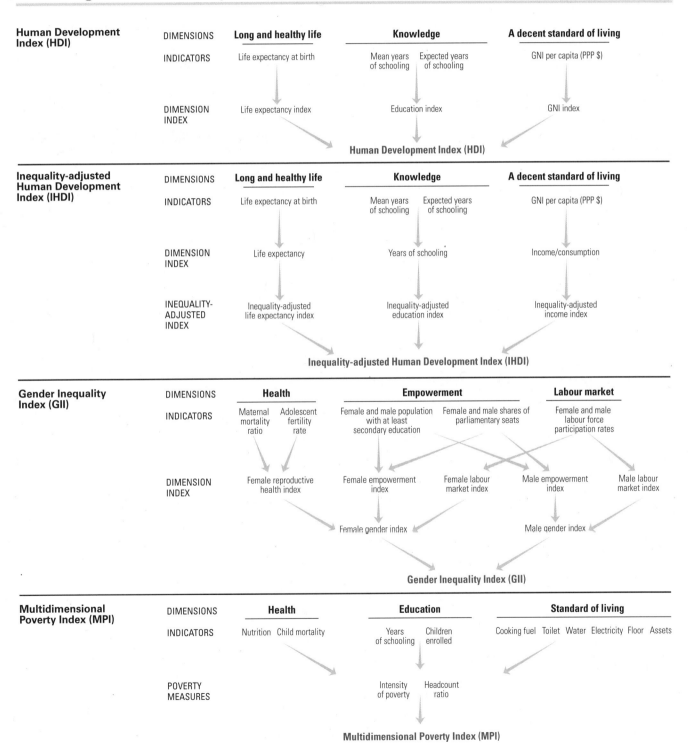

Human Development Index (HDI)

DIMENSIONS

Long and healthy life | Knowledge | A decent standard of living

INDICATORS

Life expectancy at birth | Mean years of schooling   Expected years of schooling | GNI per capita (PPP $)

DIMENSION INDEX

Life expectancy index | Education index | GNI index

Human Development Index (HDI)

Inequality-adjusted Human Development Index (IHDI)

DIMENSIONS

Long and healthy life | Knowledge | A decent standard of living

INDICATORS

Life expectancy at birth | Mean years of schooling   Expected years of schooling | GNI per capita (PPP $)

DIMENSION INDEX

Life expectancy | Years of schooling | Income/consumption

INEQUALITY-ADJUSTED INDEX

Inequality-adjusted life expectancy index | Inequality-adjusted education index | Inequality-adjusted income index

Inequality-adjusted Human Development Index (IHDI)

Gender Inequality Index (GII)

DIMENSIONS

Health | Empowerment | Labour market

INDICATORS

Maternal mortality ratio   Adolescent fertility rate | Female and male population with at least secondary education   Female and male shares of parliamentary seats | Female and male labour force participation rates

DIMENSION INDEX

Female reproductive health index | Female empowerment index   Female labour market index   Male empowerment index   Male labour market index

Female gender index   Male gender index

Gender Inequality Index (GII)

Multidimensional Poverty Index (MPI)

DIMENSIONS

Health | Education | Standard of living

INDICATORS

Nutrition   Child mortality | Years of schooling   Children enrolled | Cooking fuel   Toilet   Water   Electricity   Floor   Assets

POVERTY MEASURES

Intensity of poverty   Headcount ratio

Multidimensional Poverty Index (MPI)

The Human Development Index (HDI) is a summary measure of human development. It measures the average achievements in a country in three basic dimensions of human development: a long and healthy life, access to knowledge and a decent standard of living. The HDI is the geometric mean of normalized indices measuring achievements in each dimension. For a full elaboration of the method and its rationale, see Klugman, Rodriguez and Choi (2011). This technical note describes the steps to create the HDI, data sources and the methodology used to express income.

Steps to estimate the Human Development Index

There are two steps to calculating the HDI.

Step 1. Creating the dimension indices

Minimum and maximum values (goalposts) are set in order to transform the indicators into indices between 0 and 1. The maximums are the highest observed values in the time series (1980–2011). The minimum values can be appropriately conceived of as subsistence values. The minimum values are set at 20 years for life expectancy, at 0 years for both education variables and at $100 for per capita gross national income (GNI). The low value for income can be justified by the considerable amount of unmeasured subsistence and nonmarket production in economies close to the minimum, not captured in the official data.

Goalposts for the Human Development Index in this Report

Dimension	Observed maximum	Minimum
Life expectancy	83.4 (Japan, 2011)	20.0
Mean years of schooling	13.1 (Czech Republic, 2005)	0
Expected years of schooling	18.0 (capped at)	0
Combined education index	0.978 (New Zealand, 2010)	0
Per capita income (PPP $)	107,721 (Qatar, 2011)	100

Having defined the minimum and maximum values, the subindices are calculated as follows:

$$\text{Dimension index} = \frac{\text{actual value} - \text{minimum value}}{\text{maximum value} - \text{minimum value}}. \quad (1)$$

For education, equation 1 is applied to each of the two subcomponents, then a geometric mean of the resulting indices is created and finally, equation 1 is reapplied to the geometric mean of the indices using 0 as the minimum and the highest geometric mean of the resulting indices for the time period under consideration as

the maximum. This is equivalent to applying equation 1 directly to the geometric mean of the two subcomponents.

Because each dimension index is a proxy for capabilities in the corresponding dimension, the transformation function from income to capabilities is likely to be concave (Anand and Sen 2000). Thus, for income the natural logarithm of the actual minimum and maximum values is used.

Step 2. Aggregating the subindices to produce the Human Development Index

The HDI is the geometric mean of the three dimension indices:

$$\left(I_{Life}^{\;1/3} \cdot I_{Education}^{\;1/3} \cdot I_{Income}^{\;1/3}\right). \quad (2)$$

Example: Viet Nam

Indicator	Value
Life expectancy at birth (years)	75.2
Mean years of schooling (years)	5.5
Expected years of schooling (years)	10.4
GNI per capita (PPP $)	2,805

Note: Values are rounded.

$$\text{Life expectancy index} = \frac{75.2 - 20}{83.4 - 20} = 0.870$$

$$\text{Mean years of schooling index} = \frac{5.5 - 0}{13.1 - 0} = 0.478$$

$$\text{Expected years of schooling index} = \frac{10.4 - 0}{18 - 0} = 0.576$$

$$\text{Education index} = \frac{\sqrt{0.478 \cdot 0.576} - 0}{0.978 - 0} = 0.503$$

$$\text{Income index} = \frac{\ln(2,805) - \ln(100)}{\ln(107,721) - \ln(100)} = 0.478$$

$$\text{Human Development Index} = \sqrt[3]{0.870 \cdot 0.503 \cdot 0.478} = 0.593$$

Data sources

- Life expectancy at birth: UNDESA (2011)
- Mean years of schooling: HDRO updates (http://hdr.undp.org/en/statistics/) based on UNESCO data on education attainment (http://stats.uis.unesco.org/unesco) using the methodology outlined in Barro and Lee (2010a)
- Expected years of schooling: UNESCO Institute for Statistics (2011)
- GNI per capita: World Bank (2011a), IMF (2011), UNSD (2011) and UNDESA (2011)

Methodology used to express income

GNI is traditionally expressed in current terms. To make GNI comparable across time, GNI is converted from current to constant terms by taking the value of nominal GNI per capita in purchasing power parity (PPP) terms for the base year (2005) and building a time series using the growth rate of real GNI per capita, as implied by the ratio of current GNI per capita in local currency terms to the GDP deflator.

Official PPPs are produced by the International Comparison Program (ICP), which periodically collects thousands of prices of matched goods and services in many countries. The last round of this exercise refers to 2005 and covers 146 countries. The World Bank produces estimates for years other than the ICP benchmark based on inflation relative to the United States. Because other international organizations—such as the World Bank and the International Monetary Fund (IMF)—quote the base year in terms of the ICP benchmark, the HDRO does the same.

To obtain the income value for 2011, IMF-projected GDP growth rates (based on constant terms) are applied to the most recent GNI values. The IMF-projected growth rates are calculated in local currency terms and constant prices rather than in PPP terms. This avoids mixing the effects of the PPP conversion with those of real growth of the economy.

Estimating missing values

For a small number of countries that were missing one out of four indicators, the HDRO filled the gap by estimating the missing value using cross-country regression models. The details of the models used are available at http://hdr.undp.org/en/statistics/understanding/issues/.

In this Report, the PPP conversion rates were estimated for three countries (Cuba, Occupied Palestinian Territory and Palau), expected years of schooling were estimated for five countries (Barbados, Haiti, Montenegro, Singapore and Turkmenistan) and mean years of schooling were estimated for eight countries (Antigua and Barbuda, Eritrea, Grenada, Kiribati, St. Kitts and Nevis, St. Lucia, St. Vincent and the Grenadines, and Vanuatu). This brought the total number of countries in the HDI in 2011 up to 187, from 169 in 2010.

Technical note 2. Calculating the Inequality-adjusted Human Development Index

The Inequality-adjusted Human Development Index (IHDI) adjusts the Human Development Index (HDI) for inequality in the distribution of each dimension across the population. It is based on a distribution-sensitive class of composite indices proposed by Foster, Lopez-Calva, and Szekely (2005), which draws on the Atkinson (1970) family of inequality measures. It is computed as a geometric mean of geometric means, calculated across the population for each dimension separately (for details, see Alkire and Foster 2010).

The IHDI accounts for inequalities in HDI dimensions by "discounting" each dimension's average value according to its level of inequality. The IHDI equals the HDI when there is no inequality across people but falls further below the HDI as inequality rises. In this sense, the IHDI is the actual level of human development (taking into account inequality), while the HDI can be viewed as an index of the "potential" human development that could be achieved if there was no inequality. The "loss" in potential human development due to inequality is the difference between the HDI and the IHDI and can be expressed as a percentage.

Data sources

Since the HDI relies on country-level aggregates such as national accounts for income, the IHDI must draw on alternative sources of data to obtain insights into the distribution. The distributions have different units—life expectancy is distributed across a hypothetical cohort, while years of schooling and income are distributed across individuals.

Inequality in the distribution of HDI dimensions is estimated for:

- Life expectancy, using data from abridged life tables provided by UNDESA (2011). This distribution is grouped in age intervals (0–1, 1–5, 5–10, ... , 85+), with the mortality rates and average age at death specified for each interval.
- Mean years of schooling, using household survey data harmonized in international databases, including the Luxembourg Income Study, EUROSTAT's European Union Survey of Income and Living Conditions, the World Bank's International Income Distribution Database, the United Nations Children's Fund's Multiple Indicators Cluster Survey, ICF Macro's Demographic and Health Survey, the World Health Organization's World Health Survey and the United Nations University's World Income Inequality Database.
- Disposable household income or consumption per capita using the above listed databases and household surveys—or for a few countries, income imputed based on an asset index matching methodology using household survey asset indices (Harttgen and Vollmer 2011).

A full account of data sources used for estimating inequality in 2011 is given at http://hdr.undp.org/en/statistics/ihdi/.

Computing the Inequality-adjusted Human Development Index

There are three steps to computing the IHDI.

Step 1. Measuring inequality in the dimensions of the Human Development Index

The IHDI draws on the Atkinson (1970) family of inequality measures and sets the aversion parameter ε equal to 1.[1] In this case the inequality measure is $A = 1 - g/\mu$, where g is the geometric mean and μ is the arithmetic mean of the distribution. This can be written as:

$$A_x = 1 - \frac{\sqrt[n]{X_1 \ldots X_n}}{\bar{X}} \qquad (1)$$

where $\{X_1 \ldots, X_n\}$ denotes the underlying distribution in the dimensions of interest. A_x is obtained for each variable (life expectancy, mean years of schooling and disposable income or consumption per capita).[2]

The geometric mean in equation 1 does not allow zero values. For mean years of schooling one year is added to all valid observations to compute the inequality. Income per capita outliers—extremely high incomes as well as negative and zero incomes—were dealt with by truncating the top 0.5 percentile of the distribution to reduce the influence of extremely high incomes and by replacing the negative and zero incomes with the minimum value of the bottom 0.5 percentile of the distribution of positive incomes. Sensitivity analysis of the IHDI is given in Kovačevic (2010).

Step 2. Adjusting the dimension indices for inequality

The mean achievement in an HDI dimension, $\bar{X}$, is adjusted for inequality as follows:

$$\bar{X} \cdot (1 - A_x) = \sqrt[n]{X_1 \ldots X_n} \ .$$

Thus the geometric mean represents the arithmetic mean reduced by the inequality in distribution.

The inequality-adjusted dimension indices are obtained from the HDI dimension indices, I_x, by multiplying them by $(1 - A_x)$, where A_x, defined by equation 1, is the corresponding Atkinson measure:

$$I_x^* = (1 - A_x) \cdot I_x .$$

The inequality-adjusted income index, I_{Income}^*, is based on the unlogged GNI index, I_{Income^*}. This enables the IHDI to account for the full effect of income inequality.

Step 3. Combining the dimension indices to calculate the Inequality-adjusted Human Development Index

The IHDI is the geometric mean of the three dimension indices adjusted for inequality. First, the IHDI that includes the unlogged income index ($IHDI^*$) is calculated:

$$IHDI^* = \sqrt[3]{I_{Life}^* \cdot I_{Education}^* \cdot I_{Income}^*} =$$

$$\sqrt[3]{(1 - A_{Life}) \cdot I_{Life} \cdot (1 - A_{Education}) \cdot I_{Education} \cdot (1 - A_{Income}) \cdot I_{Income^*}} \ .$$

The HDI based on unlogged income index (HDI^*) is then calculated:

$$HDI^* = \sqrt[3]{I_{Life} \cdot I_{Education} \cdot I_{Income^*}} \ .$$

The percentage loss to the HDI^* due to inequalities in each dimension is calculated as:

$$Loss = 1 - \frac{IHDI^*}{HDI^*} = 1 - \sqrt[3]{(1 - A_{Life}) \cdot (1 - A_{Education}) \cdot (1 - A_{Income})} \ .$$

Assuming that the percentage loss due to inequality in income distribution is the same for both average income and its logarithm, the IHDI is then calculated as:

$$IHDI = \left(\frac{IHDI^*}{HDI^*} \right) \cdot HDI = \sqrt[3]{(1 - A_{Life}) \cdot (1 - A_{Education}) \cdot (1 - A_{Income})} \cdot HDI .$$

Notes on methodology and caveats

The IHDI is based on an index that satisfies subgroup consistency. This ensures that improvements or deteriorations in the distribution of human development within a certain group of society (while human development remains constant in the other groups) will be reflected in changes in the overall measure of human development. This index is also path independent, which means that the order in which data are aggregated across individuals, or groups of individuals, and across dimensions yields the same result—so there is no need to rely on a particular sequence or a single data source. This allows estimation for a large number of countries.

The main disadvantage is that the IHDI is not association sensitive, so it does not capture overlapping inequalities. To make the measure association-sensitive, all the data for each individual must be available from a single survey source, which is not currently possible for a large number of countries.

Example: Peru

	Indicator	Dimension index	Inequality measure (A1)	Inequality-adjusted index
Life expectancy	74.0	0.852	0.148	(1–0.148) · 0.852 = 0.728
Mean years of schooling	8.7	0.662		
Expected years of schooling	12.9	0.717		
Education index		0.704	0.240	(1–0.240) · 0.704 = 0.535
Logarithm of gross national income	9.03	0.634		
Gross national income	8,389	0.077	0.300	(1–0.300) · 0.077 = 0.054

	Human Development Index	Inequality-adjusted Human Development Index	Loss %
HDI with unlogged income	$\sqrt[3]{0.852 \cdot 0.704 \cdot 0.077} = 0.359$	$\sqrt[3]{0.728 \cdot 0.535 \cdot 0.054} = 0.275$	1 – 0.275 / 0.359 = 0.232
HDI	$\sqrt[3]{0.852 \cdot 0.704 \cdot 0.634} = 0.725$	(0.275 / 0.359) · 0.725 = 0.557	

Note: Values are rounded.

Technical note 3. Calculating the Gender Inequality Index

The Gender Inequality Index (GII) reflects gender-based disadvantage in three dimensions—reproductive health, empowerment and the labour market—for as many countries as data of reasonable quality allow. The index shows the loss in potential human development due to inequality between female and male achievements in these dimensions. It varies between 0—when women and men fare equally—and 1, where one gender fares as poorly as possible in all measured dimensions.

It is computed using the association-sensitive inequality measure suggested by Seth (2009). The index is based on the general mean of general means of different orders—the first aggregation is by the geometric mean across dimensions; these means, calculated separately for women and men, are then aggregated using a harmonic mean across genders.

Data sources
- Maternal mortality ratio *(MMR):* WHO, UNICEF, UNFPA and World Bank (2010)
- Adolescent fertility rate *(AFR):* UNDESA (2011)
- Share of parliamentary seats held by each sex *(PR):* Inter-parliamentary Union's Parline database (2011)
- Attainment at secondary and higher education *(SE)* levels: HDRO (2011) updates of Barro and Lee (2010b) estimates based on UNESCO Institute for Statistics data on education attainment (http://stats.uis.unesco.org/unesco/)
- Labour market participation rate *(LFPR):* ILO (2011)

Computing the Gender Inequality Index
There are five steps to computing the GII.

Step 1. Treating zeros and extreme values
Because a geometric mean cannot have a zero value, a minimum value must be set for all component indicators. The minimum is set at 0.1 percent for adolescent fertility rate, share of

parliamentary seats held by women, attainment at secondary and higher education levels, and labour market participation rate. Female parliamentary representation of countries reporting zero is coded as 0.1 percent because even in countries without female members of the national parliaments, women have some political influence.

Because higher maternal mortality suggests poorer maternal health, for the maternal mortality ratio the maximum value is truncated at 1,000 deaths per 100,000 births and the minimum value is truncated at 10. It is assumed that countries where maternal mortality ratios exceed 1,000 do not differ in their inability to create conditions and support for maternal health and that countries with 1–10 deaths per 100,000 births are performing at essentially the same level and that differences are random.

Sensitivity analysis of the GII is given in Gaye et al. (2010).

Step 2. Aggregating across dimensions within each gender group, using geometric means
Aggregating across dimensions for each gender group by the geometric mean makes the GII association sensitive (see Seth 2009).

For women and girls, the aggregation formula is

$$G_F = \sqrt[3]{\left(\frac{10}{MMR} \cdot \frac{1}{AFR}\right)^{\frac{1}{2}} \cdot (PR_F \cdot SE_F)^{\frac{1}{2}} \cdot LFPR_F},$$

and for men and boys the formula is

$$G_M = \sqrt[3]{1 \cdot (PR_M \cdot SE_M)^{\frac{1}{2}} \cdot LFPR_M}.$$

The rescaling by 0.1 of the maternal mortality ratio in the aggregation formula for women and girls is needed to account for the truncation of the maternal mortality ratio minimum at 10. This is a new adjustment introduced in *Human Development Report 2011*.[3]

Step 3. Aggregating across gender groups, using a harmonic mean

The female and male indices are aggregated by the harmonic mean to create the equally distributed gender index

$$HARM\,(G_F, G_M) = \left[\frac{(G_F)^{-1} + (G_M)^{-1}}{2}\right]^{-1}.$$

Using the harmonic mean of geometric means within groups captures the inequality between women and men and adjusts for association between dimensions.

Step 4. Calculating the geometric mean of the arithmetic means for each indicator

The reference standard for computing inequality is obtained by aggregating female and male indices using equal weights (thus treating the genders equally) and then aggregating the indices across dimensions:

$$G_{\overline{F}, \overline{M}} = \sqrt[3]{\overline{Health} \cdot \overline{Empowerment} \cdot \overline{LFPR}}$$

where $\overline{Health} = \left(\sqrt{\dfrac{10}{MMR} \cdot \dfrac{1}{AFR}} + 1\right)/2,$

$\overline{Empowerment} = \left(\sqrt{PR_F \cdot SE_F} + \sqrt{PR_M \cdot SE_M}\right)/2,$ and

$$\overline{LFPR} = \frac{LFPR_F + LFPR_M}{2}.$$

$\overline{Health}$ should not be interpreted as an average of corresponding female and male indices but as half the distance from the norms established for the reproductive health indicators—fewer maternal deaths and fewer adolescent pregnancies.

Step 5. Calculating the Gender Inequality Index

Comparing the equally distributed gender index to the reference standard yields the GII,

$$1 - \frac{HARM\,(G_F, G_M)}{G_{\overline{F}, \overline{M}}}.$$

Example: Lesotho

	Health		Empowerment		Labour market
	Maternal mortality ratio	Adolescent fertility rate	Parliamentary representation	Attainment at secondary and higher education	Labour market participation rate
Female	530	73.5	0.229	0.243	0.719
Male	na	na	0.771	0.203	0.787
$\frac{F+M}{2}$	$\sqrt{\dfrac{\sqrt{\left(\frac{10}{530}\right)\cdot\left(\frac{1}{73.5}\right)}+1}{2}}$ = 0.508		$\dfrac{\sqrt{0.229\cdot0.243}+\sqrt{0.771\cdot0.203}}{2}$ = 0.316		$\dfrac{0.719+0.787}{2}$ = 0.743

na is not applicable.

Using the above formulas, it is straightforward to obtain:

$$G_F \quad 0.134 = \sqrt[3]{\sqrt{\frac{10}{530}\cdot\frac{1}{73.5}} \cdot \sqrt{0.229\cdot0.243\cdot0.719}}$$

$$G_M \quad 0.675 = \sqrt[3]{1 \cdot \sqrt{0.771\cdot0.203\cdot0.787}}$$

$$G_{\overline{F}, \overline{M}} \quad 0.492 = \sqrt[3]{0.508\cdot0.316\cdot0.743}$$

$$HARM\,(G_F, G_M) \quad 0.230 = \left[\frac{1}{2}\left(\frac{1}{0.134}+\frac{1}{0.675}\right)\right]^{-1}$$

$$GII \quad 1 - (0.230/0.492) = 0.532.$$

Technical note 4. Calculating the Multidimensional Poverty Index

The Multidimensional Poverty Index (MPI) identifies multiple deprivations at the individual level in education, health and standard of living. It uses micro data from household surveys, and—unlike the Inequality-adjusted Human Development Index—all the indicators needed to construct the measure must come from the same survey. More details can be found in Alkire and Santos (2010).

Methodology

Each person is assigned a deprivation score according to his or her household's deprivations in each of the 10 component indicators. The maximum score is 100 percent, with each dimension equally weighted (thus the maximum score in each dimension is 33.3 percent). The education and health dimensions have two indicators each, so each component is worth ⅙ (or 16.7 percent). The standard of living dimension has six indicators, so each component is worth ⅑ (or 5.6 percent).

The thresholds are as follows:

- Education: having no household member who has completed five years of schooling and having at least one school-age child (up to grade 8) who is not attending school.

- Health: having at least one household member who is malnourished and having had one or more children die.

- Standard of living: not having electricity, not having access to clean drinking water, not having access to adequate sanitation, using "dirty" cooking fuel (dung, wood or charcoal), having a home with a dirt floor, and owning no car, truck or similar motorized vehicle while owning at most one of these assets: bicycle, motorcycle, radio, refrigerator, telephone or television.

To identify the multidimensionally poor, the deprivation scores for each household are summed to obtain the household deprivation, c. A cut-off of 33.3 percent, which is the equivalent of one-third of the weighted indicators, is used to distinguish between the poor and nonpoor. If c is 33.3 percent or greater, that household (and everyone in it) is multidimensionally poor. Households with a deprivation score greater than or equal to 20 percent but less than 33.3 percent are vulnerable to or at risk of becoming multidimensionally poor. Households with a deprivation score of 50 percent or higher are severely multidimensionally poor.

The MPI value is the product of two measures: the multidimensional headcount ratio and the intensity (or breadth) of poverty.

The headcount ratio, H, is the proportion of the population who are multidimensionally poor:

$$H = \frac{q}{n}$$

where q is the number of people who are multidimensionally poor and n is the total population.

The intensity of poverty, A, reflects the proportion of the weighted component indicators in which, on average, poor people are deprived. For poor households only, the deprivation scores are summed and divided by the total number of poor persons:

$$A = \frac{\sum_1^q c}{q},$$

where c is the deprivation score that the poor experience.

Weighted count of deprivations in household 1:

$$\left(1 \cdot \frac{5}{3}\right) + \left(1 \cdot \frac{5}{9}\right) = 2.22,$$

which is equal to a deprivation score of 2.22/10 = 0.222, or 22.2 percent.

Example using hypothetical data

Indicators	Household 1	2	3	4	Weights
Household size	4	7	5	4	
Education					
No one has completed five years of schooling	0	1	0	1	5/3 or 16.7%
At least one school-age child not enrolled in school	0	1	0	0	5/3 or 16.7%
Health					
At least one member is malnourished	0	0	1	0	5/3 or 16.7%
One or more children have died	1	1	0	1	5/3 or 16.7%
Living conditions					
No electricity	0	1	1	1	5/9 or 5.6%
No access to clean drinking water	0	0	1	0	5/9 or 5.6%
No access to adequate sanitation	0	1	1	0	5/9 or 5.6%
House has dirt floor	0	0	0	0	5/9 or 5.6%
Household uses "dirty" cooking fuel (dung, firewood or charcoal)	1	1	1	1	5/9 or 5.6%
Household has no car and owns at most one of: bicycle, motorcycle, radio, refrigerator, telephone or television	0	1	0	1	5/9 or 5.6%
Results					
Household deprivation score, c (sum of each deprivation multiplied by its weight)	22.2%	72.2%	38.9%	50.0%	
Is the household poor ($c > 33.3\%$)?	No	Yes	Yes	Yes	

Note: 1 indicates deprivation in the indicator; 0 indicates nondeprivation.

Headcount ratio $(H) =$

$$\left(\frac{7 + 5 + 4}{4 + 7 + 5 + 4}\right) = 0.800$$

(80 percent of people live in poor households)

Intensity of poverty $(A) =$

$$\frac{(7.22/10 \cdot 7) + (3.89/10 \cdot 5) + (5.00/10 \cdot 4)}{(7 + 5 + 4)} = 0.5625$$

(the average poor person is deprived in 56 percent of the weighted indicators).

$$MPI = H \cdot A = 0.450$$

NOTES

1 The inequality aversion parameter affects the degree to which lower achievements are emphasized and higher achievements are de-emphasized.

2 A_x is estimated from survey data using the survey weights,

$$\hat{A}_x = 1 - \frac{X_1^{w_1} \dots X_n^{w_n}}{\sum_1^n w_i X_i}, \text{ where } \sum_1^n w_i = 1.$$

However, for simplicity and without loss of generality, equation 1 is referred to as the Atkinson measure.

3 The GII trends calculated at five-year intervals for 1995–2011 using consistent data and methodology are available at http://hdr.undp.org/en/statistics/gii.

Regions

Arab States (20 countries or areas)

Algeria, Bahrain, Djibouti, Egypt, Iraq, Jordan, Kuwait, Lebanon, Libya, Morocco, Occupied Palestinian Territory, Oman, Qatar, Saudi Arabia, Somalia, Sudan, Syrian Arab Republic, Tunisia, United Arab Emirates, Yemen

East Asia and the Pacific (24 countries)

Cambodia, China, Fiji, Indonesia, Kiribati, Democratic People's Rep. of Korea, Lao People's Democratic Republic, Malaysia, Marshall Islands, Federated States of Micronesia, Mongolia, Myanmar, Nauru, Palau, Papua New Guinea, Philippines, Samoa, Solomon Islands, Thailand, Timor-Leste, Tonga, Tuvalu, Vanuatu, Viet Nam

Europe and Central Asia[1] (30 countries)

Albania, Armenia, Azerbaijan, Belarus, Bosnia and Herzegovina, Bulgaria, Croatia, Cyprus, Czech Republic, Estonia, Georgia, Hungary, Kazakhstan, Kyrgyzstan, Latvia, Lithuania, Republic of Moldova, Montenegro, Poland, Romania, Russian Federation, Serbia, Slovakia, Slovenia, Tajikistan, The former Yugoslav Republic of Macedonia, Turkey, Turkmenistan, Ukraine, Uzbekistan

Latin America and the Caribbean (33 countries)

Antigua and Barbuda, Argentina, Bahamas, Barbados, Belize, Plurinational State of Bolivia, Brazil, Chile, Colombia, Costa Rica, Cuba, Dominica, Dominican Republic, Ecuador, El Salvador, Grenada, Guatemala, Guyana, Haiti, Honduras, Jamaica, Mexico, Nicaragua, Panama, Paraguay, Peru, Saint Kitts and Nevis, Saint Lucia, Saint Vincent and the Grenadines, Suriname, Trinidad and Tobago, Uruguay, Bolivarian Republic of Venezuela

South Asia (9 countries)

Afghanistan, Bangladesh, Bhutan, India, Islamic Republic of Iran, Maldives, Nepal, Pakistan, Sri Lanka

Sub-Saharan Africa (45 countries)

Angola, Benin, Botswana, Burkina Faso, Burundi, Cameroon, Cape Verde, Central African Republic, Chad, Comoros, Congo, Democratic Republic of the Congo, Côte d'Ivoire, Equatorial Guinea, Eritrea, Ethiopia, Gabon, Gambia, Ghana, Guinea, Guinea-Bissau, Kenya, Lesotho, Liberia, Madagascar, Malawi, Mali, Mauritania, Mauritius, Mozambique, Namibia, Niger, Nigeria, Rwanda, São Tomé and Príncipe, Senegal, Seychelles, Sierra Leone, South Africa, Swaziland, United Republic of Tanzania, Togo, Uganda, Zambia, Zimbabwe

Note: Countries included in aggregates for Least Developed Countries and Small Island Developing States follow UN classifications, which are available at http://www.unohrlls.org/. HDRO does not include Bahrain, Barbados or Singapore in the aggregates for Small Island Developing States.

1. The former socialist countries of Europe and Central Asia that have undergone a political and economic transformation since 1989–1991 as well as Cyprus and Turkey.

Statistical references

ADB (Asian Development Bank). 2011. *Asian Development Outlook 2011: South-South Economic Links.* Mandaluyong City, Philippines. www.adb.org/documents/books/ado/2011/ado2011.pdf.

Alkire, S., and J. Foster. 2010. "Designing the Inequality-Adjusted Human Development Index (IHDI)." Human Development Research Paper 28. UNDP–HDRO, New York. http://hdr.undp.org/en/reports/global/hdr2010/papers/HDRP_2010_28.pdf.

Alkire, S., J.M. Roche, M.E. Santos, and S. Seth. 2011. "Multidimensional Poverty Index: New Results, Time Comparisons and Group Disparities." Human Development Research Paper. UNDP–HDRO, New York.

Alkire, S., and M. Santos. 2010. "Acute Multidimensional Poverty: A New Index for Developing Countries." Human Development Research Paper 11. UNDP–HDRO, New York. http://hdr.undp.org/en/reports/global/hdr2010/papers/HDRP_2010_11.pdf.

Anand, S., and A. Sen. 2000. "The Income Component of the Human Development Index." *Journal of Human Development and Capabilities* 1 (1): 83–106.

Atkinson, A. 1970. "On the Measurement of Economic Inequality." *Journal of Economic Theory* 2 (3): 244–63.

Barro, R. J., and J. W. Lee. 2010a. *A New Data Set of Educational Attainment in the World, 1950–2010.* NBER Working Paper 15902. Cambridge, MA: National Bureau of Economic Research. www.nber.org/papers/w15902.

———. 2010b. "Barro-Lee Dataset." Korea University, Seoul. www.barrolee.com.

Boden, T. A., G. Marland, and R. J. Andres. 2010. "Global, Regional, and National Fossil-Fuel CO_2 Emissions." Carbon Dioxide Information Analysis Center, Oak Ridge National Laboratory, TN. http://cdiac.ornl.gov/trends/emis/overview_2007.html

CRED (Centre for Research on the Epidemiology of Disasters). 2011. "EM-DAT: The International Disaster Database." Université catholique de Louvain, Belgium. www.emdat.be.

EBRD (European Bank for Reconstruction and Development). 2011. "Regional Economic Prospects in EBRD Countries of Operations: May 2011." London. www.ebrd.com/downloads/research/REP/rep.pdf.

ECLAC (Economic Commission for Latin America and the Caribbean). 2011. *Preliminary Overview of the Economies of Latin America and the Caribbean.* Santiago. www.eclac.org/cgi-bin/getProd.asp?xml=/publicaciones/xml/4/41974/P41974.xml&xsl=.

Emerson, J., D. C. Esty, M. A. Levy, C. H. Kim, V. Mara, A. de Sherbinin, and T. Srebotnjak. 2010. "2010 Environmental Performance Index." New Haven, CT: Yale Center for Environmental Law and Policy. www.epi.yale.edu.

Eurostat. 2010. "European Union Statistics on Income and Living Conditions." European Commission, Brussels. http://epp.eurostat.ec.europa.eu/portal/page/portal/microdata/eu_silc.

FAO (Food and Agricultural Organization). 2011. "ResourceSTAT." Rome. http://faostat.fao.org/.

———. Forthcoming. *State of Land and Water 2011.* Rome.

Foster, J., L. López-Calva, and M. Szekely. 2005. "Measuring the Distribution of Human Development: Methodology and an Application to Mexico." *Journal of Human Development and Capabilities.* 6 (1):5–25.

Gallup World Poll. 2011. "Gallup WorldView." Washington, DC. http://worldview.gallup.com. Accessed 15 June 2011.

Gaye, A., J. Klugman, M. Kovacevic, S. Twigg, and E. Zambrano. 2010. "Measuring Key Disparities in Human Development: The Gender Inequality Index." Human Development Research Paper 46. UNDP–HDRO, New York. http://hdr.undp.org/en/reports/global/hdr2010/papers/HDRP_2010_21.pdf.

Global Footprint Network. 2010. "Global Footprint Network." Oakland, CA. www.footprintnetwork.org. Accessed 15 April 2011.

Harttgen, K., and S. Vollmer. 2011. "Inequality Decomposition without Income or Expenditure Data: Using an Asset Index to Simulate Household Income." Human Development Research Paper. UNDP–HDRO, New York.

ICF Macro. 2011. "Measure DHS (Demographic and Health Survey)." Calverton, MD. www.measuredhs.com.

IEA (International Energy Agency). 2011. *World Energy Balances.* Organisation for Economic Co-operation and Development and IEA, Paris. http://data.iea.org. Accessed 15 June 2011.

ILO (International Labour Organization). 2011. *Key Indicators on the Labour Market,* 6th edition. Geneva. http://kilm.ilo.org/KILMnetBeta/default2.asp. Accessed 15 March 2011.

IMF (International Monetary Fund). 2011. "World Economic Outlook database, April 2011." Washington, DC. www.imf.org/external/pubs/ft/weo/2011/01/weodata/index.aspx. Accessed 15 April 2011.

IPU (Inter-Parliamentary Union). 2011. "Women in National Parliaments: World Classification." Geneva. www.ipu.org/wmn-e/classif.htm. Accessed 15 March 2011.

IUCN (International Union for Conservation of Nature and Natural Resources). 2010. "IUCN Red List of Threatened Species. Version 2010.4." Geneva. www.iucnredlist.org. Accessed 15 March 2011.

Klugman, J., F. Rodriguez, and H. J. Choi. 2011. "The HDI 2010: New Controversies, Old Critiques." Human Development Research Paper 1. UNDP–HDRO, New York. http://hdr.undp.org/en/reports/global/hdr2011/papers/HDRP_2011_01.pdf.

Kovacevic, M. 2010. "Measurement of Inequality in Human Development—A Review." Human Development Research Paper 35. UNDP–HDRO, New York. http://hdr.undp.org/en/reports/global/hdr2010/papers/HDRP_2010_35.pdf.

LIS (Luxembourg Income Study). 2009. "Luxembourg Income Study Project." www.lisproject.org/techdoc.htm.

OECD, AfDB, UNECA, and UNDP (Organisation for Economic Co-operation and Development, African Development Bank, United Nations Economic Commission for Africa, and United Nations Development Programme). 2011. *African Economic Outlook 2011.* Paris: Organisation for Economic Co-operation and Development. www.africaneconomicoutlook.org.

Seth, S. 2009. "Inequality, Interactions, and Human Development." *Journal of Human Development and Capabilities* 10 (3): 375–96.

UNDESA (United Nations Department of Economic and Social Affairs). 2010. *World Urbanization Prospects: The 2009 Revision.* New York. http://esa.un.org/unpd/wup/index.htm. Accessed 15 May 2011.

———. 2011. *World Population Prospects: The 2010 Revision.* New York. http://esa.un.org/unpd/wpp/index.htm. Accessed 15 May 2011.

UNDP (United Nations Development Programme)–Human Development Report Office. 2011. "The Human Development Index (HDI)." New York. http://hdr.undp.org/en/statistics/hdi/.

UNESCAP (United Nations Economic and Social Commission for Asia and the Pacific). 2011. *Economic and Social Survey of Asia and the Pacific—Sustaining Dynamism and Inclusive Development: Connectivity in the Region and Productive Capacity in Least Developed Countries.* Bangkok. www.unescap.org/pdd/publications/survey2011/download/Econimic-and-Social-Survey-2011.pdf.

UNESCO (United Nations Educational, Scientific and Cultural Organization) Institute for Statistics. 2011. "UNESCO Institute for Statistics: Data Centre." http://stats.uis.unesco.org. Accessed 15 May 2011.

UNESCWA (United Nations Economic and Social Commission for Western Asia). 2011. "Summary of the Survey of Economic and Social Developments in the Economic and Social Commission for Western Asia Region 2010–2011." Geneva. www.escwa.un.org/information/publications/edit/upload/EDGD-11-2.pdf.

UNICEF (United Nations Children's Fund). 2000–2010. *Multiple Indicator Cluster Surveys*. New York. www.unicef.org/statistics/index_24302.html.

———. 2011. *The State of the World's Children*. New York. www.unicef.org/sowc2011/. Accessed 15 May 2011.

UNSD (United Nations Statistics Division). 2011. National Accounts Main Aggregates Database. New York. http://unstats.un.org/unsd/snaama/. Accessed 15 April 2011.

UNU-WIDER (United Nations University, World Institute for Development Economics Research). 2008. World Income Inequality Database, Version 2.0c, May 2008. Helsinki. www.wider.unu.edu/research/Database/en_GB/database/.

WHO (World Health Organization). 2000–2010. *World Health Survey*. Geneva. www.who.int/healthinfo/survey/en/.

———. 2009. "Environmental Burden of Disease: Country Profiles." Geneva. www.who.int/quantifying_ehimpacts/countryprofiles.

———. 2010a. *World Health Statistics 2010*. World Health Organization Statistical Information System. Geneva. www.who.int/whois/whostat/2010/en/index.html. Accessed 15 April 2011.

———. 2010b. *World Malaria Report*. Geneva. www.who.int/malaria/publications/atoz/9789241564106/en/index.html.

———. 2011. "DengueNet." Geneva. www.who.int/denguenet.

WHO, UNICEF, UNFPA (World Health Organization, United Nations Children's Fund, United Nations Population Fund), and World Bank. 2010. *Trends in Maternal Mortality 1990–2008*. Geneva. http://whqlibdoc.who.int/publications/2010/9789241500265_eng.pdf.

World Bank. 2010. *International Income Distribution Database*. Washington, DC.

———. 2011a. World Development Indicators database. Washington, DC. http://data.worldbank.org/data-catalog/world-development-indicators. Accessed 15 May 2011.

———. 2011b. *Global Economic Prospects—June 2011*. Washington, DC. http://web.worldbank.org/WBSITE/EXTERNAL/EXTDEC/EXTDECPROSPECTS/EXTGBLPROSPECTSAPRIL/0,,contentMDK:20665990~menuPK:659178~pagePK:2470434~piPK:4977459~theSitePK:659149,00.html.